I0606281

"Here is a panorama of Christian history from the divisions of the sixteenth century to the challenges of the twenty-first. It covers political struggles in Europe and fierce debates in America. Over time the imperative to achieve the right ordering of the church, as strong among Roman Catholics and Eastern Orthodox as among the various bodies of Protestants, gave way to a passionate desire to spread the gospel throughout the world, which culminated in the numerical dominance in the Christian church of the Global South. Thomas Kidd has written a lucid analysis of the whole process, enriched by carefully selected quotations and up-to-date lists for further reading."

—**David W. Bebbington**, emeritus professor of history, University of Stirling

"Professor Thomas Kidd is a committed Christian, an evangelical Baptist rooted in the Augustinian tradition. He is also a first-rate historian. Both qualities shine through in this superb overview of church history from the Protestant Reformation until the present. Recommended with enthusiasm!"

—**Timothy George**, distinguished professor, Beeson Divinity School of Samford University

"Thomas Kidd is a master at selecting the telling detail or colorful anecdote that brings a theological trend to life. While other historians often focus on novelty—which typically means highlighting theologians who break from orthodox Christianity to teach liberal theology or outright skepticism—Kidd's balanced treatment draws attention to those who remained faithful to what he calls the great tradition of Christian theology."

—**Nancy Pearcey**, professor and scholar in residence, Houston Christian University

"In this book, Thomas Kidd delivers an outstanding survey of church history since the dawn of the Reformation. With lucid writing and impressive coverage, he strikes the right balance between exploring the key events and ideas of ecclesial history and crafting a narrative that displays the breadth of the Christian story that has become a truly global reality in the modern era. I am delighted to recommend it."

—**Paul A. Sanchez**, assistant professor of religion and assistant director of the honors program, Oklahoma Baptist University

"In recent years, two encouraging trends have emerged in the American evangelical world: a growing interest in the historic, pre-Reformation roots of Christian thought and an increasing awareness of the global church. In this book, eminent historian Thomas Kidd shows how Protestantism respected such roots and spread across the globe. Learned but written with a light, accessible touch, this book offers a compelling—warts and all—vision of church history and how God's grace has worked in and through her over time. This is scholarship that will also inspire."

—**Carl R. Trueman**, professor of biblical and religious studies, Grove City College

"Thomas S. Kidd has delivered a beautifully written and comprehensive narrative to teachers of modern church history to help guide their students. With an eye toward the deep complexities in modern church history as well as the need for amplifying often neglected voices, Kidd ably walks the reader through the spread of Christianity from a European to a world faith system. As a committed Christian and a capital historian, Kidd provides us with the best of the tradition of 'confessing history.'"

—**John D. Wilsey**, associate professor of church history and philosophy, The Southern Baptist Theological Seminary

CHRISTIAN
History

VOLUME 2

VOLUME 2

CHRISTIAN *History*

From the Reformation to the Present

THOMAS S. KIDD

Christian History, Volume 2: From the Reformation to the Present

Published by B&H Academic
Brentwood, Tennessee

ISBN: 978-1-0877-3701-0

Dewey Decimal Classification: 270

Subject Heading: CHURCH HISTORY \ PROTESTANTISM \ CHRISTIANITY

Cover design by Gearbox; Cover images from Shutterstock: The Holy Virgin, photo by Agata Dorobek; Holy Bible, photo by Moreno Soppelsa; White church, photo by Warren Price Photography, Bronze Statue of Martin Luther in Dresden, built by Adolf von Donndorf in 1885, photo by manfredxy; Architectural window, photo by Kozlik; Ancient arch, photo by Kozlik; Oldest cathedral in the world Etchmiadzin in Armenia, photo by Jana Buryskova.

Printed in South Korea

29 28 27 26 25 24 SW 1 2 3 4 5 6 7 8 9 10

CONTENTS

INTRODUCTION

This volume is an overview of Christian history from the Reformation to the present. It is animated by the conviction that much of church history centers around struggles for churches and Christians to live in accord with the "great tradition of the church." Theologian D. H. Williams has defined the great tradition as "the foundational legacy of apostolic and patristic faith, most accurately enshrined in Scripture and secondarily in the great confessions and creeds of the early church."[1] Of course, many figures in Christian history—increasingly in the nineteenth and twentieth century—have downplayed or rejected the notion of orthodox, historical, or biblical boundaries like those of the "great tradition." Critics would argue that enforcing orthodoxy is usually more about asserting power than maintaining the "faith . . . once delivered unto the saints" (Jude 1:3 KJV). Although one can readily see that power in church, state, and empire has often intertwined with claims of orthodoxy, I still believe that there is indeed a great tradition of the church. It is a historic tradition which churches are called to believe and live out. Defining the boundaries of the great tradition has never been a simple matter, regardless of the time period. But the complexity and contestedness of that boundary-setting does not mean that the great tradition doesn't exist.

Even among evangelical Protestants—my own faith tradition—Williams's definition leaves open many questions. Which points of the great tradition are essential? Which are secondary and debatable? Do post-Reformation confessions such as the Westminster Confession of Faith carry the same weight as those of the early church, such as the Nicene

[1] D. H. Williams, *Evangelicals and Tradition: The Formative Influence of the Early Church* (Grand Rapids: Baker, 2005), 24.

Creed? Are debates such as ones between Calvinists and Arminians, or between paedobaptists and credobaptists, ones that should fundamentally divide believers, or can we just agree to disagree? Much of Christian history has entailed conflict over such questions. But it is important that we decide, as Christians, whether there is a great tradition of orthodox belief and practice at all, especially when considering the subject of church history. Is there a capacious and disputed tradition of belief and practice which exists for us to defend? Or has the concept of such a tradition largely served to marginalize those whom powerful people deem as heterodox?

I have my own convictions about the great tradition. I believe that it exists, and that Christians and churches are responsible to God for being faithful to it. Knowing this, you will presumably be able to perceive my general perspective throughout the chapters of this volume, although I hope you will not find my approach picky or polemical. But it matters where I am coming from as a Christian. I am a practicing Baptist, an evangelical Christian, and a Protestant in the Augustinian tradition. I teach at an evangelical Baptist seminary. I would hope, however, that those who practice the traditions represented to some extent here, including mainline Protestants, Pentecostals, Catholics, and Eastern Orthodox, will find the descriptions of their history, beliefs, and practices to be accurate and fair, even if I do not share some of their basic convictions. I am not primarily writing as a theological umpire. I am not calling "balls and strikes" about the relative correctness of every belief or of every theological figure discussed. But I hope that you will also understand that I am no theological relativist.

I am mainly trying to offer a composite picture of important, influential, and representative Christian beliefs, thinkers, activists, trends, and practices from about 1500 to the present. And when I say "Christian," I generally mean people who identify as Christians, not just the people with whom I agree on most particulars. The meaning of "Christian" is, of course, one of the most disputed issues of all in Christian history.

Telling the story of Christian history is, candidly, a daunting prospect. I want to offer a roughly global history of Christians and Christian denominations. Doing so not only reflects the global character of God's church in the world ("all nations, and kindreds, and people, and tongues" Rev 7:9 KJV), but it also reflects arguably the most salient Christian development of the past century: the demographic shift of active Christian communities to the Global South, especially East Asia, sub-Saharan Africa, and Latin America. Traditional church history textbooks have often failed adequately to account for this shift. Much of "church history" has actually meant "the history of academic theology," and the prestigious centers of such scholarly work are still in Europe and North America. But telling a global history of Christian peoples is more difficult than telling a history of academic theology. If national histories are highly selective and episodic (and they are), then how much more selective and episodic are global histories? The experience of many peoples, nations, salient developments, and religious groups are, by definition, either neglected or left out altogether in a worldwide approach over multiple centuries.

But in this relatively brief account of five centuries of Christian history, I have tried to do some justice to the global diversity of the church, centered on stories about the fate of the great tradition. So, if you are an American reader and you find yourself wondering, why is Professor Kidd talking about Dutch Calvinists in Brazil? Or Rwandan Pentecostals? Or Baptists of Nagaland (India)? Global perspective is the reason for this regional and confessional diversity, and it reflects profound Christian realities of increasing importance in the twenty-first century. Yet amidst all the mind-boggling variety of the Christian world, there remains a center. The historic center of Christian belief, grounded in the Word of God, has been entrusted to a great cloud of witnesses and is ultimately embodied in the person of Jesus Christ. That center has held, and it will hold, by God's power.

— Chapter 1 —

The Reformation Begins

Was the Protestant Reformation inevitable? In God's providential plan, it certainly was. God used the Reformation to challenge European churches and Christians toward greater doctrinal purity and greater holiness. Protestant readers should not embrace a simplistic "good guys" and "bad guys" dualism with regard to the Reformation, however. The pre-Reformation church in the West was not as corrupt and devoid of spiritual life as it sometimes has been portrayed. And the post-Reformation Protestant churches surely did not inaugurate an era of Christian perfection. But there were serious doctrinal and ethical problems in the Catholic Church on the eve of the Reformation. The Reformation gave Christians new opportunities to pursue biblical doctrine and practice, in fuller accord with the great tradition of the church.

People generally think that they are living through times of extraordinary turmoil, but by any measure the fourteenth and fifteenth centuries in European history were times of frightening disruption and intellectual ferment. The Catholic Church had suffered competing claims to the papacy during the 1300s, when a number of popes resided in Avignon, France, an era sometimes called the "Babylonian Captivity of the Church." (Martin Luther would pick up on this label in an influential 1520 publication of the same name.) By the early 1400s, there were not just two but three claimants to the papacy. In the same period, warring Europeans saw unprecedented levels of carnage due to improvements in war-making technology, such as the invention of gunpowder.

Famine and death also haunted the continent, especially in the time of the Black Death, or the bubonic plague. The Black Death peaked in Europe from 1347 to 1351. Worldwide it likely killed hundreds of millions of people, from Central Asia to Ireland. Priests were hit especially hard by the plague, as they ministered to the dying. One priest in Tournai (in modern Belgium) noted that "no one, rich, middling or poor, was safe" but that "certainly there were many deaths among the parish priests and chaplains who heard confessions and administered the sacraments." Christians intuitively saw the plague as the judgment of God. But what was God saying to them in the pandemic?

Movements for "reform" in the church were common and widespread in the late medieval period. Indeed, the Catholic Church was probably more open to internal debate and criticism in the decades before the Reformation, which hardened battle lines between Catholics and Protestants. Catholic reformers called for changes in the papacy, in order to heal the divisions in the church caused by the split claimants in Rome and Avignon. The "conciliar" movement in the Catholic Church sought to check the quasi-monarchical power of the pope, making him subject to general councils of the church, such as the council that met in Constance (in modern Germany) in 1414 to address the papal schism. The Council of Constance, after much political maneuvering, was able to consolidate the papacy in the person of Pope Martin V in 1417, a century before Martin Luther issued his ninety-five theses.

Reform movements like conciliarism hinted at conflicts within the Catholic Church that would endure long after the Reformation, such as debates over the relative authority of the pope. Other calls for reform prior to 1517 entailed forms of proto-Protestantism, or agitation for the church to adhere more closely to the original teachings of Scripture, or of the church fathers. The Council of Constance faced such a challenge from the Bohemian leader Jan Hus, a pastor-theologian of the University of Prague (in the modern Czech Republic). Hus ran afoul of church officials for his teachings which accorded with those of the English Reformer John Wyclif. Wyclif was an early champion of biblical authority and of making the Scriptures available in vernacular languages. Inspired by Wyclif and by his own studies, Hus came to believe that the Bible trumped any earthly church authority or tradition. Most controversially, Hus insisted that Christian laypeople should receive not just the bread but also the eucharistic cup in communion. The medieval church did not allow communion in "both kinds" for laypeople. Condemned by the Council of Constance in 1415, Hus was proclaimed a "heresiarch" and burned at the stake. Hus was gone, but his native Bohemia remained a center of religious dissent for centuries afterward.

Image 1.1. *Jan Hus monument, Prague*

Christian Humanists and Scripture

Some Reformers prior to 1517 focused on improving Christian arts and education within the Catholic Church. These trends were broadly associated with the Renaissance, and more specifically, with "Renaissance humanism." The scholarly term "humanism" is somewhat unfortunate, as to modern ears it sounds like a form of secularism. Although some Renaissance humanists were skeptical about Christian doctrine, we do better to understand much of this movement as devout Christian humanism, or religiously-informed art and study of the humanities. The Christian humanist impulse is seen in the work of sculptors and artists such as Michelangelo (1475–1564), with his brilliant sculptures and Sistine Chapel frescoes. For our purposes, the most important humanist legacy was the study of ancient languages and texts, including the original languages of the Bible. The animating principle of such humanists was "ad fontes," a Latin phrase meaning "to the sources," or to the original text. This philological ideal applied not only to a new zeal for the study of ancient Greek and Roman pagan writers such as Aristotle but also of Greek and Hebrew manuscripts that illuminated the original meaning of Scripture.

For centuries, the Catholic Church had depended upon the Vulgate, Jerome's fourth-century Latin translation of the Bible. Even though the Vulgate was itself a triumph of Christian humanistic scholarship, by the 1400s it had functionally become an obstacle to fresh recovery of scriptural learning. When Reformers like Wyclif called for new translations of the Bible into vernacular languages, they were rejecting the idea that Christians should only know the Bible via the Latin Vulgate. Regular churchgoers would have learned some of the Latin Bible during mass, but the Catholic Church hierarchy resisted making the Bible available in languages that laypeople knew best. Critics also said that the Vulgate, despite Jerome's phenomenal work, was not an entirely accurate translation. The greatest Christian humanist of the period was Desiderius Erasmus (d. 1536). Erasmus's Greek New Testament of 1516, based on the earliest Greek texts available, was arguably the most influential product of the Christian humanist movement. Erasmus ultimately aligned against Luther. Yet he nevertheless abetted the Protestant Reformers' belief that studying the original texts and meaning of Scripture was one of the church's foremost responsibilities.

Pre-Reformation Mystics

Erasmus hardly meant to damage the Catholic Church. Neither did most of the proto-Reformers, or even Protestant Reformers such as Luther, who started out as a little-known Augustinian monk. The medieval era was punctuated by spiritual writers and mystics who modeled rigorous devotion to God beyond that of most laypeople, or even that of clergy and church officials. The Italian writer and Catholic activist Catherine of Siena (1347–80), for example, used her unusual influence and intense piety to call for a resolution of the papal schisms of the 1300s. She was a "mystic" in the sense that she relentlessly pursued an intense relationship with God and wrote at length about her experiences. She even related conversations in which the Father, as it were, spoke directly to her. Catherine wrote that the Father said, "I have loved both you and others before you were in existence; and that, through the ineffable love which I had for you, wishing to re-create you to Grace, I have washed you, and re-created you in the Blood of My only-begotten Son, spilt with so great a fire of love." Catherine died in 1380, and received canonization as a saint of the Catholic Church in 1461. Her devotees claimed that she had received the "stigmata" of Christ's wounds as a sign of her close identification with the Savior, but that claim was not officially accepted by Catholic authorities until centuries after her death.

Spiritual exemplars such as Catherine would serve largely as models for Catholics alone, once the Reformation ensued. But some late medieval writers would continue to inspire Protestant believers, as well. Arguably the most enduring of these writers was Thomas à Kempis (1380–1471), the attributed author of *The Imitation of Christ* (1441). Thomas was an Augustinian monk in the Netherlands and an advocate of what became known as *devotio moderna* (new devotion), or a program of Christian meditation that was intense yet accessible to laypeople. As one might expect from an Augustinian context, *The Imitation of Christ* depended heavily on the rhetoric and devotion of Augustine himself. Late medieval and early modern discussions of piety and doctrine often focused on an understanding of what Augustine had taught a millennium earlier, making him arguably the most influential exponent of the great tradition, outside of the biblical authors. Although Augustine remained

Image 1.2. *Saint Catherine of Siena Receiving the Stigmata* (c. 1513–15)

influential before and after this time, the mid-1400s to the mid-1700s represented an "Augustinian moment" for European Christians, according to historian A. D. Wright.

Thomas à Kempis offered a picture of vital devotion to the Lord above the nominal religiosity that marked so many people in Christian Europe. "O my God, everlasting Love," he prayed, "Happiness which can never have an end, I desire to receive thee with the most earnest affection, and the most suitable awe and reverence." Thomas's fervor resonated across many national and confessional boundaries in the coming centuries. *The Imitation* appealed to Continental Pietists in the 1600s and to many of the leaders of the early evangelical movement in the 1700s, including the evangelist George Whitefield. Early Methodist leader John Wesley published full and extracted editions of *The Imitation.* The shorter versions allowed rank-and-file Methodists to own pocket-sized editions of the medieval classic and also let Wesley delete theological material he regarded as erroneous. Methodist laypeople eagerly read Thomas, too. Ann Bolton, a devout Methodist from the Oxford area, used *The Imitation* in her personal and family devotions in the 1770s and 1780s, writing about the prayers inspired by *The Imitation* in her spiritual diary. Because of the work of Wesley and legions of other admirers through the centuries, *The Imitation* became the most-printed book authored in the medieval period.

The Print Revolution

The Imitation of Christ also illustrates the impact of the print revolution, which transformed the culture of information technology in the decades prior to the Reformation. Before Johannes Gutenberg developed his new printing press in the 1450s, there was already a lively, but inefficient, trade in hand-copied books in Europe. Gutenberg's press hardly eliminated this trade in copied books. Gutenberg himself was a far greater inventor than businessman, as his foray into printing books and Bibles led him to bankruptcy. *The Imitation of Christ* was originally produced in hand-written copies; starting in 1472 it also appeared in print. Scholars estimate that *The Imitation* has appeared in more than 3,000 editions in the centuries since then, in many different languages. Thomas's devotional work was already becoming popular prior to the advent of a robust print trade, but the advent of print was essential to it becoming a global Christian classic.

This was the background to Luther's Reformation, which was a revolution in doctrine and in print. It is not easy to overstate Martin Luther's importance for the Reformation, not only in the ideas that inspired it, but also the means by which those ideas spread. Luther was also the most important figure in turning the European print trade into an efficient, mass enterprise. The Reformers made sermons based on the Bible their chief means of communication, but print enabled those sermons (and commentaries, pamphlets, hymnbooks, and vernacular Bible translations) to become mobile sources of Reformation thought, ones which could communicate and inspire when the author was not physically present or long after the author was dead (witness Ann Bolton's reading of *The Imitation* hundreds of years after initial publication). Luther and other Reformers tapped into trading and financial networks to make printed communication sustainable. As Gutenberg realized to his peril, print was a capital-intensive business that struggled to become viable for a half century. The sensational debates produced by the Reformation attracted urban merchants who invested in the presses, paper, and book inventories that made the trade work. It may be an exaggeration to say that without the printing press, there would have been no Reformation. But without the printing press, the Reformation would not have had the same viral, rampaging effects.

Doctrinal Challenges

Luther and the Protestant Reformers took up critical themes that had been advanced, at one time or another, by reformist Catholics and proto-Protestant dissenters over the centuries prior to 1517. But Catholic Europe was not yet teeming with dissent or heresy in the years prior to Luther. Catholic theologians (including Luther) were generally reticent to voice harsh criticisms of the church, especially in venues that might attract attention from laypeople. But criticisms did persist, usually focusing on ethical lapses among Catholic leaders, or on what they regarded as unbiblical precepts such as purgatory. Purgatory, a Catholic doctrine officially confirmed in 1274, was the idea that there was an intermediate place after death for those who will go to heaven but who have remaining sins to be cleansed and "purged." There is no direct biblical warrant for such a belief, but its defenders pointed to Bible verses (including ones in the Apocrypha) and patristic sources that suggested prayers for the dead were appropriate. What did prayers for the dead indicate, if not that intermediate state? Eastern Orthodox churches tended not to dwell on purgatory as much as Catholics did, but nevertheless they affirmed the validity of prayers for the dead. Figures in the medieval Catholic Church became highly focused on purgatory and what Christians could do to reduce their time, or that of loved ones, in that liminal state.

Purgatory led to a heightened focus on good works, since holy deeds were the most obvious path to lessening the torments a person might endure before heaven. Some men and women decided to enter monasteries or convents, even late in life, in hopes of alleviating their purgation or perhaps avoiding it altogether. Concern over purgatory inspired pilgrimages, works of charity, prayers, and most controversially, the payment of indulgences. Indulgences, it was believed, could allow the pope to appeal to the "treasury of merit" from Christ and the saints in order to remit the temporal punishment for sins. (Forgiveness of sins was obtained via confession and God's pardoning grace.) The church could grant indulgences for people saying prayers or other godly works, but payments to the church became the most abused form of indulgences. They also became the focus of Martin Luther's initial criticisms of the church. Luther's attack was the culmination of a growing Catholic chorus against the transactional nature of the sale of indulgences. Even after the Reformation, repeated Catholic church councils have raised concerns about the abuse of indulgences, but the church still maintained that they were spiritually valid when practiced in an appropriate manner.

Martin Luther

Born in 1483, Luther did not seem destined to become a great Christian Reformer. His prosperous German family hoped he would take up a career in law or government. But as he trained in the law, Luther began to struggle with fears about his sin and God's judgment. This spiritual crisis led him to enter an Augustinian monastery. Becoming a monk and receiving ordination as a Catholic priest (1507) did not alleviate his spiritual anxieties, however. He threw himself into biblical studies and received a faculty position at the University of Wittenberg in eastern Germany. There he developed powerful series of lectures on books of the Bible, including the Psalms, Galatians, and most importantly, Romans. Reflecting the influence of Christian humanism, Luther moved from a medieval allegorical mode of Bible interpretation toward the original meaning of the Greek and Hebrew texts themselves. (We shouldn't overstate this change, however, as most traditionalist Bible interpreters have taken an allegorical interpretation approach to some parts of Scripture, such as the Song of Solomon.) The core

> 32. Those who believe that they can be certain of their salvation because they have indulgence letters will be eternally damned, together with their teachers.
>
> ---
>
> Martin Luther, *Ninety-Five Theses or Disputation on the Power and Efficacy of Indulgences*, 1517

of Luther's emerging theology was the liberating tension between the law of God, which condemns sinners, and the gospel, which forgives and restores them. In particular, Luther came to believe that all his previous strivings after righteousness had not led him to salvation but to more turmoil. He determined that God alone could justify sinners.

In 1515, Pope Leo X (1475–1521) declared a new indulgence to fund the construction of the massive St. Peter's Basilica in Rome. In Germany, the monk Johann Tetzel was one of the chief promoters of the St. Peter's indulgence. Luther believed that Tetzel's indulgences led people to assume that they could gain forgiveness, or reduced time in purgatory, without real repentance from sin. Sinners naturally feared punishment more than they regretted their sins, Luther figured.

Luther's concerns culminated in his posting of the "Ninety-Five Theses" in Latin on the door of the Castle Church in Wittenberg on October 31, 1517. The details of this alleged posting have been challenged from every conceivable angle. Suffice it to say that the posting, which was surely not a dramatic scene in the moment, probably did happen on the date in question. A university administrator may have done the actual posting, not Luther with his trusty mallet. The theses were a set of propositions about which Luther wanted to generate scholarly discussion. The theses themselves were provocative but not especially novel. What was novel—even revolutionary—was that the theses were translated into German, printed, and rapidly distributed. Luther's biting prose, circulated in print, turned the theses into a Continent-wide sensation. Although Luther initially had no notion that he was igniting anything like the "Protestant Reformation," his public criticisms of the pope and the church destabilized traditional Catholic claims about Christian authority. By early 1518, Luther already had a sense that events were exploding out of his control. He professed that he never intended his protests to generate so much popular notice. But he was already on his way to becoming one of the most famous religious leaders in all of history.

Luther intuitively realized that the controversy regarding indulgences, and his skyrocketing fame, opened unprecedented opportunities for reform of the church. Diving in, Luther generated many publications of great theological influence, not just on indulgences, but also on topics including law, grace, the cross, and the corruption of the Catholic Church. He summarized the arguments of the 95 theses in his *Sermon on Indulgence and Grace* (1518). This was the publication that introduced Luther to a mass Continental audience, as the pamphlet went through twenty-two printings in just two years and was translated into multiple languages. His work drew the attention of church authorities, including the pope, who ordered the head of the Augustinian order to "take care of the problem of Martin Luther."

Luther worried that he might fall victim to the charge of heresy that had felled Jan Hus a century earlier. Indeed, Luther had taken up some of Hus's classic concerns, such as the cup in communion for laypeople.

By mid-1518, Luther had become convinced that God justified sinners by grace alone and that people could not contribute anything toward achieving a right standing before God. In addition to dependence on the Word of God alone, this principle of justification by grace alone, through faith alone, became the signature belief of the Reformers. As Luther put it in *The Freedom of a Christian Man* (1520), true Christians were justified only by the merits of Christ. A sinner added nothing meritorious to his or her justification and salvation. Luther was careful to show that faith was not a good work. By faith the believer put confidence only in what God could do, not what a person could do. A person's soul "is justified by faith alone and not by any works; for if it could be justified by anything else, it would not need the word [of God], and consequently it would not need faith," Luther wrote.

A series of formal exchanges with papal authorities did not convince Luther to recant his views. The pope issued a bull (decree) against Luther's errors, calling on him to change his ways or to face excommunication from the church. Far from repenting, Luther publicly burned a copy of the bull in Wittenberg, leading to his excommunication in 1521. Luther was then summoned to the Holy Roman Emperor's diet (assembly) at Worms in southwestern Germany. Excommunication was both an ecclesiastical and civil punishment, and godly rulers were expected to banish the excommunicated from their domains. Luther remained steadfast, however, explaining that his conscience was "captive to the Word of God." Some scholars doubt whether Luther actually said the famous lines attributed to him at the diet: "Here I stand, I can do no other." But his sentiment reflected the quote nevertheless. The Diet of Worms declared Luther a heresy-preaching criminal and banned him from the empire. Only a clever "kidnapping" by soldiers of Frederick III, Elector of Saxony and Luther's key patron, saved Luther from death or banishment. Frederick's men deposited him at the Wartburg Castle for safekeeping.

At the Wartburg, Luther continued his phenomenal output of writing, capped by his most important work, the German translation of the New Testament. The Bible had been translated into German before but with nothing like the rhetorical power of Luther's edition. Luther's Bible was a culmination of John Wyclif's call for vernacular translations and of the Christian humanist return to original languages. Despite a looming rift between Luther and Erasmus, Luther depended heavily upon Erasmus's Greek edition of the New Testament as he composed his German edition. In his translating work, Luther also sought the help of Philip Melanchthon (1497–1560), his university colleague, closest collaborator, and spiritual confidant. Melanchthon, who had become Professor of Greek at the university at age twenty-one, was key to the intellectual defense of Lutheran doctrine.

Luther's guiding principles in the German translation included accessibility to lay readers, fidelity to the original Greek and Hebrew texts, and the primacy of salvation by grace alone. Indeed, Luther struggled at times to reconcile fidelity to the original text and his zeal for the principle of grace. Sometimes he added an additional word or two when the original text was not explicit enough, such as in the case of Rom 3:28, which he translated as "justified without works of the law, by faith *alone*," even though the Greek does not have the word "alone." Luther also made clear that he did not consider all the New Testament books to be of equal value. He particularly doubted the canonical status of James because some of its passages implied the necessity of works in addition to faith. Indeed, Catholic refutations of Luther turned to passages such as Jas 2:24, which declared that a "person is justified by works and not by faith alone." One Catholic canon law expert observed that James could not have made a more effective rebuttal to the Reformers "if he had seen Luther and his followers" with his own eyes.

Radical Reformers

Melanchthon sought to keep Luther's revolution moving forward during his detention at the Wartburg Castle. Already by 1522, Wittenberg and other German cities had begun to see outbreaks of radical fervor and iconoclasm that the more moderate, or "magisterial" Reformers, would struggle to restrain. The magisterial Reformers valued the traditional partnership between state and church authorities in the service of the Reformation instead of the Catholic Church. Radical Reformers tended to see secular oversight of the church as introducing worldly corruption. Seasons of renewal and revival within the church have almost always witnessed tensions like this dialectic. Moderate and radical Reformers have routinely fought against one another as bitterly as they did against their supposed common enemy (in this case, the Roman Catholic hierarchy). In the Reformation, those who sought to ensure that change would transpire in a respectful fashion faced off against radicals who saw caution as dalliance with sin and the forces of antichrist. Some of the most spectacular confrontations were over statues of saints and other devotional art, which some Protestants smashed as violations of the second commandment's prohibition of idolatrous graven images. (Eastern Orthodox Christians avoided this complication with the use of "icons"—flat, painted images.) Protestants questioned the propriety of statues and crucifixes, which were ubiquitous in Catholic sanctuaries. Priests who did not adhere to Lutheran criticisms of the church found themselves shouted down by radicals or barraged with rocks or feces.

Charismatic figures also began to preach across Germany, claiming direct inspiration from the Holy Spirit to push the Reformation farther than Luther or Melanchthon intended. Some of these prophetic figures came from the Reformation center at Zwickau, Germany. Luther had raised questions about the Catholic doctrine of transubstantiation (the idea that the communion elements actually became the body and blood of Christ), but he still believed that the presence of Christ dwelled in the bread and wine. The Zwickau preachers proposed that the bread and wine were just symbols of Christ's sacrifice and that there was nothing miraculous or mysterious that occurred when believers observed the meal of remembrance. More jarringly, the new prophets insisted that baptism, the other sacrament affirmed by the Reformers, was meant only for believers, not for babies. While the Protestant Reformers inveighed against the Catholic view of communion, most of them agreed with the Catholic (and Eastern Orthodox) view that infants were to be baptized. This was the common Christian practice of baptism since at least the time of Augustine. Now even baptism came into question, largely because there were no clear instances of infant baptism recorded in Scripture. Individual baptisms in the Bible included a profession of faith, something newborn babies could not do. Defenders of paedobaptism, including Luther, said that children were surely among those baptized in instances such as the "entire household" of the converted jailer in Acts 16. They contended that at baptism, children were "received into [God's] grace," as the Augsburg Confession (1530) put it.

Luther mocked the Zwickau "prophets" and their pretensions to divine inspiration. He said he would not listen to such visionaries even if they "swallowed the Holy Ghost, feathers and all." The radicals' challenge helped Luther to articulate his "two kingdoms" philosophy. Christians had to live in both the kingdom of God and the kingdom of the world. The kingdom of the world could support the kingdom of God, but no one—whether Catholics or radical Reformers—should confuse the spheres encompassed by the two kingdoms. Civil authority had to restrain crime and mischief, but it could not manifest the spiritual principles of love of God and neighbor that characterized the true church. Luther believed that Christians should expect the church to comply with all God asked of it in Scripture but that Christians could accept living under many types of earthly authorities, even ungodly ones. Luther was pragmatic and conservative when it came to matters of state, and he was idealistic and reformist regarding the church.

Luther's conservatism about the governing authorities did not comport well with the Peasants' War of the mid-1520s, even though this enormous popular uprising was inspired partly by his teachings. Scholars have debated how much the Reformation sparked the Peasants' War, but it appears that the Reformers helped to give widespread grievances over taxes and land rights a new religious focus. One of the leaders of the peasants (many of whom were actually prosperous farmers) was the controversial Reformer and foe of Luther, Thomas Müntzer (d. 1525), who was also from Zwickau. Müntzer's apocalyptic theology led him to believe that Christians should rise up against corrupt civil authority at the prompting of the Holy Spirit. Luther initially expressed some sympathy for the peasants, but as the Continent descended into chaos, Luther became a full-throated defender of law and order. He called for violent repression of the rebels. In typically vitriolic prose, Luther penned the 1525 pamphlet *Against the Robbing and Murdering Hordes of Peasants*, calling on the magistrates and their supporters to "smite, slay, and stab, secretly or openly, remembering that nothing can be more poisonous, hurtful, or devilish than a rebel." For his part, Müntzer was captured, tortured, and beheaded by government forces in 1525, with his head posted in public as a warning to other would-be visionaries and rebels.

Zwingli and the Anabaptists

Radical Reformers would continue to play a major role in the doctrinal debates of the Reformation. Some of these radicals became known as "Anabaptists," or re-baptizers. They would baptize believers who once had received infant baptism, which they no longer considered a valid form of the ordinance. Some of the earliest Anabaptist leaders emerged from the Reformed movement in Zürich, Switzerland, where Huldrych Zwingli (1484–1531) was the first prominent leader of the Reformation. In the Swiss Reformation, Zwingli took on a comparable role to Luther's in Germany. Zwingli, a parish priest in Glarus and then Zürich, was influenced intellectually by Luther, Erasmus, and Augustine. But Zwingli was trending in a more radical direction than Luther. Zwingli rejected the church's fasting requirements during Lent as a human invention. He also condemned the church's prohibition on priestly marriage, and Zwingli secretly got married several years before Luther took that step in 1525. Zwingli prohibited music and hymns in church, while Luther made hymns such as

"Ein feste Burg ist unser Gott" ("A Mighty Fortress Is Our God") among the most distinctive facets of the German Reformation. Finally, Zwingli took a similar approach to communion as did the radical Reformers: he viewed it primarily as a symbol of God's liberation of his people from the captivity of sin. At the invitation of Philip I of Hessen, Luther and Zwingli tried to hammer out a mediating position on communion at the Marburg Colloquy in 1529, but they failed to arrive at an agreement.

Some radical followers of Zwingli broke with him, over issues where they felt that Zwingli was unwilling to follow the Bible to its logical conclusion. These issues included baptism. Swiss and German Anabaptists produced the Schleitheim Confession of Faith in 1527. Anabaptist churches were not generally united but divided among regions and ethnicities. The Schleitheim Confession was an effort at giving the movement cohesion, and it provides a good sense for Anabaptist theology as it emerged from Reformation centers such as Zürich. The Schleitheim document expressed a starkly different image of Christians' place in the world than did Luther's two kingdoms. (Indeed, the differing views of Luther and the Anabaptists reflected tensions over the church and politics that would endure, in some forms, through present day.) Becoming a Christian and receiving baptism, to the Anabaptists, removed the believer from the world and placed him or her into the kingdom of Christ. There should be as little overlap between the two kingdoms as possible. Thus they advocated pacifism, refused to swear oaths, and prohibited Christians from serving as magistrates. Of course, they also repudiated infant baptism, which they characterized as the "chief abomination of the pope." Anabaptists were coming under dire persecution, and Schleitheim was a renunciation of the political aspirations held by the

> We have been united concerning the separation that shall take place from the evil and the wickedness which the devil has planted in the world, simply in this: that we have no fellowship with them [the wicked], and do not run with them in the confusion of their abomination.
>
> ---
>
> Michael Sattler, *The Schleitheim Confession*, 1527
>
> This is a more common translation of the same:
>
> "We are agreed (as follows) on separation: A separation shall be made from the evil and from the wickedness which the devil planted in the world; in this manner, simply that we shall not have fellowship with them [the wicked] and not run with them in the multitude of their abominations."

magisterial Reformers. Anabaptists occasionally showed interest in aligning with state authorities, especially in Moravia, where Anabaptist leader Balthasar Hubmaier (1480–1528), following his expulsion from Zwingli's Zürich, converted a local lord to Anabaptist convictions in the mid-1520s. For a time, Moravia was seen as a refuge for persecuted Anabaptists elsewhere in Europe. But not even Hubmaier could avoid the wrath of officials in the Holy Roman Empire, who burned him at the stake in 1528.

The number of Anabaptist martyrs between 1525 and 1625 probably ran into the thousands. Why were Anabaptists so fiercely persecuted? Partly because Catholics and magisterial Reformers alike believed that the state had a role in prosecuting heretics and religious incendiaries. Catholics and paedobaptist Protestants disagreed over many doctrinal issues, but they agreed that those who repudiated infant baptism were wildly aberrant. Moreover, the rejection of infant baptism was an emotional issue for virtually all Europeans. Promoting believer's baptism rejected the traditional ritual that was widely believed to place babies within the sacred canopy of the church and on the path to salvation.

Anabaptists were also easy to paint as dangerous radicals in other ways. For instance, Anabaptists were more likely than other Christian groups to be pacifists, or to permit female prophets and exhorters. Women were indeed vital to Catholic and Protestant congregational life, and devoted women among Catholics had a clear avenue to religious vocation as nuns. However, Protestants, who put a new emphasis on the pastor faithfully preaching the Word, did not have as clear a churchly vocation for women. Protestants denounced and closed the nuns' convents as soon as they took control of a city or region. Protestant women, such as Luther's wife Katharina von Bora, enjoyed a revered status as exemplars, mothers, and wives, and such women influenced Protestant pastors in a multitude of informal ways. But they did not usually serve as pastors or preachers themselves.

In churches that emphasized a dynamic pneumatology (theology of the Holy Spirit), women of the Reformation sometimes asserted that they could take on public roles as evangelists, exhorters, and prophets. They could do so even if they did not receive formal ordination. One such woman was the Anabaptist visionary Ursula Jost of Strasbourg, who recorded dozens of visionary messages she said she received from the Spirit during the turmoil of the Peasants' War and the outbreak of persecution against Anabaptists. The Anabaptist leader Melchior Hoffman regarded Jost as a prophetess and arranged for the publication of her visions. Such activity only fueled the magisterial Reformers' conviction that the Anabaptists were fanatics. This allowed the magisterial Reformers to cast themselves in better light as rational and sober.

The Ottoman Threat and the Augsburg Confession

Most radical Reformers had little hope of swaying political leaders to support their cause, which helped them to nurture a stronger animosity toward state involvement with churches. The political alliances of the late 1520s began to coalesce around traditional Catholic authorities and the magistrates who backed the "Protestants," a term that emerged in the late 1520s. (The early Protestants were often just called "evangelicals.") Holy Roman Emperor Charles V summoned the competing sides to a diet at Augsburg in 1530, an assembly which produced Philip Melanchthon's Augsburg Confession. Charles V hoped that the diet might actually foster reconciliation between Europe's brawling Christians.

The emperor was concerned about the imperial threat of the Ottoman Turks, who had conquered Constantinople in 1453, turning the Orthodox Church's monumental Hagia Sophia cathedral there into a mosque. The Ottomans also conquered Syria and Egypt in 1517, placing the Orthodox patriarchates (church jurisdictions) of Alexandria, Antioch, and Jerusalem under Muslim rule. Charles V did not want internal dissension to damage the European Christians' united front against Muslim power. Ottoman expansion was a serious threat in Europe, as they conquered the city of Buda and the Kingdom of Hungary in 1541. Periodic threats of Ottoman aggression in eastern and central Europe continued until their failed siege of Vienna in 1683.

In the meantime, Philip Melanchthon represented an irenic version of the new Protestant belief, and his type of reformist Christianity still resonated with a number of Catholics who remained concerned about the abuse of indulgences and similar problems. But the forces of papal primacy convinced Charles V that reconciliation was hopeless, so Melanchthon's Augsburg Confession became a cornerstone of the emerging "Lutheran" theology. It also was a reference point for other Reformed believers, even those who did not accept all of Luther's beliefs, especially regarding communion. Arguably the definitive passage of the confession was Article IV, "Of Justification." Citing Romans, Melanchthon wrote that people "cannot be justified before God by their own strength, merits, or works, but are freely justified for Christ's sake, through faith, when they believe that they are received into favor, and that their sins are forgiven for Christ's sake, who, by His death, has made satisfaction for our sins. This faith God imputes for righteousness in His sight." With God's help, Luther and his followers had recovered and reaffirmed the doctrine of justification by faith alone. In the process, European Christendom itself had shattered.

Selected Bibliography

Bainton, Roland. *Erasmus of Christendom*. New York: Scribner's, 1969.

Goertz, Hans-Jürgen. *The Anabaptists*. Translated by Trevor Johnson. New York: Routledge, 1996.

Hindmarsh, D. Bruce. *The Spirit of Early Evangelicalism: True Religion in a Modern World*. Oxford: Oxford University Press, 2018.

MacCulloch, Diarmaid. *The Reformation*. New York: Viking, 2004.

Pelikan, Jaroslav. *Reformation of the Church and Dogma (1300–1700)*. Chicago: University of Chicago Press, 1984.

Pettegree, Andrew. *Brand Luther: 1517, Printing, and the Making of the Reformation*. New York: Penguin, 2015.

Selderhuis, Herman. *Martin Luther: A Spiritual Biography*. Wheaton, IL: Crossway, 2017.

Stjerna, Kirsi. *Women and the Reformation*. Malden, MA: Blackwell, 2009.

Van Engen, John. *Sisters and Brothers of the Common Life: The Devotio Moderna and the World of the Later Middle Ages*. Philadelphia: University of Pennsylvania Press, 2008.

Wright, A. D. *The Counter-Reformation: Catholic Europe and the Non-Christian World*. 2nd ed. New York: Routledge, 2017.

— Chapter 2 —

The Reformation: Division and Reaction

As significant as Martin Luther was, he was never the singular leader of the Reformation that his legendary proclamation "Here I stand" might suggest. He depended deeply on Philip Melanchthon for intellectual leadership and spiritual support, and upon his wife Katharina, with whom he had a companionate relationship that changed the Christian view of marriage, especially for pastors. The extent to which the Swiss Reformation depended upon Luther's ideas is debated, but there is no doubt that Huldrych Zwingli took Zürich on a reformist track that paralleled and sometimes clashed with Luther's approach. In any case, Luther's death approached in the 1540s, but the movement he founded would continue after he was gone.

Luther became more rigid as he aged, and some of his worst tendencies became magnified in his later years. In particular, Luther went from promoting a moderate form of toleration for Jews to expressing vicious anti-Jewish beliefs as an old man. The transition had troubling implications for the future history of Germany and the Protestant faith. Anti-Jewish rumors and legends were common among both Catholics and Protestants in Europe. Even though Christian humanists often took a positive view of ancient Hebrew writings, they could also stereotype Europe's Jews as money-grubbing "Christ-killers," ignoring the fact that Jesus and his disciples were Jewish.

Luther's most famous anti-Jewish tract was *On the Jews and Their Lies* (1543), which apparently was inspired by Luther's failed attempts to evangelize rabbis and his impression that Jews were making inroads in proselytizing among Protestants. Whatever the cause, *On the Jews and Their Lies* displayed an irrational hatred for Jews, with raging insults of the Jewish people as "an incorrigible whore and an evil slut" and "blood-thirsty bloodhounds and murderers of all Christendom." Luther recommended to Christian rulers that Jewish synagogues, schools, houses, and sacred writings should be destroyed, their wealth confiscated, and the Jews themselves put to work in labor camps. The publication of a new edition of *On the Jews and Their Lies* in Frankfurt, Germany set the stage for a mob's attack on Frankfurt's Jewish ghetto and the expulsion of thousands of Jews from the city in 1614. Unfortunately, *On the Jews and Their Lies* did not plumb the darkest depths of Luther's anti-Jewish writings. His book *On the Ineffable Name and On the Lineage of Christ* (1543) employed the most profane and lurid descriptions of Jews that one could imagine. Luther's anti-Jewish ideas were more theological than racial, and Luther obviously did not know the lengths to which such notions would be implemented in Nazi Germany four centuries later. Yet the echoes of Luther's sentiments in the Holocaust are harrowing to contemplate.

Luther did not age gracefully, then, partly due to physical torments he endured and colorfully described in his declining years. Kidney stones were just one of his maladies. In an age that could do little to treat relatively simple ailments such as kidney stones, such conditions could lead to interminable suffering, and they did so for Luther. This does not excuse his anti-Jewish ranting (and similar fulminations against Zwingli and others), but it may put it in some context. Luther finally passed away in 1546.

Heinrich Bullinger

The next generation of Reformers had begun to emerge before Luther's death, with clearer lines separating "Lutherans" from Calvin's followers, or the "Reformed." Zwingli died in battle against Swiss Catholic forces in 1531, and he was succeeded in Zürich by Heinrich Bullinger (1504–75). Bullinger's education in the late 1510s was marked by readings of Erasmus and other key works on Christian humanism. Bullinger read Greek and Latin classics and the Greek New Testament. Luther's remarkable publications of 1520, such as *The Babylonian Captivity of the Church*, piqued Bullinger's interest in justification by faith alone. Studying Luther, the New Testament, and church fathers including Augustine, Bullinger (still in his late teens) became convinced that Luther's critique of Catholic theology and practice accorded with Scripture and the best traditions of church history. Like Zwingli, Bullinger did not agree with Luther on the real presence of Christ inhering in communion, but otherwise he found Luther a faithful guide. Also like Luther, Bullinger's work of reform began in a Catholic context, as he had been a teacher at a Cistercian monastery. Bullinger led the monks in lessons through many of the New Testament books, and many of his students became convinced of the truth of Reformed theology. In 1523 Bullinger met and began working with Zwingli in the Swiss Reformation. Bullinger was the natural successor to Zwingli as the pastor of Zürich's Reformed congregation in 1531. He was more irenic than Zwingli, yet Bullinger was also a firm defender of the magisterial Reformation against challenges from Catholics and Anabaptists (and from Lutherans on issues such as communion). Bullinger ministered in Zürich for forty-three years, securing the Reformed movement in that strategic city. He was also a key player, along with Geneva's John Calvin, in establishing a "Reformed" European cohort against "Lutherans." Lutherans and the Reformed churches disagreed on a number of issues, most pointedly on the nature of communion.

Bullinger was a prolific author, but his seminal contribution was the Second Helvetic Confession of 1566. The Second Helvetic Confession became the most influential of the sixteenth-century Reformed confessions, cited by churches from Hungary to the British American colonies. Bullinger and Calvin had worked out a Reformed agreement on the nature of communion, but they remained quietly at odds on questions such as "double predestination" (the divine decree for the elect to be saved and for sinners to be condemned) and the nature of God's covenant with the elect. The Second Helvetic Confession was sufficiently broad to encompass most views within Reformed churches. Bullinger framed the confession as being fully in line with the great tradition of the church, beginning with Scripture, but also with the testimony of church fathers, especially Augustine. The Second Helvetic Confession repeatedly commended Augustine as speaking "truly and according to Scripture." Citing Rom 3:28, the confession affirmed that believers receive "justification, not through any works, but through faith in the mercy of God and in Christ, we therefore teach and believe with the apostle that sinful man is justified by faith alone in Christ, not by the law or any works." Regarding predestination, Bullinger declared that "From eternity God has freely, and of his mere grace, without any respect to men, predestinated or elected the saints whom he wills to save in Christ." Against the Anabaptists, the confession insisted that baptism introduced children into the covenanted community of the church. "We condemn the Anabaptists," Bullinger wrote, "who deny that newborn infants of the faithful are to be baptized. For according to evangelical teaching, of such is the Kingdom of God, and they are in the covenant of God. Why, then, should the sign of God's covenant not be given to them?" If anything, the confession's condemnation of the Anabaptists was more direct than its criticism of the papacy.

John Calvin

For all Bullinger's brilliance, his colleague John Calvin (1509–64) was the most influential of Luther's European successors, and the most trenchant theologian of the Reformed movement. Indeed, Calvin and Jonathan Edwards are arguably the two greatest theologians produced by Reformed Protestant churches, which are sometimes simply known as "Calvinist." Born in France and a graduate of the University of Paris, Calvin came under similar Christian humanist influences as Bullinger before his conversion to the principle of salvation by grace alone. Calvin came to this conviction around 1533 or 1534. The new focus on justification by grace prompted Calvin, a lawyer by training, to begin writing his seminal *Institutes of the Christian Religion*, which was first published in 1536. Calvin had thought of moving to the Protestant stronghold of Strasbourg, on the French and German border, but a providential stopover at Geneva led Calvin to settle there instead at the behest of Geneva's Protestant leaders. Calvin and his Reformed colleagues were abruptly expelled from Geneva in 1538, which allowed Calvin to reach his once-expected destination of Strasbourg. There he spent formative years working with Martin Bucer, the key Protestant leader in the city. In the meantime, conditions in Geneva became favorable for Calvin's return, which took place in 1541.

Calvin and his Reformed allies transformed Geneva's church and state in accord with what they saw as the biblical model. Dispensing with the Catholic hierarchy of bishops and archbishops, Calvin substituted offices of elders, pastors, and deacons. The Reformed ministers oversaw the church and tended to the city's spiritual and physical needs. The pastors and elders of Geneva belonged to the "consistory." Blending the functions of state and church, the consistory monitored the spiritual well-being and behavior of Genevans. Around 7 percent of Geneva's whole population appeared before Calvin's consistory every year, facing questions about everything from marital disputes to insufficiently Protestant religious practices. To the consternation of many Genevans, the consistory liberally employed excommunication, especially banning people from communion, as a disciplinary tool against rich and poor alike. To critics of Calvin, this sort of oversight seems heavy-handed. But most if not all members of Geneva's consistory were committed to fostering an ethically and doctrinally sound environment in the city. Protestant refugees flowed into Geneva from around Europe, and most of them eagerly supported Calvin's program of reform and pastoral oversight.

Women in the Reformation

Although Calvin gets headline billing, Calvin's Reformation depended upon the support of thousands of clergy and laypeople whose names are little remembered today. Many of them migrated within Europe in order to escape violence or to find a congenial religious environment. In Geneva, for example, one of the Reformation's defenders was the former nun Marie Dentière (c. 1495–1561). Born in France, she moved with her family to Geneva in 1535, just before Calvin's arrival. In her 1539 polemic *A Most Beneficial Letter . . . Against the Turks, the Jews, the Infidels, the False Christians, Anabaptists, and Lutherans*, Dentière defended Reformed theology against all comers. She also took up women's roles as theological advocates in the church. "If God has given grace to some good women, revealing to them by his holy scriptures something holy and good, should they hesitate to write, speak, and declare it to one another because of the defamers of truth? Ah, it would be too bold to try to stop them." She acknowledged the different biblical roles for men and women in church and family, but also insisted that there was only one gospel, which men and women alike were to proclaim. Her *Letter* defended Calvin, then exiled in Strasbourg, over the other leaders in Geneva in 1539. The missive's incendiary tone offended many in the city, and Dentière's publisher (who had attempted to remain anonymous) was arrested and many copies of the *Letter* were destroyed. Calvin and Dentière's relationship, though supportive, was testy. Calvin undoubtedly appreciated her backing during his return to Geneva, but he was uncomfortable with her assertive, public role in the Genevan Reformed movement, calling her an "unruly" woman in 1546. Yet fifteen years later, Calvin asked Dentière to write a preface to a sermon he wrote on female clothing and modesty, and Dentière did so. No other women writers were published in Geneva in the sixteenth century.

> This is my principal cause, my lady, that has moved me to write to you, hoping in God, that henceforth women will no longer be scorned as in the past.
>
> ———
>
> Marie Dentière to Queen Marguerite of Navarre, *A Most Beneficial Letter*, 1539

Reformers elevated the roles for godly women as wives and mothers, and the Protestant insistence on the permissibility of marriage for clergy cut down on priestly concubinage, which was rife in the pre-Reformation Catholic Church. But official roles for women in religious vocations became more constrained than they were in pre-Reformation Catholic culture, exceptions such as Dentière notwithstanding. Women who had served as nuns sometimes got married, as in the case of Luther's wife Katharina von Bora, or Bullinger's wife Anna Adlischweiler. But Protestant pressure to close convents was not always effective, and nuns often found themselves in a liminal state while Protestant authorities controlled a city. Some were grudgingly allowed to keep their convent open; some preserved what amounted to Protestantized convents. Some nuns left their convents but maintained a quasi-monastic existence in homes of friendly families. Protestant leaders worried about the unreformed convents as sources of heterodoxy, or worse. One German Protestant wrote "what misery, terrible deeds must occur in women's cloisters, in erring consciences, in secret burnings, secret swearing, blasphemy, evils which may not be spoken of, for it cannot be denied that a woman is far more easily persuaded, easily misled and more cunning than a man."This type of concern about the lurid goings-on in convents became a staple of popular anti-Catholic polemics well into the 1800s.

Heresy in Geneva

As for Calvin, he addressed the range of classic Reformed theology in his writings, but he is probably best known for his robust view of God's sovereignty, including God's sovereignty over salvation and damnation. Calvin would not have placed predestination at the center of his theology, but it became a major focus in his revisions of the *Institutes*. Many Reformers taught that God predestined his chosen people to salvation, but Calvin believed that the non-elect were also condemned to hell by God's eternal decree. As Calvin noted in the *Institutes*, "To many this seems a perplexing subject, because they deem it most incongruous that of the great body of mankind some should be predestinated to salvation, and others to destruction." Pointing to passages such as Romans 9, Calvin insisted that his view was scriptural and was confirmed in the church fathers, particularly Augustine. Some in Geneva disagreed. One disputant was a former Catholic friar named Jerome Bolsec (d. 1585), who declared that double predestination fed into unbiblical fatalism about salvation. An eternal decree condemning sinners to hell would effectively make God responsible for those people remaining lost in their sin. When Bolsec publicly touted these views, Calvin had him arrested and banished from the city. Bolsec, who eventually returned to the Catholic Church, spent much of the rest of his life reviling Calvin and his successor, Theodore Beza.

The disciplinary case for which Calvin is most notorious was that of Michael Servetus (d. 1553). Servetus was a Spanish doctor who had become an Arian, or one who denied the Trinity and the eternal existence of Jesus as the Son of God. Servetus's aberrant views were abhorrent to both Catholic and Protestant authorities. The Catholic Inquisition first condemned Servetus in Lyon, France, but Servetus escaped from a Catholic prison and foolishly went to Geneva in 1553. Servetus had a self-destructive penchant for confrontation. He may have figured that going to Geneva would have either resulted in his rallying the city's growing anti-Calvin sentiment or in his martyrdom for Arianism. He got the latter. Genevan authorities condemned him to burning at the stake for heresy when Servetus refused to recant. Calvin seems to have been ambivalent about this harsh method of execution. Again, the banishment or even killing of dissenters was common in both Catholic and Protestant circles, where there was significant blurring of lines between church and state. What Geneva did to Servetus may seem extreme, but it was not unusual at the time. Calvin received the approval of key Protestant leaders, including Bullinger and Melanchthon, for Servetus's death sentence. Calvin regarded the banishment of Bolsec, the burning of Servetus, and similar episodes as tragedies resulting from people's rejection of God's Word and of God's ordained authorities in church and state.

The Spread of Calvinism

Calvin was first and foremost a preacher, and he helped to pioneer the classic Protestant and Reformed mode of painstaking exegetical preaching through Scripture. Calvin and his followers had a high view of lay Christians' capacity to understand theological truth. He would spend years, and hundreds of sermons, explicating individual books of the Bible. Calvin's followers eagerly received his preaching, and Geneva unsurprisingly became a Reformed publishing center to distribute Calvin's commentaries and sermons more widely. Perhaps the most important work produced at Geneva in the sixteenth century, however, was the English-language "Geneva Bible," published in 1560. Reformed printers had just begun to include verse numbers in Bibles. Verse numbers ("John 3:16") did not appear in the original biblical texts. But they made it easier to study the Bible and to refer to a preacher's text for yourself. The Geneva Bible included verse numbers, as well as Calvinist-themed marginal notes. These made it something like a modern "study Bible."

The Geneva Bible was wildly popular for a century among readers in England, Scotland, and the American colonies until it was gradually replaced by the (noteless) Authorized Version, or King James Bible, of 1611.

Despite Calvin's angular personality, he hoped to play a unifying role in the international Reformed community. This unifying impulse produced its greatest fruit in his partnership with Bullinger on the 1549 *Consensus Tigurinus*, the era's key Reformed statement on the meaning of communion. As we have seen, communion was the most divisive issue among Protestants. Bullinger and Calvin crafted a broad Reformed position that affirmed more than Zwingli's symbolic view but did not go as far as Luther did in insisting on the real presence of Christ in the meal. (Of course, it repudiated the Catholic view of transubstantiation.) "The notion of any kind of local presence ought especially to be set aside," the *Consensus* said. "While signs are present in this world, they are discerned by the eyes and touched by the hands, but Christ, so far as he is man, is to be sought nowhere other than in heaven, and not otherwise than with the mind and the understanding of faith." Luther had passed away in 1546, but his successors took up the banner of the real presence, lambasting Bullinger and Calvin for their errors.

The Lutheran and the Reformed factions of the Protestant movement had become permanently divided. The Reformed wing developed a more robust international following, however, partly due to the constant flow of refugees and ministers in and out of Geneva. Calvinism was overall more cosmopolitan in orientation. In places such as Scotland and Transylvania (in Romania), Reformed theology took on a legally established status. In America, Reformed and Calvinist theology animated English, Scottish, Welsh, Scots-Irish, and Dutch congregations, as well as Puritan, Presbyterian, Baptist, and (in a more contested fashion) Anglican traditions. On the American side of the Great Awakening in the 1730s and '40s, all the major revivalists across denominations were Calvinists. Lutheran theology was always more denominationally-centered and regional, but it tended to be carried abroad by German and Scandinavian immigrants.

Calvinism's wide dissemination, in addition to the Reformed advocates who took it across nations and oceans, was prompted by Calvin's writing itself. The *Institutes* were published at first in Latin and in French, showing that he had scholarly and popular audiences in mind for the book from the start. Calvin died in 1564 and was buried (according to his instruction) in an unmarked grave so as to prevent idolatrous veneration of his corpse. But the *Institutes* and Calvin's biblical commentaries would carry his legacy forward for ever-larger audiences. In 1559, Calvin completed a massive expansion of the

Institutes, now running to more than a thousand pages. Many popular editions of Calvin's best-known work would be condensations, translations, and annotations of the complete tome. Far more people consulted sections of the *Institutes* than read the 1559 edition from beginning to end. William Delaune's *Epitome* edition of the *Institutes* was more popular in England in the 1600s than the bulky original volume. In addition to English editions, Delaune's book came out in Dutch and Latin versions. By the 1580s, two decades after his death, Calvin had become by far the most widely read Reformed theologian in England. Calvin could not be ignored, even by his critics. The Dutch theologian Jacob Arminius (1560–1609), whose free will "Arminian" theology came to stand for anti-Calvinism, said he owned more of Calvin's works than those of any other writer.

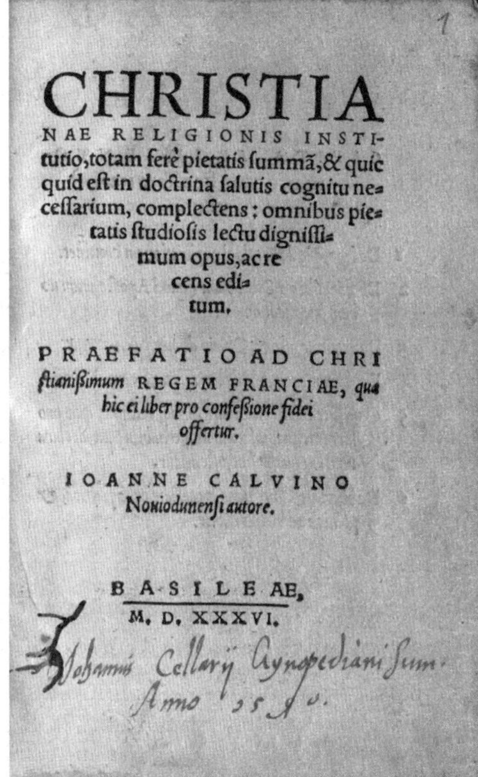
CHRISTIA
NAE RELIGIONIS INSTI-
tutio,totam ferè pietatis ſummã,& quic
quid eſt in doctrina ſalutis cognitu ne-
ceſſarium, complectens: omnibus pietatis ſtudioſis lectu dignißi-
mum opus,ac re
cens edi-
tum.

PRAEFATIO AD CHRI
ſtianißimum REGEM FRANCIAE, qua
hic ei liber pro confeßione fidei
offertur.

IOANNE CALVINO
Nouiodunenſi autore.

BASILEAE,
M. D. XXXVI.

Image 2.1. Calvin's *Institutes* (1536)

The French Reformation

Despite the movement's dynamism after Calvin's death, Reformed churches faced some of their greatest difficulties in France, the land of Calvin's birth. French Protestantism had swelled to formidable numbers by the 1560s, seeded by Calvin's network of refugees, pastors, and publications. As with Luther's phase of the Reformation, print fueled the French Protestant movement, driven by versions of the *Institutes*, the French vernacular Bible, and perhaps most frequently, the French psalter, used for congregational singing. In 1562, Catholic partisans unleashed the first of many waves of violence against French Protestants, who were called "Huguenots." France descended into the Wars of Religion for most of the rest of the 1500s, with competing sides led by nobles aligned with Protestants or Catholics. Some of the violence was committed in formal military encounters, but the Continent was also racked by Catholic vigilante attacks on Protestants, and vice versa. In

1572, Reformed partisans captured the Dutch town of Brill, for instance, and executed nineteen Catholic priests.

Later that year, France saw its worst outbreak of inter-confessional violence, in the St. Bartholomew's Day massacre of Huguenots. The French royal family had arranged for a strategic interreligious marriage between Princess Marguerite and King Henry of Navarre, which they hoped would ease tensions between the warring Catholics and Protestants. But the provocative French Protestant leader, Admiral Gaspard de Coligny, foolishly attended the wedding festivities. Several days after the wedding, Coligny was shot and nearly killed in Paris by a Catholic assassin. The attempt on Coligny's life brought the nation's simmering tensions to an overflowing boil. Royal French soldiers began executing Huguenot leaders in Paris. Catholic mobs took the cue and started a murderous rampage in Paris and in regional cities, torturing and killing some 5000 Protestants. The Protestant King Henry of Navarre, just wedded to Princess Marguerite, converted to Catholicism out of fear for his life. Henry of Navarre went on to become King Henry IV of France (r. 1589–1610). He permanently renounced Protestantism in the 1590s, to the grave disappointment of Huguenots and international supporters such as Geneva's Theodore Beza. Henry IV hoped that his return to the Catholic fold would secure peace and religious toleration in France. He was successful, at least for the time being, as he brought the Wars of Religion to an end and promulgated the Edict of Nantes (1598), which promised toleration to the Huguenots. This ostensibly permanent settlement lasted nine decades until King Louis XIV revoked the Edict of Nantes in 1685 and generated another wave of persecution against the beleaguered Huguenots. Though some Christian groups have thrived under persecution, the successive outbreaks of violence against the Huguenots hampered what otherwise could have been one of the most vibrant segments of the international Reformed community.

Anabaptists and Mennonites among the Calvinists

The Calvinist movement was arguably the most powerful theological tradition among the many strains of Protestantism. By the time of Calvin's death, it was clear that only two or three convictions united Protestants. One was hostility toward the Catholic Church. Another was justification by grace alone, and a third was the primacy of the Bible. But Protestants reached different conclusions about other important doctrines and practices, especially communion and baptism. Claims to follow the Bible brought general (though not detailed) agreement on *sola fide*, but differing understandings of communion and baptism divided Protestants into camps that were sometimes as hostile toward one another as they were toward Catholics.

As we have seen, several groups promoting believer's baptism had appeared in Switzerland and Germany in the 1520s and '30s. They followed their biblicist impulse to its logical conclusion: a literal reading of Scripture seemed to indicate that churches were to baptize only those who had personally repented and believed in Christ. The Anabaptists were fighting against a millennium of church tradition that had overwhelmingly supported infant baptism, however. The Anabaptists were also a diffuse and fractious movement which rarely enjoyed the support of friendly magistrates. Anabaptists suffered for centuries to escape the memory of the apocalyptic debacle which unfolded in Münster, Germany, in 1534–1535: the terroristic reign of John of Leiden. John declared himself the "king of righteousness" over Münster, which he renamed the New Jerusalem. He demanded that his followers obey his every command, and he banished all who would not receive believer's baptism. John also established polygamous marriage and took sixteen wives. Protestant and Catholic forces in the region eventually combined to besiege Münster. John of Leiden was captured, tortured for months, and finally executed in 1536. For centuries afterward, Anabaptists and Baptists endured accusations that they were the spawn of the "monsters of Münster."

In fact, Anabaptists were more likely to embrace pacifism than the horrifying tactics of John of Leiden. The Dutch (Frisian) Anabaptist leader Menno Simons (1496–1561) established many of his convictions about Anabaptist principles in reaction to the violent excesses of Münster. He hoped that his followers would repudiate worldly power and violence, and establish quiet, Christ-centered congregations of the baptized. Simons had been a Catholic priest, but in the early 1530s he learned about Anabaptist teachings. He broke with the Catholic Church and by 1540 had become a major teacher among the Frisian and northern German Anabaptists. Simons's key work was *The Foundation of Christian Doctrine*, in which he explained that "Young children are without understanding and cannot be taught, therefore, baptism cannot be administered to them without perverting the ordinance of the Lord; misusing his exalted name, and doing violence to his holy word. In the New Testament there are no ordinances enjoined upon infants." Simons explicitly repudiated the horrors of Münster, telling magistrates that Anabaptists would resist no authority unless the directives were contrary to the Word of God. Simons's most controversial position during his time was his view of baptism, but in the longer term, his most unusual doctrine was his rejection of the belief in Christ having two natures joined in one person. Instead, Simons, who was concerned about how Christ could take on flesh and yet remain sinless, argued that Christ really had a divine nature alone. This was a species of monophysitism, a heresy which church authorities condemned in the fifth century. Subsequent Mennonites have returned to the traditional Christian position of two natures in one person, articulated at the Council of Chalcedon in 451. Calvinists, the Anabaptists' most formidable Protestant opponents, reviled Simons and his "Mennonites" for their views on baptism, the incarnation, and their belief in humanity's free will in salvation. Calvin himself, learning about a Reformed minister's debate with Menno Simons, asked "who is stubborner than this dog, or stupider than this ass?" When Simons died in 1561, however, the Mennonites had become major players on the Anabaptist scene.

Catholic Counter-Reformation

As we have observed, many of the early Reformers such as Simons and Martin Luther began their lives and ministries as Catholics. Thus, Catholics were not uniformly hostile to the Reformation; early Catholic reformers were responsible for the Reformation. Reformed and Lutheran leaders still believed they were drawing on the best of the Christian tradition in their teachings. Augustine was the church father most commonly referenced by the Protestants. Among Catholics who remained within their church, there was a wide range of responses to the splintering of European Christendom. Some were sympathetic to Protestant critiques of church doctrine and practice, and some sought reconciliation between Catholics and Protestants. Other Catholics might have conceded that there were problems within the institutional church, but they saw breakaway Protestants as dangerous radicals who should be ruthlessly suppressed.

This range of Catholic responses to the Reformation fueled what scholars call the "Counter-Reformation," or the "Catholic Reformation." These alternative terms reflect a debate over the extent to which changes in the Catholic Church represented a reaction to the Reformation itself or were part of longer-term Catholic reform movements that preceded the Reformation. In any case, changes were afoot in the Catholic Church, and there seems little question that the pressure of the Reformation helped many Catholics to take more seriously the mandate of internal churchly and doctrinal reforms. But Reformation pressure also led some Catholics into a defensive and even paranoid fear about Protestant incursions. This was especially the case in southern European countries such as Spain and Italy, where the Reformation made few inroads.

Spain had an active Catholic Inquisition dating back decades before the Reformation. Spanish Catholics worried about a long-standing Muslim presence in their nation: the final Muslim stronghold in Granada had only fallen to the Spanish Christians in 1492. Spanish Catholics were also concerned about Jewish "conversos" who claimed to have converted to Christianity but who remained perennial objects of suspicion. In the 1500s, the Inquisition transitioned into monitoring and suppressing Protestants and outright heretics (such as Michael Servetus). During the tenure of Pope Paul IV in the mid-1550s, the pontiff instituted a comprehensive list of banned books, the *Index Librorum Prohibitorum*, which led to the burning of some 10,000 books in Venice in 1558. The prohibited titles included not only those of Protestant writers but also those of the Catholic humanist Desiderius Erasmus and vernacular translations of the Bible.

If the Inquisition reflected the rigid defensiveness of some Catholic leaders, the founding of new Catholic orders, especially the Jesuits, reflected a new missionary and educational zeal for combatting the Protestant threat. The founder of the Jesuits (the Society of Jesus) was the Basque/Spanish priest Ignatius of Loyola (1491–1556).[1] Battle wounds suffered in 1521 put Loyola into a long convalescence, which turned into months of spiritual seeking, culminating in a conversion-like experience in which Loyola devoted himself to the service of the church. Loyola went to study at the University of Paris in the late 1520s, where he briefly overlapped with John Calvin. A decade later Loyola and a circle of Catholic compatriots moved to Italy and offered their services to the pope, who officially commissioned the Society of Jesus in 1540.

The Jesuits did not initially stand out as an innovative or aggressive order. Instead, they were inspired partly by older ideals of the *devotio moderna* and the warm piety modeled by Thomas à Kempis's *The Imitation of Christ*. The full-fledged Counter-Reformation of the 1550s and '60s would greatly expand the Jesuits' focus. In his devotional zeal, however, Loyola was joined by other great Spanish writers of the 1500s, most notably John of the Cross, and John's mentor, Teresa of Ávila. Teresa authored her classic text, *The Interior Castle*, showing the steps of meditation and prayer that led to ever-increasing closeness with God. Teresa wrote that there came for her a point of intense intimacy where "God so fixes himself in the interior of this soul, that when she comes to herself she cannot but believe she was in God, and that God was in her."

---

[1] Íñigo López de Loyola was his original name.

The early 1560s saw the final sessions of the Council of Trent in northern Italy, which was a major assembly of Catholic officials that had been periodically meeting since the mid-1540s to respond to the Protestant challenge. The resulting "Tridentine" reforms firmly positioned the Catholic Church in an anti-Protestant stance, which it would officially maintain at least until the reforms of Vatican II in the 1960s. The Tridentine Creed affirmed the authority of the tradition of the church, as well as transubstantiation. In the service of the mass, it said, "there is made a change of the whole essence of the bread into the body, and of the whole essence of the wine into the blood." Once again, the differences between Europe's Christian movements were often framed as variant understandings of what transpired in the Eucharist, or communion. The Council of Trent also formalized the Latin Mass, which would be the template for Catholic services for four centuries.

Image 2.2. *Statue of Ignatius of Loyola, Pima, AZ*

Expanding Catholicism

The Council of Trent did not overtly address the need for Catholic world missions, but the renewal or founding of orders such as the Jesuits, plus the expansion of Catholic economic and military empires (especially Portugal and Spain) led to an unprecedented attempt to establish a Catholic presence around the world. Systematic Catholic overseas missionary efforts pre-dated Protestant ones by almost two centuries. Loyola's Jesuit companion Francis Xavier (1506–52) set the pace. In the early 1540s Xavier and other Jesuit missionaries followed paths created by the growth of the Portuguese empire in Africa, India, Japan, and China. Franciscans and Dominicans likewise followed Spanish expansion and conquest in the Caribbean basin and throughout the Americas, following Christopher Columbus's Spanish-sponsored explorations there starting in 1492. Spanish clerics baptized millions of people in the Americas by the mid-1500s, though many of those "converts" received little pastoral oversight. Many native converts appeared to see their adherence to the Catholic faith as tentative and contingent.

Perhaps the key breakthrough for the "indigenization" of Catholicism in the emerging mestizo culture in Central America was the reported appearance of the Virgin of Guadalupe to an Aztec Catholic convert named Juan Diego in 1531. (Indigenization refers to the process of Christianity becoming integrated with a different local culture, rather than just a product of the sending culture, which in the early modern period meant European.) The Virgin Mary, it was said, confirmed her apparitions to Juan Diego when her image miraculously appeared on the cloak Diego was wearing as he appeared before a Catholic bishop. That Mary would appear to a native of Mexico seemed to indicate that the Catholic God was not European but was present among the native peoples of the Americas, too. Father Miguel Sanchez, who recorded the account of the Virgin of Guadalupe in the mid-1600s, was also inspired by the writings of Augustine in narrating the apparitions. From figures as varied as Luther and Miguel Sanchez, the theological resources that both Protestants and Catholics found in Augustine seemed to have no end. With its ancient roots in the Middle East, North Africa, and elsewhere, Christianity had always been more than a European faith. Yet the missions of the Catholic Reformation signaled a major new era of Christian globalization.

Selected Bibliography

Baker, J. Wayne. *Heinrich Bullinger and the Covenant: The Other Reformed Tradition*. Athens: Ohio University Press, 1980.

Brading, David A. *Mexican Phoenix: Our Lady of Guadalupe: Image and Tradition across Five Centuries*. New York: Cambridge University Press, 2001.

Clossey, Luke. *Salvation and Globalization in the Early Jesuit Missions*. New York: Cambridge University Press, 2008.

Dentière, Marie. *Epistle to Marguerite de Navarre; and, Preface to a Sermon by John Calvin*. Edited by Mary B. McKinley. Chicago: University of Chicago Press, 2004.

Eire, Carlos M. N. *The Life of Saint Teresa of Avila: A Biography*. Princeton, NJ: Princeton University Press, 2019.

Gordon, Bruce. *John Calvin's Institutes of the Christian Religion: A Biography*. Princeton, NJ: Princeton University Press, 2016.

———. *Zwingli: God's Armed Prophet*. New Haven, CT: Yale University Press, 2021.

Hsia, R. Po-chia, ed. *A Companion to the Reformation World*. Malden, MA: Blackwell, 2004.

Probst, Christopher J. *Demonizing the Jews: Luther and the Protestant Church in Nazi Germany*. Bloomington: Indiana University Press, 2012.

Roper, Lyndal. *The Holy Household: Women and Morals in Reformation Augsburg*. New York: Oxford University Press, 1991.

Selderhuis, Herman J., ed. *The Calvin Handbook*. Grand Rapids: Eerdmans, 2009.

—— Chapter 3 ——

The Catholic Reformation

European Catholic missionaries began to create fully global Christian networks in the 1500s. The emerging new worlds of Catholicism could be dizzyingly complex. Take the shrine to the Virgin of Guadalupe. Devotees built this shrine sometime in the sixteenth century near Mexico City, on the spot where a temple to the Nahuatl/Aztec goddess Tonantzin ("Our Mother") had once stood. The building of Catholic churches and shrines on the sites of pagan temples, often using building materials from the demolished edifice, was standard practice, especially at Catholic missionary sites of the Americas. Mexico's Virgin of Guadalupe shrine depended on one of the same name in Castile, Spain, inspired by a Marian apparition to a Spanish rancher in the 1300s. In what became the most widespread Marian devotion in the Americas, there were influences from Spanish Castile, Nahuatl religion, and older European Catholic venerations of Mary. Yet in the 1500s, the dedication to Our Lady of Guadalupe started to become an indigenous Catholic devotional tradition. European Catholic officials affirmed this tradition with the canonization of Juan Diego (the man to whom the Virgin appeared in 1531, in the Mexican Guadalupe account) as a saint in 2002. Diego was the first indigenous person from the Americas to achieve that recognition.

Missions in the New World

Medieval European Christians and clergy struggled with questions of contextualization, or the extent to which Christianity can adapt to local culture or non-Christian religious traditions and remain faithful to the great tradition of Christian theology. The medieval church was rife with what some modern observers might consider magical or superstitious practices. But the expansion of European Christian missions and churches to the Americas, Africa, and Asia raised questions of syncretism and indigenization in ways more pressing than ever before. Missionaries and clergy worried, with some justification, that the faith of new adherents was contingent and that it often just supplemented pre-existing religious practices. The baptized "convert" who went to Catholic mass might also consult their tribe's shaman or make sacrifices to local deities. He or she might see no inherent problem with combining Catholic and indigenous religious practices. But clergy and missionaries did see problems with this hybrid faith. Especially when priests baptized large numbers of people in response to the professed affiliation of a tribal leader, the adherence of individual "Indios" to the faith could be deeply uncertain. Some native people in the Americas became devout Catholics, of course, and some maintained their Christian faith even when it was not advantageous to do so. Others turned against the colonizers and missionaries, engaging in anti-Catholic rebellions that periodically rocked Spanish colonies from Peru to New Mexico.

Christopher Columbus (1451–1506), the Italian explorer working for the Spanish monarchs, framed his New World discoveries as victories for Christendom. He wrote to Spain's Ferdinand and Isabel in 1493 that "our Redeemer has given victory to our most illustrious King and Queen, and to their kingdoms rendered famous by this glorious event, at which all Christendom should rejoice . . . with fervent prayers for the high distinction that will accrue to them from turning so many peoples to our holy faith." As with many Europeans, Columbus implied that Spain's arrival on the American scene was virtually equivalent to the Christian conversion of the native peoples there.

Shortly after Columbus began to explore the Caribbean basin in 1492, Pope Alexander VI divided the known world between the imperial powers of Spain and Portugal. This arrangement was confirmed in the Treaty of Tordesillas in 1494. Under the treaty's terms, Spain was given control of most of the Americas and the Caribbean, except for Portugal's main New World colony of Brazil. Spain's colonial possessions encompassed thousands of miles of mainland with formidable native societies, which led to the invasions by conquistadores such as Hernando Cortés in Mexico and Francisco Pizzaro in Peru. They, and the epidemic diseases they unwittingly introduced, caused massive devastation for the native peoples of the Americas. Catholic missionaries came in the conquistadores' wake, baptizing thousands of the surviving Indians and gathering them into sedentary farming communities centered on mission churches. Epidemic disease, military conquest, and the widespread enslavement of native people was not an auspicious context in which to raise up functioning indigenous Catholic congregations. Yet these jarring realities remained characteristic of many Catholic and Protestant colonies in the Americas and elsewhere for centuries.

Catholic missionaries were often complicit in the maltreatment of native peoples. Other missionaries found themselves at odds with civil or military leaders concerning the abuses. The most famous critic of Spanish imperial rule was the priest Bartolomé de las Casas (1484–1566). He had worked in Hispaniola (today's Haiti and the Dominican Republic) and Cuba and had owned Indian slaves before having his conscience stirred and divesting himself of his plantation holdings. Las Casas spent his remaining decades advocating for the protection and rights of Indians in the Americas. His best-known work was *A Short Account of the Destruction of the Indies*, published in Spain in 1552. Las Casas gave a harrowing portrait of the brutality of the Spanish conquests, concluding that "The Spaniards first set sail to America, not for the honor of God, or as persons moved and merited thereunto by fervent zeal to the true faith, nor to promote the salvation of their neighbors . . . but in truth, only stimulated and goaded on by insatiable avarice and ambition." Las Casas did convince some Catholic officials in Spain and Rome that they needed to restrain the worst exploitations. Las Casas enjoyed greater influence among Protestants than Catholics, however. Protestants used Las Casas to lambaste Catholic colonizers as exceptionally cruel. Dozens of translated editions of *The Destruction of the Indies* appeared in Germany, England, and the Netherlands, sometimes with lurid illustrations of the horrors of the Spanish New World ventures. Such propaganda would increase the sense of urgency to initiate long-delayed Protestant missions.

> The Spaniards entered like wolves, tigers, and lions which had been starving for many days, and since forty years they have done nothing else.
>
> ---
>
> Bartolomé de las Casas, *A Short Account of the Destruction of the Indies*, 1552

Virtually every mission outpost in the Catholic world struggled with the questions of syncretism and accommodation of local religion. Catholic and Protestant missionaries alike wrestled with difficulties in translating Christian terminology into native languages, which often did not have equivalents for terms such as the Trinity, sin, hell, the devil, or the one sovereign God. How much indigenous religious language could the missionaries import without diluting the essential message of Christianity? As seen in the use of pagan temples for shrines and churches, clergy often presented Christianity as a replacement for older native rituals and concepts. Sometimes "replacement" did not foster a smooth break from the past, however. For example, one of the most popular festivals in Latin America was (and is) the Day of the Dead (Día de los Muertos), which combined the Christian celebrations of All Saints' and All Souls' days. It also drew on preexisting pagan festivals to revere dead ancestors. Accommodating local traditions was an obvious way to bridge cultural and religious gaps with indigenous people. Catholic and Protestant churches were often reluctant to give indigenous men ordination as pastors or priests, though. In 1555, the Mexican provincial government banned Indians, mestizos (people of Indian and Spanish parentage), or Africans as priests, reserving that office for Europeans only.

98 Spieghel der Spaenſche Tyrannye,

Figuere Num. 17.

DE Voedſter-Moeders teer het Landt hier moeten bouvven,
Die door den ſvvaren laſt gheen Soch en konnen houvven:
Dees' mergheelooſe drooght' veroorſaeckt groote noodt,
En brengt aen menich Kindt een ontijdighe doodt.
De Mannen die ter vlucht de ſlaverny ontſluypten,
Ghekreghen zijnde, die, met Oly ſy bedruypten,
Gheghceſſelt vvierden ſy, tot 't Lichaem vvas als Bloet:
Och Godt! wat d'eene Mensch den ander hier al doet.

In

Image 3.1. *Image from Dutch edition of Las Casas's* Destruction of the Indies (1620)

Missions in the Far East

The Jesuits were aggressively evangelistic and were experimenters in "accommodationist" missions, particularly in India and China. (The Jesuits were relative latecomers to Spanish missions. Until the 1700s, much of their presence in the Americas was limited to Portuguese Brazil.) In the Portuguese colony in India, the Italian Jesuit Roberto Nobili (1577–1656) pioneered an accommodationist approach in 1606 by downplaying the European trappings of the mission and seeking to adapt a style more familiar to local Tamil culture. He adapted the habit of a Hindu priest or hermit (Brahmin) and studied religious texts in local languages. Nobili and his supporters argued that Indian converts to Christianity should be allowed to maintain any pre-existing religious practices they wished, as long as they did not directly violate Christian morals or doctrine.

Earlier conversions to Christianity among the Paravas of India offered a different model of Catholic evangelization from that of Nobili. The Paravas were a lower-caste group of fishermen in villages along the southeastern coast of India. They felt threatened by hostile and powerful Muslim and Hindu trading factions and saw "conversion" as an opportunity to court the Portuguese as protectors. Parava leaders approached Portuguese officials about baptism in 1536, and ultimately about 20,000 Paravas—effectively the whole community—received baptism. (Paedobaptists would, of course, baptize adult converts who had never received baptism as children.) Yet many of these converts understood little about Christian beliefs. When the Jesuit founder Francis Xavier began working in the region in 1542, he instructed Parava Catholics in rudimentary doctrine, teaching them to say the Lord's Prayer and the Apostles' Creed. On the whole, the Parava baptisms suggested an episode of group "affiliation" rather than individual conversions. Especially when people from non-Christian cultural backgrounds become Christians, there are typically elements of both group affiliation and individual conversion involved. Protestants have commonly wished to see more of an emphasis on the individual's changing belief than what transpired among the Paravas, however.

In China, the Italian Jesuit missionary Matteo Ricci (1552–1610) employed an accommodationist approach similar to Nobili's. He initially adopted the style of a Buddhist monk, but then switched to the garb of a Confucian scholar when he realized that it would garner more respect among Chinese officials. He studied Chinese texts and Confucian philosophy, but also taught his pupils about the latest advances in European science and technology, displaying telescopes, clocks, and bound books. Some of his prospective converts seem to have found Ricci admirable but inscrutable. "I still do not know what he is here for," said the Confucian scholar Li Zhi about Ricci. "I think it would be much too stupid for him to want to substitute his own teaching for that of Confucius. So that is surely not the reason." Indeed, Ricci was impressed by Confucian philosophy (he was less admiring of Buddhism or Taoism). He believed that like the pre-Christian teachings of ancient Greece and Rome, Confucianism reflected salutary natural philosophy. It was a stepping stone to the exclusive, revealed truth of Christianity. Christian teaching received significant resistance from Confucian and Buddhist authorities, however, who balked at the Jesuits' conceptions of grace, forgiveness, heaven, and hell.

By the time of Ricci's death in 1610, the number of Chinese Catholic converts was small, maybe around 2,500 people. Ricci and the Jesuits had built a significant foundation for the expansion of the Catholic church in China, however, and the number of converts expanded to 40,000 by 1636. In 1629, there were 26 Jesuit missionaries operating in China, with five native Chinese among them serving as assistants. Luo Wenzao was the first ordained Chinese priest. He became a bishop in 1685 but was the only Chinese bishop prior to the twentieth century. Beginning in the 1630s, the missions became the focus of the "Chinese Rites Controversy," in which critics questioned the extent to which Chinese religious terminology could be used to express Christian concepts and whether Chinese converts should be allowed to keep venerating their deceased ancestors. In 1742, Pope Benedict XIV formally banned Catholics from participating in the Chinese rites. Protestants in Europe and America eagerly followed news of the Chinese Rites Controversy, which they saw as the latest debacle caused by unreliable Catholic theology and practice.

Image 3.2. *Jesuits in China* (1667)

Catholic missionary work in Japan saw greater initial successes than in China, but then the missions encountered devastating opposition which effectively ended the public Catholic movement there for centuries. As in India and China, the Jesuits pioneered the Catholic labors in Japan, starting with the arrival of Francis Xavier in 1549. The Jesuits made special efforts to convert local chieftains with considerable results, especially on the southwestern Japanese island of Kyushu. Again, decisions to convert involved political, economic, and theological calculations for Japanese leaders, but the conversions led to remarkable scenes of mass baptisms of Japanese people. In 1574, a reported 40,000 people received baptism in just a few days. By 1600, there were around 300,000 Japanese who had at least nominally affiliated with the Catholic Church.

Japanese politics in the late 1500s were torn between competing local factions. As the Tokugawa clan began to consolidate power around 1600, the Japanese Christian movement and the Franciscan and Jesuit missionaries fell under persecution. In 1597 in Nagasaki, twenty-six missionaries and laypeople were executed by crucifixion. Similar episodes became more frequent after Tokugawa Ieyasu became the country's leader and took the office of shogun in 1603. In 1614, Ieyasu ordered the banishment of missionaries and decreed that Christianity was illegal. Japanese people who were known as Christians were sometimes executed, or tortured until they renounced the faith. The documented cases of martyrdom ran into the thousands, but the total number may have been 10,000 or more. The Japanese persecutions had a devastating effect on Catholicism. Surviving Catholics went underground and operated in small cells of "hidden" Christians. By the mid-1600s, Japan closed itself off from most contact with Europeans and remained that way until the 1800s. The best-known literary treatment of Japanese Christianity and the persecutions of the early 1600s came in Shūsaku Endō's 1966 historical novel *Silence*.

Missions in Africa

One of the most improbable success stories among the global Catholic missions was in the Kingdom of Kongo in West Africa. Churches and missionaries were often complicit in the transatlantic slave trade, and this was certainly the case with missionary orders involved in the early evangelization of West Africa. The Portuguese pioneered the European colonization and exploitation of West Africa, marked by the 1482 founding of Elmina, a slave trading hub on the Atlantic coast in present-day Ghana. The advent of the slave trade and the linguistic and cultural differences between Europeans and Africans contributed to a plodding spread of Catholicism among most West Africans during the early colonial era. Kongo was different, partly because it maintained a relatively independent status from Portuguese colonists and partly because of the extraordinary figure of Mvemba Nzinga (d. 1543), who took the Portuguese title King Afonso I in 1506. King Afonso became a devout Catholic after his baptism in 1491, though he routinely feuded with Portuguese authorities. The Kongolese nobility largely followed Afonso's Catholic commitment during the king's long reign.

The Portuguese presence in Kongo remained small in number and generally supportive of King Afonso. Afonso also sent one of his sons, Henry, to Lisbon to receive training as a priest, and in 1521, Henry became a Catholic bishop. Afonso himself was sincerely devoted to the faith, and one Portuguese priest wrote that "His Christian life is such that he appears to me not as a man but as an angel sent by the Lord to this kingdom to convert it, especially when he speaks and when he preaches." This priest also noted (favorably) that Afonso treated harshly the Kongolese who continued in pagan worship, having them burned alive along with their idols. Portuguese church officials understandably viewed Afonso's long reign (he died in 1543) as a golden age, and the church struggled to maintain its strength in Kongo and neighboring Angola for the rest of the 1500s. Catholic authorities kept sending missionaries and educators to the area, however. In 1624–1625, the Portuguese Jesuit Mattheus Cardoso published an enormously significant Portuguese-Kikongo catechism, the first surviving printed book in a Bantu language, the main vernacular linguistic group of the region. This, too, reflected the Jesuit policy of accommodation, as Catholic instruction up to that point had been in Latin or in some European language.

Image 3.3. *Kongo crucifix* (sixteenth to seventeenth centuries)

Missions in New France

The Jesuits' accommodationist philosophy also had implications for a final instance of global evangelization: that of New France, or Canada. French colonizers founded Quebec in 1608, a year after the English founded Jamestown, Virginia. French Jesuits began to arrive in Canada in the 1630s, believing that the indigenous people there had a God-given rationality that enabled them, despite their "barbaric" culture, to understand divine truth and that they needed missionaries to tell them about the Christian God. By the 1640s, the Jesuits focused on the Wendats (Hurons) as their primary evangelistic targets. They set up a mission station at Sainte-Marie, north of present-day Toronto. Borrowing from the example of Matteo Ricci and others, the Jesuits at Sainte-Marie studied native languages, but also employed European technologies such as clocks and books to impress prospective converts. The Jesuits shared the widely-held assumption that Christian culture was superior to "heathen" ones, and displaying novel technologies was a quick way to demonstrate that superiority to natives. Travel into the Canadian interior was fraught with danger, and the Jesuits and their assistants who went there saw themselves as the most devoted partisans of the Catholic Reformation. Women's religious orders also saw Quebec as a test of faith, and Marie de l'Incarnation Guyart (1599–1672) came from France in 1639 to found an Ursuline convent and school for girls. Like the Jesuits, Guyart prioritized learning native languages, and by the end of her life she had developed competency in the major indigenous dialects of the region.

The Jesuits in New France and their converts got caught in the crossfire of emerging wars between the Wendats and the tribes of the Iroquois League, a conflict that would result in the decimation of the Wendats and the destruction of the Sainte-Marie mission in 1649. As with most indigenous groups in the Americas, the coming of Europeans brought epidemic disease to the Wendats. War and epidemics created a highly unstable situation, which sometimes made native people more open to conversion. At other times the instability made Catholic missionaries a focus of resentment. Captivity among the Mohawks left Jesuit missionary Isaac Jogues with permanent injuries, but he came back to the Iroquois lands in 1646, only to suffer martyrdom by the Mohawks within a year. Other Jesuit missionaries died under similar circumstances at St. Ignace in 1649, the same year that the Jesuits abandoned and burned the Sainte-Marie mission. As the Wendats' Iroquois enemies closed in, the Jesuits baptized as many Wendats as they could, believing that they were saving the native people from hell's torments.

The destruction of the Wendats was a major setback for the Jesuits, but in the 1660s many of the region's missions relocated to areas controlled by the Wendats' enemies, the Iroquois tribes. The best-known convert among the Mohawks was Catherine Tekakwitha (1656–80), who received baptism at a village in upstate New York in 1676. She then moved to a Jesuit mission near Montreal and joined a women's confraternity whose intense piety drew both concern and admiration from the European priests. Her hardened asceticism, marked by self-flagellation, ice baths, and extended fasts, undoubtedly contributed to Tekakwitha's early death in 1680. Soon after she passed away, reports emerged of healings in response to prayers said at her grave or in connection with her relics, including her bones. The Catholic Church canonized Tekakwitha as a saint in 2012.

East-West Division

The canonization of Tekakwitha, like Juan Diego before her, signaled that by the early twenty-first century, the Catholic Church was becoming more fully global in its mindset and its roster of recognized saints. A church called "catholic" was by definition universal, but the rupture with the Protestant churches in the 1500s, combined with global colonization, energized a new worldwide scope for Catholic missions. The break with Protestants was hardly the first such division in Christendom. Most obviously, the Reformation was preceded by the East-West Schism which divided the Catholic Church from Eastern Orthodoxy in 1054, primarily over doctrinal and ecclesiastical disputes. The divide between Catholics and the Eastern Orthodox had continuing ramifications in the era of the Reformation. The conquest of Constantinople by the Ottoman Turks in 1453 reminded Catholic rulers to the west that schismatic Protestants were not the only religious-imperial threat to their interests. Muslim power was a major concern, too. After 1453, the Orthodox churches of the East became more focused on internal concerns than ever before, so contacts between Orthodox leaders and those of the Reformation were limited. (Enduring hostility between Orthodox and Catholic officials also limited their constructive interactions.) But Orthodox-Protestant exchanges did spring up after 1517 in surprising ways.

The most important figure for Orthodox connections to the Protestant world was Cyril I (1572–1638), the Ecumenical Patriarch of Constantinople. Born in Crete as Constantine Loukaris, Cyril received his education in Italy and was ordained in Constantinople in 1595. Ecclesiastical conflict in eastern Europe turned Cyril into an inveterate enemy of the Jesuits and gave him a more favorable view of Protestants. As he worked to counter Catholic proselytizing in eastern Europe, Cyril built bridges with Protestants in western Europe, including in England. He was convinced by Protestant criticisms of hierarchical church organizations, saying that he wished for Orthodox churches to manifest the biblical fidelity and "evangelical simplicity" touted by Protestants. In 1620, Cyril became the Patriarch of Constantinople, an office which remained subject to the authority of the Ottoman Empire.

Cyril appreciated the Christian humanist ideals for religious education that inspired many Protestants. He also cultivated a hard-edged anti-Catholicism, born out of violence committed against the Orthodox by Catholic authorities in eastern Europe. For example, Cyril helped to recruit a printer to set up a printing press in Constantinople, the first of its kind in the Greek Orthodox world. But because it was clearly intended as an engine of anti-Catholic propaganda, Jesuits destroyed the Constantinople press just months after it began operating. (The Jesuits and the Orthodox were locked in a long-standing battle over Christians' allegiances in the city.) Cyril looked to diplomats from Protestant countries for protection, and he gratefully gave the English ambassador in Constantinople a gift of the extraordinary *Codex Alexandrinus*, one of the earliest nearly complete manuscripts of the Bible. (It is now one of the highlights of the British Library's "Treasure Gallery" in London.) Cyril also generated rage among Catholics, and worry among other Orthodox leaders, when he signed a confession of faith in 1629 that reflected an unusual combination of Orthodox and Protestant (Calvinist) theology. Cyril's role in writing the document is disputed, but it was certainly intended to display unity with Dutch officials in Constantinople. Protestants happily published the confession in Geneva, with a somewhat misleading implication that the Orthodox world stood on the edge of its own Reformation. Cyril was caught in between threats from Catholics, Ottomans, and his enemies among the Orthodox. He said that he simply put his trust in God, concluding "if the Lord is my light and saviour, whom am I afraid of?" A decade after the publication of his notorious confession, Cyril's enemies finally brought him down. They charged him with treason in 1638 and had him executed. Shortly after his death, printers in Geneva brought out a modern Greek translation of the New Testament, which Cyril had commissioned a decade earlier. It was one of the crowning achievements of his Christian humanist and quasi-Protestant sensibilities.

Catholic Devotional Reform

As seen in the remarkable missionary efforts of the Jesuits and other orders, the Catholic Church after the Council of Trent was eager to confront the Protestant threat and its allies, such as Cyril I. After Trent, the spirit of the Catholic Reformation was embodied in the person of Pope Pius V (1504–72), who combined a ferocious anti-Protestantism with disciplined spirituality that, ironically, mimicked the devotion advocated by many Protestants. Pius V also confirmed the church's intellectual debt to Thomas Aquinas, the great thirteenth century Dominican philosopher, as its most influential theologian since Augustine. Pius made Thomas a Doctor of the Church in 1567, a rarefied category for saints who made an especially significant contribution to Catholic theology. The pope arranged for the publication of a new edition of Thomas's landmark *Summa Theologiae* in the early 1570s.

Martin Luther did not seem to have studied Thomas Aquinas closely, but he associated Thomas's scholastic philosophy with the corruption of the Catholic Church. (Other Reformers such as Zwingli and Martin Bucer were educated in the Dominican tradition and studied Aquinas meticulously.) Indeed, Luther went so far as to call Thomas "the foundation of all heresy, error, and obliteration of the Gospel." Among other objections, Luther believed that Aquinas put too much stock in humanity's ability to understand God's truth via natural law. Luther's strident denunciations of Aquinas, however, were really directed at contemporary Catholic opponents who defended practices such as indulgences and who considered themselves Thomists. Luther was adamant that while certain great theologians such as Augustine continued to offer important insights, no post-biblical author could compete with the preeminent authority of Scripture. The Thomists of the era countered that God had given the Doctors of the Church, including Thomas, special understanding of the proper interpretation of Scripture. Thomas's writings exercised heavy influence on the Jesuits, including their founder, Ignatius Loyola. The Jesuits made Thomas Aquinas their order's official theologian in the 1590s. Jesuit missionaries produced a Chinese translation of the *Summa* starting in the 1650s. The Reformation-era disagreements tended to give most Protestants a dim view of Thomas, even though the theological differences between Thomas and the Reformers were probably not as sharp as Luther suggested.

Pope Pius V and other leaders of the Catholic Reformation implicitly acknowledged that medieval lay piety was often deficient, and they sought ways to encourage serious devotion among laypeople. This desire led to the formalization of practices such as the Hail Mary prayer (Latin "Ave Maria") and the accompanying use of prayer beads, a practice known as the Rosary. Pius V issued a bull in 1569 giving an officially-approved guide to Rosary prayers. The Rosary would become one of the most familiar Catholic devotional practices. The beads on the prayer chain helped the praying person keep track of how many times he or she had said the requisite prayer. The Hail Mary was based on greetings to Mary in the Gospel of Luke:

> Hail Mary, full of grace,
> the Lord is with thee.
> Blessed art thou amongst women,
> and blessed is the fruit of thy womb, Jesus.
> Holy Mary, Mother of God,
> pray for us sinners,
> now and at the hour of our death. Amen.

The Rosary proved popular among Catholic laypeople. Pius V even attributed the major naval victory of Catholic powers over the Ottomans in the Battle of Lepanto in 1571 to an outpouring of Rosary prayers across Europe. Successive popes offered indulgences, which remained an incentive for Catholic piety after the Reformation, to those who said the Rosary.

One of the most distinctive products of the Catholic Reformation and its quest for lay devotion was an emphasis on the visual arts. Again, this was not a decisive break from the Catholic past. For example, Michelangelo had completed some of his finest works, such as his statue of David and the ceiling paintings of the Sistine Chapel, before the Reformation began. But by the end of the Council of Trent in the 1560s there was a new zeal for Catholic art which could inspire lay piety in Europe and in global missions. Catholic art and statuary often took a combative style depicting the destruction of the church's enemies, including the new Protestant heretics. Protestants, by contrast, tended to see the use of images in worship as idolatrous, and some radical Protestants advocated the destruction of icons and paintings in churches. The Council of Trent, however, recommended artwork to stimulate the piety of laypeople, many of whom were illiterate. Good Christian art could inspire such people "to adore and love God; and to cultivate piety." In this sense, the great Christian art of the Catholic Reformation was meant to reach the common people. But just as often, Catholic art and architecture of this era served to emphasize the splendor and opulence of the Counter-Reformation church.

Popes and churches commissioned huge numbers of paintings in the century after Trent, providing a living to devout and non-devout artists alike. The greatest of the Italian Catholic Reformation painters was Michelangelo Merisi da Caravaggio (1571–1610). The "Baroque" style of figures such as the Flemish artist Peter Paul Rubens tended to produce soaring, transcendent scenes, but Caravaggio's exceptional genius was in depicting biblical images that were both earthy and intensely spiritual. To his critics' dismay, Caravaggio painted works that sometimes seemed too accessible to everyday people, and he often treated iconic biblical scenes as if they were happening to regular folks in Europe at the turn of the seventeenth century. There has been debate about the quality of Caravaggio's own Christian commitment. There is no doubt that his careening life was full of turmoil, street brawls, and vendettas. He killed a man in a gang fight in 1606, ran away from Rome, and received a death sentence in absentia. The troubled Caravaggio died at age 38, but not before becoming one of the greatest artists in world history.

From global missions to individual piety, the Reformation was damaging yet invigorating to the papacy and to the nations that remained aligned with Rome. The Catholic Reformation brought much-needed change and activism to the Catholic Church. The church now defined itself in opposition to Protestants, as well as to the Eastern Orthodox

Image 3.4. Caravaggio, *The Calling of St. Matthew* (1599–1600)

and the Ottoman Empire. This combination of vitality and belligerency led to centuries of war, persecution, and internal struggles for the fate of nations. Perhaps no place in Europe endured such a harsh, compelling history of struggles over the Reformation, however, as the British Isles.

Selected Bibliography

Chidester, David. *Christianity: A Global History*. San Francisco: HarperSanFrancisco, 2000.

Greer, Allan. *Mohawk Saint: Catherine Tekakwitha and the Jesuits.* New York: Oxford University Press, 2005.

Hastings, Adrian. *The Church in Africa, 1450–1950.* New York: Oxford University Press, 1996.

Hsia, R. Po-chia, *A Jesuit in the Forbidden City: Matteo Ricci, 1552–1610.* New York: Oxford University Press, 2010.

———. *The World of Catholic Renewal, 1540–1770.* 2nd ed. Cambridge: Cambridge University Press, 2005.

Kitromilides, Paschalis. "Orthodoxy and the West: Reformation to Enlightenment." In Michael Angold, ed. *The Cambridge History of Christianity*, vol. 5, *Eastern Christianity*, 187–209. New York: Cambridge University Press, 2008.

McGinn, Bernard. *Thomas Aquinas's "Summa Theologiae": A Biography.* Princeton: Princeton University Press, 2014.

Rapley, Elizabeth. *The Lord as Their Portion: The Story of the Religious Orders and How They Shaped Our World.* Grand Rapids: Eerdmans, 2011.

Tingle, Elizabeth C. *Indulgences After Luther: Pardons in Counter-Reformation France, 1520–1720.* New York: Routledge, 2015.

Vermander, Benoît, S.J. "Jesuits and China." *Oxford Handbooks Online.* New York: Oxford University Press, 2015.

— Chapter 4 —

Reform in the British Isles

The Reformation in England stands apart from the rest of the early Protestant movement because of the nation's unusual, enduring contest for the religious allegiance of the monarchy. This struggle lasted from the 1530s to the 1690s, from Henry VIII's original break with the papacy to the Glorious Revolution settlement that finalized England's Protestant commitments. Because the Reformation in England was initiated in top-down fashion by Henry VIII, it played out differently there than in (for example) Luther's Germany or Calvin's Geneva. In Germany and Geneva, magisterial concerns flowed out of theological ones. The creation of the Anglican Church was the most distinctive denominational result of the Reformation. The Reformation in England had theological roots, based on concerns that dated at least to John Wyclif's call for a Bible in English in the late 1300s. The Wyclifite critique of the Catholic Church in England bred a proto-Reformed movement called the "Lollards." Lollard was a term of derision, meaning "mumbler." English church authorities reacted harshly against the Lollards and banned English vernacular translations of the Bible. The Lollards failed to get the traction that Luther's Reformation did, partly due to the unavailability at the time of printing technology to disseminate Wyclifite works rapidly and cheaply.

Seeds of Reform

The Reformation of the 1500s, however, would eventually transform the whole church-state order of the British Isles. Scholars at the University of Cambridge began meeting at the White Horse Inn in the early 1520s to discuss reform in education, church, and theology. We should not imagine that this celebrated group represented a massive groundswell behind English Protestantism, however. When King Henry VIII became familiar with Luther and the early Reformation, his response was generally hostile. During the 1520s, England did not look likely to align with the emerging magisterial Reformation, or to give political-ecclesiastical support to the Protestant movement. Henry was a stout defender of Catholicism, and the Catholic Church seemed as strong in England as anywhere on the Continent.

However, seeds of change were being planted in the English monarchy and the church. Perhaps most critically, the Oxford scholar William Tyndale (d. 1536) was inspired by Christian humanism, Erasmus, and Luther to create a new English translation of the Bible, despite the prohibition on vernacular editions. Tyndale, concerned that he would not be able to complete his work in England, went to Germany in 1524. Evading German authorities' attempts to suppress it, Tyndale secured a German printer for his New Testament translation in 1526. Soon copies of Tyndale's translation, as well as associated tracts and commentaries, began to proliferate in illicit versions across England. Church officials banned Tyndale's New Testament as a "pestiferous and most pernicious poison." The Bishop of London oversaw a public burning of seized copies of Tyndale's Bible at St. Paul's Cathedral. As elsewhere, no technology boosted the English Reformation more than printing. In their small, cheap editions, Tyndale's New Testaments and other works proved impossible to stop.

> Concerning all I have translated or otherwise written, I beseech all men to read it for that purpose I wrote it – even to bring them to the knowledge of the Scripture.
>
> ———
>
> William Tyndale, *Preface to the New Testament*, 1534

It also helped that Tyndale was a genius of Scripture translation and master of the English language. Only William Shakespeare, born in 1564, has had as much influence on the form of the English language as Tyndale did. Scholars have noted that Shakespeare's style was indebted to Tyndale, too, via the Geneva Bible. (The Geneva Bible's New Testament depended substantially on Tyndale's translation.) Most subsequent New Testament translations in English, including the Geneva translation and King James Bible, were influenced by Tyndale's rhetoric. Phrases such as "the powers that be" and "fight the good fight" have become commonplace English sayings that many people do not recognize as biblical, much less as coined by Tyndale. Tyndale never finished his Old Testament translation, and only sections of it were published in his lifetime. But Tyndale's Old Testament, too, made a great impact on the English Bible. Tyndale would be martyred by strangulation in Brabant (modern Belgium) in 1536. In *Foxe's Book of Martyrs*, the popular compendium of those who died for the Protestant cause, Tyndale was recorded as saying before his death, "Lord! Open the King of England's eyes."

Reform from the Top

A personal matter of conscience was indeed beginning to propel Henry VIII (1491–1547) toward breaking with Rome. Henry had married his dead brother's widow, Catherine of Aragon, but their inability to produce a male heir began to make Henry think that their marriage violated biblical principles such as the prohibition in Lev 20:21 against marrying your brother's wife. Not coincidentally, Henry had also become enamored with a new prospective wife, Anne Boleyn, who was sympathetic to Protestantism. The pope, however, would not grant the annulment of Henry's union with Catherine. Henry and his chief assistant, the Protestant-leaning Thomas Cromwell (1485–1540), began crafting a legal justification for rejecting papal authority. Meanwhile, Anne Boleyn became pregnant, and Henry and Anne secretly got married. Thomas Cranmer (1489–1556), the recently-appointed Archbishop of Canterbury (the top church position in England), annulled Henry's marriage to Catherine and declared Anne as the new queen. In 1534, Henry secured the Act of Supremacy, which formalized the separation from Rome and made him the supreme authority over the church in England.

The break with Rome generated little public criticism, partly because such criticism would likely end a person's political career, if not their life. The most principled defender of England's continued alignment with Rome was Thomas More, Henry's former Lord Chancellor and a pious Catholic. More had persecuted Protestants during his short tenure as Lord Chancellor, and he was William Tyndale's chief intellectual adversary. More privately opposed the annulment of Henry's marriage to Catherine, and he resigned as Lord Chancellor because he would not take the oath affirming Henry's supreme authority over the English church. He declined to attend Queen Anne's coronation. Thomas Cromwell used More's association with the prophetess and nun Elizabeth Barton of Kent to orchestrate More's final downfall. Barton had prophesied (in the king's presence) that Henry would die if he went through with his marriage to Anne Boleyn. Barton was subsequently executed for treason. Thomas More ultimately would not renounce papal authority, and he was beheaded at the Tower of London in 1535.

The changes wrought on the Continent by the early Reformation had destabilized the Catholic Church, and it set the stage for England's rupture with the papacy, too. But however principled Henry's concerns were about his marriage to Catherine, he was hardly a man of theological insight like Luther or Calvin. Thus, the English Reformation began as a jurisdictional squabble over a narrow matrimonial question. Questions about grace, salvation, and the structure of the church were not front and center. But many Protestants in England wanted to bring those questions to the fore. Repeated attempts to do so shaped the course of the English Reformation from 1534 onward.

Reforming the English Church

In the wake of the Act of Supremacy, the formidable Thomas Cromwell assumed papal-like authority in England, even helping to engineer Queen Anne's demise via trumped-up charges of unfaithfulness to the king. Cromwell was committed to demolishing the Catholic Church in the British Isles, too, and by 1540 he had arranged for the destruction of many monasteries and shrines. He ordered the iconoclastic renovation of churches. Cromwell fatally misjudged matters when he encouraged Henry's marriage to Anne of Cleves for political reasons. Henry found the new Anne deeply unsatisfactory as a marriage partner. Cromwell's standing with Henry collapsed, and in 1540, Cromwell was executed on allegations of heresy and treason. Henry began to consider Cromwell as an extremist Protestant. The king and Archbishop Thomas Cranmer began to chart the middle way between Catholicism and a thoroughgoing Reformation. Henry authorized the execution of both Catholic partisans and radical Protestant leaders.

The last ten years of Henry's reign saw enormous instability and a whipsawing course of the Reformation. This volatility resulted from Henry's poor health and erratic preferences. Despite occasional vacillations about Protestantism itself, Henry was not going to submit to Rome again. His son Prince Edward was raised by principled Protestant tutors, and when at age nine the prince became King Edward VI (r. 1547–53), England seemed positioned to become a vanguard of the Reformation. England in young Edward's early years as king was actually governed by a group of Protestant officials, including Archbishop Thomas Cranmer. Cranmer sensed that England could give new leadership to the international Reformed movement. He brought in luminaries such as Martin Bucer and Peter Martyr Vermigli (an Italian Protestant who had taken refuge in Bucer's Strasbourg) to become professors at Cambridge and Oxford, respectively. Cranmer even tried to recruit Philip Melanchthon to Cambridge, but that was not to be.

Cranmer was responsible, in consultation with Bucer and Vermigli, for successive editions of the English-language Book of Common Prayer. Cranmer's prayer book was not far behind the King James Bible in its effects on the rhetoric of English-speaking Christianity. For example, the marriage rite of the 1550s reads, "Dearly beloved friends, we are gathered together here in the sight of God, and in the face of his congregation, to join together this man and this woman in holy matrimony . . ." Many people in English-speaking nations can still recite parts of this marriage ceremony, without realizing that it comes from the Book of Common Prayer. The 1549 version explicitly rejected the authority of the pope, but some English Protestants remained unhappy with the prayer book's Catholic trappings. In particular, the 1549 prayer book acknowledged that the communion service was "commonly called the Mass," instead of rejecting the term outright. The 1552 edition of the prayer book reflected a more ambitious synthesis of Reformed theology and got rid of terms including "Mass," and "altar" for the Lord's table. Still, some thoroughgoing English and Scottish Reformers were dismayed by lingering Catholic practices in the Anglican tradition, such as kneeling for communion. The fierce Scottish Reformer John Knox (d. 1572) insisted that people should take communion while seated, to emphasize that the ritual was a memorial meal, not the idolatrous worship that Catholics ostensibly practiced.

The prayer book became one of the most controversial texts of the English Reformation. The Catholic Queen Mary, who acceded to the throne in 1553, banned Cranmer's prayer book and reinstituted the old Catholic services. Shortly after renouncing Protestantism and then reversing course by renouncing Catholicism, Cranmer was burned at the stake in Oxford in 1556. Finally, when Elizabeth I, a moderate Protestant, became queen in 1558, she authorized a new prayer book that combined the features of Cranmer's 1549 and 1552 editions. The new Elizabethan edition took out some of the most aggressively anti-Catholic language, such as a prayer that the English Church would avoid the "detestable enormities" of the pope. During Elizabeth I's long reign as queen (r. 1558–1603), the Book of Common Prayer became a fixed element of English Christianity. When King Charles I tried to enforce Anglican liturgy on Scottish Presbyterian churches in the 1630s, however, the prayer book became a major source of controversy again. The Scottish fracas produced one of the most memorable scenes of the Reformation in Britain. In 1637, when the minister of St. Giles Cathedral in Edinburgh began reading the communion service from the English prayer book, a Scottish woman named Jenny Geddes reportedly threw a stool at the minister's head and yelled "daur ye say Mass in my lug [ear]?"

Protestant, Catholic, Protestant Again

The wildest vacillations of the Reformation in England came eight decades before Geddes threw her chair. King Edward VI's accession seemed to herald a new day for the Protestant movement, but he died unexpectedly in 1553, setting the stage for Mary, the daughter of Henry VIII, to become queen. Mary's rigid commitment to Catholicism meant exile for many English and non-English Reformers alike. She married King Philip II of Spain, securing a diplomatic union with a major Continental Catholic power. She also formally reunited the Church of England with Rome, via Cardinal Reginald Pole, who became Archbishop of Canterbury after Thomas Cranmer was removed for opposing Mary's accession. Even though he knew it would not save him from execution, the doomed Cranmer pitifully repudiated all of his Protestant advocacy. But then he changed his mind, declaring his fidelity to the Protestant movement from the pulpit at Oxford's University Church. He dramatically shoved his writing hand into the flames when he went to the stake, declaring his shame for his brief renunciation of the Lord's (Protestant) cause. Reginald Pole went about refitting churches with Catholic icons, and church authorities separated thousands of married priests from their wives. Pole realized that some features of the pre-Reformation church were not coming back, however, and he talked of commissioning a Catholic-friendly English translation of the Bible.

As illustrated by Cranmer's demise, by the mid-1550s Mary's regime enacted a program of executing recalcitrant Protestants for heresy. In this age, intra-confessional and colonial violence was the rule, not an exception. Yet Mary's reign was undoubtedly "bloody," as Protestants came to call it. Almost three hundred Protestants suffered martyrdom in the last years of her rule. John Foxe, one of the exiled Protestant ministers, compiled a harrowing record of the executions in his *Book of Martyrs*. The book became one of the most enduring Protestant best-sellers in the English-speaking world. Queen Mary and Cardinal Pole died on the same day in 1558, setting the stage for Elizabeth's accession and the official return of English Protestantism. Elizabeth herself was not as visibly devoted to Protestantism as Mary had been to Catholicism, but the new queen was known to read the Greek New Testament daily, an indication of her rigorous Christian humanist education.

Intense English Protestants were again disappointed by the "Elizabethan Settlement," but at least the queen and her officials were repudiating Catholicism. In addition to a new version of Cranmer's prayer book, in 1563 the church issued a revised list of the Thirty-nine Articles, which encapsulated the doctrinal beliefs of the Church of England. (The Articles were also based on an earlier compilation by the prolific Cranmer.) A finalized list of the Thirty-nine Articles appeared in 1571 and were included in the Book of Common Prayer. The Thirty-nine Articles took broad but strong Reformed positions on issues such as predestination: "predestination to life, is the everlasting purpose of God, whereby (before the foundations of the world were laid) he hath constantly decreed by his council secret to us, to deliver from curse and damnation, those whom he hath chosen in Christ out of mankind." It took a mediating Protestant position on the Lord's Supper, saying that when done in faith, communion was a spiritual partaking of the body and blood of Christ. Yet the Articles explicitly denied transubstantiation as "repugnant to the plain words of Scripture." Against the Anabaptists, the Articles affirmed infant baptism and they argued against Christian pacifism and against Christians holding their property in common. In good Protestant fashion, the articles declared that the Scriptures "containeth all things necessary to salvation: so that whatsoever is not read therein, nor may be proved thereby, is not to be required of any man."

Reform in Scotland, Wales, and Ireland

Elizabeth's Settlement, then, reflected a firm commitment to Protestantism generally, but she disappointed many who wanted to see biblical reforms go much further. She kept Continental and Scottish Reformers at arm's length. England's place in the vanguard of the international Reformed movement faded. By contrast, Scotland's Reformation had deep international connections to the Reformed community, partly due to John Knox's time spent on the Continent in the mid-1550s, when he worked alongside John Calvin and other Reformed leaders. But Scottish Reformers struggled for years to displace Catholic authorities such as Queen Mary of Guise to no avail. In 1558, Knox published an incendiary tract, *The First Blast of the Trumpet against the Monstruous Regiment of Women*, which was directed against Queen Mary of England and Mary of Guise. The new English queen, Elizabeth, took exception to this tirade against female rulers as well.

Knox returned to Scotland in 1559, and his confrontational preaching fueled a surge of revolutionary Protestant fervor and iconoclasm. In 1560, Knox and his allies in church and state began transforming the Church of Scotland into the Protestant "Kirk," a new Presbyterian system based on Calvin's Geneva. The early Reformers in Scotland implemented massive changes to the church as a revolutionary movement against the Scottish monarchs. By contrast, in England the Reformation largely depended upon the tolerance of the monarch for change. By the time that James VI (the future James I of England) became King of Scotland in 1567, the Kirk had become deeply Reformed and the king (whatever his reluctance about it) had to work within that Protestant reality. The reforms in Scotland were more radically Protestant and internationalist than in England, reflected by the Kirk's adoption of Heinrich Bullinger's Second Helvetic Confession of Faith. The struggle for the Reformation in Scotland was also less violent, with only a couple dozen instances of Catholic or Protestant martyrdom. Scotland was divided culturally between the lowland English-speaking population and Highlanders, who spoke Gaelic. The Highland clans' reception of Protestantism was somewhat mixed, but certain key chiefs adopted the new faith. In 1567, Protestant Highlanders published Gaelic translations of the *Book of Common Order* used by the Kirk and of John Calvin's smaller catechism. The whole Bible was not translated into Gaelic until 1801, however.

In other parts of the British Isles, the reception of Protestantism ranged from a great success in Wales to rejection in Ireland. Both places endured the vacillations caused by the changing English monarchs, who claimed sovereignty in Wales and Ireland. Both the Book of Common Prayer and the Bible were translated into Welsh by the 1580s, which put an indelible Protestant imprint on Welsh culture. Popular Catholicism declined rapidly in Wales, unlike in Ireland. English authority, both civil and ecclesiastical, was taken as more of an affront in Ireland. The country was racked by war with the English for much of the late 1500s. Despite efforts to ban observance of the mass, Irish nobles and Catholic church leaders made common cause with forces of the Catholic Reformation on the Continent. By the late 1500s, Ireland was developing a unique, popular Catholic culture that rested uneasily alongside the official Protestantism of the English empire. The only Irish Protestant stronghold was created via Scottish settlements in Ulster, or the area now known as Northern Ireland. These settlers were committed to Presbyterianism, and they became the cultural hearth of the "Scots-Irish" people who dominated British migration to the American colonies in the 1700s. Tensions between Catholics and Protestants would be a defining mark of Northern Ireland's culture, well into the twentieth century.

Puritan Reform

In England, Reformers inspired by the likes of Calvin in Geneva and Knox in Scotland were thankful that Elizabeth I had turned the nation back to Protestantism. They were continually dissatisfied with failures to fully reform the Church of England, however. The English church establishment called their Reformed critics "precisionists" or "Puritans." The latter name stuck. Puritans sought complete reform of the Church of England, but authorities within the church often saw the Puritans as representing a threat as dire as English Catholics. The Church of England remained too "popish," in the Puritans' terminology. They wanted to see the church focus on the preaching of the Word of God, to simplify church rituals in accord with biblical forms, and to reduce the church hierarchy into a simpler presbyterian system of governance. Some Puritans went so far as to say that the local congregation was the only form of church governance contemplated in Scripture. Thomas Cartwright (1535–1603) was one of the first church leaders to advocate publicly for ecclesiastical reform on the presbyterian model. For his efforts, Cartwright was removed from his professorship at the University of Cambridge in 1570.

Queen Elizabeth sometimes struggled to find church leaders who were sufficiently anti-Catholic but who were not sympathetic to the Puritans either. She made an ill-fitting choice of Edmund Grindal (1519–83) as Archbishop of Canterbury in 1575. He was one of the clergy exiled to the Continent during Queen Mary's reign and had developed sympathies for the international Reformed community. Grindal fell out of favor with Elizabeth when he refused to stamp out the practice of "prophesying," which basically entailed special church meetings where preachers could give extended, expository biblical sermons. These meetings were a primary outlet for Reformed clergy and laypeople and Elizabeth wanted them to stop, seeing them as potentially subversive. Grindal and other Puritan-leaning church officials disagreed. Grindal reminded the queen that "public and continual preaching of God's word is the ordinary means and instrument of the salvation of mankind." He pointedly told the queen that he would rather offend her than offend God. The provocative Grindal was placed under house arrest at Lambeth Palace, the archbishop's official residence in London, and Elizabeth ordered an end to prophesying.

One of the most scandalous examples of Puritan frustration with the established church came in the "Martin Marprelate" tracts of the late 1580s. These were hilarious and bawdy attacks on the corrupt "prelates" of the Church of England. Their authorship has been much debated, but a Puritan member of Parliament, Job Throkmorton, seems to have been one of the chief composers. Throkmorton and his associates, including a wealthy Puritan widow named Elizabeth Crane, arranged for the tracts to be surreptitiously printed at locations including Crane's house. The tracts' printer soon left England, while Crane spent time in Fleet Prison for her involvement. The search for the tracts' authors led to the arrest of Throkmorton, as well as a broader network of presbyterian ministers, including Thomas Cartwright. Many leading Puritans disapproved of the sensational Marprelate tracts, which among other things implied that the new Archbishop of Canterbury was in a homosexual relationship with an official at Cambridge.

The Marprelate tracts further undermined the prestige of Church of England officials, but they gave the government an excuse to crack down on Puritans, too. In 1588 (the same year the Marprelate tracts began to appear), the seemingly miraculous English defeat of the Spanish Armada suggested to establishment officials that God must be blessing England and its church, despite the precisionists' scurrilous satires. English officials also made an example of a number of Puritans who were truly radical, and sometimes deranged. In 1591, a small group of Puritans declared a man named William Hacket to be a messiah and "king of Europe," and they announced that Elizabeth was hereby deposed. Hacket was executed by hanging, then drawn and quartered. Such episodes helped establishment critics to cast the whole Puritan movement as rank fanaticism. Some Puritans had also become separatists, or those who believed that the Church of England was entirely apostate. Separatists contended that true believers should abandon the state church and set up independent congregations of the godly. In an era of close links between church and state, separatism was viewed as sedition, and three English separatists were executed in 1593. Anti-Puritans argued that separatism was the logical consequence of Puritanism.

Such episodes hinted at the persecution of Puritans that was to come in the 1620s and '30s. Anti-Puritan persecution would surge again in the 1660s under the restored English monarchy, after the interlude of Oliver Cromwell's Puritan-friendly Protectorate and the English Civil War. In the later years of Elizabeth's reign, however, there was a continuum of opinion in England that ran from staunch defenders of the Elizabethan church on one end to radical separatists on the other. In between were ministers and theologians such as Cambridge's William Perkins (1558–1602), who believed that full reform could take place within the confines of the established church. To Puritans like Perkins, separation was unnecessary. Perkins, as a Puritan defender of the Elizabethan Settlement, became the most popular theologian in England and one of the most influential thinkers of the whole English Reformed tradition.

Perkins was known for advocating "covenant" theology. For Perkins, the covenant of grace entailed God's determination to grant saving faith to the elect. It applied only to those predestined to salvation by God's election, and those truly chosen would necessarily respond to God's gracious offer. Christ's atoning sacrifice provided forgiveness for the elect, who like the rest of humankind had violated the covenant of works. The covenant of works remained central for Perkins because the sources of God's moral law, especially the Ten Commandments, gave regenerate people a perfect template for obedience. The Holy Spirit gave the regenerate person a new ability and inclination to obey God's laws. The covenant of works was also the basis for what Puritans believed was a deserved sentence to eternal hell for unregenerate sinners. Certain scholars have argued that Puritans such as Perkins were introducing a subtle form of works-righteousness by their emphasis on the law and covenant of works. Others have insisted that Perkins's view on salvation by grace alone was in substantial continuity with Reformed predecessors, most notably Calvin. All mainstream Reformers understood that grace hardly negated the importance of law. Yet God's unilateral gift of grace, not law, was the only path to salvation. In any case, a distinction between the covenant of grace and covenant of works became a hallmark of the Puritan movement. Richard Sibbes (1577–1635), one of Perkins's successors as a Cambridge theologian and preacher, said that in order to understand the core message of God's grace, "we must appeal from Sinai to Sion, from the Law to the Gospel, from Moses to Christ." The tension between grace and works lingered in the Puritan movement, sometimes resulting in debilitating controversies such as the "antinomian" or "free grace" crisis that racked Puritan Massachusetts in the 1630s.

> II. The moving or efficient cause of predestination to life is not the foresight of faith or of perseverance, or of good works, or of anything inherent in the persons predestined, but only the will of God's good pleasure.
>
> ---
>
> *The Lambeth Articles*, 1595

One of the reasons that Perkins, Sibbes, and others were able to remain comfortably within the Church of England was that the Thirty-nine Articles affirmed Reformed doctrines such as predestination. When Arminian professors at Cambridge criticized the doctrine of predestination in the mid-1590s, the Archbishop of Canterbury approved a Cambridge-authored document known as the Lambeth Articles. The articles buttressed the church's commitment to Reformed theology, especially predestination. The first of the nine terse articles simply affirmed that "God from eternity hath predestinated certain men unto life; certain men he hath reprobated." The anti-Arminianism of the Lambeth Articles became even clearer in its ninth affirmation, that "it is not in the will or power of every one to be saved." Queen Elizabeth, always hesitant about connecting the Church of England with the international Calvinist movement, ordered the archbishop to suspend the articles. Thus, they were not published until much later, but the existence of the Lambeth Articles was comforting to Reformed English leaders such as Perkins. Perkins tended not to quibble about church polity, focusing on a proper understanding of salvation, the covenants, and the place of morality in a regenerate person's life. As long as Reformed leaders stuck to theology, followed the queen's orders, and remained quiet on issues such as presbyterian church government, they could remain in official church positions under Elizabeth.

Anti-Reformation Stirrings

There was a strong element of anti-Reformed thought and aesthetics within the Church of England, however. That element would at times make the church a decidedly uncomfortable place for stricter Reformed clergy. One of the exemplars of this anti-Reformed strain was Lancelot Andrewes. In 1601, Andrewes became Dean of Westminster Abbey, the great burial place for monarchs and a quasi-cathedral standing in the shadow of Parliament. The abbey became one of the great symbols of English nationalism and a visible reminder of the nation's union of church and state. Andrewes wanted to steer the Church of England away from association with the Continental Reformation and away from doctrines such as predestination. It was not so much that Andrewes denied the predestination of the elect. (He rejected the predestination of the damned to reprobation, however). He just saw theological squabbling over such inscrutable doctrines as unseemly. Andrewes preferred a focus on the sacraments, ceremonies, and the beauty of Anglican worship, such as what transpired in the great English sanctuaries like Westminster Abbey.

When James VI of Scotland became King James I of England in 1603, the status of the English Reformation became more uncertain. Elizabeth was no Puritan, but she was ruthlessly anti-Catholic. Her long tenure made England more secure in its Protestantism than ever before. James would come to appear more sympathetic than Elizabeth to the Catholic Church, even after Catholic terrorists led by Guy Fawkes plotted in 1605 to blow up Parliament's opening session, where the king and his family would have been in attendance. James's wife Anne of Denmark was indisputably friendly to Catholicism and may have privately converted to it. Allegations about the Stuart kings' Catholic sympathies (or

Image 4.1. *Engraving of Westminster Abbey* (1780)

their open Catholicism, in the case of King James II), would trouble English Protestants throughout the 1600s. James I, however, proved to be savvy in negotiating the ecclesiastical politics involved in governing the British Isles.

The Authorized English Bible

The most important religious product of James's tenure was the Bible translation to which he lent his name. James promised moderate Puritans in 1604 that he would sanction a new English Bible. He wanted it done in the best traditions of Christian humanism, correcting translation errors in previous vernacular editions and free from the pointed Calvinist commentaries in the Geneva Bible. Between 1604 and 1611, dozens of theologians and biblical scholars worked on the king's monumental translation project.

As the translators explained in the preface to the Authorized Version (as it came to be called in the 19th century), they were not creating an entirely new translation, but were seeking "to make a good one better, or out of many good ones one principal good one." They wanted this Bible to be familiar to readers and preachers, a source of unity in the church, and a model of Christian scholarship. The KJV's language was already old-fashioned when it was published, being molded by English rhetoric of the 1500s, especially from Tyndale. Their rich and diverse sources extended well beyond Tyndale, however. The translators consulted the original languages, previous official Anglican versions, the Geneva Bible, and more remarkably, the Catholics' English language Douay-Rheims Bible. The Douay-Rheims New Testament had been published in 1578 (an Old Testament translation had followed in 1610, too late for the KJV translators). These varied sources made the KJV traditional in rhetoric, yet current with the best philological scholarship. Its respect for the English vernacular, its lovely, transcendent phrasing, and its widespread acceptance made the King James Bible the most influential book ever published in English. The translators' reverence for the task of handling "God's word, God's testimony, God's oracles, the word of truth, [and] the word of salvation" made it the most important edition of the Bible since the Vulgate.

The era of mass Bible distribution by missionaries and Bible societies lay in the future. The KJV, however, illustrated a century-long trend toward widespread availability of the vernacular Bible in Protestant nations. The Douay-Rheims signaled the Catholic Reformation's impulse to produce its own vernacular editions, though generally with more deference to Jerome's Vulgate than in Protestant Bibles. How widespread was Bible knowledge for ordinary laypeople? For literate, devout Protestants, the practice of individual Bible reading was now within reach. The KJV enhanced the widespread availability of English vernacular editions begun by the Geneva Bible. By the mid-1600s there may have been a million copies of English-language Bibles in circulation. Ministers and theologians might not have believed that all people were equally capable of understanding the Bible, but Protestants still praised individual believers who searched the Scripture for themselves. Tyndale had encouraged believers to "endeavor thyself to search out the meaning of all that is described [in Scripture] . . . note everything earnestly, as things pertaining unto thine own heart and soul." Even for non-literate Protestants, hearing the Word preached, read, and sung in one's own language had become normal.

The year that the King James Bible was published, an Anglican funeral sermon extolled the personal piety of the deceased, a woman named Mary Swaine. Taking the Gospel account of Mary and Martha as his point of departure, the minister said "How often did [Swaine] fall at Christ's feet to pray unto him? She prayed, not three times a day, with Daniel, but continually. I have often observed her, that all the time she was not employed in household business, she spent it in meditation and prayer . . . Her whole care and desire was (with Mary) to sit at Christ's feet, to hear God speaking unto her, or else to speak unto God by prayer." As funeral sermons sometimes do, this memorial likely presented an idealized piety. Nevertheless, Swaine's prayer life was shaped by models in Scripture (Daniel and Mary), and the basis of her meditations was undoubtedly the Bible, too. Whether Mary Swaine just heard the Bible preached and sung, or whether she could read it for herself, we do not know. But after 1611, meditating on God's truths in the Bible became one of the most representative features of Protestant piety. As the eccentric English theologian William Chillingworth memorably put it in 1637, "the Bible only, is the religion of Protestants."

Selected Bibliography

Brownlee, Victoria. *Biblical Readings and Literary Writings in Early Modern England, 1558–1625*. Oxford: Oxford University Press, 2018.

Dawson, Jane. *John Knox*. New Haven, CT: Yale University Press, 2015.

Heal, Felicity. *Reformation in Britain and Ireland*. Oxford: Oxford University Press, 2003.

Jacobs, Alan. *The Book of Common Prayer: A Biography*. Princeton, NJ: Princeton University Press, 2013.

MacCulloch, Diarmaid. *Thomas Cranmer: A Life*. Rev. ed. New Haven, CT: Yale University Press, 2017.

Marshall, Peter. *Heretics and Believers: A History of the English Reformation*. New Haven, CT: Yale University Press, 2017.

Patterson, W.B. *William Perkins and the Making of a Protestant England*. Oxford: Oxford University Press, 2014.

Peters, Christine. *Patterns of Piety: Women, Gender, and Religion in Late Medieval and Reformation England*. Cambridge: Cambridge University Press, 2003.

Ryrie, Alec. *The Origins of the Scottish Reformation*. Manchester, UK: Manchester University Press, 2010.

Wilcox, Helen, "The King James Bible in Its Cultural Moment." In Kevin Killeen, Helen Smith, and Rachel Willie, eds., *The Bible in Early Modern England, c.1530–1700*, 455–68. Oxford: Oxford University Press, 2015.

Woolsey, Andrew A. *Unity and Continuity in Covenantal Thought: A Study in the Reformed Tradition to the Westminster Assembly*. Grand Rapids: Reformation Heritage Books, 2012.

— Chapter 5 —

The Fate of the Reformation into the 1600s

By 1617, the original Reformers had passed away, and "the Reformation" was transitioning into historical memory. In that year, Protestants from across Europe, especially in Germany, held "jubilees" marking the beginning of Luther's Reformation. Catholic authorities including Pope Paul VI responded by declaring a sort of counter-jubilee focused on prayer and acts of penance for the preservation of the true faith against heretics. In Protestant churches, Luther was hailed as a new Moses, or Elijah, or Noah.

A century after Luther, tensions still ran high between Catholics and Protestants. Indeed, the year 1618 would see the beginning of the Thirty Years' War, a complex, horrific conflict that changed Europe permanently. Protestant-Catholic rivalry was not the whole story of the war, but it was a determinative factor. The early 1600s also saw increasing tensions between Protestant factions, who were divided by regions and by theological disputes. The Catholic Church's control of western Europe was broken forever due to the Reformation, but what alignments would replace it remained a source of violent conflict.

Image 5.1. *Luther medal* (1661)

Ongoing Reforms in Germany

In Germany, disagreements persisted between Lutherans and the Reformed churches. The allegiance of a prince often determined the allegiance of his realm. Friedrich III (1515–76), the Elector Palatine, sought in the early 1560s to fashion a broad-minded Reformed consensus in the German churches and recruited leading Reformed thinkers as professors at the University of Heidelberg. One of these was Zacharias Ursinus (1534–83), a protégé of Philip Melanchthon. Friedrich III commissioned Ursinus to craft a new Reformed statement of doctrine, the 1563 Heidelberg Catechism. It opened with the question and answer,

"Q. What is your only comfort in life and death?

A. That I am not my own, but belong with body and soul, both in life and in death, to my faithful Saviour Jesus Christ."

Though Lutheran partisans would not accept the Heidelberg Catechism, it went on to become one of the most influential Reformed documents and was translated into dozens of languages. The Reformed figures at Heidelberg made common cause with Heinrich Bullinger in Zürich, and they championed Bullinger's Second Helvetic Confession (1566). After John Calvin's death in 1564, Heidelberg emerged as one of the vital centers of Reformed thought on the Continent. Some have labeled this phase of the movement as the "Second Reformation." Reformed leaders were generally more effective at sustaining international connections than were Lutherans, despite Lutheranism's growing sway in Scandinavia. King Christian III of Denmark and Norway (r. 1534–59) had made Lutheranism the national faith in 1537, and in 1593, the Protestant Church of Sweden formally aligned with Lutheranism by affirming the Augsburg Confession (1530).

Ongoing Reforms in the Low Countries

In western Europe's Low Countries, the late 1500s saw the emergence of a southern Catholic state that became Belgium and a northern Protestant state that took the name "the Netherlands." Dutch Reformed belief into the early 1600s was highly diverse, but the need for Protestant unity helped the Netherlands become one of the most religiously tolerant nations of Europe. This made the Netherlands one of the key centers of Anabaptism, as well as Arminian theology, alongside Calvinism. West Friesland, in the far north of the Netherlands, became a special stronghold for Anabaptist Mennonites, who often preached in the Frisian language to reach rural and poor people there, following the example of their Frisian founder, Menno Simons.

Dutch pluralism did not necessarily entail peace between churches. The most heated theological controversy among Dutch Protestants in the early 1600s was over Arminian theology. Arminian theology was named for Jakob Hermanszoon (latinized as Jacobus Arminius). Arminius was not an obvious candidate to become the most influential anti-Calvinist thinker of his age, as he had studied with Calvin's successor Theodore Beza in Geneva. Arminius became a pastor in Amsterdam in 1588 and then a professor at the University of Leiden. By the time he arrived in Amsterdam, he had become skeptical about Beza's version of Calvinism, which included double predestination and the doctrine of limited (or definite) atonement, the idea that Christ died only for the elect. Arminius posited that some people, by free will, could be damned even after God graciously offered them salvation. Calvinists taught that when God initiated a gracious work of regeneration in a sinner's heart, it was by definition effective ("irresistible") to save that person. God's will could never be thwarted by humans.

As an insider among Dutch Calvinists, Arminius's views were enormously controversial. Yet because of the relatively free climes of the Netherlands, Arminius was able to avoid punishment. Arminius cultivated an international anti-Calvinist platform. He wrote against English theologian William Perkins's views on predestination. In doing so, he took on the most popular English Calvinist writer of the era. Arminius could not square rigid predestination with the Bible's description of God desiring "all men to be saved." (1 Tim 2:4 KJV)

How could it be, Arminius asked, that God "desires that a person believe in Christ whom he desires to be alien to Christ, and to whom he has decreed to deny the necessary assistance for faith?" Arminius's treatise against Perkins helped him to secure a place as one of the most influential Protestant critics of Calvinist theology ever. Just as not all Calvinists have agreed with Calvin, not all "Arminians" have been in complete accord with Arminius's theology. (Arminius, for example, never fully repudiated predestination, especially for the elect.) But his name came to stand for a theology in which human will played a prominent role, at least in the ability to reject God's grace.

The Dutch Reformed leaders' Synod of Dordt (1618), which produced the "Canons of Dordt," sought to counter a 1610 statement by the Dutch "Remonstrants," or supporters of Arminius. The Remonstrants argued that election entailed only God's foreknowledge of the faith of the elect, and that Christ had died for all people, not just the elect. Meeting at Dordrecht (spelled Dort or Dordt in English), Dutch representatives met with international Calvinist delegates representing countries from England to Germany. They denounced Arminian theology and formalized tenets of newly-threatened Calvinist orthodoxy in the Canons of Dordt. Going straight to the point, the first section of the Canons of Dordt was on predestination. They made clear that the "cause or fault" of unbelief lies with the condemned sinner. The faith of the elect, however, proceeded from the eternal decree of God. "Before the foundations of the world were laid," God chose the elect for salvation, not because of their merit, but because of God's good pleasure. The force of that eternal decree could not "be interrupted, changed, recalled, [or] broken off." In classic Protestant fashion, the synod concluded by exhorting preachers to think and speak through the Bible alone, "according to the analogy of faith," or in harmony with the entire Scripture. The Synod of Dordt placed the Dutch Reformed Church in the vanguard of the international Reformed movement, a status it would retain for centuries, partly due to a Dutch Calvinist diaspora in places such as the United States and South Africa.

Jansenism

Divisions between Arminians and Calvinists stoked swirling religious animosities in Europe. As powerful as the divisions were between Catholics and Protestants, and between Catholics and Orthodox Christians, splits within these communions continued to trouble the churches, too. Even after the Council of Trent, many Catholic reformers kept insisting that the Roman church needed major bureaucratic and spiritual changes in ways that seemed to echo Protestant critiques. Certain Catholics even showed interest in quasi-Calvinist reforms. The chief advocate of Calvinist-style theology among European Catholics was the Dutch Catholic bishop Cornelius Jansen (1585–1638). As was typical among Protestants and reformist Catholics, Jansen was profoundly influenced by reading the works of Augustine. Jansen's growing doubts about human nature—informed by Augustine's dim view of humanity—put him at odds with much of the spirit of the Catholic Reformation. In particular, the Jesuit order insisted that while sin was a debility, sin did not ruin humanity's reason or its capacity to choose the good.

Jansen wanted to reform the Roman Church, and he had little patience for Protestants per se. Jansen urged Catholics to take the Bible, especially as interpreted by Augustine, as their chief guide. Jansen and his followers were virtually unique among the advocates of the Catholic Reformation in suggesting that the laity should read the Bible for themselves. Jansen's most influential and controversial work was titled (tellingly) *Augustinus*, through which he sought to reintroduce Catholics to Augustine's views on predestination, election, and God's sovereign initiative in saving sinners. *Augustinus* was only published posthumously, however, and as a faithful bishop Jansen would have undoubtedly been troubled at the enormous conflict between his "Jansenist" followers and Jesuits that ensued for decades in the Netherlands and France.

Jesuits across Europe reviled *Augustinus*, giving the treatise a much greater notoriety than if they had just left Jansen's memory alone. Officials of the Roman Inquisition determined that *Augustinus* challenged papal authority. In 1643, a papal bull condemned Jansen's work. Jansen's popularity, or notoriety, continued to spread in western Europe, with special interest in Jansenism developing in Paris. The Cistercian nuns of the Abbey of Port-Royal turned their convent and schools into centers of Jansenist devotion, despite increasing pressure from King Louis XIV for Catholics to repudiate Jansen's thought. Jacqueline Pascal, one of the Port-Royal nuns, influenced her brother, the great French mathematician and theologian Blaise Pascal, to become one of the leading proponents of French Jansenism. Pope Clement XI abolished the Port-Royal abbey in 1708, and the nuns at Port-Royal were forced to leave in 1709. The French Jansenist theologian Pasquier Quesnel compared the nuns' suffering to that of Christ. "The world crucifies you," he told the Port-Royal nuns, "that is to say, its maxims, its morals, its crimes, that its spirits and even its false virtues are insupportable to you." A bull by Pope Clement XI also condemned Quesnel in 1713, signaling the end of papal toleration of Jansenist theology.

The Thirty Years' War

Any theological controversy in Europe in the 1600s could have enormous stakes. Debates over theology could precipitate persecution, official condemnations, or even war. The rise of Europe's modern nations and their military-imperial ambitions presented new temptations for the politicization of religion. The cataclysm of the Thirty Years' War demonstrated this potential all too well. Tensions between Catholics and Protestants, and between rival Catholics and rival Protestants, intertwined with rivalries between empires and noble families to make the Thirty Years' War one of the most complex conflicts in human history. The spark for the war came in Bohemia (modern Czech Republic), when Protestants in Prague tossed representatives of the Catholic House of Habsburg out of a third-story window. This was the "defenestration of Prague." (The act mimicked a similar episode in Prague involving proto-Protestant Hussites two centuries earlier.) The defenestrated Habsburg officials survived the fall, which Catholics cited as a remarkable providence of God. Protestants widely saw the defenestration of Prague and start of European war as the beginning of the downfall

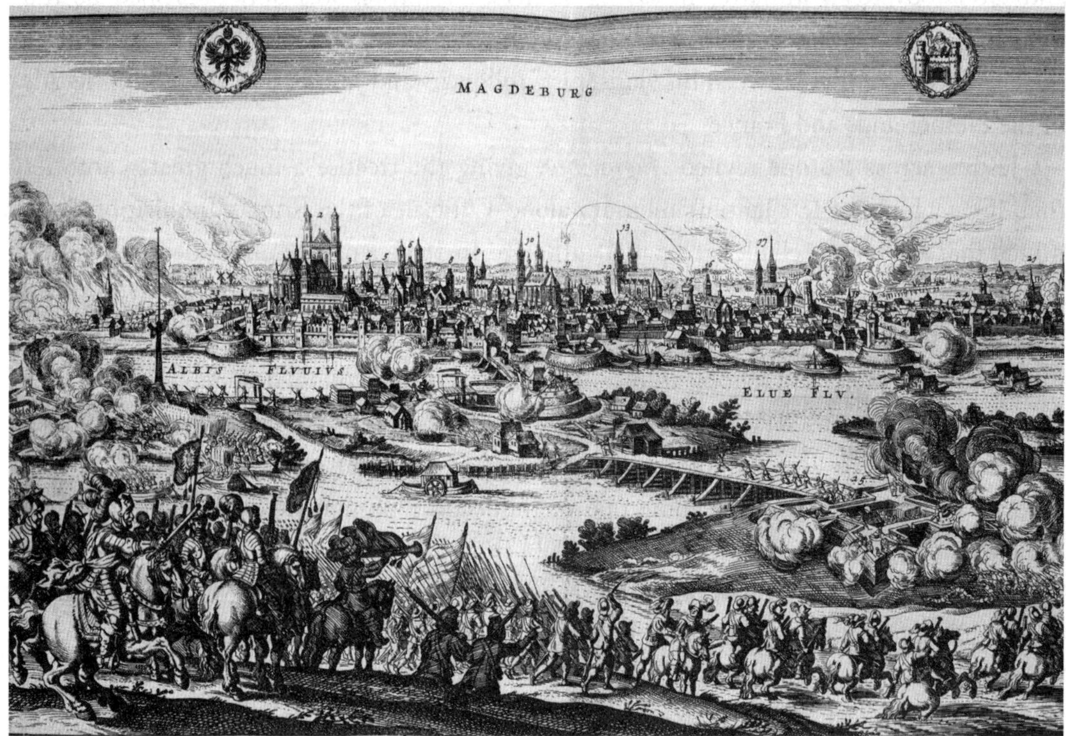

Image 5.2. *Siege of Magdeburg*

of Antichrist, a force which they associated with Catholic power. John Arrowsmith, a Puritan minister, regarded the unfolding of the Reformation and the beginning of the Thirty Years' War as the "happy time of Antichrist's drooping." He noted that the sword of recent judgments in Europe "began to be unsheathed in Bohemia, which was the seat of the first open and authorized Reformation," meaning that of the Hussites. Arrowsmith, the future Regius Professor of Divinity at Cambridge, thought it was obvious that the defenestration and subsequent war represented a partial fulfilment of Rev 6:1–2, in which the rider on a white horse "went forth conquering, and to conquer" (KJV).

After 1618, it appeared that Protestants in Bohemia might secure a trans-European Protestant alliance stretching from Britain to Transylvania. But Protestants were routed at the Battle of White Mountain near Prague in 1620. After White Mountain, other Protestant strongholds in central Europe came under attack. Heidelberg was destroyed in 1622, and its Protestant churches and the University of Heidelberg closed. Frederick V, the great Protestant prince and Elector Palatine, became a refugee in the Netherlands. Protestants were expelled from Inner Austria in the late 1620s, signaling the downfall of the Lutheran church there, where it had once thrived. Perhaps the most horrific episode of the war for Protestants was the sack of Magdeburg in 1631. The city was razed, and the majority of its 20,000 Protestant inhabitants died by summary execution or in the fires that destroyed most of Magdeburg's buildings.

A key Protestant refugee from the Czech lands was the Bohemian pastor and educator Jan Comenius (1592–1670). He and thousands of others associated with the Czech Unity of the Brethren fled to Poland in the aftermath of the Battle of White Mountain. Comenius was one of the most ingenious Protestant Reformers of the era. Inspired by Christian humanist ideals, he believed that through comprehensive moral and educational reform the church could prepare the way for the millennial kingdom of Christ on earth. Comenius wrote widely on topics including diplomacy, war, and the history of the Unity of the Brethren, but he is best known today for

> In order to educate the young carefully it is necessary to take timely precautions that their characters be guarded from the corruptions of the world, that the seed of honour sown in them be brought to a happy growth by pure and continuous teaching and examples, and, lastly, that their minds be given over to the true knowledge of God.
>
> ———
>
> Jan Comenius, *The Great Didactic*, 1657

his writings on education. Comenius was one of the first thinkers ever to propose an age-graded system of universal education.

Some of the remaining Czech Protestants would also reassemble in Saxony on the estates of the Lutheran noble Nicholas von Zinzendorf. These Czech pietists became known as the Moravian Brethren, or Moravians. The Moravians would have a major impact on the history of missions and the evangelicals of the Great Awakening in the 1700s.

Part of the difficulty for Protestants resisting Catholic imperial power was that Lutherans and the Reformed often distrusted one another as much as they did Catholics. Episodes such as the Synod of Dordt kept highlighting theological divides between the Lutherans and the Reformed. Although the Reformed delegates at Dordt focused on the teachings of Jacobus Arminius and his followers, Lutherans noticed that Dordt condemned views of predestination and free will that were common in Lutheran circles, too. For a century since the Marburg Colloquy of 1529, Lutherans and the Reformed were at odds over such doctrines, as well as their views of the Lord's Supper. The disaster at the Battle of White Mountain and encroaching Catholic power in central Europe produced glimmers of Lutheran-Reformed rapprochement, at least for survival if nothing else. At the Leipzig Colloquy in 1631, virtually all German Protestant princes attended and agreed to create a pan-Protestant army to fight against Catholic power. Lutheran and Reformed theologians there emphasized their overwhelming agreement on Philip Melanchthon's Augsburg Confession (1530). Despite continuing differences on predestination and the Lord's Supper, Lutheran and Reformed leaders vowed to "show each other Christian love in the future." Such resolve would not last, however. Several years after Leipzig, one of the key Lutheran leaders there opposed military support for Calvinist princes. Such support was "tantamount to rendering feudal service to the devil, the originator of Calvinism," the Lutheran leader said.

The end of the Thirty Years' War in 1648 saw much of Europe return to the boundaries that existed in 1624. It was a dispiriting end to a seemingly pointless conflict. After the Thirty Years' War, there was a growing sense of weariness over religious strife, yet Europe could not escape it. Some scholars attribute a rise in skeptical philosophy and biblical criticism, as represented by René Descartes (who fought in the war), Thomas Hobbes, and Baruch Spinoza, to the fatigue that followed 1648. Descartes remained a faithful Catholic, but his emphasis on individual reason as the path to truth anticipated more radical attacks on Christian tradition. Catholic and Protestant imperial foes still battled one another over the next century and a half, but rival factions within the Catholic and Protestant communions also took up arms against one another, even within the same nation. This was the case in the mid-1600s when rival English Protestants fell into a civil war over politics and religion.

Division in the English Churches

As in the Netherlands, Reformed leaders in England were concerned about the rising influence of Arminian thought in the Church of England. King James I's allegiance vacillated in the Arminian-Calvinist struggle, for he had intervened on the side of the anti-Arminian faction in the Netherlands in the late 1610s. But in England, the aging king found himself boosted by Arminian allies. The Arminians William Laud and Lancelot Andrewes gained increasing prominence in King James I's last years, and they helped turn Prince Charles, the heir to the throne, into a committed Arminian. Repeated royal pronouncements banned the discussion of predestination from English pulpits, paralleling Catholic efforts to suppress Jansenists in France. As the Bishop of London and then Archbishop of Canterbury, Laud took the church in a harsh anti-Puritan direction. Charles I, who became king in 1625, developed a contemptuous relationship with Parliament, and he began trying to govern England via executive fiat. Outspoken Puritan ministers fell under more persecution. In northern England, an aggressive Arminian archbishop even banned the works of William Perkins, the great covenant theologian who had died three decades earlier.

The once-capacious church of Elizabeth's reign was narrowing. The narrowing put many Puritans in a bind. Should they leave England and seek religious freedom elsewhere? This was not a new dilemma, as early English Reformers such as William Tyndale had left for the Continent almost a century earlier. Puritan leaders such as Thomas Cartwright had also fled England during Elizabeth's reign. Amidst the escalating persecution of the 1620s, Puritans and other dissenters now had colonies in America to consider as possible escapes, too.

Even before William Laud's persecutions, dissenters began to leave England during the early years of King James I's reign. Some of these were separatists who believed that true believers should abandon the Church of England and start their own congregations. Some separatists also became Baptists, believing that infant baptism was a vestigial product of Catholic corruption. Christians had overwhelmingly practiced infant baptism since the time of Augustine. During the early Reformation, however, Anabaptist groups on the Continent began to advocate for the baptism of believers only. It was only a matter of time before certain English Christians rejected paedobaptism, too.

One of the key figures in the early English separatist and Baptist movements was John Smyth. Smyth started out as a Church of England minister with Puritan convictions. But he was removed from his pastorate and began preaching to a separatist congregation in Gainsborough, England. Separatist congregations like Smyth's were illegal, and the Gainsborough separatists fell under persecution. By 1608, they had fled to Amsterdam, where Dutch authorities granted more liberty to sectarian groups. Smyth developed connections with Dutch Mennonites, and they may have helped to convince him that infant baptism was unbiblical. He denounced paedobaptism and baptized himself by affusion. Smyth soon died, but a part of his Baptist congregation under Thomas Helwys returned to England by 1612, meeting for worship in north London. Helwys published a tract criticizing James I and calling for religious liberty, which resulted in him being put in jail, where he died around 1616.

Another faction of Smyth's separatists had broken off from his congregation and gone to Leiden in the Netherlands, setting the stage for the separatist migration to the Plymouth Colony in the New World. Sailing on the *Mayflower*, the colonists arrived in Plymouth in 1620. Before disembarking, the colonists signed the "Mayflower Compact," committing the colony to pursue "the glory of God, and advancement of the Christian faith, and honor of our king and country." The site of the Plymouth settlement had been a Patuxet Indian village, but the Patuxets had been decimated by an outbreak of epidemic disease. Such epidemics were all-too-common phenomena which marked the initial encounters between European colonizers and Native Americans.

Even many Puritans saw separatists as fanatics, and Puritans did not want to get conflated with separatists by Church of England critics. Yet separatists and Puritans both faced an increasingly unfriendly environment in England, especially with the ascension of Charles I to the throne, and Laud becoming Bishop of London in 1628. Most Puritans would not ultimately leave England, but a group of prominent Puritans led by lawyer John Winthrop founded the Massachusetts Bay Company in 1629. The historian Perry Miller classically argued that Winthrop's Puritans were on an "errand into the wilderness," setting up a model church and state that would serve as a "city on a hill" and a model to the Reformed community in England. Winthrop quoted Jesus's city on a hill metaphor in his "Model of Christian Charity" oration, which cast a vision for the Puritan mission in America. Other scholars have portrayed the Puritan migration to Massachusetts as a more fearful, inwardly-focused retreat by a group of persecuted sectarians.

In any case, about 21,000 English people came to New England during the 1630s, in what historians call the "Great Migration." Research suggests that most of the original English colonists, largely composed of families of middling or wealthy status, had little reason to come to Massachusetts other than religious conviction. Some of the settlers did return to England in the 1640s when the English Civil War broke out and circumstances became more favorable for Puritans in England. Puritans also founded Connecticut, and there were significant numbers of Puritans in early English colonies including Maryland, Virginia, Bermuda, and Barbados. Puritans also founded a colony at Providence Island, off the coast of Nicaragua, in 1629, but it was conquered by Spain in 1641. Because of Massachusetts's outsized role in the future history of the United States, scholars generally portray it as the paradigmatic Puritan colony.

Unlike most free settlers in the southern and Caribbean colonies, the vast majority of the early Puritan migrants came as part of kin groups, often in nuclear families. Nathaniel and Lydia Tilden, for example, were fifty-two and forty-seven years old, respectively, when they sailed for New England in 1635. Lydia had already borne twelve children, five of whom died (not an unusual percentage for the time) before the family left England. The other seven children came with their parents to New England. Like many of the Puritan migrants, the Tildens were relatively prosperous. Nathaniel had served as mayor of their small English town. The cause of Puritanism and the looming specter of persecution seem to have inspired the Tildens and thousands of English people like them to go to the New World.

Winthrop and the Puritan migrants envisioned Massachusetts as a place where they could build a godly church and state from the ground up. English Reformers had constantly struggled against precedent and extrabiblical tradition and were frustrated at every turn by the impediments to fully implementing biblical reforms. In the New World they would face no such impediments, especially because Winthrop was able (literally) to bring the Massachusetts charter with him. This symbolized an unusual level of independence for a fledgling colony. John Cotton (1585–1652), one of the brightest of the Puritan luminaries at Cambridge University, came to Boston, Massachusetts, after being forced out of his church. Cotton cited William Perkins in his belief that the Word of God offered a platform, not only for theology, but for fields of knowledge including ethics and government. "It is very suitable to God's all-sufficient wisdom, and to the fullness and perfection of Holy Scriptures, not only to prescribe perfect rules for the right ordering of a private man's soul to everlasting blessedness with himself, but also for the right ordering of a man's family, yea, of the commonwealth too, so far as both of them are subordinate to spiritual ends," Cotton wrote. Puritans like John Cotton believed that they had a unique opportunity to manifest the whole counsel of Scripture in the Massachusetts churches and government. Above all, they sought to preach the gospel in unimpeded clarity.

Early Colonial Struggles

The Puritans' biblicist vision was soaring. They strictly intended to base their entire system of church, state, and law on the Bible. But the New Englanders' vision immediately crashed into the realities of theological disagreement and dissent and the horrors of war against Native Americans. Even though settlers in New England were broadly Reformed, latent disagreements surfaced by the mid-1630s. In particular, tension within Puritanism between grace and works fueled what scholars often call the "antinomian controversy." Some believe the episode might be better called a "free grace controversy." John Cotton was one of the key players in this dispute, but historians have focused primarily on the role of Cotton's congregant Anne Hutchinson (1591–1643). Hutchinson and her family had gone to Massachusetts to follow Cotton, their pastor in England.

Hutchinson was a charismatic religious figure in her own right, and she began hosting small group discussions in her home. Originally intended only for women, they soon attracted men who found Hutchinson's Bible teaching compelling. Hutchinson would not likely have run into trouble for teaching in this private capacity alone. However, she began to criticize most of Boston's ministers (except for a select group including pastors John Cotton and John Wheelwright) for ostensibly teaching a form of works-righteousness and implying that Christians contributed to their own salvation. Hutchinson and Cotton took a stricter line on the doctrine of monergism, or the idea that there was nothing whatsoever people contributed to their salvation, not even "cooperation" with God's gracious work. Regeneration and faith were works of God alone, who took exclusive, unilateral action to save the elect. Hutchinson's opponents might have agreed with her in principle, but they suggested that salvation typically proceeded in a predictable order, usually in the church. Conversion typically happened under gospel preaching, so someone wishing to be saved should sit under such preaching. Hutchinson and Cotton warned against such "preparationist" teaching. "Before regeneration we are not active at all in any spiritual Christian action," Cotton wrote. If critics objected to such a stark view of grace, Cotton exclaimed, "Let Calvin answer for me!"

As a laywoman, Hutchinson was a more vulnerable target for critics of the free grace theology. Historians have debated whether John Winthrop and the Puritan authorities' attacks on Hutchinson were rooted in misogyny. Her place as a woman certainly did not strengthen her position, but Puritans were quite capable of treating dissent by male pastors in the same way they did with Hutchinson. In any case, Hutchinson's criticism of the Boston pastors was not well received. They labeled her and her followers as "antinomians," or those who rejected God's moral law. Cotton distanced himself from Hutchinson, while her brother-in-law John Wheelwright defended her and was subsequently banished from Massachusetts. Wheelwright's high-stakes banishment was probably the climax of the free grace controversy, but scholars' fascination with Hutchinson has tended to make her (understandably) the center of the antinomian controversy. In a dramatic showdown with John Winthrop and other Puritan judges, she testified that she had the gift of prophecy and that God had revealed his free grace to her by an "immediate revelation" of the Holy Spirit. This was the final straw for the judges, who heard echoes of radical sectarianism in such claims. Hutchinson was also banished from Massachusetts.

Like Hutchinson, the minister Roger Williams (d. 1683) had come to Massachusetts as a Puritan, but when he arrived he was already developing separatist convictions about the illegitimacy of the Church of England. Williams shuttled between the Plymouth Colony and Massachusetts, becoming increasingly uncomfortable with the colonists' churches and their treatment of Native Americans. He believed that colonists were stealing Native Americans' lands because they refused to acquire territory through mutual agreements and purchases. Massachusetts authorities became alarmed by Williams, and in 1636 they banished him. Williams went on to found the Rhode Island colony, south of Massachusetts, which is where expelled dissenters often went when they left the Puritan colonies. Williams committed Rhode Island to religious liberty, believing that it was biblical to maintain a "wall of Separation between the Garden of the Church and the Wilderness of

> God requires not uniformity of religion to be enacted and enforced in any civil state. Such enforced uniformity sooner or later is the greatest occasion of civil war, of the ravishing of conscience, of the persecution of Christ Jesus in his servants, and of the hypocrisy and destruction of millions of souls.
>
> ---
>
> Roger Williams, *The Bloody Tenent of Persecution for Cause of Conscience*, 1644

the world." Government interference with the church, or with the conscience of individuals, injected worldly influence into the kingdom of God. Williams briefly became a Baptist, and he helped establish the colonies' first Baptist church in Providence, Rhode Island in 1638. Williams was too much of a quibbler to stick with any denomination for long, so despite receiving believer's baptism, he did not fully identify with the Baptists either.

Evangelism in the Colonies

England had started establishing colonies fairly late in European imperial context, but in 1607 the Virginia Company founded the first permanent English colony in North America. Virginia was not founded with a religious mission per se, although Christianity was omnipresent among the Virginia colonists. Virginians erected what presumably was the first Protestant church building in North America soon after founding Jamestown. Some of the Jamestown colonists gestured toward evangelizing the Native Americans of the colony, but conflicts over land and resources dominated the early relations between the two groups. A horrific 1622 war between Virginians and the Powhatan Indians nearly destroyed the colony, making it an inauspicious environment for evangelism.

Like many European colonists, the Puritans in Massachusetts professed a desire to evangelize Native Americans. The seal of the Massachusetts Bay Company featured a Native American man saying, "Come Over and Help Us," quoting from Paul's vision of the man from Macedonia in Acts 16:9. But conflict over land and supplies developed quickly between New Englanders and their Indian neighbors, leading to ravaging wars and long-term resentments. Nevertheless, in the 1640s the Puritan missionary John Eliot (1604–90) worked with Native American translators to produce the so-called Eliot Bible, a Massachusett-language edition of the Geneva Bible. This was the first version of the Bible published in the English colonies. Also, in 1670 Hiacoomes, of the Wampanoag Nation, became the first Native American person to receive ordination as a pastor in England's American settlements.

Colonial Upheaval and Salem Witchcraft

By the 1690s, New England entered an era of cultural anxiety and decline. The founding generation of Massachusetts was passing away: John Winthrop had died in 1649, for example. The second and third generations of Puritans seemed not as committed to the Puritan mission as the original settlers were, at least according to the pastors of New England. Then in the 1680s English authorities revoked Massachusetts' precious charter, which Winthrop had secured to give the Puritans autonomy from English meddling. In a whipsawing series of events, the "Glorious Revolution" of 1688–89 saw the relatively peaceful removal of the Catholic King James II in England, which prompted the overthrow of royal government in Massachusetts, too. A new Massachusetts charter required the colony to tolerate other Protestants, including Quakers, Baptists, and Anglicans. Before the 1690s, such groups were not welcome in Massachusetts, which had even executed some aggressive Quaker missionaries starting in the late 1650s. The enforced toleration of the 1690s effectively signaled the end of the great Puritan experiment in Massachusetts.

At the same moment, Massachusetts endured the scourging experience of the Salem witchcraft controversy. English colonists (and Europeans generally) still assumed the existence of witches and demons, who might attack Christians with their malevolent powers. Reformed pastors such as England's William Perkins wrote popular guides on the biblical methods of detecting witchcraft. Perkins regarded as superstitious folk methods such as the "water test," in which a person who floated in water was proven to be a witch. Perkins preferred confession of crimes by accused witches, or at least the testimony of multiple witnesses. Inexplicable physical convulsions experienced by a group of adolescent girls in Salem, Massachusetts, and subsequent investigations, spiraled out of control in a series of accusations of witchcraft against dozens and then hundreds of people in eastern New England. The Salem judges accepted "spectral" evidence in which witnesses described encounters where the spirits of the accused pressured them to make covenants with the devil. Innocence was not presumed, and courts denounced the accused who would not admit to being witches. Twenty people—almost all of them older women—were eventually executed before authorities halted the proceedings.

Salem was hardly the biggest outburst of accusations and executions in the history of Europe and its colonies. For example, scholars estimate that some nine hundred accused witches died in a series of trials around Würzburg, Germany, between 1626 and 1631. Hundreds more died in the "great noise" of witch prosecutions in Sweden in the 1660s and '70s. Salem was one of the last great outbursts of witch executions in history, however. Belief in witches endured in America, but prosecutions after Salem tended to focus on isolated individuals instead of dozens of people at one time. Witchcraft accusations remain a live issue in parts of the developing world today, especially in areas of sub-Saharan Africa and the islands of Oceania. Influenced by the naturalistic philosophy associated with the Enlightenment, however, many elites in Europe and America took a muted or skeptical approach to witchcraft and demonology by the mid-1700s. In 1768, the great English Methodist leader John Wesley wrote with trepidation that "most of the men of learning in Europe, have given up all accounts of witches and apparitions as mere old wives' fables. I am sorry for it. . . . They well know (whether Christians know it or not) that the giving up of witchcraft is in effect giving up the Bible." We might not share Wesley's concern about the decline of witchcraft accusations, but there was no question that Salem occurred during a great cultural transition between the passing of the medieval world and the beginnings of a more secular "modernity." Supernatural phenomena that most Europeans once took for granted were now coming under enlightened scrutiny.

Selected Bibliography

Anderson, Virginia DeJohn. *New England's Generation: The Great Migration and the Formation of Society and Culture in the Seventeenth Century*. New York: Cambridge University Press, 1991.

Atwood, Craig D. *Theology of the Czech Brethren from Hus to Comenius*. University Park: Pennsylvania State University Press, 2009.

Cunningham, Andrew, and Ole Peter Grell. *The Four Horsemen of the Apocalypse: Religion, War, Famine and Death in Reformation Europe*. Cambridge: Cambridge University Press, 2000.

Howard, Thomas Albert. *Remembering the Reformation: An Inquiry into the Meanings of Protestantism*. Oxford: Oxford University Press, 2016.

Hutton, Ronald. *The Witch: A History of Fear, from Ancient Times to the Present*. New Haven, CT: Yale University Press, 2017.

Kostroun, Daniella. *Feminism, Absolutism, and Jansenism: Louis XIV and the Port-Royal Nuns*. Cambridge: Cambridge University Press, 2011.

Nischan, Bodo. "Reformed Irenicism and the Leipzig Colloquy of 1631," *Central European History* 9, no. 1 (March 1976): 3–26.

Pettit, Norman. *The Heart Prepared: Grace and Conversion in Puritan Spiritual Life*. 2nd ed. Middletown, CT: Wesleyan University Press, 1989.

Stanglin, Keith D., and Thomas H. McCall. *Jacobus Arminius: Theologian of Grace*. Oxford: Oxford University Press, 2012.

Van Kley, Dale K. *The Jansenists and the Expulsion of the Jesuits from France, 1757–1765*. New Haven, CT: Yale University Press, 1975.

—— Chapter 6 ——

The English Civil War, Pietism, and the Early Enlightenment

In 1637, Jenny Geddes threw her stool at the minister of St. Giles Cathedral in Edinburgh for "saying Mass," that is, for using the new English prayer book's liturgy. That altercation heralded looming disaster for the stubbornly incompetent King Charles I (r. 1625–49). The English Civil War, like the Thirty Years' War then ending on the Continent, was born out of political, religious, and imperial factors. The conflict led to King Charles being deposed and ultimately beheaded. The English Civil War was a time of major religious change, but by the late 1650s, many in England were eager for stability. The Puritans had their day for most of the 1640s and '50s. The "Restoration" of the House of Stuart in 1660 boded ill for Reformed believers in England and Scotland alike.

England at War

Charles's ill-conceived attempt to impose Anglican piety in Scotland led to massive unrest there, but the Scots beat back royal attempts to restore order. The Presbyterian Scots signed the National Covenant in 1638, committing themselves to defending Scotland from the Anglican incursions of the king and his bishops. The Reformed, anti-monarchical forces in Scotland became known as the Covenanters. The Covenanters invaded northeastern England in 1640, scoring a decisive victory over Charles's army at the Battle of Newburn.

In 1641 Ireland also erupted in rebellion, as Irish Catholics sensed an opening to vanquish their English and Scottish Protestant colonizers. The Protestant-Catholic violence was especially acute in Ulster (Northern Ireland), where more than ten thousand Protestants died in the unrest. Charles wanted to invade Ireland as well, but resistance against him in England soared, partly due to fears that he would side with Irish Catholics. Leaders of Parliament seized political control in London in 1642, when the king withdrew from the city and looked to raise support in the English provinces.

Reformed Leaders and Documents

In 1643, Parliament commissioned a synod of English and Scottish ministers to meet at Westminster to propose reforms in the Church of England and to create a new confession of faith for British Protestants. The result was the Westminster Confession of Faith (1646), the most influential Reformed confession in the English language. The Westminster Confession's influence turned out to be more enduring in Scotland and America than in England due to ongoing churchly turmoil in the latter. The confession affirmed Reformed distinctives, including double predestination: "By the decree of God, for the manifestation of His glory, some men and angels are predestinated unto everlasting life; and others foreordained to everlasting death." Westminster delegates denied papal or kingly authority over Christ's church and associated the pope with Antichrist. "There is no other head of the Church but the Lord Jesus Christ. Nor can the Pope of Rome, in any sense, be head thereof: but is that Antichrist, that man of sin, and son of perdition, that exalteth himself, in the Church, against Christ." They affirmed infant baptism, which prompted Calvinistic Baptists to produce their own confessions, such as the influential Second London Baptist Confession (1689), based on Westminster but with Baptist caveats about believer's baptism. The Second London Baptist Confession also used the Savoy Declaration (1658), an English Congregationalist statement of faith and church order, which likewise drew upon Westminster.

Despite its controversial assertions, Westminster opened with a classic Protestant statement on the Bible as the "Word of God written." The Bible was marked with "entire perfection," and the "authority of the Holy Scripture, for which it ought to be believed, and obeyed, dependeth not upon the testimony of any man, or Church; but wholly upon God (who is truth itself) the author thereof: and therefore it is to be received, because it is the Word of God." The nineteenth-century German Reformed church historian Philip Schaff said that Westminster represented "the best confessional statement of the evangelical doctrines of justification, adoption, sanctification, saving faith, good works, and assurance of salvation."

In 1648, a military purge of moderates from Parliament set the stage for Charles's trial and execution the following year. At his death, moderate Anglicans hailed Charles as a Christian martyr and a victim of Puritan fanaticism. The army general Oliver Cromwell (1599–1658) became the head of the new English Republic, or Commonwealth. Cromwell needed as much support from a range of Protestants as he could get, so he instituted a bold program of toleration. In 1650, England stopped requiring attendance at parish churches, opening the way for English people to attend a congregation of their choice.

Baptists such as Thomas Helwys had been arguing for religious toleration since the early 1600s, and the turmoil of the Civil War and Cromwell's Interregnum allowed for previously-unknown levels of religious freedom. This freedom generally remained limited to trinitarian Protestants, however. Sectarian groups like the Quakers grew by leaps and

Image 6.1. *Assertion of Liberty of Conscience by the Independents of the Westminster Assembly of Divines* (1847)

bounds during the 1650s, even though they still endured frequent harassment from local officials. The Quaker evangelist George Fox preached the Quakers' distinctive message in his travels through England, Ireland, the Netherlands, and English colonies in America and the Caribbean. Quaker evangelists made a special effort to reach people of African background in the colonies. Fox and other Quakers insisted that they did not want to make slaves rebellious, as critics often charged. But the Quakers were among the earliest Christian groups to criticize New World slavery, and to encourage "Friends" (as they called themselves) to emancipate enslaved people.

Baptists found more consistent protection under Cromwell's rule than did Quakers. Some Baptists even got put on committees to review the competence of local ministers. Cromwell's 1653 *Instrument of Government* demanded only that "the Christian religion, as contained in the Scriptures," be taught in English churches. Since small numbers of Baptists were entrusted with monitoring that biblical religion was indeed taught, it was clear that Cromwell saw long-despised Baptists as fitting within his capacious concept of orthodox Protestantism. Partly due to the influence of the Calvinist minister John Owen (1616–83), arguably the most powerful theologian of Cromwell's rule, Arminians now found themselves more likely targets of official scorn than Calvinistic Baptists did.

Owen started his career as an Anglican minister but ran afoul of William Laud's persecution of Puritans. During the 1640s, he developed congregationalist convictions against church hierarchy, and became an inveterate foe of Arminian theology. Owen's first book, *Theomachia . . . or, A Display of Arminianism* (1643), was published at the behest of the House of Commons, signaling Owen's growing political sway. He served as a chaplain in Cromwell's army, and in church and academic positions in Oxford in the 1650s. Owen was a relentless writer, penning some eighty books totaling eight and a half million words. The Anglo-Canadian theologian J.I. Packer has called Owen "puritanism's theological Everest." Owen was one of the chief drafters of the Congregationalist Savoy Declaration in 1658. Like most Puritans, Owen's career fell on hard times with the Restoration of the English monarchy in 1660. He devoted much of his remaining years to the defense of English "dissenters," who did not wish to be part of the Church of England. Much of Owen's work was for the benefit of Reformed pastors and laypeople, including devotional works such as *On the Mortification of Sin in Believers* (1656). In it, Owen wrote that "my heart's desire unto God, and the chief design of my life in the station wherein the good providence of God hath placed me, are, that mortification and universal holiness may be promoted in my own and in the hearts and ways of others, to the glory of God; that so the gospel of our Lord and Saviour Jesus Christ may be adorned in all things."

Some Reformed clergy had supported Charles II's return as king, but the Act of Uniformity of 1662, and related statutes regulating the established church, represented a crackdown on Reformed pastors. A new version of the Book of Common Prayer made clear in its first sentence that the Restoration Church of England meant to be the true *via media* between Catholicism and radical Protestantism. "It hath been the wisdom of the Church of England, ever since the first compiling of her Publick Liturgy, to keep the mean between the two extremes, of too much stiffness in refusing, and of too much easiness in admitting any variation from it." More than two thousand Puritan pastors were removed from their churches for failing to comply with the Act of Uniformity and the requirements of the new prayer book.

John Owen had already lost his position as the Dean of Oxford's Christ Church Cathedral in 1660, but the "Great Ejection" of 1662 led to the removal of many more Puritan leaders. These included the popular writers Richard Baxter and John Flavel. Baxter had served as parish minister at Kidderminster and was the author of classic works including *The Saints' Everlasting Rest* (1650). Flavel had ministered in Dartmouth, England, until 1662. After his removal he continued to serve as a dissenting pastor in a variety of secret and formal capacities. Flavel's spiritual writings often focused on Christian vocational issues, such as *Husbandry Spiritualized* (1669). His writings on Christian devotion and vocation became among the most enduring Puritan classics in Britain and America, well into the 1800s. Flavel's works were also translated into languages including Dutch, Latin, Welsh, and Czech. After 1660, the Church of England took a decisive step back from its leadership in the international Reformed community, but Puritan writers such as Flavel and Owen remained major influencers in that network.

The era's Puritan writer of the most lasting popularity was John Bunyan (1628–88), a tinker (repairer of metal utensils) and veteran of Cromwell's army. Bunyan went through years of spiritual struggle before joining a separatist congregation in Bedford, England, in 1655. Bunyan's journey to conversion took a critical turn when "three or four poor women" of the Bedford church witnessed to him about the "new birth, the work of God on their hearts; also how they were convinced of their miserable state of nature." Bunyan marveled at how they spoke with "such pleasantness of scripture language." He realized that these women inhabited a new-born spiritual world that he did not know. Hearing preaching at Bedford and reading the Bible and Protestant classics such as Luther's *Commentary on Galatians* brought Bunyan to the threshold of conversion. He realized that his solitary struggle for justification was futile and that "my righteousness was Jesus Christ himself." With this realization, he felt as if spiritual chains fell off his legs and he was loosed from his "afflictions and irons."

Bunyan began to preach even before he broke through to assurance of salvation, and he was arrested for illegal preaching in 1660. Because Bunyan refused to stop, he ended up serving twelve years in prison. He was free to write in jail, however, and among his prison writings was *Grace Abounding to the Chief of Sinners* (1666), his spiritual autobiography and second most popular work. He also began composing *The Pilgrim's Progress* (1678), the spiritual allegory which became one of the most famous books ever written in English. By the end of his prison term, Bunyan was appointed as a pastor in his Bedford congregation. He also adopted Calvinist Baptist convictions. Bunyan died just prior to the beginning of the Glorious Revolution in 1688, the event which led to the removal of James II as king.

Few works outside of the Bible have ever approached the literary and spiritual influence of *The Pilgrim's Progress*. It has been translated into more than 200 languages and went through some 1300 editions by the year 1938. It influenced thinkers and writers across a religious spectrum, including Benjamin Franklin, Herman Melville, and the Romantic artist William Blake. Bunyan and Blake are both buried in Bunhill Fields, the extraordinary nonconformist burial ground in London. Bunhill Fields is the location of the graves of other major figures such as John Owen, Susanna Wesley (the mother of John and Charles Wesley), the Baptist pastor and theologian John Gill, the author Daniel Defoe, and the hymnist Isaac Watts.

> What God says is best, indeed is best, though all the men in the world are against it.
>
> John Bunyan, *The Pilgrim's Progress*, 1678

The Restoration and Act of Uniformity drew a permanent line in English religion dividing "Anglicans" from "nonconformists," or "dissenters," who for a variety of reasons could not conform to the Anglican way. Evangelical and Calvinist Anglicans remained a presence in the Anglican Church, but the Church of England never again would take a definitive leading role within the international Reformed community. In the mid-1700s, figures such as John Wesley and George Whitefield would seek to re-energize the Anglican Church from within (though Wesley and Whitefield would bitterly disagree about whether evangelical renewal should include Calvinist theology). In the meantime, Presbyterians, Congregationalists, Baptists, Quakers, and other dissenting groups after 1660 found themselves fighting merely to be tolerated by the English religious establishment. Toleration improved somewhat after the 1660s, but people could not hold public office in English towns unless they took communion in an Anglican church. That rule would not change until the nineteenth century.

Image 6.2. *Watercolor by William Blake, of a scene from John Bunyan's* The Pilgrim's Progress (ca. 1824–27)

The Glorious Revolution, Religious Toleration, and Enlightenment

The persecution of Protestant dissenters stood in tension with the widespread Protestant hostility toward Catholics in England. This hostility endured despite the Stuart kings' attachment to Catholicism. Charles II converted to Catholicism on his deathbed, and his brother and successor James II was openly Catholic, to the dismay of Anglicans and dissenters alike. James's enemies accused him of plotting to make England Catholic again, conjuring memories of Queen Mary's violent reign in the 1550s. James's son-in-law and daughter, William and Mary of the Netherlands, invaded England in 1688, replacing James II in a largely bloodless coup that most English Protestants were pleased to see happen. James's forces made more of an effort to maintain power in Scotland and Ireland. James's (bloody) losses in Ireland in the early 1690s scuttled the Irish Catholic dream of having a British Catholic monarch. Periodic "Jacobite" rebellions, which sought to return the Stuart line to the throne, racked Scotland and other parts of the British Isles through the mid-1700s. The most significant religious outcome of the Glorious Revolution was the Act of Toleration (1689), which suspended penalties against dissenters' worship as long as they promised to support the British monarch. The act did not afford the same freedom to Catholics.

Among the chief theorists of religious toleration in the Glorious Revolution was John Locke (1632–1704). Locke was the most influential English figure of the "Enlightenment."

The Enlightenment has become a disputed term among historians. They note that the movement was hardly unified, and "Enlightened" thought may not have represented unqualified progress culturally or intellectually. The traditional use of the term Enlightenment ("Aufklärung" in German) carried anti-Christian implications about a supposed dark period of blind faith that preceded it. More recent scholarship has clarified that some advocates of the Enlightenment, particularly in Britain and America, were quite friendly to faith. Some have argued that the Enlightenment, for example, influenced the early evangelical movement of the 1730s and '40s, with its focus on the individual and its confidence about a Christian's ability to understand the mysteries of the "new birth" in Christ. However, it still seems appropriate to regard the long-term trend toward a naturalistic understanding of the world and an increasing emphasis on the potential of science and rational analysis as representing something we call the Enlightenment.

Locke studied at Christ Church, an Oxford college, where he regularly heard the preaching of John Owen. Locke also had a distinguished Puritan ancestor, Anne Locke, who was a friend of the Scottish Reformer John Knox and a translator of John Calvin's works into English. John Locke was not a Puritan in the mode of Anne Locke or John Owen, however. Instead, he positioned himself as a defender of *The Reasonableness of Christianity as Delivered in the Scriptures*, as he put it in a 1695 publication. Yet Locke was also representative of a deistic trend in learned English circles. Deists in the 1700s represented a wide range of beliefs, from mere rationalist Christianity to strident agnosticism. Locke's doubts about traditional faith were muted, but he was still an inspiration for radical skeptics such as Scotland's David Hume (1711–76), who declared that his belief in religion ended when he read Locke. Locke preferred an ethics-centered version of Christianity and was reluctant to affirm the doctrine of the Trinity. Many figures in the Anglo-American Enlightenment, including Benjamin Franklin and Thomas Jefferson (1743–1826), affirmed Christianity in an ethical sense. Yet Franklin and Jefferson balked at doctrines such as the Trinity, which might seem (in the critics' eyes) to contradict reason and the unitary nature of God. Locke's belief in toleration was rooted in a spirit of Christian forbearance toward all who supported England's Protestant establishment. This did not include Catholics, so Locke's canopy of toleration did not cover them.

Scotland's Enlightenment, with the notable exception of the skeptic Hume, may have been the most friendly to traditional Christian belief of all the Enlightenment tributaries. The Scots' contributions were also arguably the most influential segment of the Enlightenment for America's Founding Fathers. Following Descartes, Locke, and other major philosophers, however, Scotland's Enlightened philosophers still assumed that reason was a primary, if not the unique, means of discerning truth. Divine revelation, to Christian traditionalists, would affirm the same truths as reason did because God was behind both reason and revelation. The defenders of the Enlightenment, even those from a Calvinistic background, put inordinate weight on the unaided power of reason. Some traditional Christian pastors and theologians warned about excessive dependence on human understanding, however. For example, the Scottish pastor-theologian Thomas Halyburton (1674–1712) posthumously published the enduring treatise *Natural Reason Insufficient; and Revealed Necessary to Man's Happiness* (1714). Halyburton, a professor of divinity at the University of St. Andrews, critically engaged with Locke as he defended the proposition that the "faith whereby we assent unto, and receive the Word of God, to his glory and our salvation, is faith divine and supernatural." Reason was not enough; supernatural revelation alone could supply the complete truth about God and man.

The Scottish Enlightenment was best known for its emphasis on common sense morality, or the idea that each person possessed a God-given sense of right and wrong. This philosophy is often called Scottish Common Sense Realism. Again, this theory was not intended to oppose revelation. It was more of a result of centuries of conflict over the Reformation. Many moral philosophers desired to find a universal basis for ethics that did not depend only on divine revelation. One of the main exponents of commonsense ethics was Francis Hutcheson (1694–1746), professor of moral philosophy at the University of Glasgow. In writings such as his *Inquiry into the Original of Our Ideas of Beauty and Virtue* (1725), Hutcheson argued that prior to reason, human beings had an inborn inclination to approve moral acts and to disapprove immoral ones. People did not always behave in accord with their inborn benevolent sentiments because of selfish passions, misguided beliefs, or corrupt culture. But to Hutcheson, those inconsistencies did not negate the reality of a universal moral sense which God implanted in all humanity. Hutcheson's humanistic views on moral sense often became associated with theologians and pastors drifting away from Calvinist theology. Calvinists routinely warned that the fall of humankind had dealt a terrible blow to people's ability to perceive and act upon God's law. Even the staunch Arminian John Wesley exclaimed that Hutcheson's optimistic view of human nature "cannot stand unless the Bible falls. I know both from Scripture, reason, and experience that his picture of man is not drawn from life."

David Hume went much further than the moderate Hutcheson. Hume's religious views were too radical for him to secure a faculty position in Scotland, but his job as a librarian at the University of Edinburgh facilitated his wide-ranging writing career. Hume's key intervention in religion was his argument against miracles. He asserted that we should never accept second-hand evidence or testimony about alleged violations of laws of nature (such as the resurrection of a dead person), especially alleged ones that happened long ago. Testimonies about miraculous occurrences could never outweigh the weight of the laws of nature themselves. Hume's argument was the epitome of a new skepticism rising in Europe. By the mid-1700s, intellectual unbelief (though not necessarily atheism) was becoming a viable option, even in a place as culturally Christian as Scotland.

Higher Criticism and Enlightenment on the Continent

Hume's skepticism was enabled in part by biblical higher criticism, which began to emerge on the European Continent by the 1670s. Higher criticism was different from textual, or lower criticism. Textual criticism was the focus of Christian humanists who sought to understand the original languages of the Bible and to use the best and earliest manuscript sources of the Bible. Textual criticism paired easily with reverence for the Bible as the inspired Word of God. Higher criticism, however, often took a more skeptical view of the Bible, treating it as any other ancient text with associated problems of authorship and historical reliability.

Some scholars were interested in both lower and higher criticism. For example, the French Catholic priest Richard Simon (1638–1712) became one of his era's leading experts on Hebrew, Syriac, and comparative ancient religions. In his *Histoire Critique du Vieux Testament* (1678), Simon developed the theory that Moses could not have written the whole Pentateuch, but that the five books were a pastiche derived from sources including Moses and "public scribes" of Israel. The latter were still guided by the Holy Spirit, but they preserved oral traditions rather than directly recording history as it happened. Simon insisted that Protestant figures such as Luther and Calvin lacked an accurate understanding of Hebrew and the Old Testament, as did church fathers including Augustine. Simon was hardly an anti-Christian skeptic like the rabidly anticlerical French writer Voltaire (1694–1778), but his work still suggested that some traditional understandings of the Bible would not stand up to scholarly research. Catholic officials in France found such implications alarming enough to order copies of Simon's *Histoire* to be burned.

Simon's work was informed by that of Baruch Spinoza (1632–77), but Spinoza's philosophy took a much bigger step than Simon's toward functional atheism. Spinoza did believe that God existed, but not in a personal sense. He did not believe that God governed history.

Historian Jonathan Israel has argued that Spinoza deserves more recognition as the father of the "radical Enlightenment" of reason, materialism (the reality of matter alone), and anti-providentialism. Spinoza grew up in a Jewish family in Amsterdam, but in his mid-twenties he was expelled from his family's synagogue for heterodox beliefs. In 1670, Spinoza anonymously published his *Theologico-Political Treatise*, in which he reviled the coercive power of state-backed religion. Free inquiry about religious tradition and the Bible would liberate people from superstition and forced belief, he proclaimed. As with Locke, Spinoza believed that the chief value of Scripture was its moral code, but that much of the Bible related to circumstances that were not relevant to later times and places. As Hume would later argue, Spinoza did not see the biblical miracles as literal events, but only poetic descriptions meant to inspire devotion in common, uneducated people.

Spinoza doubted that Moses wrote much or any of the Pentateuch, and he further surmised that the historical books of the Hebrew Bible were written and/or compiled by later authors and editors. He made a similar argument for the prophetic books. Spinoza's claims about the Pentateuch were not entirely new, but his thoroughgoing critique of the Old Testament's sources was shocking. The study of Scripture was similar to the study of any other artefact, he insisted. "By allowing no other principles or data for the interpretation of Scripture and study of its contents except those that can be gathered only from Scripture itself and from a historical study of Scripture," Spinoza proclaimed, "steady progress can be made without any danger of error." Spinoza wanted to free Europeans from their outdated reverence for Scripture, and he was especially keen to see governments stop policing heresy. The heart of Scripture was its injunction to love one's neighbor. Authorities should leave people alone to worship God (or not) as their conscience dictated.

The French philosopher Pierre Bayle (1647–1706) reached similar conclusions to Spinoza's about toleration. Bayle's experience was permanently shaped by the revocation of the Edict of Nantes in 1685 and the subsequent crackdown by the French government on the Protestant community there. Bayle grew up in a Protestant family, briefly converted to Catholicism as a young man, then re-converted to Protestantism. Because of these vacillations, Bayle had to flee to Geneva. After returning to teach at a Protestant academy in France, he finally settled in Rotterdam, in the Netherlands, where he died in 1706. Bayle was best known for his *Dictionnaire Historique et Critique*. Aside from his skepticism, Bayle was hard to label with theological precision. The many editions and translations of his dictionary popularized his skepticism for many readers in the 1700s. Thomas Jefferson was one of many figures who owned an English translation of Bayle's dictionary, which Jefferson regularly recommended to friends. Bayle believed the persecutorial spirit of governments sprung from their failure to observe the love of neighbor commanded in Scripture. "If the multiplicity of religions prejudices the state," he wrote, "it proceeds from their not bearing with one another but on the contrary endeavouring each to crush and destroy the other by methods of persecution."

French Protestantism and Persecution

Bayle was haunted by the government oppression of his fellow Huguenots, a persecution which came in its full fury just after he left France for good in the early 1680s. The Huguenots' relationship with the French state had been uncertain for the better part of a century, despite the freedoms guaranteed to Protestants by the Edict of Nantes (1598). Protestant unrest had led to the 1628 French government conquest of La Rochelle, the port city that was the nation's greatest Protestant stronghold. But French Protestants had seen nothing like the disaster of the revocation of the Edict of Nantes. The revocation was one of the most aggressive actions taken during the reign of King Louis XIV (r. 1643–1715), who saw himself as the embodiment of God-ordained monarchical authority. Protestant churches and schools were closed, and Protestant parents were forced to have their children baptized in the Catholic Church. Protestant pastors were given the choice between leaving the country or converting to Catholicism; the government even quartered French troops in recalcitrant Protestants' homes to constantly pressure them to renounce the Reformed faith. Out of desperation, political calculation, or other motives, many French Protestants did formally declare themselves to be Catholics (as Bayle had once done). Bayle lamented that the revocation and subsequent persecution showed that the French Catholic Church was "still animated as much as ever with a spirit of cruelty and fraud."

Protestant dissenters and Enlightenment advocates of religious liberty would point to the savage treatment of French Protestants as the era's emblem of religious intolerance. This point of agreement did not always lead to harmony between Enlightenment philosophes and Christian dissenting leaders. Indeed, one of Bayle's greatest objects of scorn in his *Dictionnaire* was the Huguenot pastor and theologian Pierre Jurieu (1637–1713), who taught at the same Protestant school as Bayle. Jurieu also fled to Rotterdam when their academy was suppressed in 1681. Bayle and Jurieu proposed starkly different postures toward the French state, with Bayle arguing that French Protestants should demonstrate their loyalty to Louis XIV and thereby win religious toleration. Jurieu, however, had no hope for reform in the French church and state, which he increasingly associated with Antichrist. From Rotterdam, Jurieu aided attempts to undermine the French government. He promoted the interests of William of Orange, soon to be the new King of England. Jurieu argued that Huguenots should engage in armed resistance if necessary to defend their right to freely assemble. Jurieu also disagreed with Bayle's notion of toleration as a good unto itself. Jurieu still believed that godly government should promote biblical truth. Jurieu's writings on prophecy and Christian devotion were popular in English editions. His prophetic interpretations enjoyed a brief renaissance a century later amidst the anti-Christian horrors committed during the French Revolution.

The crackdown on the Huguenots inspired many prophetic writings like Jurieu's and fueled millenarian resistance among some French Protestants, especially in the mountainous Cévennes region of southern France. There, Protestants known as the Camisards fought in resistance against French Catholic forces from 1702 to 1715. The trauma and dislocations following the revocation of the Edict of Nantes generated radical Protestant movements led by would-be prophets, including a teenage shepherdess named Isabeau Vincent (fl. 1670–90). For several months in 1688, Vincent and her followers asserted that she would speak prophecies while asleep, reciting Scripture and singing psalms. In the years following the revocation, a number of French Protestants had reportedly heard mysterious psalm-singing coming from the skies, and psalm-singing was one of the distinctive practices of Continental Reformed churches.

Vincent assured her Protestant hearers that if they withstood Louis XIV's onslaught, God would honor their courage and their churches would thrive again. Her messages showed the influence of Jurieu's writings, even though her age, gender, and slumbering prophecies made her ministry more controversial than Jurieu's. She claimed inspiration from the Holy Spirit, citing Joel's prediction that God would pour out the Spirit on all flesh, and that "your sons and your daughters shall prophesy." Vincent would eventually be arrested and forced into a Catholic convent, but the prophetic movement she represented hardly ended there. A number of the "French Prophets" eventually fled France and went to Switzerland, Germany, and England. By 1706, London alone had twenty-four French Protestant churches, and Protestants associated with the French Prophets would have a controversial influence on the Great Awakening in England.

The Pietists

The French Prophets were illustrative of the Spirit-fueled religious "enthusiasm" that rationalist writers such as John Locke despised. In between the cool rationalism of Locke and the radical prophecies of an Isabeau Vincent, many Protestants sought a warm, worshipful, and communal faith that engaged the mind and the heart. This desire undergirded the Pietist movement, centered in Germany in the 1600s. One of Pietism's chief forerunners, the theologian Johann Arndt (1555–1621), was born in the late stages of Luther's Reformation. Arndt became the most widely-read German devotional writer of the 1600s, due especially to his book *True Christianity* (1606). In the next century and a half, Arndt's book would be printed in more than a hundred editions and translated into at least nine languages. He played a major role in developing the Pietist (and later evangelical) understanding of an individual's repentance and conversion to faith in Christ. "Repentance or true conversion," Arndt wrote, "is a work of God of the Holy Spirit, through which the human being recognizes his sins from the law and the anger of God against these sins." Early English Methodist leaders John Wesley and George Whitefield, among others, were deeply influenced by reading Arndt. The Methodists would go farther than Arndt, however, in teaching that the new birth of conversion came at a single identifiable moment.

Following Arndt's lead, German Pietists put more focus than earlier Reformers on a personalized, internal life of faith beyond mere understanding of doctrine or church attendance. Pietists encouraged transformation by God through rigorous devotion in community with other Christians. Philipp Jakob Spener (1635–1705) was arguably the most influential Pietist leader and writer, due to his 1675 classic *Pia Desideria*. Spener was concerned that the German Protestant churches might be doctrinally correct but were cold and lifeless, especially for the laity. He urged pastors to instruct their congregations in vital piety, not just abstract doctrine. Spener further proposed that German believers should meet in small fellowships, or *collegia pietatis*, for teaching, prayer, and the encouragement of charitable works. Spener's model was

> It is of the utmost importance that the office of the ministry be occupied by men who, above all, are themselves true Christians and, then, have the divine wisdom to guide others carefully on the way of the Lord.
>
> ———
>
> Philipp Jakob Spener, *Pia Desideria*, 1675

an important complement to the distinctively Protestant focus on the Word of God preached. As important as teaching the Word was, mere doctrinal assent led to an incomplete and immature Christian life. Pietist conventicles spread rapidly in German cities in the late 1600s, attracting large numbers of male and female townsfolk. Women sometimes even led the private conventicles, which drew concern from anti-Pietist authorities, who called the meetings a "cancer" and the "Pietist weed."

In 1694, Spener helped to found the University of Halle, which became the period's key center for Pietist education and missions. One of Spener's protégés, August Hermann Francke, became Halle's most entrepreneurial leader, turning the university into a unique center of Pietist ventures, including an orphanage, a medical dispensary, and a missionary hub. The Halle Pietists were among the first Protestant groups to establish missionary and educational works outside of Europe. The Halle mission in India, founded in 1706 in the Danish colony of Tranquebar, attracted attention around the Protestant world. More than a hundred and fifty years after the Jesuits had pioneered Catholic missions in India, Protestants were finally becoming active in South Asia as well.

Conclusion

Protestant-Catholic hostilities remained a major story in France and other nations, but by 1700, Protestant churches were generating new reform movements of their own, including Pietism. This desire for further reform was a sign of Protestantism's maturation and institutionalization in the centuries after 1517. Protestants also began to take fledgling steps toward expansion and evangelism beyond Europe's borders. Most immediately, this was happening in Protestant-affiliated colonies around the Atlantic world. But Halle and Tranquebar signaled the growing global ambitions among devout Protestants such as Francke.

Selected Bibliography

Andrews, Edward A. "Tranquebar: Charting the Protestant International in the British Atlantic and Beyond." *William and Mary Quarterly*, 3rd ser., 74, no. 1 (January 2017): 3–34.

Bingham, Matthew C. *Orthodox Radicals: Baptist Identity in the English Revolution*. Oxford: Oxford University Press, 2019.

Bracken, H.M., "Pierre Jurieu: The Politics of Prophecy." In J.C. Laursen and R.H. Popkin, eds., *Millenarianism and Messianism in Early Modern European Culture*, vol. 4, 85–94. Dordrecht, NL: Kluwer Academic, 2001.

Broadie, Alexander, and Craig Smith, eds. *The Cambridge Companion to the Scottish Enlightenment*. 2nd ed. Cambridge: Cambridge University Press, 2019.

Garrett, Clarke. *Origins of the Shakers: From the Old World to the New World*. Baltimore: Johns Hopkins University Press, 1998.

Gleixner, Ulrike. "Pietism." In Ulinka Rublack, ed., *The Oxford Handbook of the Protestant Reformations*, 329–49. New York: Oxford University Press, 2016.

Israel, Jonathan I. *Radical Enlightenment: Philosophy and the Making of Modernity, 1650–1750*. New York: Oxford University Press, 2001.

Shantz, Douglas, ed., *A Companion to German Pietism, 1660–1800*. Leiden: Brill, 2014.

Treasure, Geoffrey. *The Huguenots*. New Haven, CT: Yale University Press, 2013.

Ward, W.R. *Christianity under the Ancien Régime, 1648–1789*. Cambridge: Cambridge University Press, 1999.

—— Chapter 7 ——

New World Colonies

During the sixteenth to eighteenth centuries, European powers scrambled to control as much territory in the Western Hemisphere as they could. Their colonial struggles almost always had religious implications, ones that furthered the Protestant-Catholic conflicts of the Reformation era. For a variety of reasons, Spain and Portugal took a lead over the English and French in establishing New World colonies, starting with Christopher Columbus's explorations in the Caribbean on behalf of the Spanish crown in the late 1400s. Portuguese sailors explored Brazil starting in 1500, and they began colonial organization of the territory in 1534. French Huguenots briefly joined the French Brazilian colony at Fort Coligny, where in 1557 they held what was likely the first Protestant service in the Western Hemisphere. In the early 1600s, the Dutch and Portuguese began to fight over their worldwide colonial possessions, including Brazil. For a time, the Dutch West India Company controlled parts of Brazil in the name of the Netherlands and of Reformed Protestantism. Whereas Protestant and Catholic allegiances had taken firm root in Europe by the early 1600s, in the New World many allegiances remained up for grabs. The presence of the native peoples of the Americas, as well as increasing numbers of enslaved peoples from Africa, made the New World colonies volatile and diverse, including in religious matters. Colonization and plantation slavery forced European Christians to confront novel ethical and theological questions, even as they continued to play out their old rivalries dating to the Reformation.

Protestant Colonies in the Caribbean

Protestants had long dreamed of extending the Reformation faith around the world, but they despaired as they watched Catholic nations expand colonial power through the early 1600s. The Protestant-aligned Dutch West India Company established footholds around the Atlantic basin, including in New Netherlands (New York) in the 1620s, and Brazil in the 1630s. At its height, Dutch colonial Brazil ("New Holland") extended some 900 miles along the east coast of South America. This substantial territory allowed Dutch Calvinists finally to attempt to extend what they called *Nadere Reformatie*, or "Further Reformation," to the New World and to challenge the long-standing control of Brazil by Portuguese Catholics. They also hoped to introduce the as-yet "heathen" populations of native Brazilians and Africans to the true Protestant religion. Catholics living under Dutch rule, however, as well as Africans and native Brazilians, often resisted Calvinist overtures.

Adding even greater complexity to the colonial Brazilian religious scene were the thousands of Sephardic Jews who lived there. (Sephardic Jews are originally from the Iberian Peninsula—Spain and Portugal—from which they were mostly expelled in the 1400s amidst anti-Semitic violence and paranoia.) Some of these Jews established the Kahal Zur Israel synagogue in Recife, Brazil, in 1636, the first synagogue in the Western Hemisphere. Many of those Jews would be expelled from Brazil in the 1650s when the Portuguese defeated the Dutch there. One group of the exiled Jews went to New Amsterdam in 1654, which would soon be conquered by the English and renamed New York City. The threat of violence and need for migration were ever-present factors for European-background Jews.

Dutch Calvinists saw Brazil as a challenging place for establishing stable churches. This made the few successful pastors in Dutch Brazil even more revered. In the 1630s Fredericus Kesseler was the most distinguished Dutch Calvinist pastor in the colony. As historian D.L. Noorlander notes, Dutch Reformed officials sent Kesseler to Brazil from the German-speaking Reformed congregation in Amsterdam. As Sephardic Jews had made Recife their religious center in Brazil, so also Kesseler turned Recife briefly into a Brazilian Geneva. (Recife was the Dutch West India Company's colonial capital.) Kesseler helped to form a Brazilian *classis*, the most important governing unit in the Dutch Reformed churches. Although the classis in Recife operated under church officials in Amsterdam, it was a unique New World institution (the North American colonies did not get a classis until 1679). Kesseler closely monitored the work of the Dutch Reformed churches and ministers in the colony. By the early 1640s, the Dutch Reformed church had more than twenty congregations in Brazil. As in the Netherlands, the established Dutch Reformed denomination was the only one whose churches could operate publicly, though the Dutch system allowed latitude for private observance by other Christian groups and Jews. Wherever possible, the Dutch Reformed churches offered services in Portuguese to cater to the existing Catholic-background population, and the West India Company suffused the colony with Protestant Bibles, catechisms, and anti-Catholic polemics. They also banished Jesuit priests from Dutch Brazil. They allowed other Catholic clergy to remain until 1640, when they also ejected Catholic orders including the Franciscans, leaving only parish priests to serve the Catholic population. Partly due to the perception that the Dutch Reformed clergy represented Dutch imperial power, the Dutch enticed few Portuguese Catholics into the Protestant fold. Instead, the Portuguese population rose up against Dutch authorities in Brazil in 1645, initiating a long struggle for the colony which finally put it back under Portuguese control in 1654.

The short-lived New Holland colony in Brazil was typical of the religious and cultural instability faced by New World colonies. Tumultuous ethnic and religious diversity fueled Protestant-Catholic tensions. Colonies in the Caribbean saw similar diversity and accompanying tensions. As we have already noted, English Puritans founded Providence Island in 1630 off the coast of Nicaragua to establish an English colonial foothold in a Caribbean basin dominated up to that point by the Spanish empire. Unlike Massachusetts, which had slaves but not slave plantations, Providence was a slave-centered colony from the start. Most of the Caribbean colonies—whether founded by the English, Spanish, or French—depended heavily on slave labor on plantations. The prospect of great profits from sugar did not make it easy for Puritan proprietors to keep the focus at Providence Island on faith. English sailors used Providence as a base for privateering expeditions against Cartagena, Colombia (founded in 1533 on the northern coast of South America). "Privateering," ubiquitous in the colonial Caribbean, was a euphemism for state-sanctioned piracy. The English saw capturing Spanish ships as a part of the godly cause against the global forces of Antichrist. Providence Island's vulnerable location and privateering activities made it virtually inevitable that it would fall to Spanish attack, which it did in 1641. The Spanish quickly held Catholic services in the English church on the island to celebrate their conquest.

Catholicism in New Spain

On the Central American mainland, Mexico City became the key administrative and religious center in the sprawling "Viceroyalty of New Spain." By the 1600s, Catholicism had begun to mature there into a religious culture that took on its own attributes, separate from the Catholic life of Europe. The reported apparitions of Mary to Juan Diego that formed the basis of the devotion to Our Lady of Guadalupe had transpired in 1531, but the formalization of the devotion—including published accounts describing the apparitions—did not begin until the mid-1600s. Spanish Catholic officials were concerned to keep the Catholic Church in Mexico within the bounds of European Catholic orthodoxy. Saints played an important role in that effort. Philip of Jesus was the first person born in Mexico to be beatified (a specially blessed status and often a first step toward sainthood) and later canonized as a saint. Philip was born to Spanish parents in Mexico City in 1572 and martyred in Japan in 1597.

Image 7.1. Statue of Saint Philip of Jesus, Mexico City

Although the devotion of Our Lady of Guadalupe is more popular, Saint Philip of Jesus (San Felipe de Jesús) became a patron saint of Mexico City and an important figure tying Mexican Catholicism to the Iberian and global Catholic church. Philip had briefly joined the Franciscans in Mexico before leaving the ministry and becoming a merchant, which took him to the Philippines. He rejoined the Franciscans there and ended up being executed as part of the celebrated "Twenty-Six Martyrs of Japan," where he had gone on a voyage in 1596. After Philip's beatification in 1627, Mexico City authorities sponsored special feast days for him annually on February 5. Religious and political officials participated in an elaborate and expensive celebration for the Blessed Philip in 1629, including a parade, fireworks, and a masquerade. By 1652, a Mexico City priest described the capital of New Spain as a veritable "Jerusalem, Saintly City, and birthplace of St. Philip." Such saintly devotions have been a hallmark of Catholicism, especially since the Reformation. They have helped turn Mexico and similar areas into places with profoundly Catholic cultures, even if the level of individual Mexicans' religious devotion varied widely.

Devotions like those of Philip of Jesus sometimes competed with other national traditions for regional supremacy and for attention in Europe. One competing national tradition to that of Philip was the devotion to Saint Rose of Lima, who in 1671 became the first person born in the Americas to be declared a saint. Rose (born in 1586 in Lima as Isabel Flores de Oliva) consciously adapted the ascetic example of Catherine of Siena. Indeed, her intense program of self-discipline (which included self-flagellation and relentless fasting) disturbed some observers at the time, just as the piety of the Mohawk saint Catherine Tekakwitha would do six decades later in Canada. Inquisition officials regarded Rose as fastidiously humble and almost incapable of receiving praise. They contrasted this modesty with the flamboyance of other would-be female saints who claimed, among other things, to have endured mystical pregnancies and to have the power of levitation. Rose's piety attracted the notice of key church officials. She worked as a nurse among the poor, including people of Spanish, native Peruvian, and African backgrounds, and she became enormously popular among rank-and-file Peruvians. Her fame only increased as prayers to Rose of Lima, and access to her relics, became associated with healings and other miracles. Her elite promoters and her vast popular support turned Rose of Lima into a Peruvian national icon as well as an object of Catholic admiration around the world. Dozens of Catholic parishes in the United States alone are dedicated to her today. In 1917, on the three hundredth anniversary of her death, one observer declared that "The people of Peru love their Saint Rose madly . . . he who does not love her is not Peruvian."

Image 7.2. *Portrait of Saint Rose of Lima,* ca. 1700s

As a general rule, the further one ventured from the centers of colonial power, such as Recife, Brazil; Mexico City; or Boston, Massachusetts, the more difficult it was for Christians to create stable churches. This was especially the case for the Catholic Church, which despite efforts to affirm the faith of colonists, remained a heavily hierarchical version of Christianity centered in Rome. The Jesuits and Franciscans relished taking their missionary message into frontier regions, whether the interior of Canada or the antagonistic atmosphere of Japan. In New Spain, perhaps the most difficult and audacious mission was in distant New Mexico. Spanish travelers and explorers, including Francisco Vásquez de Coronado, had already explored New Mexico by the 1540s. In 1607 (the same year the English founded Jamestown, Virginia), the Spanish founded Santa Fé, which became the capital of the "Kingdom" of New Mexico. Santa Fé still only had a couple hundred Spaniards living there a quarter-century after it was founded. Hundreds more mixed-blood people of Spanish and Native American background worked as servants and slaves in the region.

Franciscan priests sought to convert local Indian peoples, especially the widely-dispersed Pueblo Indians of New Mexico. Hundreds of Pueblos lived in Spanish mission communities and attended mass. As with most Native Americans, the arrival of Europeans had brought disease and duress to the Pueblos, whose population dropped precipitously during the mid-1600s. This led a number of Catholic Pueblos to return quietly to native Puebloan religious practices, which the Franciscans considered "sorcery." The missions to the Pueblos, like those to the Chinese in the same decades, raised difficult questions about conversion, adherence, and syncretism. Catholics tended to have a more communal view of what conversion entailed, seeing Christian affiliation as a matter of baptism and group adherence to Christian practices, especially the mass. Protestants tended to focus on individual conversion, wrought by the regenerating power of the Holy Spirit. Proselytes who possessed pre-existing non-Christian religious beliefs and systems often did not "convert" in ways that were as thorough as missionaries hoped. Some converts among groups like the Pueblos undoubtedly made a heartfelt commitment to Catholic faith. Others seem to have taken more of a transactional view: the Spaniards clearly possessed great spiritual and worldly power. It made sense for Indians to adhere to the Spaniards' god in hope that things would go well for them. When adoption of Christianity did not stave off famine, disease, or attacks from other Indians, some Pueblos thought about returning to the old ways. By the mid-1650s, there were roughly enough Franciscan missionaries (forty-six) for each of the Pueblo villages in New Mexico, but in communities distant from Santa Fé, pastoral oversight was often insufficient.

All these conditions made New Mexico ripe for rebellion by the 1670s. The Pueblos suffered attacks from neighboring Apaches, who showed little interest in the missionaries' appeals. Pueblos who engaged in traditional spiritual practices sometimes suffered terrible retribution from the priests or Spanish officials. In 1675, the Spanish executed three Pueblos for sorcery and whipped forty-three other Pueblos for involvement with pagan practices. One of those who received a whipping was a Pueblo religious leader named Popé (fl. 1630–90). Over the next several years Popé developed a plot to expel the Spanish and their missionaries from New Mexico. The Pueblo Revolt exploded in 1680, as Pueblos launched coordinated attacks on Spanish towns and missions. Popé commanded that his Pueblo followers destroy the mission chapels, including crosses, the icons of Mary, Jesus, and the saints, and "everything pertaining to Christianity." Some Pueblos apparently engaged in reverse baptisms, taking to rivers to repudiate their adherence to the Catholic Church. Others reportedly proclaimed that "God and Santa Maria were dead." More than twenty

Franciscans were martyred in the uprising. The Spanish were indeed expelled from New Mexico, with most survivors making their way down the Rio Grande to El Paso. The Spanish did not return to Santa Fé for thirteen years.

The Pueblo Revolt was the most successful Indian rebellion in North American history. Its circumstances were not unique, however: colonization and evangelization often made for a deadly mix for Indians and Europeans alike. English colonists at Virginia suffered a devastating war with the dominant Powhatan Indian tribe in 1622, one that effectively ended the existence of the Virginia Company and turned Virginia into a royal colony. Massachusetts and Connecticut, along with some Native American allies, nearly wiped out the whole Pequot tribe of southern New England in the mid-1630s. Then in the mid-1670s Massachusetts faced an existential threat from combined Native American forces led by the Wampanoag chief Metacom (1638–76), who was called "King Philip" by the English. Religion was a factor in all these conflicts, partly because all European powers came to the New World with at least the nominal intention of converting Native Americans to Christianity. War and effective evangelism do not typically go hand-in-hand, however.

Catholic Success in New France

The Jesuit and Ursuline missions in New France, led by figures such as Marie de l'Incarnation Guyart in Quebec, were relatively successful compared to other Protestant and Catholic efforts in the New World in the 1600s. This was partly because France had among the mildest imperial ambitions in North America. Military conquest was not much of a priority, at least until the Seven Years' War in the 1750s. Instead, the French wanted to tap the vast resources of fish and fur on the Atlantic coast and in the interior of Canada and the "Pays d'en Haut," or the "upper country" west of Montreal into the Great Lakes region. French Jesuits did encounter violence with Native Americans, especially in wars between the Wendats and the Iroquois League that doomed the Sainte-Marie Mission in Ontario in 1649. But the Jesuits' fate in New France was not as tied to French military and imperial aims, and for much of the 1600s the order was able to evangelize in relative peace and autonomy.

The greatest documentary record of these missions was *The Jesuit Relations* (*Relations de la Nouvelle France*), published from the 1630s to the 1670s in Paris to stir financial support for the New World missions in France. Like all missionary reports, *The Jesuit Relations* were promotional in nature. Yet they provided a wealth of information about early contact between the Catholic missionaries and their evangelistic targets in America. The Jesuit Paul Le Jeune (1591–1664), the superior of the New France missions beginning in 1632, wrote several of the accounts in the *Relations*. Le Jeune's parents had been French Calvinists, but he converted back to Catholicism in his teens and joined the Jesuit order shortly thereafter. Le Jeune and the other Jesuits used the *Relations* to appeal to elite Catholic society in Paris, who would have the financial means to make the Jesuit missions viable. Like all Catholic leaders in France, the Jesuits had to be mindful of antagonism toward Calvinist-leaning Jansenist theology, which was denounced by the pope in 1643. Still, Le Jeune and other Jesuit missionaries were influenced by the theology of Augustine, which had animated much of the thought of Cornelius Jansen, the Dutch Catholic bishop and founder of the Jansenist movement. Accordingly, Le Jeune painted a rather grim picture of native Canadian people in their unconverted state. "The Savages, being filled with errors, are also haughty and proud . . . They are void of the knowledge of truth, and are in consequence, mainly occupied with the thought of themselves." More optimistic French Catholic missionaries criticized Le Jeune for depicting native people as if they shared only the barest biological similarity with the rest of humanity and none of humanity's natural virtues. Yet Le Jeune also noted that the missionaries (including himself) struggled with lack of devotion and temptations of the flesh. He conceded that in some ways, native Canadian culture was less corrupt than that of greedy and vain France.

English Ambitions in the New World

English colonization developed more slowly than had Spanish incursions in the Americas. Even the meager early efforts at English colonization were interrupted by the English Civil War in the mid-1600s. English colonization forcefully resumed in the 1660s and '70s, however, along with efforts to bring English Protestantism to the New World. This phase of colonization saw the English conquest of the key sugar island of Jamaica from the Spanish, and the creation of mainland English colonies including Carolina (1670) and Pennsylvania (1681). Jamaica was somewhat of an afterthought in the "Western Design" campaign of English Puritan leader Oliver Cromwell. In this campaign, Cromwell initially sought to expel the Spanish from as much of their Caribbean territory as possible, with a special desire to take Hispaniola (present-day Dominican Republic and Haiti). When the English were defeated at Hispaniola in 1655, they turned their attention to Jamaica, which would become one of the most lucrative colonies in the English empire. When they seized Jamaica, the English demanded that all Catholic priests and devotional literature be removed from the island, mimicking the treatment the English had received when the Spanish took Providence Island fourteen years earlier. Conquest often echoed enduring animosities related to the Reformation. Cromwell encouraged settlement in Jamaica by "all such professing the Protestant Religion." Puritans were always eager to have principled Reformed Protestants settle in any new English colony. Thus a recruiting broadside in Massachusetts in 1656 appealed for settlers to relocate to Jamaica. Cromwell, the broadside said, desired to have the island "inhabited by a stock of such as know the LORD, and walk in his fear." But reports about sickly conditions on the island undercut mass English emigration of any kind in English Jamaica's early years. Cromwell's death, followed by the Restoration of the English monarchy in 1660, put the English Puritan movement on the defensive in the home country and around the globe. The dream of a Caribbean Puritan colony remained elusive.

Starting in the early 1660s, the Church of England received virtually all official government support in Jamaica. Like most of the southern mainland and Caribbean English colonies, Jamaica would have a formal Anglican establishment. The extent that the Church of England reached the poor whites and Africans who worked on the cocoa and sugar plantations—not to mention the pirates who used Jamaica as a base—was doubtful, however. Still, Jamaica's early capital Port Royal had a diverse range of churches, including Quaker and Presbyterian meetinghouses, a Jewish synagogue, and even a Catholic chapel. More than half of Port Royal was destroyed in an earthquake in 1692, however, setting the stage for the emergence of Kingston, Jamaica, as the political and ecclesiastical center of the colony.

The Church of England and Slavery in the New World

The goals of empire, plantation slavery, and Christian conversion mixed uneasily together across the colonial South and Caribbean, just as they had at Providence Island. These clashing aims became more acute as Anglican efforts at evangelism increased simultaneously with the population of enslaved people in the Caribbean and mainland South. Christopher Codrington (1668–1710), named governor of the Leeward Islands (including the Virgin Islands) in the eastern Caribbean in 1698, added to the complex ties between Protestantism and slavery in the New World. Codrington was told by English officials to make the "conversion of negroes" a priority, but Codrington knew that many white Caribbean planters would oppose the baptism of enslaved people from Africa. Too many planters still believed, according to long-standing (if not universal) Christian legal tradition, that enslavement was for non-Christian peoples alone.

Meanwhile, the Glorious Revolution of 1688–89 and the Act of Toleration had given new legal protections to dissenters from the Church of England. This meant that defenders of the Church of England had new reasons to protect their church against the incursions of Baptists, Quakers, and other non-Anglicans. The Church of England wanted to keep up with the pace of empire in places such as the Caribbean islands. Led by Anglican minister Thomas Bray (d. 1730), many Church of England officials worried that the colonial church in the New World lacked spiritual vigor. Anglicans needed steady doses of devotional material in addition to competent ministers and missionaries. To further these aims, Bray helped to found the Anglican Society for the Propagation of the Gospel in Foreign Parts (SPG) in 1701. Bray saw the SPG as fighting against rivals on all sides, as the "Enemy has now entered through our breaches into the very heart of our city (as St. [Augustine] calls the church of God)." The stability of true Protestant religion was menaced by "Atheists, Deists, and Socinians on the one hand, or secretly and dangerously undermined by enthusiasts and antinomians on the other."

"Socinianism," which took its name from the radical Italian theologian Faustus Socinius in the late 1500s, became a catchall term in Europe and America for a range of anti-Trinitarian and anti-Calvinist beliefs. Deism was likewise a somewhat vague term which generally connoted skepticism about traditional Christian doctrine, or a simple belief in a creator God without the trappings of controversial Christian doctrines such as the Trinity. Perhaps the most scandalous Socinian work in England at the time of the SPG's founding was John Toland's hyper-rationalist *Christianity Not Mysterious* (1696). Many Protestants saw Socinianism and deism as way stations to outright atheism, though few people in Anglo-America would have embraced atheism or agnosticism yet. Still, establishmentarian Anglicans like Bray and the SPG believed that some of the greatest threats to Protestantism were coming from within. They feared that the Act of Toleration and the growth of dissent and heresy could badly damage the Church of England.

Christopher Codrington appreciated the work of the SPG, especially as it applied to the English Caribbean colonies and the enslaved population. Codrington was an Oxford-educated, third-generation planter from Barbados, which was one of the earliest English colonies in the Caribbean. He and SPG missionaries such as the French Huguenot-turned-Anglican Francis Le Jau (1665–1717) sought to make inroads in slave conversions, but in such a way that would not threaten slavery as an institution. Le Jau had fled from

France after the revocation of the Edict of Nantes in 1685, became an Anglican, and studied theology at Trinity College, founded in 1592 as the center of Protestant learning in Dublin, Ireland. Le Jau then served as an Anglican minister at Montserrat in the Leeward Islands, where he met Codrington. Le Jau lamented that the Caribbean planters feared that if their slaves received baptism, the planters would have to view the enslaved people as "Christian Brethren" and treat them humanely. Ministers like Le Jau wanted to help planters see that they could keep their enslaved people as property, while showing concern for their eternal fate.

The wealthy Codrington was so enamored with the concept of Christianizing slavery in the New World that he deeded some of his Caribbean plantations to the SPG when he died in 1710, thus converting the SPG into a slaveholding institution. This signaled a growing—but still contested—interest among leaders of the SPG in converting enslaved people in the New World and not just bolstering Anglican faith among English people. Until the early 1700s, few Anglicans had contemplated how the growing numbers of enslaved people, especially those from Africa, fit into plans for a Christian English empire. Now some in the SPG began to consider what a Christian mission to slaves might require.

With Codrington's passing, Francis Le Jau carried on the fraught vision of Christian slavery. Le Jau had moved to South Carolina in 1706. The Carolina colony, founded in 1670, had a nominal Anglican establishment, but was in reality religiously diverse, even among white settlers. In addition to its growing number of enslaved people, South Carolina (which separated from North Carolina in the early 1700s) was a primary New World haven for Huguenot exiles. Few of the charter European settlers discovered that making a living in America was as easy as they might have expected. One Huguenot wrote from Carolina, three years after the Edict of Nantes was repealed, speculating that God had deprived them of the "pleasures of life because we had abused them, [and] does not want wealth to expose us again to the same abuses and to the same effects of his wrath."

Although Francis Le Jau was no longer technically part of the French Protestant movement, his French background and experience in the Leeward Islands gave him excellent preparation for the religious and cultural milieu he encountered in the Charleston area. Though the colony was still relatively young, farms of rice and indigo (a source of purple dye) led South Carolina planters to capture and import ever-greater numbers of enslaved people. Some slaves were Native Americans, but the long-term trajectory was toward South Carolina becoming a "black majority" colony. Le Jau and other SPG leaders also believed that the Anglican Church needed to evangelize African people in America, most of whom had little Christian background at all. Le Jau encountered huge obstacles against including Africans and African Americans in the church. Masters balked at slaves attending services, getting baptized, or getting married as Christians. Le Jau contended that Christianizing slaves would not undermine the slave system, but instead would make for more content and obedient slaves. Le Jau went on to own several people as slaves himself. He required slaves who approached him for baptism to promise that they were not seeking baptism in hopes of securing their freedom from slavery.

The Society of Friends and the Question of Slavery

Christian arguments against slavery per se were rare in church history until the 1700s. The Quakers, or Society of Friends, were one of the first Christian groups to register objections to slavery as it was developing in the New World colonies. Early Quaker leaders such as George Fox were familiar with the horrid violence and death rates associated with New World slavery. That familiarity, in addition to the Quakers' socially-leveling beliefs, made the group a vital source of Christian antislavery thought. Quaker resistance to slavery was part of their broader matrix of radical beliefs and practices, such as allowing women to serve as itinerant evangelists. Quakers also debated the relative authority of the Bible, a topic that generally went unquestioned among devout Protestants. For Quakers, Scripture's authority was complemented by the "Inward Light" of God that dwelled in every person. Not every person recognized or embraced the Inward Light, but those who did could be transformed by the saving power of Christ. Though Quakers would become more polite and restrained in worship by the 1700s, the early Quakers in England, Ireland, America, and the Caribbean were charismatic in style (allegedly "quaking" with fervor), apocalyptic in theological focus, and aggressively evangelistic. They were used to flouting social conventions.

Despite the Quakers' commitment to pacifism, colonial American authorities often saw the Friends as a menace. A number of colonies banned them or tried to silence their prophesying in the streets, which was one of the Quakers' most notorious tactics. Massachusetts, which had one of the heaviest religious establishments in America, went so far as to execute several Quaker missionaries who returned to the colony after being banished during the years 1659 to 1661. Dutch authorities in New Netherlands (New York) generally maintained a lighter form of establishment than the New England Puritans did, but still did not tolerate open condemnation of the Reformed Church. Dutch officials warned the people of New Netherlands to report activities of Quaker preachers in the colony. In 1657 this

Image 7.3. *Society of Friends meetinghouse*

injunction elicited the remarkable Flushing Remonstrance, a key early document on religious freedom in America. The remonstrance declared that the people of Flushing should refuse to obey the anti-Quaker decree and should offer the Quakers hospitality, in accord with the dictates of Christian conscience.

Quakers had an active presence in America and the Caribbean for decades before the founding of Pennsylvania in 1681. William Penn (1644–1718) was the son of a prominent aristocrat and naval officer, Admiral William Penn, who had been one of the key leaders in Cromwell's Western Design. Due in part to debts the king owed to his father, William Penn the son was able to secure a charter for his much-needed Quaker refuge. Along with Rhode Island, Pennsylvania offered religious liberty for all Christians and non-Christians alike to meet publicly, without fear of persecution. This made the colony one of the most religiously diverse in America, with a full range of Protestant groups including German Lutherans and Pietists centered at Germantown, Pennsylvania. Philadelphia would become the key denominational center in colonial America, too, with organizations like the Philadelphia Baptist Association, founded in 1707.

The Quakers in England and America were riven by bitter theological divides, often related to the weight of personal revelation versus the authority of Scripture. This was the heart of Quaker leader George Keith's criticisms of the Philadelphia Meeting of [Quaker] Ministers. Keith believed that the Pennsylvania Quakers depended too heavily on their spiritual experiences and not enough on Scripture. Keith stridently denounced Quaker leaders, leading both Philadelphia and London Quakers to bar him from their meetings. Keith eventually converted to Anglicanism and became affiliated with the Society for the Propagation of the Gospel.

> To buy souls and bodies of men for money, to enslave them and their posterity to the end of the world, we judge is a great hinderance to the spreading of the Gospel, and is occasion of much war, violence, cruelty and oppression, and theft and robbery of the highest nature. . . .
>
> ---
>
> George Keith, *An Exhortation and Caution to Friends Concerning the Buying or Keeping of Negroes*, 1693

Keith, like Francis Le Jau and Christopher Codrington, had to confront the question of Anglican missions and slavery as part of his SPG work. Before abandoning Quakerism, Keith took a strong stance against the slave trade (if not slavery itself) in the pathbreaking treatise *An Exhortation and Caution to Friends Concerning the Buying or Keeping of Negroes* (1693). This was one of the first printed antislavery works in American history. Suggesting the Quakers' broad view of the atonement, Keith wrote that "Blacks and Tawnies [Native Americans] are a real part of mankind, for who Christ hath shed his precious blood, and are capable of salvation, as well as White Men; and Christ the Light of the World hath (in measure) enlightened them." Christians, therefore, should not "bring any part of mankind into outward bondage, slavery or misery," but should instead seek the "inward and outward" liberty of all. Keith seems to have muted his qualms about slavery after his switch to Anglicanism, however. Presumably he adopted the ideas about Christianizing slavery advanced by Le Jau, Codrington, and the SPG.

Conclusion

The New World colonies presented Catholics and Protestants, then, with new ethical challenges, not least questions of conquering native peoples, and using native and African peoples as slaves. Christians sought to promote their faith in the colonial setting, but the colonial setting also molded faith in ethically damaging ways, ones that would take centuries to address and rectify.

Selected Bibliography

Bray, Thomas. *A Course of Lectures upon the Church Catechism.* Vol. 1. 2nd ed. Oxford: 1707.

Conover, Cornelius. "Catholic Saints in Spain's Atlantic Empire." In *Empires of God: Religious Encounters in the Early Modern Atlantic*, edited by Linda Gregerson and Susan Juster, 87–105. Philadelphia: University of Pennsylvania Press, 2011.

Gerbner, Katharine. *Christian Slavery: Conversion and Race in the Protestant Atlantic World.* Philadelphia: University of Pennsylvania Press, 2018.

Goddard, Peter A. "Augustine and the Amerindian in Seventeenth-Century New France." *Church History* 67, no. 4 (Dec 1998): 662–81.

Graziano, Frank. *Wounds of Love: The Mystical Marriage of Saint Rose of Lima.* New York: Oxford University Press, 2004.

Keith, George. *An Exhortation and Caution to Friends Concerning the Buying or Keeping of Negroes.* New York, 1693.

Kidd, Thomas S. *American Colonial History: Clashing Cultures and Faiths.* New Haven, CT: Yale University Press, 2016.

Noorlander, D.L. *Heaven's Wrath: The Protestant Reformation and the Dutch West India Company in the Atlantic World.* Ithaca, NY: Cornell University Press, 2019.

Pestana, Carla Gardina. *The English Conquest of Jamaica: Oliver Cromwell's Bid for Empire.* Cambridge: Harvard University Press, 2017.

Weber, David J. *The Spanish Frontier in North America.* New Haven, CT: Yale University Press, 1992.

Chapter 8

Skepticism, Devotion, and the Enlightenment

The "Enlightenment" in Europe and its American colonies represented a tectonic shift away from a largely unquestioned cultural system of broad Christian belief to a surge of doubts about Scripture, the churches, and traditional doctrines such as the Trinity. Not that traditional belief became marginal or badly damaged. In some ways, Christian devotion in Europe and America was more robust by the time of the American and French Revolutions than it had been a century earlier. But Christian devotion was becoming more of a choice than a cultural or familial inheritance. Religion as individual choice was a hallmark of the emergent modern and secular world. Secularism has rarely meant the absence of religion or Christianity as a whole, but it has often entailed the rise of skepticism or irreligion as a viable cultural option. The Enlightenment helped to make the choice between faith and skepticism more conspicuous than ever.

English Enlightenment

British Protestants had hoped that the "Glorious Revolution" of 1688–89 had secured their nation for Protestantism and established the Church of England as the ideal "via media" between Catholicism and radical Protestant sectarianism. In theological terms, however, the

Glorious Revolution represented the opening salvo in a centuries-long Anglo-American debate over the best kind of Protestant doctrine and piety. John Locke's defense of religious toleration, his muted deism, and his belief in the established position of the Church of England put him at the center of the debates over the nature of Protestant faith at the beginning of the English Enlightenment. The Church of England had aspired to anchor the future of Protestantism. It did officially serve as such an anchor in Britain. Despite this anchoring, the English Enlightenment also served irrevocably to fracture Protestant thought and practice in England. In matters of faith, the center could not hold. In the words of the dissenter and novelist Daniel Defoe, by the early eighteenth century, England was facing a "horrid invasion of atheists, deists, and heretics."

This instability in church and culture did not result from a lack of Anglican efforts to craft a moderate version of Protestant faith for all English-speaking people. Those efforts were headlined by the works of John Tillotson (1630–94), the Archbishop of Canterbury from 1691 to 1694. Tillotson was a champion of broad Protestant unity that ran from non-conformists (i.e. non-Anglicans) to deists and Socinians, with "latitudinarian" Anglicans such as himself occupying the generous center of British religious life. Tillotson reflected a trend toward de-emphasizing controversial doctrines in the name of peace and charity among Protestants. He was relentlessly hostile toward atheism and Catholicism, however, believing that both were intolerable if Britain was to sustain its Protestant character. There were more actual Catholics in Britain than atheists, of course. The Catholics included King James II, whose faith was one of the main reasons for his removal in the Glorious Revolution.

Tillotson focused on Christian ethics as the key to a happy life and a flourishing society. As an Arminian, he insisted that God gave everyone a real choice to receive grace and to live virtuously. Devotion to God was eminently reasonable, according to Tillotson. Putting good works at the center of Christian devotion did not negate justification by faith alone, he insisted. Tillotson acknowledged that Paul "vehemently and frequently" asserted the doctrine of justification by faith, but argued that this "does not thereby exclude the necessity of works of righteousness and obedience to the moral precepts of the Gospel, as the condition of our continuance in the favor of God." The suggestion that good works somehow contributed to a person's good standing with God led evangelicals and Calvinists to disparage Tillotson's understanding of soteriology. The Calvinist evangelist George Whitefield, who became the best-known preacher of the First Great Awakening, put it bluntly when he averred that Tillotson "knew no more about true Christianity than Mahomet [Muhammad]." And " as to . . . our Justification by Faith alone (which is the doctrine of Scripture and of the Church of England), he certainly was as ignorant thereof as Mahomet himself," Whitefield concluded, seemingly doubting Tillotson's salvation.

Despite Tillotson's desire to focus on Christian behavior and offer "latitude" for differing Protestant beliefs, a growing controversy over deism and Socinianism marked English religious life. John Toland's *Christianity Not Mysterious* (1696) was probably the best-known Socinian or deist tract of the era. Tillotson had spoken out against deism and Socinianism, yet editions of *Christianity Not Mysterious* quoted Tillotson for its epigraph: "We need not desire a better evidence that any man is in the wrong, than to hear him declare against reason." "Reason" was the watchword of the British Enlightenment. There was more consensus about the reasonableness of Christian morality than about the veracity of its metaphysical and miraculous claims.

Toland (1670–1722) grew up in a Catholic family in Ireland, but he rejected Catholicism as a teenager and studied at the Presbyterian-affiliated Scottish universities in Glasgow and Edinburgh. Later he studied at Dutch universities, where he fell under the influence of higher critical thought in the tradition of Pierre Bayle, Richard Simon, and Baruch Spinoza. Toland returned to England in the early 1690s and became affiliated with John Locke. In *Christianity Not Mysterious*, however, he went further than Locke in asserting that no religious truth could contradict reason. (Locke had allowed that some revealed biblical truth, such as Christ's divinity, might complement reason but not accord with it fully.) Toland framed himself as a new-style Protestant Reformer, seeking to further purify Christianity from the corruptions of money-grubbing priests. "To all corrupt clergymen . . . who make a mere trade of religion, and build an unjust authority upon the abused consciences of the laity," he wrote, "I'm a professed adversary." Toland's views were so inflammatory that for years he had to dodge being arrested for heresy in England and Ireland. He enjoyed relationships with powerful politicians and writers, including Anthony Ashley Cooper (1621–83), the third earl of Shaftesbury, who became an important skeptical writer, too. Later in life, Toland tinkered with pantheism. He composed an epitaph for himself which read, "His spirit is joined with its ethereal father from whom it originally proceeded; his body likewise yielding to nature is laid again in the lap of its mother."

Starting with writers such as Toland and Spinoza, public criticism of Scripture and traditional theology soon became a fixture of Western thought. It was more alarming to traditionalists, however, when figures within church leadership began to turn against aspects of the great tradition of theology, including the doctrine of the Trinity. Others rejected key beliefs of the Reformation, such as justification by faith alone. Tillotson had already begun to question the latter doctrine in the late 1600s. Samuel Clarke (1675–1729), rector of St. James Church, Westminster, inveighed against Trinitarian theology in *Scripture Doctrine of the Trinity* (1712). In this work, Clarke made a public defense of views on the Trinity held by his friend, the great scientist and mathematician Isaac Newton. Like Toland, Clarke positioned himself as a reformer against the non-rational accretions of Christian theology. Through an exhaustive examination of Scripture passages and church history, Clarke concluded that the Son "is not self-existent, but derives his being or essence, and all his attributes, from the Father, as from the Supreme Cause." This was a new articulation of Arianism, or the idea that the Son is divine, but subordinate to and not co-eternal with the Father.

Clarke's argument against the traditional Nicene and Athanasian view of the Trinity met many challenges, including from powerful figures within the Anglican Church. Probably the most influential of these was Daniel Waterland (1683–1740), the Master of Magdalene College, University of Cambridge, where Isaac Newton was the Lucasian Professor of Mathematics. Waterland called the Nicene view of the Trinity the "Catholick" view, in this context meaning it was both biblical and historic. If the new critics of the Trinity would set aside their undue regard for unaided reason, Waterland said, they might see the truth that God was three eternally co-existent persons, and of one divine substance. The critics should "contentedly submit their fancies to God's written word," Waterland wrote, "interpreting it according to its most obvious and natural meaning." Waterland readily admitted that some complex issues in Scripture, such as the Trinity, could raise doubts and confusion. In such cases, he said, "there is no safer guide to take with us, than the concurring judgments of the Ancients; nor any more dangerous than warmth of imagination, or a love of novelties." Scripture was the foundational rule for doctrine, but when Scripture did not afford absolute clarity, early church history was an indispensable aid to interpretation, according to orthodox theologians such as Waterland who modeled a classic method of recourse to the great tradition.

Clarke's book was hardly the only entry in what became an avalanche of Arian, Socinian, and deist publications through the 1730s in England. These included works such as *A Discourse of Freethinking* (1713) by Anthony Collins, the lawyer and friend of Locke; and the internationally renowned *Christianity as Old as the Creation* (1730) by Matthew Tindal, a lawyer and onetime Catholic. David Hume's works in the mid-1700s would introduce a controversial skeptical perspective into the traditionally Presbyterian milieu of Scotland, too. One can glimpse the effects of the deistic writers on a popular level in Benjamin Franklin's autobiography. Franklin (1706–90) grew up in a Puritan family in Boston, Massachusetts. As a teenager the bookish boy began to read authors such as Locke, Collins, and Anthony Ashley Cooper. By the age of fifteen, Franklin said (writing much later in his life) that he had begun to doubt the reliability of Scripture. His devout father gave him some anti-deist works to read, but these ironically steered Franklin more deeply into skepticism. "I soon became a thorough deist," Franklin concluded.

Not all was heading toward skepticism, however. In addition to Waterland's formidable efforts in defense of orthodoxy, Anglican bishop Joseph Butler (1692–1752) advanced the most enduring apologetic defense of Christianity from within the Church of England, with his *Analogy of Religion, Natural and Revealed* (1736). The *Analogy of Religion* was one of the most powerful anti-deist works, and remained influential for more than a hundred years. Its reputation did not endure much into the twentieth century, partly because its argument was so focused on the deists' acceptance of God as creator but not as the inspirer of Scripture. That type of deism also became less common in the twentieth and twenty-first centuries, as outright materialism, agnosticism, and atheism became more fashionable (as Butler would have predicted). The idea of "nature's God," Thomas Jefferson's phrase in the Declaration of Independence, reflected the deistic God of nature, but not revealed truth. That idea of nature's God turned out to be a way station on a journey to more radical kinds of skepticism and unbelief.

> Unbelievers must be forced to admit the external evidence for Christianity, *i.e.*, the proof of miracles wrought to attest it, to be of real weight and very considerable. . . .
>
> ———
>
> Joseph Butler, *The Analogy of Religion, Natural and Revealed*, 1736

Quoting Origen, Butler contended that "he who believes the Scripture to have proceeded from Him who is the Author of Nature, may well expect to find the same sort of difficulties in it, as are found in the constitution of nature." Moreover, Butler argued, "he who denies the Scripture to have been from God upon account of these difficulties, may, for the very same reason, deny the world to have been formed by Him." If deists insisted that nature reflected God's perfections better than did Scripture, Butler countered that one could just as easily discern troubling or perplexing aspects of the natural world, especially the world as tainted by the fall of Adam and Eve. Belief did not require a perfectly harmonized understanding of Scripture or nature, but just probable warrant to believe. Butler influenced major writers and leaders of the eighteenth and nineteenth century, including the Romantic poet Samuel Taylor Coleridge, the Anglo-Catholic theologian John Henry Newman, and British prime minister William Gladstone. Reading Butler sometimes turned skeptics back to traditional faith. This was the case for the Methodist pastor and apologist John Bayley, an Englishman who grew up in a Christian family but (like Ben Franklin) imbibed skeptical writings by his teenage years. After moving to the US, however, Bayley began attending Methodist services and reading Christian apologetics. Butler's *Analogy of Religion* was decisive, and Bayley returned to the Christian faith around 1839.

Anglican theology in the early to mid-1700s ran across an extraordinarily wide spectrum. Little else held the Anglican Church together other than shared Englishness and an institutional structure headed by the Archbishop of Canterbury and the monarch. Latitudinarians like Tillotson believed that Christian ethics would serve as the point of unity, but disagreements over theology and practice disappointed the latitudinarians' hopes. Butler represented the theologically traditionalist Anglican battle against the deist menace inside and outside of the church. But even Anglican conservatives such as Butler resisted evangelical Anglican piety, represented by revival leaders George Whitefield and John Wesley, in the 1730s. In the meantime, the deist craze of the early 1700s began to peter out. Butler and others helped to demonstrate that many deists were holding Scripture to a higher critical standard than they did other realms of knowledge. Scotland's great skeptic David Hume, perhaps improbably, functioned as something of an ally to Butler. Both were really anti-deist writers, though Hume was fundamentally anti-Christian, too. Hume recognized his ironic commonalities with Butler and praised Butler as one of the new philosophers who "have begun to put the science of man on a new footing," especially on the grounds of morality and ethics. Hume was likely not an out-and-out atheist, but like Butler he doubted the deists' serene confidence in their ability to discern natural religious precepts. Unlike Butler, however, Hume doubted whether Scripture really gave people warrant for belief, especially in its claims of miracles.

Image 8.1. *David Hume*, Esqr. (1820)

Butler and especially Hume made deism look more like a stopover on the way to agnosticism than a theological home. Hume's great significance was to make agnosticism a live option for Anglo-Americans in the Age of Revolutions (1770s to the 1820s).

Enlightenment and Resistance in France

Radical skepticism became an even more prominent option in eighteenth-century France than in Britain. The Catholic Church in France remained formidable through the nation's Revolution of 1789, though groups such as the Jansenists and Jesuits fiercely debated the extent to which Augustinian and Reformed-style theology should influence the church. The French church and crown cracked down on the Augustinian Jansenists in the 1710s, but Jansenism's wide popularity made it an enduring force in French religious culture into the 1790s. The Jesuits also fell under increasing criticism in Europe and in the New World in the 1760s. Much of the controversy surrounded a sense that the Jesuits were functioning as an alternative to the imperial power of Spain and Portugal, especially in the Rio de la Plata missions or "reductions" in Brazil, Argentina, Bolivia, and Paraguay. The Jesuits attracted more than a hundred thousand native South Americans to those missions by the 1730s, but the Jesuits' unusual autonomy and resistance against the colonial slave trade led them to fall out of favor with European monarchs and the pope. In 1767 the King of Spain expelled the Jesuits from Spanish territories. The final blow came in 1773 when the pope completely dissolved the Jesuit order.

Pietist renewal movements also played a controversial role in French religious life starting in the late 1600s. Arguably the most influential of the French mystics was Jeanne-Marie Bouvier de la Motte-Guyon, known as Madame Guyon (1648–1717). Guyon grew up as a Catholic, but her intense mystical piety fell under scrutiny of Catholic officials, even as it attracted many devotees among Protestants. She endured a number of church trials and imprisonments, including years in the Bastille prison in Paris, for allegedly teaching the heresy of "Quietism." Although critics tended to caricature Quietist beliefs as hopelessly inactive, writers such as Guyon did generally focus more on the interior life than on Christian action. Guyon advocated a form of perfectionism through rigorous spiritual discipline. "Prayer is the guide to perfection," she wrote in *A Short and Easy Method of Prayer*, her classic devotional work. "The one great means to become perfect, is to walk in the presence of God." Guyon's cousin, the theologian and Catholic archbishop François Fénelon (1651–1715), helped to popularize Guyon's writings. But in 1699, as Guyon languished in

Image 8.2. *Ruins of San Ignacio Miní mission, Argentina*

jail, the pope condemned Fénelon's *Maxims of the Saints*, which had defended Guyon's brand of Pietism.

The quasi-Calvinist Jansenist movement also remained a potent but persecuted force within the French Catholic Church, even after the pope condemned the theology of the Jansenist Pasquier Quesnel in 1713. Popular unrest in Paris over the suppression of Jansenist beliefs became focused on miracles at the gravesite of a saintly, ascetic Jansenist leader named François de Pâris, who died in 1727. His grave at the cemetery of Saint-Médard instantly became a healing pilgrimage site for Jansenists. It was not unusual in Catholic cultures for this type of devotion to saints—whether officially recognized or not—to express both piety and popular resistance against the strictures of church officials. The miracles at the cemetery seemed, to the embattled Jansenist faithful, to prove that God was behind their movement, whatever the pope and his French cronies said. The scenes at Saint-Médard also reflected the persistent interest among European Christians in a wondrous, charismatic form of Christianity. Like the "French Prophets" among Protestants, some of the Jansenists experienced trances and convulsions that they attributed to a powerful work of the Holy Spirit. Alarmed French officials closed the cemetery in 1732. Historian Dale Van Kley has demonstrated that the Jansenist challenge from within French Catholicism helped to destabilize the "divine right" claims of the French monarchy and prepare France for its 1789 revolution.

We should not imagine, then, that French religious culture was bereft of deep and even radical Christian commitment during the "siècle des Lumières," or age of Enlightenment. But starting in the mid-1700s, France did become a hotbed for some of the most extreme, vicious anti-Christian skepticism seen during the European Enlightenment. Indeed, the aggressive posture of the French church and state toward dissenters within and outside of the French Catholic Church (whether Huguenots, Jansenists, or skeptics) made the philosophes' critiques of religion more strident than in England, where there was more toleration after 1689. Indeed, admiration for tolerant England was one of the passions of Voltaire (born François-Marie Arouet in 1694), the best-known figure among the skeptical philosophes. Voltaire's satirical writings had already gotten him thrown in the Bastille in the 1710s. Voltaire successfully negotiated temporary exile to England instead of another jail sentence, resulting in his scandalous *Letters Concerning the English Nation* (1733).

In the *Letters*, Voltaire expressed esteem for the relative freedom of thought in England. "An Englishman, as one to whom liberty is natural, may go to heaven his own way," Voltaire proclaimed. Voltaire may have underestimated the power of the Church of England, but he was enamored with the rise of anti-Trinitarian, rationalist religion in England. He especially admired Samuel Clarke, who along with Isaac Newton had helped to revive the "principles of Arius." Clarke, according to Voltaire, was "the most sanguine stickler for Arianism." He was "rigidly virtuous, and of a mild disposition, [and] is more fond of his tenets than desirous of propagating them." Voltaire was no atheist, unlike some of the more radical French skeptics, but he was hostile to providential readings of history or nature. Probably Voltaire's most enduring contribution was his satirical novel *Candide, ou l'Optimisme* (1759). A popular novel can sometimes make a greater mark for one's religious or philosophical perspective than can a nonfiction treatise. (One thinks of the enormous influence of the Christian-themed novels of C. S. Lewis and J. R. R. Tolkien in the twentieth century, for example.) That fictional impact was certainly the case with *Candide*, which became a fixture of the canon of western literature. Voltaire used Candide's misadventures as an attack on the theological optimism of Gottfried Wilhelm Leibniz, an early figure of the German

Enlightenment. Voltaire did not develop a sophisticated philosophy of anti-providentialism in *Candide*, but the novel became a seminal contribution to the rich French tradition of existentialism. Life does not have any overarching purpose, existentialists would say. You should just make the best of whatever circumstances in which you find yourself.

Voltaire was not as famous for his criticism of the Bible, but his critical views were representative of the trajectory of the skeptical Enlightenment. He grew up in a committed Catholic family but became exposed to "Enlightened" Catholicism in his Jesuit schooling. Voltaire seems to have become skeptical about the veracity of the Bible by his late teens and was conversant with the work of English deists and skeptics including Clarke, Matthew Tindal, and John Toland. Voltaire's biblical criticisms were amplified by the work of his mistress, Émilie du Châtelet. She was better known for her scientific research, but she also privately produced biblical criticism that no doubt influenced Voltaire's views. After Du Châtelet's death, Voltaire traveled through Europe. In Geneva, he came under the influence of liberal Protestant pastors including Paul Moultou, who became a great devotee and collaborator with the French philosophe Jean-Jacques Rousseau.

By the time Voltaire turned sixty, he had become convinced that much of institutional Christianity was horribly corrupt. What he called "l'infâme" ("the infamous") in the church needed to be destroyed. In a flood of skeptical attacks on the Bible, penned in his sixties and seventies, Voltaire ridiculed the Old and New Testaments. Like many higher critics after him, Voltaire questioned the canon of Scripture, noting that there were other "gospels" recognized by church fathers, and that there were probably older Christian sources than the ones included in the New Testament. Also like many Unitarians after him, Voltaire did not reject Jesus per se, but preferred to see Jesus as a simple carpenter and moral teacher instead of the second person of the Trinity. Such views remained scandalous in the 1770s, but their articulation and dissemination across Europe and America made higher criticism of the Bible more fashionable, and a more viable intellectual stance.

While Voltaire had journeyed to Geneva later in life, Jean-Jacques Rousseau (1712–78) had been born there to a Protestant family. In his late teens, however, Rousseau converted to Catholicism (decades later he would re-convert to Protestantism, though neither branch of Christianity seemed to make much difference in Rousseau's life). Moving to Paris, he encountered leading philosophes including Denis Diderot (1713–84), who encouraged Rousseau's writing career. Rousseau and Voltaire eventually became philosophical and personal rivals, with Voltaire championing reason, and Rousseau touting sensibility or conscience as the guide to truth. Like Voltaire, however, Rousseau became skeptical about traditionalist understandings of the Bible. Speaking of his re-conversion to Protestantism, Rousseau wrote that the Christian gospel was "the same for all Christians . . . the fundamentals of dogma only differing over points that men attempted to explain but were unable to understand." He came to believe that religion's importance was primarily in its social utility, and that the government should play a strong role in determining the faith of a nation for its social good.

Rousseau believed that European nations ought to enforce what he called a "civil profession of faith," or civil religion, including essential features of theistic religion. The points of this civil profession included belief in God, an afterlife, divine punishment of the wicked, and reverence for the law. He also believed in religious toleration, even though he recommended an active, even persecutorial role for government in enforcing the basic tenets of civil religion. Rousseau unpacked these ideas in his landmark *The Social Contract* (1762), in which he proposed that the laws of a nation should reflect the "general will" of the people at large. Writers such as Rousseau might hold skeptical views of traditional Christianity, but they also realized that Christian assumptions were so deeply woven into European society that dispensing with them could lead to murderous chaos. Such chaos would be seen in the radical phase of the French Revolution, which came a decade and a half after Rousseau's death in 1778.

Although Voltaire and Rousseau still believed that religion had social utility, some radical philosophes by the mid-1700s had begun to cross the line into outright atheism. The term "atheism" remained more a catch-all term for heretics or people who lived godless lives. Certain radical European figures also began to advocate materialist philosophy. They denied the existence of anything spiritual or divine. Many consider the Paris philosopher Denis Diderot to be the first clearly atheist writer in early modern European history. Arguing that he was just following the materialist implications of Descartes, Newton, and others to their logical end, Diderot contended that nature itself was self-contained and not created by a divine agent outside of it.

The Influence of Enlightened and Christian Thought

Despite its radical trajectory, it would be a mistake to see the Enlightenment as a unidirectional force toward secularism or skepticism. Scholars have argued that some of the most powerful Christian traditionalists of the era, including leading evangelicals and Catholics, were influenced by patterns of Enlightenment-style thinking. Even the Eastern Orthodox tradition, though it remained largely cut off from both Protestant and Catholic theological influences, showed interest in Enlightened thought and schooling. Following in the humanist footsteps of Cyril I, the Patriarch of Constantinople, Patriarch Cyril V in the 1750s commissioned Eugenios Voulgaris (1716–1806) to turn the Athonite Academy in Greece into a center of Enlightenment learning. Voulgaris was the epitome of the devout yet rationalist Christian figures of the Enlightenment era. As a clergyman and teacher, Voulgaris promoted the study of Greek classics as well as Enlightenment writers including Descartes, John Locke, and Gottfried Wilhelm Leibniz. Voulgaris and others also helped to introduce Newtonian science at the Athonite Academy, and at the patriarchal school in Constantinople.

Strains of Christian thought, as well as Enlightenment traditions such as government by consent of the people, influenced all the major global revolutions of the late eighteenth century. This was obviously the case with the American Revolution, but also the French Revolution, where Jansenist criticisms of royal authority had eroded the sacred aura of the French monarchy for decades prior to the outbreak of revolution in 1789. Even in southwestern India, the Portuguese colony of Goa saw a grinding controversy over toleration, racial equality, and the region's Catholic Church. These led ultimately to the Pinto Revolt of 1787, one of the biggest indigenous revolts in world history, and a product of impulses within both Catholicism and Enlightenment philosophy. Priests such as the Italian-educated Josè António Gonçalves helped to fuel the revolt and its resentment against intransigent Portuguese officials in the church and the colonial regime in Goa. Gonçalves and other leaders declared that the Goan people themselves should enjoy the right of self-rule. Clearly influenced by the American Revolution, which had begun a decade earlier, a number of Goans rose up against the Portuguese. They sought to establish independence and a Goan-elected legislative government. The colonial regime crushed the uprising, and the priests involved were jailed. The point was made, however: some saw a deep connection between Enlightenment, revolutionary principles, and the Christian faith.

Haiti's celebrated revolutionary leader Toussaint Louverture (1743–1803) demonstrates a similar intertwining of traditional Christian faith, Enlightenment principles, and revolutionary ideology. Louverture grew up as a slave in the French colony of Saint-Domingue. He received his freedom around 1776 and went on to become the most prominent military leader of the Haitian Revolution against the French regime in Saint-Domingue. The Haitian Revolution was the most successful slave rebellion of the era. Louverture was a talented political and military leader, and his motivations for revolutionary leadership were influenced by Enlightenment and Christian ideals of self-governance and ethnic equality. (The broader Enlightenment's record on racial equality was mixed, with some like David Hume arguing that there was a clear racial hierarchy in the world, with whites at the top.) Louverture's father was reportedly a prince in an African kingdom, but he was forced into slavery and sent across the ocean to Saint-Domingue. There Louverture's father converted to Catholicism. Louverture received a modest classical Christian education from a free black tutor, who himself had been schooled by Catholic missionaries. Louverture may have studied the works of the Abbé Raynal, the French critic of slavery and a former Catholic priest. Some have suggested that Louverture was a private devotee of vodou, an African-based religion popular in Haiti. But he made Catholicism the official religion of Haiti in his 1801 constitution. Hostile French and Haitian officials soon arrested and deported Louverture to France, where he died in prison in 1803, the same year that Haiti achieved full independence from France.

Conclusion

As this chapter has demonstrated, it no longer suffices to portray the "Enlightenment" as uniformly skeptical or anti-Christian. The Enlightenment was too diffuse of a movement to make simplistic claims about its religious and intellectual ramifications. But it remains tempting to overstate the influence of Enlightenment thinking at the expense of the great tradition of Christian theology. For example, scholars of the Scottish educator, Presbyterian pastor, and Princeton president John Witherspoon (1723–94) have tended to exaggerate his dependence on the Scottish Common Sense school of moral philosophy, as represented by Francis Hutcheson and other humanistic figures of the Scottish Enlightenment. More recent scholarship has emphasized, however, that Witherspoon remained traditionally Presbyterian and Calvinist. He held those somber beliefs in tension with the relatively optimistic view of humanity's moral and rational nature coming out of the Common Sense philosophy. Witherspoon readily conceded that "the truths of the everlasting gospel are agreeable to sound reason." He thought it was exceedingly dangerous to make reason the primary standard of truth, however. Reason was "insufficient to bring us to the knowledge of God," he warned. For that knowledge, we need divine assistance and divine revelation. It was not unusual for Christian thinkers influenced by Enlightenment principles to maintain similar views to those of Witherspoon, who was an advocate of a Christian Enlightenment.

Selected Bibliography

Bruneau, Marie-Florine. *Women Mystics Confront the Modern World: Marie de l'Incarnation (1599–1672) and Madame Guyon (1648–1717)*. Albany: State University of New York Press, 1998.

Butler, Joseph. *The Analogy of Religion*. London, 1736.

Daniel, Stephen H. *John Toland, His Methods, Manners, and Mind*. Kingston, ON: McGill-Queen's University Press, 1984.

Gargett, Graham, "Voltaire and the Bible." In *The Cambridge Companion to Voltaire*, edited by Nicholas Cronk, 193–204. New York: Cambridge University Press, 2009.

Griswold, Charles L. "Liberty and Compulsory Civil Religion in Rousseau's *Social Contract*." *Journal of the History of Philosophy* 53, no. 2 (April 2015): 271–300.

The Exemplary Life of the Pious Lady Guion. Translated by Thomas Digby Brooke. Dublin, Ireland, 1775.

Hazareesingh, Sudhir. *Black Spartacus: The Epic Life of Toussaint Louverture*. New York: Farrar, Straus, and Giroux, 2020.

Larsen, Timothy. *Crisis of Doubt: Honest Faith in Nineteenth-Century England*. Oxford: Oxford University Press, 2006.

Lehner, Ulrich L. *The Catholic Enlightenment: The Forgotten History of a Global Movement*. New York: Oxford University Press, 2016.

Mailer, Gideon. *John Witherspoon's American Revolution*. Chapel Hill: University of North Carolina Press, 2017.

Rivers, Isabel. *Reason, Grace, and Sentiment: A Study of the Language of Religion and Ethics in England, 1660–1780*. 2 vols. Cambridge: Cambridge University Press, 1991, 2000.

Tillotson, John. *The Works of the Most Reverend Dr. John Tillotson*. 2 vols. London, 1722.

Van Kley, Dale K. *The Religious Origins of the French Revolution, From Calvin to the Civil Constitution, 1560–1791*. New Haven, CT: Yale University Press, 1996.

Waterland, Daniel. *Eight Sermons Preach'd at the Cathedral Church of St. Paul, in Defense of the Divinity of our Lord Jesus Christ*. London, 1720.

Witherspoon, John. *The Works of John Witherspoon*. Edinburgh, 1805.

Young, B.W. *Religion and Enlightenment in Eighteenth-Century England: Theological Debate from Locke to Burke*. Oxford: Oxford University Press, 1998.

Chapter 9

The Early Evangelical Movement

A hallmark of "Enlightenment" learning was greater familiarity with cultures and religions around the globe. Figures such as the Venetian merchant Marco Polo and the Italian explorer Christopher Columbus had been introducing Europeans to those world cultures since the late medieval period, but the 1700s saw greater levels of engagement in trade, Christian missions, and study of non-European peoples than ever before. The idea of a global "catholic" church had been a staple of the great tradition of Christian theology since Jesus told his followers to make disciples of all nations. But as connections with people around the world became more direct than ever, the image of a transnational communion of saints became more tangible and specific. For people enmeshed in the ongoing conflicts between Catholics and Protestants, news from around the world also fueled a powerful sense of worldwide religious conflict, one that many still interpreted as a titanic struggle between the forces of Christ and Antichrist. Then in the 1730s, new communications networks also began to forge a new sense of a transnational Protestant revival. "Revival" and "awakening" were generally synonyms. Both indicated an outpouring of the Holy Spirit on a church or a region, leading to large numbers of conversions (or rededications) in a short period of time.

The "Chinese Rites" Controversy

Catholics and Protestants in Europe watched with fascination as the "Chinese rites" controversy over Catholic missions unfolded in the early 1700s. As we have seen, Jesuits and other Catholics had pioneered evangelistic work in China in the late 1500s and employed an accommodationist strategy which emphasized similarities between traditional Confucian culture and Christianity. In 1692, the Chinese emperor Kangxi issued a decree of toleration for Christianity, explaining that Europeans' doctrine was benign and had no tendency to "excite sedition." The Jesuits in China faced classic missionary questions: how much accommodation to indigenous religious ritual or belief amounted to harmful syncretism? To what extent should missionaries require native proselytes to adapt to cultural mores of the sending European nations? Could Christian doctrine be captured in the traditional religious terminology of a non-Christian culture? Confucianism presented special difficulties because it was not a monotheistic religion but more of a system of philosophy and ethics. Confucianism was sacred to Chinese adherents, but it was not focused on the worship of one god. Thus, to the Catholic accommodationists, Confucianism could complement Christianity rather than representing a competing religious system. Other Catholics, including figures among the Jansenists and Franciscans, regarded the Jesuits as dangerously flexible about basic Christian beliefs. Critics saw the Jesuits as too willing to allow Chinese converts to continue in practices such as venerating ancestors. Decades of debate over Jesuit missionary practices in China and India culminated in bulls issued by Pope Benedict XIV in 1742 and 1744 which condemned accommodationist tactics in missions.

The events of the Chinese Rites Controversy generated interest across Europe and in its colonies. For example, the Philadelphia-based *American Weekly Mercury* noted the 1742 papal bull in which, as the report phrased it, "all the idolatrous ceremonies of the Chinees which are converted to the Roman Catholick Religion are damned." The paper also noted that the Jesuits were angry about the bull dampening their missions. Not all Chinese proselytes aligned with the Jesuits flourished, either. In a notorious 1722 case, a Chinese Catholic named John Hu accompanied the French Jesuit missionary Jean-Francois Foucquet on a trip to France, where Foucquet planned to study and translate a collection of Confucian classics with Hu's assistance. The plan went terribly awry, as Hu struggled to adjust to living in France. Foucquet became convinced that Hu was insane and had him placed in an asylum. Finally other French Catholics intervened and arranged for Hu's release and passage home to China. The Catholic Church's difficulties in China understandably reduced the number of Chinese Catholics by the late 1700s. But the church did appoint dozens of Chinese priests. Catholicism showed halting signs of becoming an indigenized religion in China, despite troubles between the Vatican, its missionaries, and Chinese converts such as John Hu.

Christianity in India

In India, the Catholic Church experienced similar struggles as in China, but with a major difference: Portugal served as a primary colonial power in India, until the British East India Company took a dominant role there starting in the mid-1700s. The Christian landscape in India was further complexified by India's Thomas Christians, who traced their roots back to the legendary missionary journeys of the Apostle Thomas in the early AD 50s. The Thomas Christians had theological and liturgical connections to the Orthodox churches of Syria, and they used Syriac as their language of worship. European Catholics regarded the Thomas Christians as doctrinally suspect and syncretistic, as the Thomas Christians avidly participated in Hindu rituals. The dominance of Hinduism in India raised similar questions about accommodation as Confucianism had in China. One controversial model of accommodation was offered by the Italian Jesuit missionary Constantine Joseph Beschi (1680–1747), who took the Tamil name Veeramamunivar. Beschi helped to indigenize Catholicism into Tamil culture by writing works such as his epic poem *Thembavani* (1726), based on the life of Joseph (Tamil "Valan") from the gospels. In the Tamil culture of southeast India, Beschi is still regarded as a major literary figure today.

As noted earlier, India was the site of one of the earliest overseas missions established by Protestants. The Halle Pietist work at Tranquebar was begun in 1706 under the auspices of a Danish colony. Tranquebar missionaries distributed the Bible and Pietist works in translation to the Tamil-speaking people in the region. Like Beschi, the German Pietist missionary Bartholomäus Ziegenbalg (1682–1719) made major efforts to learn the Tamil language. Cultivating linguistic expertise, especially in languages largely unknown in Europe, was always one of the most difficult aspects of the missionary enterprise. Driven by a Lutheran zeal for the vernacular Bible, Ziegenbalg translated the New Testament into Tamil in 1715. Ziegenbalg and the Halle Pietists emphasized "heart religion," a signature of the Pietist movement. Mere adherence to the church and Christian ritual was not enough, they taught converts. One's heart had to change to become a true disciple of Jesus. Tamil Protestants readily received the message of salvation by God's grace alone and the transforming power of Christ in one's heart. They struggled to overcome the rigid caste hierarchies of traditional Indian society, however, despite the missionaries' urging to disregard caste divisions in the body of Christ. The Tranquebar mission continued well after Ziegenbalg's death in 1719. Over the hundred and forty years of the Tranquebar station's existence, Halle sent 57 missionaries who baptized some 35,000 people. Tranquebar had symbolic value to European and American Protestantism well beyond those numbers, however. It inspired Protestants from a range of denominations to imagine new possibilities for global missions.

The Moravian Missions

One of those influenced by Tranquebar's example was Count Nicholas von Zinzendorf, founder of the Moravian Brethren. Zinzendorf was born in 1700 to a German noble family. In the 1720s he established a Pietist village and refuge on his estate in German Saxony, bordering on Moravia in today's Czech Republic. He called the town "Herrnhut," or "the Lord's Safekeeping." Some of the Pietist settlers and refugees who came to Herrnhut were descended from followers of the Czech proto-Reformer Jan Hus. In 1727 Herrnhut experienced an intense revival of prayer and worship, inspired partly by the devotion of an eleven-year-old orphan named Susanne Kühnel. One observer recorded that "through Susanne Kühnel an extraordinary movement arose in their assembly . . . So powerful a spirit prevailed among the children as is beyond words to express."

> Preach chiefly to such heathens, who never heard the gospel. We [are] not to build on a foundation laid by others nor to disturb their work, but to seek the outcast and forsaken.
>
> ---
>
> Count Nicholas von Zinzendorf, "Instructions to Missionaries," in George Henry Loskiel, *History of the Missions of the United Brethren among the Indians of North America*, 1794

Bolstered by the example of the Tranquebar mission and fueled by the intense piety growing out of the Herrnhut revival, Moravians committed to a missionary program of unprecedented scope for Protestants. They often followed the paths of the Danish empire, the only Lutheran power that had a significant non-European colonial presence. In the 1730s and '40s, Moravians established a global missionary network in places from Greenland to South Africa, and arctic Russia to Ceylon (Sri Lanka). In Greenland, the Moravians evangelized the indigenous Inuit people and established New Herrnhut, which eventually became the core of Nuuk, the capital city of Greenland. By the early 1760s, there were some five hundred Inuit people baptized into the Moravian church.

Moravians also created missionary works in mainland North America and in the Caribbean. They sent missionaries to the Caribbean island of St. Thomas in 1732, which marked a major transition point for the conversion of African, Afro-Caribbean, and African American people to Protestantism. Some West African people, especially the Kongolese, were familiar with Catholicism prior to their (usually forced) migration across the Atlantic in the "Middle Passage." Millions of enslaved people in chains took this journey across the Atlantic from the 1500s to the 1800s. But exceedingly few of the African slaves knew about Protestant Christianity before arriving in America and the Caribbean. Small numbers of African converts came into the Anglican Church and other Protestant denominations before the 1730s, but those gains were tiny compared to the burgeoning numbers of enslaved people overall.

One of the most consequential Moravian converts in St. Thomas was a former slave named Rebecca (1718–80). She had previous exposure to both Catholicism and the Dutch Reformed denomination, but she was persuaded to follow the Moravians' teaching. Even though she was not yet twenty years old, Rebecca became a kind of lay evangelist and Bible teacher for the Moravians, ministering especially to enslaved women on St. Thomas. She also married one of the Moravian missionaries. Their mixed-race union drew unwanted attention from hostile white masters. She and her husband were convicted on trumped-up charges, including inciting slave insurrection. A surprise visit to the island by Count Zinzendorf himself led to Rebecca and her husband's release. Rebecca viewed Zinzendorf's arrival as God's providential plan to have her released from prison. She told correspondents that she was grateful that her trial had given her the opportunity to testify to her faith in Christ before the island's magistrates.

Rebecca's remarkable life in the Atlantic World continued as she and her husband moved to Moravian settlements in Germany. Her husband died on the journey, however, and she remarried another Moravian named Christian Jacob Protten, a native of West Africa and child of a Danish father and an African mother. From then on, Rebecca became known as Rebecca Protten. Rebecca also took a prominent role in the Moravian Church in her European context, and even received ordination as a deaconess, probably making her the first black woman to receive such ordination in Western Christendom.

In the final major move of her life, Rebecca and Christian Protten relocated to West Africa, to the town of Christiansborg on the Gold Coast (modern Ghana). This was the center of the Danish slave trade in the eighteenth century. In Christiansborg, the Prottens taught school and maintained an uneasy relationship with both Moravian Church and Danish colonial officials. Rebecca died in West Africa in 1780, her life having ended back at a chief point of departure for the millions of forced migrants to the Americas. For Rebecca, and for many enslaved or formerly enslaved people, faith in Christ gave a new sense of purpose to worldly circumstances that were exploitative and degrading.

The Moravians' theology, especially as articulated by Zinzendorf, was strongly pietistic, being as focused on devotion and experience as doctrine. As illustrated by the multi-ethnic communities in which Rebecca Protten labored, European-background Moravians were also equality-minded, especially when it came to race relations in the church. Like most Christian groups in the 1700s, however, the Moravians generally did not denounce slavery itself. One of the most distinctive aspects of Moravian devotion was their "blood and wounds" theology, in which the blood and wounds of Christ—especially the side wound

Image 9.1. *Moravian baptism* (1757)

he received on the cross—became a primary focus in worship. Attention to the blood and wounds was not new in Christian worship or art, and Catholics in particular had a long-standing tradition of employing images of the crucified, suffering Christ in worship. But the devotion to Christ's blood and wounds attracted special attention from the Moravians, including in art, hymns, and devotional cards representing the side wound.

Though their global numbers did not match those of larger Protestant denominations, Moravians played a pioneering role in three major developments in church history. One was the rise of the Protestant missionary movement. Second was the conversion of much of the African population of North America and the Caribbean to some form of Protestantism. The third was the First Great Awakening, beginning in the 1730s. The Moravians were key early players in the Great Awakening, including in England, where Moravian pastors and missionaries made a great impact on John Wesley and George Whitefield. By the early 1740s, however, many core evangelical leaders began to distance themselves from the Moravians, worried by charges that the Moravians were enthusiastic radicals teaching aberrant theology, including the blood and wounds theology. ("Enthusiasm" in this period was a term suggesting religious frenzy or madness.) Mainstream evangelicals were concerned by the Moravians' common references to the Holy Spirit as "mother."

Awakening, Revival, and the Reformation of Manners

Despite their controversial beliefs, the Moravians were part of the broader Pietist impulse across Europe and America. They, too, were driven by the quest for "heart religion," and by Philipp Jakob Spener's ideal of the *collegia pietatis*, the small groups for worship and prayer that would transform nominal Christian adherence into the personalized devotion of brothers and sisters in Christ. Pietism was one of the main tributaries for the evangelical movement that began with the revivals of the 1730s and '40s. Indeed, it is difficult to trace the precise beginnings of the First Great Awakening because revivalistic movements already had been happening in places such as Herrnhut since before the 1720s. The revivals of the First Great Awakening spanned many places in Europe, North America, and the Caribbean. Many of the earliest incidents of revival, however, transpired in Continental European locales with strong Pietistic influences. The revival movements typically had connections to the complex interplay of Catholic-Protestant imperial rivalries. Protestant groups prayed fervently for the defeat of Catholic powers and for their liberty to worship God as Protestants.

For example, a Halle-inspired children's prayer movement broke out in Silesia (southwestern part of modern Poland) in 1708, especially in Glogau and Breslau. Halle network leaders promoted an account of the revival, *Praise Out of the Mouths of Babes*, which was printed in London and Boston editions. Hundreds of children, and thousands of onlooking adults, would gather for emotional prayer against the "overflowing wickedness of this age." They used devotional guides by Pietist luminaries including Johann Arndt. Their prayers focused more on the "reformation of manners" than conversion per se, however. Circulating accounts of revival, in this instance going from Silesia to London and to Boston, were essential for creating the expectation of more revival. Accounts like the children's prayer revival encouraged more prayer for awakening, giving Pietists and evangelicals a conviction that they were participating in a transnational renewal movement. They had a shared interest with countless brothers and sisters in Christ, most of whom they would not meet personally in this life. But through print, they could identify with them and seek to replicate their revival experiences.

As we have seen, the embattled French Protestant community also produced a diaspora cohort broadly known as the "French Prophets," who seeded the proto-evangelical movement with an intense, charismatic spirituality. Critics—including some other French Protestants—pointed to the extremes of the French Prophet radicals to condemn the whole movement. But their dreadful persecution in France, combined with their Pietist heart religion, made many French Huguenot refugees desire a purer form of Protestant faith. One of their most influential publications was the collection *A Cry from the Desart: or, Testimonials of the Miraculous Things Lately Come to Pass in the Cevennes* (London, 1707, also published there in French-language editions). Like the accounts of the Silesia children's revival, *A Cry from the Desart* emphasized God's miraculous inspiration of "children of both sexes, who [all] of a sudden became preachers," such as the teenage French shepherdess Isabeau Vincent. Many Protestants in the 1700s associated miraculous claims with credulous Catholics, but there was an undeniable fascination among other Protestants with wondrous and miraculous events that confirmed their faith. Children mysteriously empowered to preach the gospel—and to denounce Catholics—definitely qualified as Protestant signs and wonders.

A common problem with such charismatic renewal movements was knowing where to draw the line. What we call "cessationist" theology became formalized after the advent of the modern Pentecostal movement in the early twentieth century. But there were certainly early modern Protestants who believed that most or all miracles had ceased with the age of the apostles. Some of the French Prophets and their allies, to the contrary, began to teach that any of the biblical gifts or miracles might still be in operation today. Believers should pray to receive them, they insisted, whether they be prophecies, healings, tongues, or even resurrections from the dead. It was hardly just marginalized people or French refugees who promoted such beliefs. Arguably the most prominent of the radical prophets in London was John Lacy, a Presbyterian justice of the peace. Lacy's interactions with refugee French Protestants convinced him that God had re-inaugurated all the biblical gifts and miracles. In a preface to *A Cry from the Desart*, Lacy wrote that "if there has been a Diffusion of the Holy Ghost in the Cevennes, it may be the first fruits and dawn of the first Resurrection," alluding to Rev 20:5. Some of the prophets (allegedly including Lacy) predicted the physical resurrection of one of their company, Thomas Emes, who had died. This bold forecast drew much scorn from conservative Protestants, especially when the appointed day came and went, and Emes remained in his grave in Bunhill Fields, the celebrated London burial ground for dissenters.

For Protestants, and especially for Pietists and evangelicals, there was also an enduring tension between the aims of conversion and moral reform. For those who expected an imminent apocalypse, social reform efforts seemed effectively fruitless. But one did not need to be preoccupied with the world's end to emphasize spiritual renewal over social transformation. True conversion would, of course, lead to increasing sanctification of the individual, and hopefully the moral transformation of families, churches, and societies. There was no way to separate the goals of conversion and moral reform entirely. However, movements for Protestant renewal in the seventeenth and eighteenth centuries engaged in a subtle standoff between the priorities of the "reformation of manners" and individual conversions. Making matters more complex, non-evangelical Christians could readily participate in moral reform movements, even if they considered the preaching of conversion and the "new birth" in Christ as enthusiastic and unnecessary. The London-based Society for the Reformation of Manners was founded in the early 1690s. It was championed by latitudinarian Anglicans, including Archbishop John Tillotson. The Society also included non-Anglican Protestants, pulling together a broad cross-section of English-speaking Christians advocating the suppression of vices including Sabbath-breaking, public drunkenness, and prostitution. By the mid-1720s, the Society claimed to have secured tens of thousands of prosecutions against such offenses. The laws against Sabbath breaking and other public sins had often gone unenforced in earlier decades. Christian reform movements like these pursued social flourishing through laws against vice, or the promotion of wholesome, God-honoring living. Evangelicals did not seek, first and foremost, to turn people into flourishing citizens, but into born-again converts, who would go on to live according to God's moral laws. Tensions between moralism and revival were ever-present.

The colony of Massachusetts would become arguably the center of the First Great Awakening in America. For decades before the 1730s, however, it was not clear whether moral reform or revival was the answer to the perceived spiritual lassitude of the people of New England. By the 1670s, Puritan pastors had begun to perfect the "jeremiad," a sermonic form deriving its name from the somber warnings of the prophet Jeremiah. Many pastors in New England had come to believe that the colonists had lost the fervor that marked the charter generations of settlers in Massachusetts and Connecticut. The jeremiads were especially common on special occasions like election days. In them, pastors warned the people that if they did not repent and turn back to God, severe judgments were in store. Puritan pastor Michael Wigglesworth's poem "God's Controversy with New England" (1662) put it well when he wrote (in the voice of the Lord), "Except you seriously, and soon, repent,

Image 9.2. *West Parish Congregational Church, Barnstable, Massachusetts* (originally built 1717)

I'll not delay your pain and heavy punishment." As if in response, Massachusetts faced the repeated blows of King Philip's War (mid-1670s), the loss of John Winthrop's original Massachusetts charter (1689), and the Salem witchcraft controversy (1692). Pastors warned that more wrath was coming if they did not abide by God's moral laws.

The concept of the reformation of manners became part of New England's civic law, too. In 1711, the Massachusetts legislature passed an "Act against Intemperance, Immorality and Prophaneness, and for Reformation of Manners." It especially focused on the regulation of establishments selling alcohol to ensure that they did not become "nurseries of vice and debauchery." The tradeoff between works and grace was a perennial issue in puritan and Reformed theology. By the third generation of puritan settlement in New England, leading ministers leaned heavily toward an emphasis on works. They never taught that good works would save people, but they touted the value of "godly walking" as the test of an obedient Christian life. Many Puritans put little stock in assurance of salvation, or a discernible moment of conversion, though most churches still required a testimony of God's work in one's life for full membership. In New England, the Puritans also represented the established Congregationalist Church, so they functioned there more as a parish-based religion. If one's family was part of a puritan parish in Massachusetts or Connecticut—and most white families were—you were baptized as an infant, and expected to live according to biblical morality. If you did, you could have reasonable confidence that you were part of God's elect, as you "owned" God's covenant of salvation and walked as a God-honoring member of the church. Laws enforcing the reformation of manners targeted marginal colonists who by drunkenness, profanity, or Sabbath breaking disrupted the puritan vision of godly community.

Even as Massachusetts leaders ramped up the reformation of manners, some pastors warned that moral reform was hopeless without the regenerating power of the Holy Spirit. Few would question the value of the moral law in itself, but dating back to the so-called antinomian crisis of the 1630s, some did question whether puritan ministers put too much focus on moral obedience. These critics said that a clear understanding of the need for forgiveness, regeneration, and conversion was more pressing than moral exhortation. In the late 1600s, Samuel Torrey (1632–1707), the puritan minister of Weymouth, Massachusetts, sounded the alarm and called on his fellow colonists not just to seek moral reform but an outpouring of God's Spirit for revival and deliverance. In his election sermon *Man's Extremity, God's Opportunity* (1695), Torrey reminded New Englanders of God's promises to pour out his Spirit on rising generations in passages such as Joel 2:28 and Isa 44:3. "God hath laid this promise of his Spirit in the foundation of the Faith, Hope and Confidence of his people," he said. "The Accomplishment of it, is the great thing which they are to believe and pray for . . . therefore he hath directed his Church to wait upon him for Salvation, until he pour out his Spirit," citing Isa 32:15. Torrey even predicted that if the church prayed for Spirit-led revival, God would work "a glorious resurrection of religion" in New England.

Torrey died in 1707, so he did not live to see the torrents of revival that arrived in the mid-1730s. But other pastors took up the banner of prayer for an outpouring of the Holy Spirit, and laypeople joined in those prayers. Revival-like episodes had transpired among Protestants for decades from the Continent to the American colonies. Aside from special episodes like the Silesian children's revival, these were usually limited to one town or church. Starting in the late 1600s, Congregationalist churches began holding regular "covenant renewal" services, which sometimes took on the fervor of revivals. These events were especially targeted at "children of the church," or people who had received baptism and grown up in the church but had never joined as full members. Such people became especially common after the so-called Halfway Covenant of 1662, which permitted baptized non-members to have their own children baptized, instead of reserving infant baptism only for the children of full church members. Far more New Englanders had been baptized as infants than had joined as full members. Samuel Danforth Jr. (1666–1727), wrote that a 1705 covenant renewal at his church in Taunton, Massachusetts led to an "unusual and amazing Impression, made by GOD's SPIRIT on all sorts among us, especially on the young men and women." Hundreds of people in the small town made new commitments to Christ and the church. Danforth reckoned that the "time of the pouring out of the SPIRIT upon all flesh, may be at the door." Baptized but unregenerate people became the primary target of the covenant renewal services, and they were also the key evangelistic focus of the Great Awakening revivalists.

New England Awakens

The drumbeat of revival became louder in New England in the 1720s, as figures including Jonathan Edwards's grandfather Solomon Stoddard and Edwards's father Timothy saw significant revival activity. This was prior to the 1734–35 awakening in Jonathan Edwards's own Northampton, Massachusetts church, which historians often regard as the beginning of the First Great Awakening proper. There was also a notable revival in New England in 1727 in response to an earthquake in the region, which many interpreted not only as a geological phenomenon but also as the voice of God warning people of worsening judgment.

The Northampton revival signaled a new beginning, however, because it produced Jonathan Edwards's seminal *A Faithful Narrative of the Surprising Work of God.* Edwards (1703–58), a Yale graduate, had become the senior pastor of the Northampton Congregationalist church in 1729, when his grandfather Stoddard died. The revival at Northampton began in 1734. Edwards's revival account received much attention in Britain as well as in the American colonies. There was something far different about a local revival that was contained within a particular church and a publicized revival that became an international template for what one might expect God to do in a season of awakening. Edwards's revival received so much publicity because of Edwards's powerful writing style, but *A Faithful Narrative* also indicated the development of a print network bolstering the incipient international evangelical movement. Northampton, Massachusetts was a significant town in the Connecticut River Valley region, but it was marginal in the wider British Empire in the mid-1730s. Thus, the distribution of *A Faithful Narrative* depended on the support of Benjamin Colman (1673–1747), the most influential pastor in Boston at the time of the Great Awakening, and of dissenting pastors in London, including the great hymn-writer Isaac Watts. *A Faithful Narrative* was addressed as a letter to Colman, but it was published first in London in 1737. In time it was translated into other languages and published in centers of the evangelical movement across the world, becoming arguably the most influential extrabiblical description of a revival in Christian history.

Edwards traced the beginnings of the awakening to an "unusual flexibleness" he sensed among the congregation's young people. The deaths of certain youths also sobered their friends and focused the survivors' attention on eternal things. Edwards encouraged them to begin meeting in Spenerian-style small groups for "social religion." Edwards was a thorough Calvinist, so he also attributed the people's growing spiritual concerns to a "great noise" going on in New England about the dangers of Arminian doctrine, which Calvinists typically associated with belief in works-righteousness. This controversy over Arminianism gave him an opportunity to re-emphasize the principle of "justification by faith alone."

Finally, at the end of 1734, Edwards wrote that "the Spirit of God began extraordinarily to set in, and wonderfully to work amongst us." Numbers of people began to experience conversion simultaneously. He was especially struck by the testimony of a young woman previously known as one of the "greatest company-keepers," or frivolous socializers, in Northampton. Now she spoke of "a glorious work of God's infinite power and sovereign grace" in her life, and Edwards reckoned "that God had given her a new heart, truly broken and sanctified." The conversions multiplied and spread from Northampton to towns across the region. He also connected the Connecticut River Valley revivals to those happening in New Jersey, led there by pastors associated with the Tennent family of Presbyterians and by the Dutch Reformed pastor Theodorus Frelinghuysen (1691–1747) of New Brunswick.

Edwards was stunned by the scope of the Northampton revival, which crossed boundaries of age, class, and race. He noted that "several Negroes . . . appear to have been truly born again." Edwards, like a number of the key revivalists of the Great Awakening, was a slave-owner. Slavery was less prominent in colonial New England because the climate there was not conducive to large plantations. Yet New Englanders still enslaved significant numbers of Native Americans and African Americans, and many pastors such as Edwards owned slaves, usually as household servants. Edwards was critical of the practices of the transatlantic slave trade, but he never condemned slavery outright. Yet he also sought to include African Americans, including his own enslaved people, in church life and the revivals. The Northampton church admitted nine African Americans into full church membership during his time there.

Edwards was fascinated by converts' spiritual experiences, and sought in *A Faithful Narrative*, *Religious Affections* (1746), and other writings to distinguish between the work of the Holy Spirit and fleshly enthusiasm. Edwards was one of the most powerful intellects in Christian history, yet he was supremely concerned with matters of the heart, the sanctification of one's desires, and what he called the "affections." The converts in revival experienced what Edwards described as a new "spiritual sense," or a new ability to see and apprehend divine things by the gracious power of the Spirit. Edwards explained that "the Holy Ghost influences the godly as dwelling in them as a vital principle, or as a new supernatural principle of life and action." This vital principle is not active in the unregenerate person. The Spirit enlivened one's love for God, one's delight in God's Word, and one's daily experience of God's presence. Sometimes, especially during conversion and revival, the Spirit's presence might generate strong "impressions" in the mind and heart related to salvation and the truths of the Word. Edwards always steered clear of sanctioning visionary experiences of the "bodily eyes," or physical sight. But he certainly acknowledged that converts might have dramatic impressions made on the mind, such as the terrors of hell, or of the power of Christ's death and resurrection. "Some, when they have been greatly affected with Christ's death, have at the same time a lively idea of Christ hanging upon the cross, and of his blood running from his wounds," he explained in *A Faithful Narrative*.

Edwards often presented women as having exemplary spiritual experiences, and he did so in *A Faithful Narrative*. He focused on accounts of a four-year-old named Phoebe

Bartlett and a young woman named Abigail Hutchinson, who passed away not long after her conversion. Hutchinson had struggled with skepticism about the Bible's reliability and with her sins against God. But once she broke through to conversion, she "continued whole days and whole nights in a constant ravishing view of the glory of God and Christ, having enjoyed as much as her life could bear." Edwards constantly spoke of the convert's new sense of "sweetness" in contemplating the glory of God. Hutchinson experienced that sweetness in waves of ever-deeper glory and delight. She "was filled with a more exceeding sweetness; she likewise gave me such an account of the sense she once had, from day to day, of the glory of Christ, and of God in his various attributes, that it seemed to me she dwelt for days together in a kind of beatific vision of God," he recalled. She suffered terribly in her physical body as her death approached, and yet she longed to die and to be with Christ. When death finally came, Hutchinson seemed uniquely prepared for it, with her spirit focused on gaining Christ without the encumbering "clog" of her weak body. She was "a very eminent instance of Christian experience," Edwards concluded.

Conclusion

Across the Protestant world, stretching from Poland to the American colonies, signs of revival had begun to appear in the early 1700s. The Pietist and Puritan legacies gave the emerging evangelical movement deep spiritual resources on which to draw. Figures such as Samuel Torrey reminded Christians that real Christian transformation did not come through efforts to be moral, but through an outpouring of the Holy Spirit for conversions and revival. Accounts of revival—especially Edwards's revival in Northampton—began to coalesce into an expectation that the Spirit would bring awakening in far-flung parts of the world. God's people should pray for the promised outpouring of the Spirit, the new evangelicals believed. Soon the Spirit did come, in ways that Christians across Europe and America found unprecedented and "surprising."

Selected Bibliography

Atwood, Craig D. *Community of the Cross: Moravian Piety in Colonial Bethlehem*. University Park: Pennsylvania State University Press, 2004.

Garrett, Clarke. *Origins of the Shakers: From the Old World to the New World*. Baltimore: Johns Hopkins University Press, 1987.

Hempton, David. *The Church in the Long Eighteenth Century*. New York: I.B. Tauris, 2011.

Kidd, Thomas S. *The Great Awakening: The Roots of Evangelical Christianity in Colonial America*. New Haven, CT: Yale University Press, 2007.

McClymond, Michael J. *Encounters with God: An Approach to the Theology of Jonathan Edwards*. New York: Oxford University Press, 1998.

Praise out of the Mouth of Babes. London: J. Downing, 1708.

Prince, Thomas. *The Christian History*. Boston, 1743–1745.

Sensbach, Jon F. *Rebecca's Revival: Creating Black Christianity in the Atlantic World*. Cambridge: Harvard University Press, 2005.

Spence, Jonathan D. *The Question of Hu*. New York: Knopf, 1988.

Swensson, Eric Jonas. *Kinderbeten: The Origin, Unfolding, and Interpretations of the Silesian Children's Prayer Revival*. Eugene, OR: Wipf and Stock, 2010.

Ward, W.R. *The Protestant Evangelical Awakening*. New York: Cambridge University Press, 1992.

Wiggin, Bethany, ed. *Babel of the Atlantic*. University Park: Pennsylvania State University Press, 2019.

—— Chapter 10 ——

A Transatlantic Revival

The evangelist George Whitefield (1714–70) was not born with a silver spoon in his talented mouth. His mother had suffered through the death of her first husband and a disastrous second marriage. George helped his mother run the Bell Inn in Gloucester, England, serving drinks, cleaning rooms, and attending his Anglican parish school. His mother hoped for a better future for her bright son, so she arranged for him to attend Oxford University as a "servitor," or a student who paid his way through school by doing menial tasks for wealthy students. His Anglican background supplied him with resources to nurture his surging spiritual interest in college. He read classics of Christian devotion like Thomas à Kempis's *The Imitation of Christ*, and William Law's *A Serious Call to a Devout and Holy Life* (1729).

Leaders of the Awakening

Aside from the Bible, the pivotal text in Whitefield's spiritual transformation at Oxford was Henry Scougal's *The Life of God in the Soul of Man* (1677). Providentially, Whitefield had befriended the future Methodist leader Charles Wesley (1707–88), who recommended the book to him. John and Charles Wesley, Whitefield, and other devoted students became part of what critics called the "Holy Club" at Oxford. This coterie of students (John had graduated in the late 1720s) became the devotional and organizational core of the Methodist movement, which would have a transformational effect on the Church of England from the 1730s forward. Charles gave Whitefield suggestions for devotional reading, including Scougal. Like many early evangelicals, Whitefield tried to adopt a rigorous program of devotion to achieve a right standing with God, but he found that he kept stumbling back into sinful habits. Somehow he could not find reconciliation with the Lord.

The work of Scougal, a Scottish theologian and minister who had died in the late 1670s, revealed the essential problem to Whitefield. *The Life of God in the Soul of Man* showed him that he had put the cart of devotion before the horse of conversion, as it were. (The Wesleys would realize that they, too, had made a similar mistake.) As important as it was to pray, fast, and minister to the poor, these activities contributed nothing to one's salvation and could even distract from it. Without conversion and regeneration, ascetic devotion became a form of idolatry. There was no true power for devotion without the transforming might of God's Spirit. Moral effort was not enough, Whitefield realized. He must become a "new creature."

Scougal's insistence (following John 3 and similar passages) that one must be born again punctured Whitefield's sense that he was becoming a good Christian by his own merit. It first made him angry, then despondent. Whitefield recalled that he finally held Scougal's book in his hand and spoke these words aloud: "Lord, if I am not a Christian, if I am not a real one, God, for Jesus Christ's sake, show me what Christianity is, that I may not be damned." The desire to move from mere Christian adherence into "real" Christianity was arguably the defining impulse of evangelical piety. Although figures such as Whitefield and Jonathan Edwards would remain ordained pastors in established, parish-based denominations (Anglican and Congregationalist, respectively), they were also renewing the principle that one could not be a Christian by virtue of infant baptism or Christian heritage. To be saved, one must be born again.

Whitefield's Scougal-inspired prayer that God show him how to be a real Christian was a seminal moment in his testimony. He went through months of travail as he wrestled with conversion and forgiveness. His health was badly compromised, and Whitefield feared he was under satanic attack. Evangelicals—led by the Wesleyan Methodists—would come to see the conversion process as far simpler than what older puritan teaching held. But in the mid-1730s it was still conventional for conversion to take weeks, if not months or years, to resolve into some assurance of salvation. It was also common, particularly in Calvinist circles, for the penitent to wonder, as Whitefield wondered, whether God would indeed save him. Over time such doubts effectively vanished in evangelical piety. Later evangelicals often seemed to imply, or overtly teach, that God would certainly save anyone who asked for forgiveness through Christ. But for Whitefield, the puritan legacy remained strong. He was candidly uncertain about whether he desired salvation, and whether God would save him even if he did want it. The struggle made him physically ill, and some of his fellow students worried that he was losing his mind. Finally, during Lent in 1735, he received a spiritual impression that "when Jesus Christ cried out 'I thirst,' his sufferings were near at an end." Whitefield took this as a sign from the Holy Spirit, and he threw himself on his bed, shouting "I thirst, I thirst!" This was his spiritual breakthrough. Citing 2 Pet 1:19, he said that "the Day Star arose in my heart," and he was born again.

Whitefield already had a great deal of experience in Christian piety before his conversion. What was new was the joy and freedom he experienced in walking with the Holy Spirit. He now had what Edwards would describe as a new spiritual sense, or a "feeling presence" of the Spirit. Evangelicals took a high view of the Bible, but that was nothing new in the broader Protestant and Reformed traditions. What was new for evangelicals was the close attention they gave to a discernible conversion experience, the assurance of salvation that was available to converts, and the daily experience of guidance from the Spirit. In the first years following his new birth in Christ, Whitefield could not get over the joy-filled reality of being filled with the Spirit. In one of his diaries written the year after his conversion, Whitefield meticulously recorded episodes of being "full of the Holy Ghost," feeling "joy in the Holy Ghost," and sometimes counting the hours in which he was consciously filled with the Spirit. The Spirit's presence struck Whitefield most dramatically about his newly converted state. This vital pneumatology became representative of much of the broader evangelical movement. Of course, a belief in the Holy Spirit was a staple of the great tradition, but many evangelicals emphasized that true believers could have a "feeling possession" of the Spirit. They taught that Spirit could be a more tangible presence in a believer's life than many other Christians recognized.

Across Europe and America, people who became key figures in the First Great Awakening were experiencing conversion in the 1720s and '30s. Rumblings of the expansive, transatlantic awakening of the 1730s and '40s began to appear at least by the late 1720s. We have already noted the Moravian revival at Herrnhut in 1727. That same year New England experienced its biggest revival prior to Edwards's Northampton awakening. "Revival" is not a term precisely used in the Bible, though Protestants looked to the outpouring of the Spirit and the large numbers of conversions in the Book of Acts as models for what might happen today. Psalm 85 also prayed, "Wilt thou not revive us again: that thy people may rejoice in thee?" (KJV). That verse suggested that "revival" applied to the rejuvenation of believers already in the church. In the most heightened moments of revival, one was likely to see large numbers of people experiencing conversion for the first time, as well as people already converted having their faith reinvigorated. Great Awakening revivalists attributed all such responses to an outpouring of the Holy Spirit, citing verses such as Isa 44:3, "For I will pour water upon him that is thirsty, and floods upon the dry ground: I will pour my spirit upon thy seed, and my blessing upon thine offspring" (KJV). Of course, we can also point to more earthly factors in revival, such as the media sensation created by Whitefield's ministry. Printed reports of revival across Europe and America created greater expectations of and prayers for more revival.

It can often be difficult to discern the workings of God's providence in history outside of what is revealed in Scripture. The Great Awakening is something of an exception. It is no stretch to conclude, as historian Mark Noll puts it, that "something was going on" in the far-flung conversions and revivals that began to appear in the 1720s. One might posit that people in these revivals were responding to similar early modern cultural and theological prompts that fostered revival. But that does not preclude the conclusion that God was also initiating and superintending a massive international series of revivals which led to the conversion of untold thousands of people, and which permanently changed the Protestant landscape.

In the late 1710s, the minister William Tennent, Sr. decided to move his family from Northern Ireland (Ulster) to the American colonies. His oldest son Gilbert had been born in 1703, the same year that John Wesley and Jonathan Edwards were born. Around the time that the Tennents moved to America, Gilbert entered a long spiritual struggle that he called a "law work," which entailed a deep sense of his guilt before God. In America in the mid-1720s, however, Tennent broke through to conversion and became a Presbyterian pastor. Soon he partnered with the Dutch Reformed pastor and immigrant Theodorus Frelinghuysen in early revival preaching in New Jersey. Inspired by the older Frelinghuysen's successful conversionist ministry, Gilbert Tennent committed himself to "stand upon the stage of the world as it were, and plead more faithfully for [God's] cause, and take more earnest pains for the *Conversion of Souls*."

At almost exactly the same time as Whitefield's conversion, Wales's Howell Harris (1714–73) experienced the new birth, too, partly through reading Richard Allestree's devotional classic *The Whole Duty of Man* (1658). Harris became convinced that "Christ died for me, and that all my sins were laid on him." Soon he "felt some insatiable desires after the salvation of poor sinners," and he began holding evangelistic meetings from house-to-house.

Harris was a tireless itinerant, but he struggled to settle on a denominational or theological home. It may seem odd, given the Wesleys' commitment to Arminian theology, but Harris became one of Wales's standard-bearers for the Calvinistic brand of Methodism exemplified by George Whitefield. Also in Wales in 1735, the powerful evangelist Daniel Rowland (1711–90) was converted under the Welsh preacher Griffith Jones. One of Rowland's mentors noted how fearsomely Rowland preached on sin, the law, and the threat of damnation. This mentor advised Rowland to "apply the Balm of Gilead, the blood of Christ, to their spiritual wounds . . . If you go on preaching the law in this manner, you will kill half the people in the country." Like Wesley and Whitefield in England, Rowland and Harris immediately recognized the other as a brother in the cause of the gospel. With passing years their relationship became more fraught, however, until the Welsh preachers finally became estranged in 1750. Sadly, the gospel often did not preserve unity in the face of differences over theology, personality, or ministry tactics. Despite such difficulties, Wales became one of the greatest centers of evangelical revival during the era.

Sarah Osborn (1714–96), who became arguably the key lay leader in Rhode Island's Great Awakening, experienced conversion in 1737. A fierce sermon by the pastor of Newport's First Congregationalist Church drew her into a crisis over her sins. She saw in mortifying terror the "depravity of my nature and how I was exposed to the infinite justice of an angry God," she wrote. After days of wrestling with the fear of damnation, Osborn came into a confidence that God would save her. She cried and trembled as exclamations of praise poured out of her. Soon thereafter, at a communion service, she was overwhelmed by images of Christ suffering for her sins. The experience was so intense that she got on the floor and leaned on her pew. In her mind she saw her "dearest Lord in his bitter agony in the garden, and then crowned with thorns, spit upon, buffeted, beaten black and blue, and at last nailed to an accursed tree, and all to free me from the torments I had so lately dreaded." After speaking to the pastor at First Church Newport, she was admitted to full membership.

> He was the author, and he will be the finisher of my faith. And so he makes me hang on the faithfulness of a covenant God, who will not deceive nor make any ashamed of their hope, that put their trust in him.
>
> ———
>
> Sarah Osborn, *The Nature, Certainty, and Evidence of True Christianity*, 1755

As historian Catherine Brekus explains, Osborn grew up in the puritan tradition where conversion was an expectation for full church membership. Newer evangelicals, especially in the Wesleyan tradition, confidently asserted the availability of assurance of salvation. For Osborn, 1737 was followed by years of uncertainty, until the height of the Great Awakening in New England brought her to a new confidence about forgiveness and right standing with God. One of the most prolific diarists of the eighteenth century, Osborn admitted that after 1737 she "backslid" into old habits like gossip, dancing, and card playing. Her intense experiences surrounding her conversion came to seem like delusions. When George Whitefield came to preach in Newport, she, like most of the town's residents, went to hear him. It "stirred me up," she wrote. But it was Gilbert Tennent's preaching thereafter that gripped her with new fears about hypocrisy and raised basic questions about whether she was truly saved. She exchanged letters with Tennent. Like Daniel Rowland, Tennent had a reputation for preaching the condemning terrors of the law, but his pastoral counsel to Osborn was encouraging. "I like your experiences well," he told his "dear friend." "They seem to me to be scriptural and encouraging, and I think you may humbly take comfort in them and give God the glory of his pure grace." Evangelical religion, to Osborn and Tennent, was both experiential and biblicist. Mere rational assent to biblical doctrine was not true faith, but neither was groundless, subjective spirituality. Real Christianity was an affective response to the truths revealed in Scripture. Scripture also guided those struggling to gain assurance. Tennent telling Osborn that her "experiences" were "scriptural" reflected well the common characteristics of evangelical piety: the truths of the Word prompting true experiences in the Spirit.

Women and Missions in the Awakening

Women such as Sarah Osborn played a critical role in the evangelical movement. As in most Christian churches, women usually composed a majority of attendees of evangelical congregations and revival meetings. Women's experiences are often obscure or lost to history, which tends to capture documents associated with pastors and theologians far more than those associated with laypeople, especially women. Almost no churches, whether Catholic, Orthodox, or Protestant, ordained women as pastors until the mid-nineteenth century. Even then, it was usually just the most liberal Protestant churches alone who ordained small numbers of female pastors. But women like Sarah Osborn and the Moravian leader Rebecca Protten (who did receive ordination as a deaconess) exercised great influence in their churches. They did so as spiritual exemplars, teachers, evangelists, organizers, advisers to ordained clergy, and as mothers and wives. Despite chronic health problems and poverty, Osborn would go on to lead extraordinary prayer meetings at her Newport home in the mid-1760s that attracted hundreds of people, including enslaved people. She carefully deferred to ordained leaders, but her revivalist work was essential to the evangelical movement in Rhode Island.

Evangelicalism was a missionary faith, too, inspired by the example of the Moravians. Evangelicals were chastened by the reality that the Catholic Church had done vastly more missionary work than Protestants in the two and a half centuries since the Reformation. (Partly this was a product of the institutional strength of the Catholic Church compared to most Protestant churches, which had few organizations like the Catholic missionary orders.) To some like Sarah Osborn, evangelism and missions could simply mean reaching out to unchurched people in one's town, such as the enslaved and free black community of Newport. But evangelicals also had a desire to reach the "ends of the earth" with the gospel. George Whitefield would manifest that desire in his relentless travels and crossings of the Atlantic, work which took him to an early grave in 1770. But Whitefield first caught inspiration for transatlantic ministry from the Wesleys, who urged him to go to the colony of Georgia (founded in 1732) as a missionary.

John and Charles Wesley

John Wesley (1703–91) and Whitefield were both known for the saying "the world is my parish." In the mid-1730s, Wesley heralded to the recently-converted Whitefield the unparalleled missionary opportunities in the New World. There were people in the American South from all parts of the globe, plus the "known and unknown natives of this vast continent." Who would reach these diverse peoples with the gospel? Although the bulk of Whitefield's ministry would eventually be among English speakers in Britain and America, he found Georgia a fresh and enticing prospect. He would make Georgia the home of his Bethesda orphanage, the great charitable enterprise of Whitefield's career. Bethesda was inspired by the example of August Hermann Francke and the Halle Pietists in Germany, whose vast network of Christian reform projects included an acclaimed orphanage.

John Wesley had actually not received assurance of salvation before he became a (short-lived) missionary to Georgia. Even as Wesley was telling Whitefield he needed to go to the New World, Wesley was not clear about his own standing before God. Wesley seems to have imbibed a focus on the merit of good works from certain Anglican leaders. He may have thought (like Whitefield in his early Methodist phase) that good deeds, including missions, would help save him. But Wesley was caught up short in his pretensions when, having arrived in Georgia, he had a fateful conversation with a Moravian leader there, August Spangenberg. (The Moravians had established a station in Georgia in 1735.) Spangenberg asked him "Do you know Jesus Christ?" Wesley hesitated, saying he knew Jesus was the savior of the world. Spangenberg agreed, but he asked again, "Do you know he has died to save you?" Wesley stammered that he hoped so. He started to realize that even serving as an overseas missionary was not enough to address the fundamental gulf between sinful people like him and a holy God.

John Wesley's Georgia ministry ended in sordid controversy over his failed courtship of a seventeen-year-old girl. He left the colony, never to return to America, at the end of 1737. His ego was bruised; his spiritual state unsettled. "I went to America, to convert the Indians, but oh! who shall convert me?" he asked. In England, Wesley preached the necessity of the new birth in Christ, even though he was not certain whether he had experienced it himself. Peter Böhler (1712–75), a Moravian leader from Frankfurt, told Wesley that his turmoil suggested he did not possess saving faith. Wesley responded that if Böhler was correct, then surely he should stop preaching. The Moravian advised instead that he should "preach faith until you have it." Whether this was good advice or not, Wesley was gaining clarity about the doctrine of salvation by faith alone. He began to teach that precept to others. He also began to believe that a person could reasonably expect to be converted in a moment's time. One could know that he or she had this transformative experience, he reasoned, since it was all a work of God's power and grace. You could know for sure if you were saved.

Finally in 1738, Wesley went to a Moravian meeting at Aldersgate Street, London. Illustrating the ongoing connection to the Reformation in the early evangelical movement, the speaker was reading from Martin Luther's preface to Romans. "When he was describing the change which God works in the heart through faith in Christ," Wesley wrote, "I felt my heart strangely warmed. I felt I did trust in Christ, Christ alone, for salvation; and an assurance was given me that He had taken away my sins." For Wesley this might have been more an infusion of crystalline assurance than conversion per se, but nevertheless the moment has taken on legendary status in the evangelical and Methodist movements. Even though Wesley—like most of the prominent British and Anglo-American evangelical leaders—would break with the Moravians over differences in theology and practice, the Moravians were decisive in leading Wesley to a sure understanding of salvation and assurance.

John's brother Charles broke through to assurance at around the same time, via similar Moravian influences. Charles wrote that "I found myself at peace with God, and rejoiced in hope of loving Christ." Immediately he penned one of the many hymns and poems that would represent his most salient contribution to evangelical culture. The hymn was probably "Christ the Friend of Sinners," which touched on signature themes of evangelical spirituality.

> "Where shall my wandering soul begin?
> How shall I all to heaven aspire?
> A slave redeem'd from death and sin,
> A brand pluck'd from eternal fire . . .
> Come, O my guilty brethren come,
> Groaning beneath your load of sin!
> His bleeding heart shall make you room,
> His open side shall take you in."

The image of Christ's side wound reminds us again how much Moravian piety influenced the faith of early English evangelicals. Wesley would pen other classics such as "And Can It Be that I Should Gain?," "Christ the Lord is Risen Today," "Come, Thou Long Expected Jesus," and "O For a Thousand Tongues to Sing." Some of his hymns remain standards today, even in churches that employ contemporary worship styles. Along with Isaac Watts's hymns, Charles Wesley's songs supplemented or replaced psalm-singing in the musical repertoire of many English-speaking churches during and after the Great Awakening. Singing had always been an essential practice in churches, but in evangelical churches, hymn-singing became even more poignant and personalized for the average layperson.

The Ministry of George Whitefield

George Whitefield's fame as a scintillating preacher had begun to spread in England before he left for Georgia. Whitefield's trip was better-fated than John Wesley's, but he was never going to stay there long. Whitefield was a rolling stone, and he longed to follow up on signs of revival he had left behind in London. Back in the city, Whitefield fellowshipped again with the Moravians and the Wesleys, who often held intense worship meetings at a prayer society in Fetter Lane. This international assembly hit the heights of fervor at New Year's 1739, when the Methodists and Moravians held a "love-feast," a worship meeting centered on a fellowship meal. John Wesley noted that the "power of God came mightily upon us." Some cried out in joy, and others crumpled to the ground, overwhelmed by the Spirit's power. Many attendees, including Whitefield, stayed up all night together, ushering in the new year with praise.

Evangelicals had a ready template for what might happen in such awakenings because of the popularity of Jonathan Edwards's *A Faithful Narrative*. Isaac Watts and other English evangelicals had arranged for the account's inaugural publication in 1737 in London, and by 1738 it had circulated widely among British evangelicals, read by John Wesley, Howell Harris, and many others. It soon appeared in editions in Boston, Edinburgh, Amsterdam, and Magdeburg (Prussia), too, and Wesley would later produce an abridgment of *A Faithful Narrative*, as well as a number of Edwards's other works. Versions of *A Faithful Narrative* would become even more popular during the Second Great Awakening in the 1800s. Through *A Faithful Narrative* and works such as *The Distinguishing Marks of the Spirit of God* (1741), Edwards exerted enormous influence in marking out boundaries of what phenomena might be expected in true revival.

The intensity of the Great Awakening regularly tested the limits of tolerable revival experiences, however, and radical evangelicals were often willing to accept certain phenomena as legitimate that moderates regarded as illicit or dangerously chaotic. For example, Charles Wesley was alarmed when he encountered the charismatic Isaac Hollis, one of the disciples of the French Prophets in England. While Wesley was staying at Hollis's house, Hollis began trembling and he "gobbled like a turkey-cock." He was speaking in tongues, a practice regularly discussed in the Book of Acts and 1 Corinthians, but which only made rare appearances in church history until the Pentecostal revivals of the early twentieth century. Wesley, disturbed by Hollis's outburst, prayed out loud for Hollis that he would be liberated from what Wesley assumed was a demonic spirit.

In addition to perusing revival accounts like Edwards's, and reading Whitefield's wildly popular travel journals, leaders of the evangelical movement corresponded with each other. This, too, fed the growing sense of a transnational awakening. Whitefield told Howell Harris of a "great pouring out of the Spirit, at London," while Harris told Whitefield about a "great reformation" happening in Wales through the preaching of Daniel Rowland. (People at the time did not speak of "the" Great Awakening, though they routinely spoke of a "great awakening" happening in one place or another.) Whitefield soon received Anglican ordination as a priest, an office he would hold the rest of his life. But he corresponded with non-Anglican pastors too, including Philip Doddridge (1702–51), pastor of an Independent congregation in Northampton, in the East Midlands of England. Doddridge was a hymn-writer, too, but he would be best known for *The Rise and Progress of Religion in the Soul* (1745), an enduring classic of evangelical spirituality which he dedicated to Isaac Watts. Doddridge urged readers to "turn yourself to Christ . . . Would you therefore, Oh Sinner, desire to be saved? Go to the Savior. Would you desire to be delivered? Look to that great deliverer." Whitefield would find relatively little support among non-Anglicans in England, despite Doddridge's friendship. Among his most avid supporters, however, were Presbyterians in Scotland and non-Anglican Protestants in America, including evangelicals among the Congregationalists (such as Edwards), Presbyterians (such as Tennent), and Baptists.

Whitefield's audiences in England grew bigger as his fame spread, and he started to attract hostility from many Anglican authorities, too. Some churches closed their doors to him, which led him to take his sermons into the fields. Few churches could hold the kinds of crowds Whitefield was drawing anyway, especially in cities like London. At about the same time he regularly began field preaching, he also stopped using notes. It may be misleading to say that Whitefield preached "extemporaneously," because he had a rotation of highly-polished, memorized sermons he gave in different locations. But he also modified the sermons depending on how the Spirit was prompting him, or how the audiences were reacting. Whitefield had a background in the theater, and he brought dramatic techniques into his preaching. Of course, there is always a performative aspect to a sermon, but few preachers have ever used theatrical methods to such great effect as Whitefield. The revivalist would take on biblical characters' roles in the midst of sermons, in order to emphasize the pathos of the passage and to enthrall audiences.

Image 10.1. *George Whitefield* (1738)

There is no reason to suggest that Whitefield was being insincere. Given how Whitefield labored relentlessly for decades, to little personal financial profit, it would be hard to imagine that he did not sincerely believe the biblical precepts he taught. Instead, he believed that a revivalist should cultivate an effective style of communication to present biblical truth as effectively as possible. Some have characterized Whitefield's preaching as shallow, but it was actually filled with rigorous theology and references to the great tradition of Christian history. It was not unusual for him to refer to figures including the church fathers Tertullian or Polycarp, or Reformers such as Luther. But he was also preaching in a cultural context where familiarity with the Bible and with Christian history was much higher than it is in the contemporary United Kingdom or United States. He could expect even many unchurched people to understand such references.

Whitefield's spectacular rise to fame made him the most influential and controversial evangelical figure of the era. His enemies called him an "enthusiast," or a religious fanatic. Even some cautious evangelical leaders worried about aspects of Whitefield's ministry, such as his reliance on spiritual "impressions" for guidance and insight. Figures such as Isaac Watts and Jonathan Edwards warned Whitefield that depending on such internal, unmediated prompts risked confusing flesh with the Spirit. John Wesley also rejected Whitefield's Calvinist beliefs, doctrines which Whitefield put front and center in his sermons. Wesley and Whitefield were also two of the biggest names in the emerging English evangelical cohort. One imagines that their rift was about personality as much as theology. In any case, by 1739 John Wesley used the casting of lots (a practice he employed regularly to make decisions) to determine that he would denounce Whitefield's Calvinism publicly. In his sermon and tract *Free Grace*, Wesley declared that by denying that people had free will to accept Christ's offer of forgiveness, the Calvinists represented God as "worse than the devil." Why would God condemn people who could not choose to receive grace?

Even as opposition to Whitefield mounted, he entered one of his most extraordinary seasons of ministry when he returned to America in late 1739. He met key Pietist and evangelical leaders such as Gilbert Tennent and Theodorus Frelinghuysen. He made a business connection with Benjamin Franklin, who became Whitefield's most important American publisher, despite Franklin's decidedly non-evangelical religious views. As Whitefield headed south from Pennsylvania and New

Image 10.2. *John Wesley* (ca. 1730–56)

Jersey, he met a mixed reception in Maryland and Virginia. In Annapolis, Maryland, an Anglican lawyer named Stephen Bordley left one of the best descriptions of Whitefield's physical presence, from a critical perspective. Whitefield's voice was "strong and clear, but not musical, and he has a little of the West Country twang.[1] He is very young, has a well turned person, a fine set of teeth . . . and a sweet and agreeable turn of countenance, but the beauty of this is somewhat lessened by a prodigious squint with his left eye." Most portraits reflected Whitefield's crossed eyes, a condition he developed after a childhood illness. Bordley thought that Whitefield's two main topics in preaching were the work of the Holy Spirit and the deficiencies of other pastors. "In short, he has the best delivery with the worst divinity that I ever met with," the doubtful lawyer concluded.

Entering the lower South, Whitefield had to confront enslaved people more directly than before in his life. This began his own problematic relationship with slavery, and by the mid-1740s he had become an owner of enslaved people himself. In the meantime, however, Whitefield's southern sojourn led him to publish a letter indicting southern slave masters for their "cruelty to the poor negroes." Whitefield, like Jonathan Edwards, had concerns about the abuse of enslaved people, especially in the transatlantic slave trade. Unlike many other slave masters, Whitefield and Edwards wanted to introduce enslaved people to the gospel, believing that the slaves were human beings with souls. Therefore, they needed forgiveness through Christ. But Whitefield, Edwards, and a number of other American evangelical leaders did not condemn slavery itself, believing that the Bible's household regulations allowed Christians to own slaves, as long as they did not treat the slaves harshly.

Whitefield saw some of his greatest triumphs as he preached in New England in the fall of 1740. When he gave his farewell sermon in Boston, it drew at least twenty thousand people, an assembly larger than the entire population of the town. In Northampton, Whitefield was delighted to meet Jonathan and Sarah Edwards. Jonathan was thrilled to have Whitefield speak at his church, but he took the opportunity to caution Whitefield about spiritual impressions and about judging other pastors to be unconverted. Tennent had given a sermon on unregenerate pastors, too, which became *The Danger of an Unconverted Ministry* (1740), perhaps the most controversial sermon of the Great Awakening.

Of course, many ministers did not appreciate such talk about unconverted pastors because it fundamentally challenged their spiritual state and qualifications for ministry. Many Protestants had touted the need for conversion for full church membership (not to

---

[1] That is, an accent of people from the west of England.

mention for becoming a pastor). But prior to the First Great Awakening, the most tangible qualification a man needed to become a minister (including for Whitefield) was a college education. Now the ground shifted in a more populist direction. Revivalists divided their audiences, including clergy, into converted and unconverted people alone. The distinction was a revelation to many hearers, clergy and laypeople alike. The Connecticut farm woman Hannah Heaton, for example, traced the beginning of her conversion to hearing sermons by Tennent and Whitefield. "Mr. Whitefield laid down the marks of an unconverted person," she wrote. "O strange it was such preaching as I never heard before." She began to think her "nature must be changed but how to attain it I knew not." Like Whitefield a half decade earlier, she was realizing her need for a transformative experience of God's grace and power. After a long period of struggle, and torment with fears of hell, Heaton had a vision of Jesus with "the eyes of my soul . . . His face was full of smiles he looked white and ruddy and was just such a savior as my soul wanted," she thought. She was converted and felt that she "had a new soul & body both." Such conversion, in its myriad forms, was the paradigmatic experience of the Great Awakening and the evangelical movement.

Selected Bibliography:

Brekus, Catherine A. *Sarah Osborn's World: The Rise of Evangelical Christianity in Early America*. New Haven, CT: Yale University Press, 2013.

Coalter, Milton J., Jr. *Gilbert Tennent, Son of Thunder: A Case Study of Continental Pietism's Impact on the First Great Awakening in the Middle Colonies*. Westport, CT: Greenwood Press, 1986.

Hindmarsh, Bruce. *The Evangelical Conversion Narrative: Spiritual Autobiography in Early Modern England*. New York: Oxford University Press, 2005.

Jones, David Ceri. *"A Glorious Work in the World": Welsh Methodism and the International Evangelical Revival, 1735–1750*. Cardiff: University of Wales Press, 2004.

Kidd, Thomas S. *George Whitefield: America's Spiritual Founding Father*. New Haven, CT: Yale University Press, 2014.

Lacey, Barbara, ed. *The World of Hannah Heaton: The Diary of an Eighteenth-Century Farm Woman*. Dekalb, IL: Northern Illinois University Press, 2003.

Noll, Mark A. *The Rise of Evangelicalism: The Age of Edwards, Whitefield, and the Wesleys*. Downers Grove: IVP, 2003.

Rack, Henry D. *Reasonable Enthusiast: John Wesley and the Rise of Methodism*. London: Epworth, 1989.

Scott, John Thomas. *The Wesleys and the Anglican Mission to Georgia, 1735–1738: "So Glorious an Undertaking."* Bethlehem, PA: Lehigh University Press, 2021.

Strivens, Robert. *Philip Doddridge and the Shaping of Evangelical Dissent*. London: Routledge, 2016.

—— Chapter 11 ——

A Vibrant and Contested Awakening

The Great Awakening was a major turning point in Christian history. This was not just because of the incredible number of conversions that transpired under the preaching of Whitefield and other revivalists. Those conversions had incalculable eternal consequences, but the Great Awakening also sent Anglo-American and world Christianity careening in unpredictable directions. The Great Awakening reshuffled denominational alignments, sparking the ascendancy of the Baptists, Methodists, and other upstart evangelical denominations. These two denominational families would become evangelical behemoths in America, and the Methodists also became a major factor in British religion. The United States and United Kingdom would also become the world's greatest engines of evangelical missions and benevolence. Also, the Great Awakening marked a turning point for African Americans, and for African peoples in the Caribbean, who would become deeply influenced by evangelical Protestantism, especially in the Methodist and Baptist traditions.

The Growth of the African American Church

The hundreds of African-descended converts who became church leaders, evangelists, and missionaries were essential to the spread and growth of black Christian churches. As a general rule, these leaders (such as Rebecca Protten among the Moravians) were more effective at reaching African-background people than European-background evangelists were.

The same rule applied to the evangelization of indigenous people in the Americas. "Native apostles" were on balance more effective recruiters for their faith than were whites who attempted the difficult work of cross-cultural evangelism. Pioneering figures in the spread of evangelical Christianity among blacks were heavily influenced by white evangelists such as Whitefield, but the strongest momentum for the Christianization of African people in North America and the Caribbean came from black missionaries.

African American church leaders such as the Baptist pastor David George were critical to the explosive spread of evangelical religion among the diaspora of African peoples in the broader Atlantic World. George was born into slavery in Virginia in 1742, as the most sensational phase of Whitefield's revivals was starting to wane. George and his siblings suffered the abuse and violence that was endemic to American slavery. His most painful memory was seeing his enslaved mother whipped as she knelt and begged for mercy. George eventually ran away from his Virginia master. He ended up on another slave plantation in Silver Bluff, South Carolina, near the Savannah River and the Georgia border. He was careless about the things of God until a black preacher named Cyrus made him realize his need for forgiveness. Fearing that God would condemn him to hell, George came to realize that only God's grace could save him. George came under the influence of the great black Baptist evangelist and missionary George Liele (1750–1828), as well as "Brother Palmer," presumed to be Wait Palmer, a Baptist pastor from Connecticut. Palmer had also helped bring Shubal Stearns (1706–71), the founder of the Sandy Creek Baptist Church in North Carolina, into the Baptist fold. Palmer baptized David George in a creek, and George became the pastor of the Silver Bluff Baptist Church around 1773. Silver Bluff was the first enduring African American-led congregation in America.

The War for Independence disrupted plantation life in the South. David George's family fled first to British-occupied Savannah, Georgia, and then to Charleston, South Carolina, after the city fell to the British in 1780. Many African Americans aligned with the Loyalist side of the Revolutionary War, especially after British authorities in Virginia offered freedom to any runaway slaves who fought for the British army. George finally evacuated Charleston with the British and made his way to Nova Scotia in 1782. When George settled in Shelburne, Nova Scotia, he began ministering to the refugee black population there, despite harassment from hostile whites. George saw a considerable revival in the little Baptist communities of Nova Scotia, and he worked as a regional itinerant as well as a pastor in Shelburne. He preached to both whites and blacks, noting in one place that a "white sister was converted there . . . she came up afterwards, gave her experience to our church, and was baptized, and two black sisters with her." Baptists were famous and controversial for the way they reserved baptism for people who had already experienced conversion. It was also not unusual for Baptist churches in the Revolutionary era to be mixed-race congregations, in places from Nova Scotia to South Carolina. David George's extraordinary journeys continued in 1792, when he and much of his congregation relocated to Freetown, Sierra Leone. George became one of the most influential religious leaders in West Africa until his death in 1810.

George Whitefield in Scotland

A half century before David George went to Sierra Leone, George Whitefield finished his most astounding work in America, although he would come back five more times before his death in Massachusetts in 1770. In the early 1740s, Whitefield turned his attention to Scotland, the stronghold of Presbyterianism and the established "Kirk," or Church of Scotland. The revivalist enjoyed much support from established Scottish ministers, although he had to negotiate relations with secessionist Presbyterians who were open to revival but vociferously opposed the Kirk. Scotland and Northern Ireland had deep revival traditions that went back at least to the early 1600s. Scots and Scots-Irish people had become familiar with what the poet Robert Burns called "Holy Fairs," or large outdoor celebrations of the Lord's Supper. These events often became both large community gatherings and intense scenes of revival. The epicenter of the summer 1742 revival in Scotland was a weekend communion celebration at Cambuslang, which drew as many as twenty thousand people to the small parish outside Glasgow. Only a fraction of the vast assembly was admitted to the communion tables, however. Those who gave convincing evidence of conversion received communion tokens, which served as their means of admission to the Lord's Supper.

After the Cambuslang communion service, the whole assembly moved to a natural outdoor amphitheater where Whitefield preached one of his standard sermons on Isa 54:5, "Thy Maker is thy husband; the Lord of hosts is his name." He proclaimed the hope of a believer's union with Christ, which he compared to the intimacy of marital love. Cambuslang's local minister recorded more than 100 conversion testimonies emerging from the Cambuslang "Wark." A number of them mentioned the sermon on "Thy Maker is thy husband" as the most memorable moment of the revival. One woman in her late twenties, Margaret Lap, had heard Whitefield preach before, but "Thy Maker is thy husband" made the biggest impact on her, and she couldn't get it off her mind. Her conversion travail took

Image 11.1. *Communion Token* (1843)

months to get through, but it concluded one weekday morning when she woke up to the words of the sermon surging into her mind. She became overwrought with love for Christ and was convinced that God had made Christ her spiritual husband.

Organizing Revival

Many of Whitefield's converts had their lives changed forever, and they were integrated as full members into congregations. Others fell away after their burst of initial fervor. Whitefield was always an evangelist first, and the lasting results of his revival work are comparatively hard to document with precision. He often made little organized effort to "follow up" on converts. The greatest innovator of the era with regard to evangelical organization was undoubtedly John Wesley. Methodism began as a Pietist reform movement within the Church of England, but it would become a distinct global denomination, separate from the Anglican Church. Wesley functionally broke with the Church of England with great reluctance in the mid-1780s. By the early 1740s, however, he was already consolidating his followers into a Methodist network that would form the basis for the new denomination. Because Wesley and his lieutenants were far better organizers than the Calvinistic Methodists like Whitefield and Howell Harris, "Methodist" would become inextricably tied to Wesley, his brilliant organizational system, and his staunch Arminian theology. Wales was an exceptional context theologically, where Methodist usually continued to mean "Calvinist" and Whitefieldian.

Like so many Christian reformers of the 1700s, Wesley's organizational model was inspired by Philipp Spener's *collegia pietatis*, or devotional small groups. While he wanted Methodists to keep attending their Anglican parish, Wesley also urged them to be members of Methodist societies for prayer and spiritual accountability, called "classes." Methodist classes were more like house churches than a modern concept of "classes" would suggest. Class leaders, both men and women, offered discipleship and pastoral counsel to members. "Bands" were small groups divided by sex, marital status, and age. By 1744, John and Charles Wesley met with other Methodist leaders for what the movement regards as the first annual conference in England. Although John would not readily admit it, the Methodists were starting to act like a separatist faction within the Anglican Church. Under Wesley's guidance, the Methodists insisted that their leaders affirm the classic Reformation doctrine of salvation by faith alone. On the issue that caused Wesley's great break from Whitefield, however, they proclaimed a general atonement for all sinners. The Savior who "died for all, hath died for me!" as one of the Wesleys' hymns put it. "Loving to every man Thou art . . . God is not hate, but God is love!" By such assertions the Wesleys made clear that a belief in Christ's death for all people, and not just for the predestined elect, would be a signature of Methodist faith.

Divisive Revival

As the Great Awakening entered the early 1740s, views of the revivals began to fall into three main camps. Older histories of the Awakening saw just two camps, the "Old Lights" and the "New Lights," the former opposing the revivals, and the latter supporting them. But the actual responses were more complex. They ranged from vociferous opposition, to cautious support, to uncritical zeal for the revivals. These groups were antirevivalists, moderate evangelicals, and radical evangelicals. Antirevivalists opposed the revivals because they saw them as a threat to the established order of the churches and to the prestige of long-serving ministers. Or they might squirm at the evangelicals' talk about the discernible work of the Holy Spirit. Or they might reject the evangelical understanding of the new birth. Some antirevivalist paedobaptists believed that the new birth happened when an infant was baptized. In works such as *Seasonable Thoughts on the State of Religion in New-England* (1743), Boston's arch-antirevivalist (and a future proponent of universal salvation) Charles Chauncy (1705–87) highlighted the most extreme behavior of the radical revivalists. He tarred the whole evangelical movement as fractious spiritual frenzy.

One of the problems with the catchall term "New Lights" is that the moderate and radical evangelicals fought against each other as ferociously as did the antirevivalists and their evangelical opponents. Moderate evangelicals were pleased with the revivals, but they were worried about the awakeners' excesses, such as questioning the salvation of established ministers. They also retained a firmly hierarchical view of church life and did not relish the wild scenes in some revivals where "exhorters," including women, African Americans, children, and uneducated men, testified to the work of God in their lives. The moderates adopted views that would become known as "cessationism," or the idea that the miraculous signs and wonders of the New Testament had ceased sometime around the final codification of the canon of Scripture. Radicals, however, were eager to promote ecstatic phenomena such as revelatory dreams, visions, and healings. Some like Whitefield depended on such charismatic experiences in early ministry, but curtailed the focus on them later when he became chastened by criticism, even by moderate evangelicals.

Jonathan Edwards, too, would become more moderate over time. His 1741 "Sinners in the Hands of an Angry God" sermon in Enfield, Connecticut, produced a frenzied reaction from the audience that seemed like the epitome of "enthusiasm." But Edwards also offered the most sophisticated evangelical analysis of how to test revival phenomena. In 1741, Edwards delivered the commencement address at Yale College, his alma mater, and spoke to the intense controversy over the revivals that had engulfed the school and much of New England. This address became his publication *Distinguishing Marks of a Work of the Spirit of God* (1741). This, along with Edwards's other revival writings, became an indispensable guide for evangelicals seeking authentic revival. Edwards posited that people put too much focus on the ecstatic phenomena in order to validate, or condemn, the revivals. He reserved judgement on the more extreme manifestations of revival, however, and focused on testing the lasting fruit of the awakenings. The mere fact that a revival had "unusual and extraordinary" effects could not determine, one way or the other, whether it was a true work of the Spirit. In the longer term, believers should consider if the revival

> That extraordinary influence that has lately appeared on the minds of people abroad in this land, causing in them an uncommon concern and engagedness of mind about the things of religion, is undoubtedly, in the general, from the Spirit of God.
>
> ---
>
> Jonathan Edwards, *The Distinguishing Marks of a Work of the Spirit of God*, 1741

raised the "esteem" of Jesus, operated against "Satan's kingdom," brought about "greater regard to the Holy Scriptures," and enhanced "love to God and man." If a revival produced such fruits, then the revival was a work of the Spirit, whether its original manifestation was quiet and sober or edgy and emotional. As of 1741, Edwards was confident that the bulk of the Great Awakening qualified as a legitimate work of God. Backsliding in his own church would make him question that confidence by the mid-1740s, however.

Edwards and other moderate evangelicals were also concerned by the wave of church separations and illicit congregations that came out of the Great Awakening. The radical movement never took coherent form as an alternative denomination. For a time, however, New England saw the formation of dozens of independent congregations devoted to promoting true revival. These Separate congregations might come out of churches with an antirevivalist pastor, or even one with a moderate evangelical pastor, if he tried to clamp down on extreme revival phenomena. For instance, some clergy refused to allow radical itinerant preachers to speak at their church. One of the most notorious of the itinerants was James Davenport (1716–57), a Yale graduate from Long Island, who denounced unconverted ministers by name and who led crowds of poor whites, African Americans, and Native Americans singing through the streets of New England towns. When New England colonies began passing anti-itinerant laws in the early 1740s, they were often designed with Davenport in mind. Davenport eventually flamed out—literally—when he held a book- and clothes-burning in New London, Connecticut in 1743, at which he contributed his own pants to the fire. Even his most devoted followers concluded that Davenport's zeal had turned into foolish chaos. He began working to salvage his pastoral career, explaining that he had been under a delirium-inducing fever at New London.

The Separate congregations were beleaguered, since it was technically illegal to start a new church without the approval of establishment authorities in Massachusetts or Connecticut. Separatists and early Baptists such as John Smyth had faced this same problem a century earlier in England. The spirit of the Reformation often fostered church separations, but even most Protestant authorities disdained to allow any Christian group to start new congregations. Yet the spate of church separations in the Great Awakening fueled a new campaign for full religious liberty. This campaign for religious freedom was the most significant political movement to emerge directly from the revivals. Following principles articulated earlier by figures such as Roger Williams, the radical evangelicals contended that the government should not meddle in the affairs of the church. Civil government should not play favorites in matters of doctrine or denomination. True believers, they argued, should be allowed to preach the gospel freely in their own churches, with no fear of persecution from the government. They were fighting against centuries of establishmentarian precedent, however, so the Separates did not find a welcoming response.

Baptists in America

Most Separates started new congregations or house churches simply in the name of gospel purity. Yet some of these radical evangelicals began to evaluate other aspects of their faith and practice, aside from just proclamation of the gospel. The existing Baptist churches of the colonies tended to be small, and were often resistant to the revivals. Some Baptist churches, like Philadelphia's First Baptist, were split so badly by the Great Awakening that not even the church's pastors could agree on how to respond. Most significantly for the future of the Baptist movement, however, some of the Separates who came out of paedobaptist churches began to reconsider the practice of baptism. Some of them concluded that baptizing infants was a root of many troubles in churches. Separate Baptists saw no clear instances of infant baptism in the Bible. Baptizing infants also introduced those children into a quasi-membership status, a status that had no connection to conversion. This meant that most churches had people who considered themselves to be part of a church but were unregenerate. The Separates insisted that God intended church membership only for converted believers and touted the ideal of a regenerate and (then) baptized church membership. The new Separate Baptists typically had originated by separating from an established church, but then they went a step further than other Separates. They became convinced that church membership was only for converted believers who received baptism after their conversion. Baptism was a public sign of the inward work of the Spirit.

The Separates revolutionized the Baptist movement in America, which by the 1760s had been commandeered by radical evangelicals emerging from the Great Awakening. Some of the pre-existing Baptist churches, especially General Baptists who embraced Arminian theology, dwindled dramatically in the mid-1700s. Calvinist Baptists such as David George became the wave of the Baptist future. One of the most influential of the early Baptist converts was Isaac Backus (1724–1806). Backus came from a respected farming family in Norwich, Connecticut. In 1741, not long after Edwards delivered the "Sinners in the Hands of an Angry God" sermon in Enfield, Backus was converted "while mowing alone in the fields." The Spirit overcame him and enabled him to "see the perfect righteousness of Christ and the freeness and riches of His grace." The pastor at Norwich, Benjamin Lord

(1694–1784), was a moderate evangelical, but Backus and his mother (also recently converted) became concerned that the Norwich church had members who gave no clear indication of regeneration. Lord also became increasingly hostile toward the itinerant preachers, such as Davenport, whom the radicals were constantly inviting to speak before church assemblies. Like many of the radical evangelicals, Backus and his allies started meeting in a Separate assembly committed to revival and the work of the Spirit, as they saw it. Unlike some ephemeral Separate meetings, Backus's church built a meetinghouse. Within a decade it was challenging Lord's Congregationalist fellowship as the most popular church in town.

Backus himself began preaching to Separate assemblies in the mid-1740s. He itinerated through southeastern New England before settling at a new Separate church in Middleborough, Massachusetts, in 1748. His church members immediately ran afoul of established church officials, who demanded that they pay tithes to support the Congregationalist church in town, which they of course did not attend. Backus was threatened with jail time, and other members had property confiscated. At least one woman in his church spent more than a year in jail for refusing to pay the religious tax. Back in Norwich, his mother and brother likewise spent time in prison for tax evasion. Such personal experience with persecution made Backus and other Separates and Baptists inveterate enemies of religious establishments and fearless advocates for church-state separation.

Opposing the established churches of New England was a relatively easy decision, compared to Backus's struggle over the proper mode of baptism. As we have seen, there was little disagreement among Protestants, Catholics, and Orthodox churches that the children of Christian parents were proper subjects for baptism. Those Christian churches would baptize adults, too, but only if they had not been baptized as an infant. This was common when indigenous people in the Americas, or enslaved people of African background, joined Christian churches. But for people of European background, infant baptism was standard practice. Continental "Anabaptists" had begun to question this view of baptism during the sixteenth-century Reformation. Backus and other paedobaptist Separates were challenged to consider whether infant baptism was really scriptural by new Baptists emerging from the radical evangelical movement. Certain members of Backus's congregation urged him to study the subject to discern whether infant baptism was warranted. He began to suspect that infant baptism was a holdover from the pre-Reformation Catholic Church. Backus himself received "believer's baptism" by immersion in 1751. For several years, he tried to keep his church together as a mixed Baptist and paedobaptist congregation, but it did not work. Finally in 1756 he became the pastor of the First Baptist Church of Middleborough. For the rest of the eighteenth century, Backus would be the most influential Baptist leader in New England and one of America's most persuasive advocates for religious liberty.

Longtime Baptist organizations in America, such as the Philadelphia Baptist Association (founded 1707), maintained an important organizational and doctrinal role for Baptists. Virtually all Baptists in America after the First Great Awakening were moderate or strict Calvinists. Indeed, the vast majority of the American revivalists in the Great Awakening were Calvinists, too, until Wesleyan Methodists became a more conspicuous presence in the US after the American Revolution. But Separate Baptists like Backus permanently changed the Baptist landscape. Their aggressive evangelism brought the Baptist tradition powerfully into the South starting in the mid-1700s. The South in the colonial era was widely regarded as the least religious part of British Protestant America. The decades following Great Awakening started to change that image, and the South began a long journey to becoming America's Bible Belt, with high rates of religious affiliation among both whites and blacks by the time of the Civil War.

The most influential figure for introducing the Baptist faith in the backcountry South was Shubal Stearns, also of Connecticut. Stearns's religious pilgrimage was quite similar to Isaac Backus's. Stearns experienced conversion, joined a Separate congregation, and then adopted Baptist convictions at almost exactly the same time as Backus, through the influence of the Separate Baptist minister Wait Palmer. While Backus remained in New England, Stearns went to the South. With other Separate Baptist missionaries, Stearns founded the Sandy Creek Baptist Church in North Carolina in 1755, as well as the Sandy Creek Baptist Association in 1758. Stearns and Sandy Creek would preside over a massive expansion of the Separate Baptist movement across the Carolinas, Georgia, and Virginia. They were aggressive proselytizers and rigorous biblicists. Like the Puritans before them, they sought to create congregations based strictly on a New Testament model, though they would have disagreed with the Puritans about the correct mode of baptism. In addition to practicing believer's baptism, the Separate Baptists observed the Lord's Supper weekly. Like Moravians and Methodists, they held love feasts. They also practiced other rituals such as feet washing, a practice noted in the New Testament but rarely observed except by sectarian groups. The Separate Baptists had elders and deacons, and some had women serving as deaconesses, and even some eldresses, who exercised pastoral oversight for women in a congregation. Over time it became more common for Baptist churches to have just one elder, instead of multiple elders, and to call that one elder a "pastor." In the US antebellum period, Primitive Baptist churches—strict Calvinist descendants of the Separate Baptists—maintained the name "elder" for pastors, however, as in "Elder Shubal Stearns."

As seen in David George's conversion and the establishment of the Silver Bluff Church, evangelicals in the era of the Great Awakening began to make inroads among the African American and Afro-Caribbean populations. The Moravians led this initiative, bolstered by figures such as Rebecca Protten. The Moravians especially focused on the Danish colonial Virgin Islands, where they baptized more than 10,000 people in the second half of the eighteenth century. Moravians also established mission stations on the north coast of South America, in modern-day Guyana and Suriname. They made converts in British Caribbean colonies, including the lucrative, slave-worked sugar island of Jamaica, where they founded a station in 1754. British colonial Antigua became the primary center of Moravian evangelism outside of the Danish islands, however, with some three thousand blacks baptized there by Moravian missionaries as of the mid-1780s. Given the strength of Moravian and Methodist evangelism on the island as of 1800, one might regard Antigua at that time as the greatest stronghold of Afro-Protestantism in the western hemisphere.

Baptist Revival and Growth among African Americans

In mainland British North America, we have seen how figures such as George Whitefield and Jonathan Edwards included African-background people in their revival work, but their outreach was rendered problematic by owning enslaved people themselves. White evangelicals in the South, such as the Virginia Presbyterian minister Samuel Davies (1723–61), likewise had a conflicted relationship with enslaved people. Davies, like Edwards, owned small numbers of slaves, even as he wrote effusively about the devotion of enslaved converts. Davies eagerly let enslaved people hold worship meetings at his house, and he wrote that "sometimes, when I have awaked about two or three a-clock in the morning, a torrent of sacred harmony poured into my chamber." Some of the slaves stayed all night at his house, presumably in part because they would have to work all day in the fields and had no spare time for worship meetings. Davies also happily admitted dozens of slaves to full church membership and to the Lord's Supper. But this egalitarian bent in the church did not, to figures such as Davies, change the social or legal standing for enslaved people, including the people he owned.

Still, the evangelical message was beginning to spread among African people in America and the Caribbean. Once African American and Afro-Caribbean figures such as

David George and Rebecca Protten became pastors and evangelists, the trickle of African-background converts started to become a flood. As we have seen, the former slave and Baptist evangelist George Liele was instrumental in David George's conversion. Liele also became the pastor at an African American church outside of British-occupied Savannah, Georgia, in 1778. At the end of the American Revolution, Liele left the mainland South and went to Jamaica. In 1784 he began pastoring a church in Kingston and was especially successful at reaching poor and enslaved Jamaicans. His church was also the first non-Anglican chapel built in Jamaica. Liele received no salary as a pastor, but he reported that "I preach, baptize, administer the Lord's Supper, and travel from one place to another to [proclaim] the gospel, and to settle church affairs, all freely." He faced harassment and persecution from whites, who feared slave rebellion in a colony where the population was overwhelmingly black and enslaved. Jamaica would face constant rumored and actual slave rebellions throughout the colonial era, culminating in an uprising known as the "Baptist War" in 1831–32. In the meantime, Liele baptized some four hundred converts in the first seven years of his church work in Kingston. Liele also faced internal theological controversies, such as a group within the church which claimed to be speaking in tongues. Liele regarded their claimed experiences as ludicrous, and the tongues-speakers left the church.

Liele published a Baptist (or "Anabaptist") church covenant, derived from a similar document he brought from Georgia. It affirmed believer's baptism by immersion in a "river, or a place where there is much water, in the name of the Father, the Son and of the Holy Ghost." The Jamaican Baptists also practiced the washing of feet, as well as prayers and anointing with oil for the sick. Although the Baptist church in Jamaica would become a refuge for many enslaved people, and sometimes a center of slave resistance, Liele's covenant included provisions designed to put slave masters' minds at ease. No slave could join the church, it said, without a letter of approval from his or her master. Slaves were also singled out for exhortations of obedience to masters, in accordance with the New Testament's household regulations.

Baptist congregations operated as autonomous entities and maximized their evangelistic flexibility. They multiplied rapidly in Jamaica. Moses Baker, a free African American from New York, was no devoted Christian when he first arrived in Jamaica. He had evacuated the North American mainland with the British in 1783. (The end of the Revolutionary War was a key moment in the spread of African American evangelical faith around the Atlantic World.) But Baker's wife Susannah and then Moses himself, experienced conversion, and Baker received baptism from Liele. A Quaker slaveowner paid Baker to serve as an evangelist and pastor among the slaves on his Jamaica plantation. His church quickly grew to some 1400 baptized members by the early 1800s and thousands more who were not members but who listened to Baker's preaching. Jamaica authorities grew nervous about the rapid growth of the Baptist churches and had Liele and Baker jailed for sedition, but they were acquitted.

Whitefield's Final Years

Such patterns of evangelical growth continued well after the First Great Awakening and through the beginning of the Second Great Awakening in the early 1800s. Both awakenings were punctuated by moments of incredible fervor and growth, such as New England in 1740, Scotland in 1742, or the camp meeting revivals in Kentucky and Tennessee in the early 1800s. But evangelicals had also developed clear patterns for conversions, revivals, and outpourings of the Holy Spirit that shaped their global movement from the 1730s forward.

After 1742, the focus of Whitefield and other key evangelical leaders turned somewhat toward politics and imperial affairs, or what we would call "civil religion." Whitefield offered pastoral assistance to a British colonial expedition against the French fortress at Louisbourg on the Canadian coast in 1745. Even antirevivalists cheered him for doing so. In 1746, Whitefield preached *Britain's Mercies, and Britain's Duty* in Philadelphia, celebrating the recent British defeat of Jacobite rebels in Scotland. The Jacobites would have placed the Stuart Pretender, Bonnie Prince Charlie, on the British throne. The Jacobite cause was rooted in resentment over the removal of the Catholic King James II in the Glorious Revolution in 1688–89. Many British leaders viewed Jacobitism as a grave threat to the nation's commitment to Protestant faith. *Britain's Mercies* allowed Whitefield to present himself as a loyal British Protestant, after enduring years of accusations that he was a disloyal fanatic. *Britain's Mercies* became one of his best-selling sermons ever. One observer noted that the sermon showed the revivalist was "as sound and zealous a Protestant, as truly loyal a subject, as now he is a grand and masterly orator." Was Whitefield becoming as much of a political British patriot as an evangelical revivalist?

Perhaps he was, but Whitefield also kept crossing the Atlantic and preaching the gospel of the new birth wherever he went. His preaching remained deeply affecting through the end of his life. Among his final converts was the African American musician John Marrant (1755–91) of Charleston, South Carolina. Sometime in 1769 or '70, Marrant took a dare from a friend and tried to interrupt a packed Whitefield meeting by blowing his French horn.

Instead, Whitefield looked Marrant straight in the eye and named his text, "PREPARE TO MEET THY GOD, O ISRAEL" (Amos 4:12 KJV). The power of the word physically felled Marrant, who passed out for thirty minutes. Whitefield counseled Marrant after he woke up, telling him that "Jesus Christ has got thee at last."

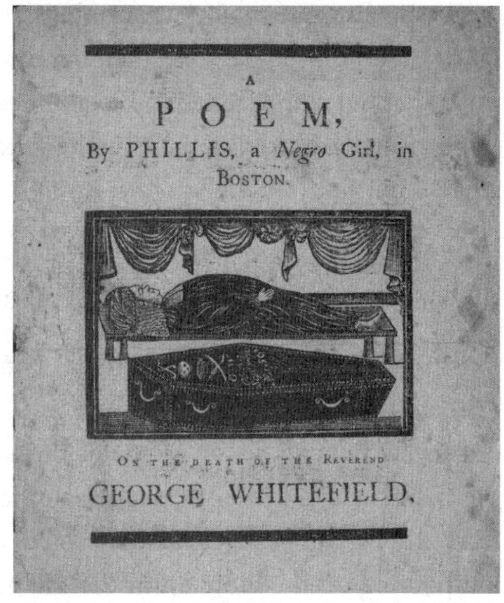

Image 11.2. *Phillis Wheatley elegy* (1770)

Marrant went on to become an ordained minister in the Methodist "Connexion" sponsored by Selina Hastings, the Countess of Huntingdon. (She was Whitefield's leading patron.) Marrant ministered in Nova Scotia around the same time as David George, bolstering the colony as an evangelical stronghold, especially for African American refugees. The Countess similarly sent a black missionary named David Margrett to preach to enslaved people in South Carolina and Georgia in 1774 after he studied at the Countess's theological college in Wales. Margrett's background is obscure, but he was likely a fugitive slave from somewhere in Britain's colonies. In America, Margrett indiscreetly denounced slavery in his preaching and had to flee the colonies. The Countess was likely chagrined by this development because she shared Whitefield's accommodating views on slavery. She inherited the enslaved people who worked at Whitefield's Bethesda Orphanage in Georgia when he died.

Whitefield passed away in 1770 in Newburyport, Massachusetts. John Wesley preached at a memorial service for him in London, as they had tentatively restored their friendship in the 1760s. Perhaps the most celebrated elegy for Whitefield, however, was penned in Boston by the enslaved teenager Phillis Wheatley (1753–84), the first published African American woman. Wheatley would make pointed comments later about the injustice of American slavery, but in this poem she extolled Whitefield and the gospel he preached.

> Thou didst, in strains of eloquence refin'd,
> Inflame the soul, and captivate the mind.
> Unhappy we, the setting sun deplore!
> Which once was splendid, but shines no more . . .

Regarding Christ and people of African descent, she wrote,

> Take him, ye Africans, he longs for you;
> Impartial Savior, is his title due;
> If you will choose to walk in grace's road,
> You shall be sons, and kings, and priests to God.

In an alternative version of the poem, that final line read, "He'll make you free, and kings, and priests to God." But evangelicals—and Protestants generally—were just beginning their decades-long struggle over the morality of slavery itself. The connection between evangelical belief and freedom for slaves would be hotly and violently disputed.

Selected Bibliography

Brooks, Joanna, and John Saillant, eds. *"Face Zion Forward": First Writers of the Black Atlantic, 1785–1798*. Boston: Northeastern University Press, 2002.

Carretta, Vincent. *Phillis Wheatley: Biography of a Genius in Bondage*. Athens: University of Georgia Press, 2011.

Catherall, Gordon A. "British Baptist Involvement in Jamaica, 1783–1865." PhD Thesis, University of Keele, UK, 1970.

Catron, John W. *Embracing Protestantism: Black Identities in the Atlantic World*. Gainesville: University Press of Florida, 2016.

Cox, Francis A. *History of the Baptist Missionary Society, 1792–1842*. 2 vols. London, 1842.

Dayfoot, Arthur Charles. *The Shaping of the West Indian Church, 1492–1962*. Kingston, Jamaica: University of the West Indies Press, 1999.

Frey, Sylvia R., and Betty Wood. *Come Shouting to Zion: African American Protestantism in the American South and British Caribbean to 1830*. Chapel Hill: University of North Carolina Press, 1998.

Kidd, Thomas S. and Barry Hankins. *Baptists in America: A History*. New York: Oxford University Press, 2015.

Lockley, Tim. "David Margrett: A Black Missionary in the Revolutionary Atlantic." *Journal of American Studies* 46, no. 3 (Aug 2012): 729–45.

Marsden, George. *Jonathan Edwards: A Life*. New Haven, CT: Yale University Press, 2003.

McLoughlin, William G., ed. *Isaac Backus on Church, State, and Calvinism*. Cambridge: Harvard University Press, 1968.

Sanneh, Lamin. *Abolitionists Abroad: American Blacks and the Making of Modern West Africa.* Cambridge: Harvard University Press, 1999.

Sparks, Elder John. *The Roots of Appalachian Christianity: The Life and Legacy of Elder Shubal Stearns.* Lexington: University Press of Kentucky, 2001.

Winiarski, Douglas L. "Jonathan Edwards, Enthusiast? Radical Revivalism and the Great Awakening in the Connecticut Valley." *Church History* 74, no. 4 (2005): 683–739.

Chapter 12

Faith and the Age of Revolutions

The decades from the 1770s to the 1790s have become known as the Age of Revolutions. The successive convulsions of the American and French revolutions triggered a host of political and intellectual changes that ushered the West from the early modern to the modern period of history. The Age of Revolutions had cascading effects across the world, in events such as the Haitian Revolution (1791–1804) and a series of independence movements in Latin America, weakening the power of European empires in the western hemisphere. But the Age of Revolutions, with its signature emphasis on liberty, also fostered a new era of religious skepticism, liberal philosophy, and higher criticism of the Bible. Traditional Christians committed to the great tradition of the church were ready to respond to those challenges, however.

George Whitefield's death in 1770 raises a counterfactual: If he had lived, would he have supported the patriot side in the American Revolution? Perhaps not. Whitefield was British, and spent most of his life in England, even though he was constantly traveling through and across the British empire and the North Atlantic world. He retained his Anglican ministerial credentials, and the Church of England was one of the key organizations that gave cohesion to the empire. But he was friends with Ben Franklin and had supported Franklin's early patriot advocacy against the Stamp Act. Indeed, patriot leaders attempted to enlist Whitefield's memory in one of the early campaigns of the war. Continental Army soldiers, including the future traitor Benedict Arnold, stopped in 1775 at Newburyport, Massachusetts, as they were heading north on a campaign into Quebec. After a Sunday service at First Presbyterian Church, the officers descended into the crypt, which held Whitefield's remains. Opening his tomb, they took some of the revivalist's clerical vestments, snipped them into pieces, and handed them out among the soldiers. As far as we know, none of the officers ever explained what this apparent relic-taking signified. It seemed strange for Protestants to take such an action as saints' relics were associated with Catholic devotion. In any case, Arnold and the other officers appeared to be suggesting that their cause was the same as Whitefield's: the cause of Christ and of liberty.

American Christians are familiar with their nation's tendency to sacralize the American founding. Many Americans have embraced a national civil religion, or civil spirituality, which sometimes blends in uncomfortable ways with traditional Christian belief. In modern America, many evangelical Christians have become the most ardent devotees of such civil religion. Anglo-American evangelicals in the 1770s were more ambivalent about the American Revolution than many are today, however. Some evangelical pastors in America were firm advocates of independence. British-based evangelicals such as John Wesley were adamantly opposed to it. Wesley's bestselling *A Calm Address to Our American Colonies* (1775) offered little sympathy for the colonists' grievances. The tract was so reviled in the colonies that the controversy virtually stopped Wesleyan Methodist growth in America for a decade. The small number of Native American evangelicals, such as the Mohegan pastor Samson Occom (1723–92), tended to advise wartime neutrality to other Native Americans, believing (correctly) that little good would emerge from the war for Indian peoples. African American evangelical leaders such as South Carolina's David George tended to align with the British in the Revolution, believing that the British were more open to freedom for enslaved people than were the American patriots.

Still, the majority of politically-active white American evangelicals supported the Revolution, including influential pastors such as Oliver Hart (1723–95) of First Baptist Church, Charleston, South Carolina, the Philadelphia Presbyterian pastor and Continental Congress chaplain George Duffield (1732–90), and many Congregationalist pastors in New England, such as Ammi Robbins (1740–1813), minister in Norfolk, Connecticut, and chaplain to a Continental Army regiment. The army chaplains during the war were disproportionately evangelical, too. They explained that biblical injunctions to obey and honor the king (Romans 13, 1 Peter 2) were not absolute prohibitions on resistance or even rebellion. Christian patriots pointed to instances in Scripture when godly people refused to obey unjust commands by rulers. Evangelicals may have gotten used to resistance against government authorities during conflicts generated by the Great Awakening. Leaders of the established churches in America, including the Anglican Church, were often hostile toward the revivalists. Separate and Baptist churches in particular had plenty of experience at resisting government, or at least government-backed religious authorities. Some historians have even posited that the Great Awakening was so rooted in popular resistance that it became a sort of test run for the Revolution itself.

This is an intriguing thesis. The Great Awakening surely played some kind of preparatory role for the Revolution. Most historians of the late colonial era see the Great Awakening as one of the greatest social and cultural upheavals of the entire period. It gave many evangelical Americans their first taste of resisting official authorities, including the state-backed established church pastors who did not support the revivals. All this happened just three decades before the Revolution. But we shouldn't push the connection too far. The Revolution was most obviously caused by friction over imperial administration and tax policy in the colonies. Moreover, the most visible American patriot leaders were not evangelicals, nor were most of them profoundly influenced by the revivals. Some notable patriot leaders, such as Samuel Adams and Patrick Henry (1736–99), did have deep evangelical backgrounds. Others like Ben Franklin, Thomas Jefferson, and Thomas Paine (author of *Common Sense*) had skeptical views of Christianity. Such leaders were still adept at using theological rhetoric, and sometimes the Bible itself, to persuade Americans to support independence. Franklin and Whitefield had a sincere but "mere civil friendship," as Franklin called it. Franklin consistently rebuffed Whitefield's overtures for him to put his faith in Christ, however.

Still, there were religious dynamics everywhere in the patriots' invocations of the "sacred cause of liberty." In certain episodes, religion did play a causal role in crises leading to American independence. Most notably, the British caused widespread fury in 1774 when they granted the Roman Catholics of Quebec (which Britain recently conquered from the French in the Seven Years' War) their freedom of religion. For the British administration, this was a pragmatic way to keep Quebec stable. To the colonists, the Quebec Act seemed like an endorsement of the still-loathed Catholic Church, and perhaps even evidence of a Catholic conspiracy unfolding in the British administration. The Continental Congress, which was starting to function as an American national legislature, was astonished that British Parliament had endorsed "a religion that has deluged your island in blood and dispersed impiety, bigotry, persecution, murder and rebellion through every part of the world."

Fear of Catholic power remained fresh, as the great struggle of Britain against France and Spain in the Seven Years' War had only concluded in the 1760s.

Some American evangelicals were willing to support the American cause, but they called for political and moral reforms to accompany independence. Some evangelicals, especially in the North, insisted that God would never bless the Americans' fight against British oppression so long as Americans defended slave owning. Also, evangelicals who had suffered under religious persecution by the established churches were not keen to endorse the rebellion, unless they had reasonable confidence that the harassment of dissenters would stop. Isaac Backus spoke for many when he asked in 1773, "how can any reasonably expect that HE who has the hearts of kings in his hand, will turn the heart of our earthly sovereign to hear the pleas for liberty, of those who will not hear the cries of their fellow-subjects, under their oppressions." In Virginia, such appeals went a long way toward securing equal treatment for Christian denominations. In 1786, the Virginia legislature adopted Jefferson's Bill for Establishing Religious Freedom, which ended the Anglican establishment there. In New England, the struggle for religious liberty lasted longer, and Massachusetts would not give up its established church until 1833.

Overall, the leaders of the American Revolution were friendly to traditional religious beliefs, even if they were not themselves committed Christians. Paine would become the most controversial anti-Christian polemicist in America in the 1790s. Yet in 1776 he used an analysis of 1 Samuel 8 (God's warnings to the Israelites about a king) in a key section of his wildly popular *Common Sense*. This was the tract that clinched the American argument for independence. Arguably the most famous speech of the Revolution, Patrick Henry's "Liberty or Death" oration, was liberally peppered with citations from the Bible, especially the prophet Jeremiah. When Jefferson and Franklin were commissioned to design a national seal for the new United States, they both wanted (but did not get) an image of the Israelites crossing the Red Sea in Exodus. Jefferson's Declaration of Independence, which many Americans have revered as a kind of quasi-scripture, used robust theological (though not specifically Christian) language in its proposition that rights come from God, making those rights sacred and unalienable. Conversely, the US Constitution of 1787 stands out for its relative silence about God or theological claims. The First Amendment's prohibition on a national "establishment of religion," and its guarantee of "free exercise of religion," were welcome developments for American skeptics and dissenting evangelicals alike.

Religion and the French Revolution

The French Revolution seems more a product of the secular, radical Enlightenment than the American Revolution. Especially in its extreme phases, the French Revolution was fanatically anticlerical and anti-Christian. But there were powerful Christian sources behind the Revolution, as well. Among the most frequent challengers to the French tradition of the divine right of kings were Jansenist Catholics, who battled regularly with the Vatican and French church officials over their freedom to criticize the established church's corruption. The Jansenist tradition fueled a belief in balanced power between king and the legislature. Jansenists also drew on a Protestant/Huguenot tradition from the Reformation era known as the "monarchomachs" (those who fight against the king). These included figures such as Calvin's successor Theodore Beza, who argued that kings had a contractual obligation to rule justly, or they forfeited the right to rule. The monarchomachs provided critical ideological background to the Glorious Revolution in England in 1688, as well as France's Revolution. The French Jansenist and jurist Gabriel-Nicolas Maultrot (1714–1803) published his three-volume *Origin and Just Limits of the Temporal Power* (1789) to counter the theory of the divine right of kings. Like the American patriots, Maultrot reasoned that Christians only had to obey kings who ruled justly. Prohibitions on resistance, like that in Romans 13, could never be absolute.

Jansenist criticism of Louis XVI and his pro-monarchical church authorities helped to undermine support for the French king and church. They made the crown's claims to divine authority seem more opportunistic than sacred. The French government was in deep financial distress, and the king seemed incapable of responding to the crisis. The storming of the Bastille, a symbol of French monarchical authority, and the creation of the French National Assembly signaled the beginning of the end of France's *ancien régime*, along with its feudal nobles and autocratic kingly rule. In August 1789, the Assembly issued the "Declaration of the Rights of Man," one of the most representative statements of Enlightenment thought ever. Although it referenced God as the "Supreme Being," the document chiefly focused, as its name suggests, on the "sacred rights of man." Liberty, it explained, "consists in the freedom to do everything which injures no one else." The document gave little attention to moral duties that liberty required.

The National Assembly wished to reform the French Catholic Church, but their plans turned radical when they proposed that the people should elect France's bishops and that even Protestants and Jews should participate in the church elections. Church lands were seized, and the pope was no longer permitted to meddle in affairs of the French church. (The pope condemned this move.) "The Civil Constitution of the Clergy," adopted in 1790, asserted that "No church or parish of France nor any French citizen may acknowledge . . . the authority of an ordinary bishop or of an archbishop whose see [governing authority] shall be under the supremacy of a foreign power." The Assembly required French priests to swear to abide by the Civil Constitution. Remarkably, about half of the French Catholic clergy agreed to do so. The other half did not, and dissident clergy began to be portrayed as enemies of the Assembly and of the French people. King Louis XVI, a committed Catholic, resisted the Civil Constitution as well, which accelerated his downfall.

By 1792 France descended into war and radical anticlerical extremism. The scale and murderous anti-Christian chaos of the Reign of Terror would have few parallels until the twentieth century's communist regimes in Russia, China, and Eastern Europe. Believing it had a right to enforce the revolution against the enemies of the French people, the Assembly

Image 12.1. *Execution of Louis XVI* (1793)

began mass executions by guillotine of aristocrats and priests. The king and queen and most of the French royal family fell victim to the guillotine's blade in 1793. The Assembly (now the National Convention) closed all Catholic churches that did not have a priest who swore to uphold the Civil Constitution. The harsh French policies precipitated unrest, including revolts in the Vendée region and in the city of Nantes, both in western France. Revolutionary authorities sent tens of thousands of soldiers to suppress the revolts. They began a genocidal crusade against the people of western France. Drowning became the preferred method of execution there, beginning with priests who objected to the Civil Constitution. Thousands of French people, including women, children, and the elderly, were drowned or killed by whatever lurid means the executioners could devise. Perhaps one-seventh of the whole Vendéen population was exterminated in the murderous campaign.

The targeting of the priests was animated by the Jacobins' (French radicals) and French philosophes' hostility toward institutional Christianity. Decades before the Revolution, the atheist Denis Diderot had written of wanting to use the "guts of the priest to strangle kings." Although philosophes such as Diderot and Voltaire had already passed away, their virulent anti-Christian writings had prepared the way for the guillotine. The Anglo-Irish philosopher and member of British Parliament, Edmund Burke (1729–97), wrote in *Reflections on the Revolution in France*, his classic critique of the French Revolution, that the Jacobins "preferred atheism to a form of religion not agreeable to their ideas. They succeeded in destroying that form; and atheism has succeeded in destroying them." Burke presciently penned those words in 1790, even before the radicals began their murderous campaigns a couple years later. Cathedrals and churches were closed or turned into secular temples devoted to the cult of Reason. The Christian calendar was abolished, and revolutionaries who tried to curb the anti-Christian frenzy were denounced themselves and taken to the guillotine.

By 1799, France had been left bloodied and exhausted by the revolution. The French were ready for a leader who would restore order and dignity to the nation. That leader emerged in the general Napoleon Bonaparte (1769–1821), who took control of the government and led as an emperor for fifteen years. Bonaparte was not devout himself, but he realized that the Revolution had drastically underestimated Catholicism's importance among the French people, so he brokered a new relationship between the papacy and the French government. This renewed cooperation was symbolized by Napoleon's coronation as emperor at Notre-Dame Cathedral in Paris in 1804, with Pope Pius VII in attendance. Napoleon placed the crown on his own head, however. This was not a precise re-enactment of Charlemagne's coronation as Holy Roman Emperor by Pope Leo III in AD 800, but it certainly signaled a return to a friendlier church-state relationship in France.

The French Revolution in Eastern Perspective

Throughout much of the Christian world, the horrors of the French Revolution generated Christian resolve to renew the churches and to keep Enlightenment-style secularism and libertinism at bay. Such concerns animated church authorities from Catholics in France, to Congregationalists in the United States, to Eastern Orthodox authorities in the Ottoman Empire. In Constantinople, the Orthodox Patriarch Gregory V, alarmed by the French Revolution and by Napoleon's campaign against Egypt (which began in 1798), waged a decades-long struggle against Enlightened secularism. Patriarchal encyclicals warned against secularist Jacobinism as a "disease." Anthimos, the Orthodox Patriarch of Jerusalem, wrote a fiery treatise called *Paternal Instruction* (1798), which posited that French libertinism was the latest in a long series of demonic challenges to the true (Orthodox) church. These challenges included Roman Catholicism (the "Latin heresy"), and the "Lutherans, Calvinists, Luthero-Calvinists, Evangelicals and others without number; this heresy engendered its own destruction, so that it might become clear that it was rotten and unstable." Now the devil had "devised in the present century another artifice and pre-eminent deception, namely, the much vaunted system of liberty, which perhaps on the surface appears to be good, so as to deceive if possible the chosen people [Matthew 24:24]. It is, however, a trap of the devil and a destructive poison." The patriarch insisted that God had raised up the Ottoman Empire as a bulwark for the true church, as well. Despite the Islamic faith of the Ottomans, they offered shelter to the Orthodox churches. Orthodox authorities eagerly supported the Ottoman Empire's war against Napoleon and the French, which started in 1798.

Russian Orthodox Christians found themselves in a somewhat different position in the 1700s, as they lived under rulers including Tsar Peter the Great, and Empress Catherine the Great. They affirmed Orthodoxy but also wanted to strengthen the Russian state, sometimes at the expense of the church. Catherine ruled from 1762 to 1796 and was particularly interested in connecting Russia with broader Enlightenment-style trends drawn from western Europe's cultural centers such as Paris. She corresponded with Voltaire, while Diderot and other philosophes visited her court. Catherine enacted a number of enlightened reforms, including some guarantees of religious liberty to Catholics, Protestants, and Muslims. More ominously, Catherine's administration required Jews to resettle in a strip of western Russia that included present-day Poland, Ukraine, and Belarus. Jews in these areas suffered under poverty and discrimination. These Jews' relocation to eastern Europe would later turn it into the "bloodlands," or the focus of Nazi Germany's genocidal "final solution."

Catherine's commitment to Enlightenment principles did not extend to anything that might represent a threat to the Russian state. This concern over Enlightenment radicalism grew more acute with the outbreak of the French Revolution. In suppressing the writings of the radical reformer Alexander Radishchev (1749–1802), Catherine explained that the "author, infected and full of the French madness, is trying in every possible way to break down respect for authority and for the authorities, to stir up in the people indignation against their superiors." She also claimed that his writing was "in direct opposition to the law of God, the Ten Commandments, Holy Scripture, Orthodoxy, and the civil law." (This was an odd complaint coming from an empress who had taken many lovers and who was probably a deist or agnostic, despite her professed Orthodox faith.) She would not countenance revolutionary sentiments, especially after 1789. She had Radishchev exiled to Siberia and had copies of his objectionable book burned.

The Bible and Enlightened Higher Criticism

Figures such as Catherine feared that Enlightenment skepticism and French radicalism would damage the state. Many church leaders worried about French radicalism's effects on the political influence of traditional churches. Other Christians, especially Protestant educators and pastors, opposed radical Enlightenment developments in biblical scholarship that we now associate with "higher criticism." These developments were not new, but in light of the anticlerical fanaticism of the French Revolution, the higher critical thought of the late 1700s seemed even more menacing to many traditional Christians. Higher criticism is often portrayed chiefly as a nineteenth-century phenomenon, but fundamental challenges to the Bible dated at least to the writings of Baruch Spinoza in the 1670s. Nevertheless, anti-traditionalist views of the Bible became more common in the mid-1700s, seeping into European centers of biblical scholarship, including the University of Halle. Halle had been the stronghold of Pietist reform and education, but by the 1750s it was also becoming a center of higher critical thought. The leader of critical biblical studies at Halle was Johann Salomo Semler (1725–91), whom some regard as the father of German higher criticism. He was an essential forerunner to Friedrich Schleiermacher, whose work in higher criticism is better known today than Semler's.

Semler believed that God spoke through the Bible, but not through all of it. Free inquiry, untethered from tradition, would reveal which parts of Scripture were essential to the Christian message. Unlike critics who focused on the centrality of the Synoptic Gospels, Semler posited that the Gospel of John and Paul's letters to the Romans, Galatians, and Corinthians, contained the most essential Christian doctrines. Semler made a distinction between the Bible and the "Word of God." The latter represented the divine truth which "makes all men in all times wise unto salvation." Not all the books of the Bible were the Word of God, he surmised. In his *Treatise on a Free Inquiry of the Canon* (1771), Semler expressed doubts about the divine inspiration of parts of the Old Testament. Should Christians "accept the books of Ruth, Esther, Esdras, and Nehemiah as containing clear signs of the divine, salvific, and indispensable truth? Or must they accept these books simply because the Jews have been in the habit of gathering them, alongside other ancient documents and scriptural records of their nation?" Semler asserted a stark distinction between relics of Judaism and the transcendent truths of Christianity, a distinction that cast doubt on the value of much of the Hebrew Bible. He similarly did not see how one could reconcile the bloody scenes in a book such as Revelation with the "divine universal love" that lay at the heart of Christianity.

Semler's views were challenged on multiple fronts, including by more radical skeptics who saw no point in defending any part of the Bible as authoritative. The German pantheist Gotthold Ephraim Lessing (1729–81), for example, was perplexed by Semler's continued belief in Christ's resurrection, despite his skeptical views of other parts of Scripture. Traditionalist Lutherans, conversely, insisted that for Luther's doctrine of *sola scriptura* to stand, one must assume the authority of the whole Bible and not pick out preferred parts as more inspired than others. Semler and the Hamburg Lutheran minister and theologian Johann Melchior Goeze (1717–86) studied under the same theology professor at Halle. After their university studies they went in opposite directions with regard to the Bible. Goeze argued for the verbal inspiration of the whole Bible, and he warned that one should never make human reason the final arbiter of biblical truth. Human intellect was badly damaged by sin, and Christians needed the Spirit to illumine the truths contained in the Bible, Goeze insisted. Such debates over the inspiration of the entire Bible would mark trends in biblical interpretation into the twenty-first century.

Despite traditionalist Lutheran efforts to stem the tide of higher criticism, its influence continued to grow in the late 1700s. Johann Philipp Gabler (1753–1826), another key higher critic, taught theology at German universities in Altdorf and Jena. Altdorf had a long history of heterodox theology. In the 1610s it had become notorious as the German center of Socinian (anti-trinitarian) theology. Almost two centuries later, Gabler asserted a basic difference between "biblical" and "dogmatic" theology, the former based on objective study of the text, the latter on dogmatic preconceptions. Many higher critics assumed that the study of the Bible was a scientific discipline, guided by a scholar's rationality rather than Christian theological tradition. In this view, "tradition" was often an obstacle to advances in new knowledge and improved understanding of the Bible. Gabler saw dogmatic theology as the enemy of biblical truth. Like Semler, he also assumed that the New Testament superseded the Hebrew Bible and that much of the Bible was mythical. It was therefore relevant only to the place and time in which it was written. Even for the New Testament, Gabler proposed, "we must investigate what in the sayings of the Apostles is truly divine, and what perchance merely human." Gabler believed that biblical scholars were best positioned to determine the usefulness of any section of Scripture.

Prussian authorities became concerned in the 1780s about theologians and pastors who promoted the "miserable, long-refuted errors of the Socinians, deists, naturalists and other sectarians, and spread them among the people with impertinent impudence under the much abused banner of 'enlightenment.'" In 1788, the Prussian king issued warnings that any pastors or professors promoting heretical doctrines would lose their jobs. Enforcing such warnings proved difficult, however, as many Lutheran pastors and theology professors opposed greater restrictions on religious thought. The policy put a spotlight on writers such as the eminent German philosopher Immanuel Kant (1724–1804), who could only publish his *Religion within the Boundaries of Mere Reason* (1793) via a clever outmaneuvering of censors. Kant's theology was rationalist, to be sure, but he remained relatively sympathetic to traditional belief, or what Gabler had dismissed as "dogmatic" theology.

Higher critical theory was more muted in Britain and America, partly due to the surging evangelical movement in those countries, and partly due to effective Christian apologetics, led by Joseph Butler's classic anti-deist work *Analogy of Religion* (1736). A similarly powerful apologetic work was William Paley's *A View of the Evidences of Christianity* (1794). Paley (1743–1805), the Anglican Archdeacon of Carlisle, focused on the historical evidences for Christ as the risen Messiah, and the reliability of the gospel accounts. "We have the authenticity of these books established by more and stronger proofs than belong to almost any other ancient book whatever," Paley wrote. (He made similar arguments defending Paul's letters.) *A View of the Evidences* was a huge success, published in cities including Dublin, Ireland, Boston, Philadelphia, New York, and many editions in London. Even Paley did not insist that the Gospels were written by the traditional authors assigned to them, however. He and similar apologists figured that proving authorship was exceedingly difficult. Paley also popularized an enduring argument for intelligent design in *Natural Theology: or, Evidences of the Existence and Attributes of the Deity* (1802). If one finds a watch, Paley argued, one should assume there is a watchmaker. Likewise, if the creation reflects orderly design (which it does), there must be a powerful creative intelligence behind it.

Skeptical writings were hardly unknown in Britain and America, of course. Thomas Jefferson's only full-length book, *Notes on the State of Virginia* (1785), was published in French, English, and American editions. Even though Jefferson muted his skepticism to protect his political ambitions, *Notes* raised questions about the historicity of Noah's flood and speculated that perhaps all of humankind (especially Africans) was not created at the same time, thus undermining the traditional Genesis account. The American patriot leader Ethan Allen (1738–89) of Vermont published the harsh *Reason the Only Oracle of Man* (1784), one of the first skeptical publications by an American-born writer. Allen asserted that reliable transmission of the biblical texts was impossible due to the obscurity of their origins and the insurmountable difficulties of accurately interpreting the texts which have survived, which themselves are not the originals.

Allen's publication was a commercial flop, but there was an emerging market for skeptical writings in Britain and America, as illustrated by Thomas Paine's *The Age of Reason* (1794). Paine was one of the most compelling writers of the Age of Revolutions and was already widely known for his books *Common Sense* and *The Rights of Man* (1791), his refutation of Edmund Burke's critique of the French Revolution. Paine went to France to participate in the Revolution. For a time, Paine served as a member of France's National Convention, despite his inability to speak French. As with many early supporters of the Revolution, however, the radical Jacobins eventually turned against Paine. He was jailed and only avoided execution due to a clerical error at the prison. Written at around the same time as his confinement, *The Age of Reason* was concise and punchy, but in America its attacks on traditional belief generated as much outrage as they did sympathy. In Britain, publishers risked prosecution for sedition if they published *The Age of Reason*, but that probably enhanced the pamphlet's popularity.

> [The Bible] is a history of wickedness, that has served to corrupt and brutalize mankind; and, for my part, I sincerely detest it, as I detest everything that is cruel.
>
> ———
>
> Thomas Paine, *The Age of Reason*, 1794

Paine opened *The Age of Reason* with a rousing statement of his deist creed: "I believe in one God, and no more . . . I do not believe in the creed professed by the Jewish church, by the Roman church, by the Greek church, by the Turkish church, by the Protestant church, nor by any church that I know of. My own mind is my own church." To Paine, creation alone was the word of God, and most of the Bible obscured the truth about God rather than revealing it. The only passages in the whole Bible that "convey to us any idea of God" were those on creation in Job and Psalm 19. Paine's irreverent style provoked a huge response, with dozens of authors issuing rejoinders to Paine for years afterward. Among them was Elias Boudinot (1740–1821), former president of the Confederation Congress, the director of the US Mint, a devout Presbyterian, and a founder and early president of the American Bible Society. In *The Age of Revelation* (1801), Boudinot refuted Paine point-by-point, arguing that Paine lacked basic expertise on biblical criticism and the Bible's historicity. "He has barely vamped up, in a parade of language, the well-answered objections of the Deists," Boudinot lamented. Paine had just added "the ludicrous and blasphemous reveries of debauchees and drunkards over their cups."

Image 12.2. *Thomas Paine* (1793)

With his bestselling work, Paine made higher criticism of the Bible a fixture of Anglo-American popular culture, despite the howls of derision from traditionalists such as Boudinot. By the 1790s, there was also a fixed presence of radical biblical skepticism among theology professors, especially in European universities. This signaled a new drift (or fleeing) away from the great tradition of the church. Among the most significant of these skeptical professors was Friedrich Schleiermacher, who taught at the universities of Halle and Berlin. Schleiermacher grew up in a Moravian family in Silesia (southwestern modern Poland). He began to doubt basic Christian doctrines as a student at Halle, but he never definitively renounced his Moravian upbringing. (This became a common pattern in higher critical thought: many scholars who had grown up in more traditionalist backgrounds did not necessarily condemn Christianity, but they believed they had developed a more sophisticated version of their childhood faith.) Following figures such as Gotthold Ephraim Lessing, Schleiermacher concluded that the history of religion and the creeds of dogmatic theology would not lead to divine truth.

Anticipating the great Romantic era of the nineteenth century, he posited that philosophy, feeling, and intuition were more authentic paths to knowing God than creeds and old-fashioned readings of Scripture. Schleiermacher believed that theology was inescapably personal and subjective, making a radical application of the "religion of the heart" taught by the Moravians. "Each student of theology must form one's own clear historical vision for oneself, concerning both information about the total career of Christianity and information about the moment of history in which one lives," he wrote in his *Brief Outline of Theology as a Field of Study* (1811, 1830). Schleiermacher envisioned modern theologians inquiring about the canonical status of every part of Scripture. Unlike many later Bible scholars and critics, Schleiermacher did not jettison the concept of canon altogether. Indeed, to some of his critics' consternation, Schleiermacher saw the Gospel of John as a reliable account of the life of Jesus. Otherwise, he argued that a "connected presentation" of Jesus's actual life was largely inaccessible. Schleiermacher continued to expand the perceived gulf between the text of the Bible and an individual Christian's knowledge of Jesus. If our confidence in the Bible was fundamentally undermined, he wrote, "we would not lose anything essential: Christ remains the same and our faith in him remains the same." Schleiermacher's convictions were Christocentric, but not biblicist.

Liberal figures such as Schleiermacher, perhaps understandably, receive a great deal of attention in the history of theology. They represented intellectual change, which is often regarded as a more fascinating topic than intellectual stasis. In other words, histories of theology tend to prize innovators such as Schleiermacher over those who saw themselves as preserving theological tradition. Schleiermacher was a major contributor to elite theology in Europe and America for the next two centuries. But it is easy to overstate Schleiermacher or other higher critics' significance, especially in light of the enduring power of the great tradition of Christian theology.

In the early nineteenth century, Germany went through its own evangelical and pietist revival of the sort that was happening in the United Kingdom and America at the same time. These revivals not only renewed Protestants' commitment to what they regarded as authentic Christianity, but they also helped many to stay faithful to the historic doctrines of Christianity. The "German Awakening" was not just a populist movement, either, as it had major backers on German theological faculties. To cite just one of them, Georg Christian Knapp (1753–1825) was a theology professor at Halle for five decades, from 1775 to 1825. He and Schleiermacher overlapped briefly as colleagues at Halle before Schleiermacher transitioned to Berlin. Semler was also one of Knapp's professors, and subsequently a colleague. Knapp likewise dabbled in theological liberalism, but he experienced a traditional religious awakening of his own in 1794. A student later wrote that "Knapp recognized that he was on the wrong path and perceived his own need for a savior and redeemer. His own inner life, his faith, and his piety then began, just as the New Testament stipulates that they must." Knapp understood this as his moment of the new birth, the experience described in John 3.

Knapp served in Halle's extensive charitable, missionary, and Bible distribution endeavors. He also tried to reassert the legacies of the Pietist pioneer Philipp Jakob Spener and of Halle's founder August Hermann Francke, whose writings had fallen into some obscurity. Knapp also defended the veracity of Scripture, including (for example) Gospel accounts of Jesus delivering people from demonic possession. These were just the sort of supernatural episodes that drew guffaws from higher critics, but Knapp urged traditionalist German Christians to willingly face opposition from "philosophers and the *Aufklärer* [Enlighteners], and all the opprobrium and derision that they will redound upon them from mockers." Knapp's *Lectures on Christian Theology* were popular in Germany, but it was even more so in the United States. In 1831 they appeared in a translation by Leonard Woods, a Calvinist professor at Andover Theological Seminary in Massachusetts. Knapp's lectures became one of the most popular theological texts in American seminaries for the rest of the nineteenth century, appearing in twenty American editions over the course of four decades.

In the lectures, Knapp positioned himself as revitalizing the tradition of the Reformers with regard to the authority, inspiration, and sufficiency of the Bible. To Knapp, the "infallibility" of the Scripture was "grounded on the fact, that the authors of the Bible were rendered infallible by divine influence." He opposed those theologians who "rely unduly upon unaided reason in matters of faith." The Reformers had battled against Catholic theologians who denied the sufficiency of Scripture alone to guide Christians in the truth. Now, theologians such as Knapp confronted liberal theologians who rejected the inspiration of the Bible, or who at least believed they could judge via reason, science, or feelings which parts of Scripture were divinely inspired and which were not. This type of struggle, again, shaped much of the academic study of the Bible into the contemporary era.

Selected Bibliography

Chalamet, Christophe, ed. *The Challenge of History: Readings in Modern Theology*. Minneapolis: Fortress, 2020.

Clogg, Richard. "The 'Dhidhaskalia Patriki' (1798): An Orthodox Reaction to French Revolutionary Propaganda." *Middle Eastern Studies* 5, no. 2 (May 1969): 87–115.

Kidd, Thomas S. *God of Liberty: A Religious History of the American Revolution*. New York: Basic Books, 2010.

Kloes, Andrew. *The German Awakening: Protestant Renewal after the Enlightenment, 1815–1848*. Oxford: Oxford University Press, 2019.

Knapp, Georg Christian. *Lectures on Christian Theology*. Translated by Leonard Woods. London, 1831.

Mariña, Jacqueline, ed., *The Cambridge Companion to Friedrich Schleiermacher*. New York: Cambridge University Press, 2005.

Nisbet, Hugh Barr. *Gotthold Ephraim Lessing: His Life, Works, and Thought*. Oxford: Oxford University Press, 2013.

Tackett, Timothy. *The Coming of the Terror in the French Revolution*. Cambridge: Harvard University Press, 2015.

Thaler, Roderick P. "Catherine II's Reaction to Radishchev." *Slavic and East-European Studies* 2, no. 3 (Autumn 1957): 154–60.

Van Kley, Dale K. *The Religious Origins of the French Revolution: From Calvin to the Civil Constitution, 1560–1791*. New Haven, CT: Yale University Press, 1996.

Chapter 13

Protestants and New Global Missions

The revivalist George Whitefield's passing in 1770 marked a major transition point for the Anglo-American evangelical movement. He was the most visible leader of the movement that he, more than anyone else, had helped to start. In 1770, it remained unclear whether Whitefield and Jonathan Edwards's form of Calvinist activism would become the norm in evangelicalism. John Wesley's Methodists advocated strict Arminianism, as did new evangelical sects such as the Freewill Baptists, which began growing in America around the time of the Revolution. But the 1785 publication of the English Particular Baptist Andrew Fuller's *The Gospel of Christ Worthy of All Acceptation* signaled that moderate Calvinist faith would fuel much of the evangelical growth, missions, and reform movements (including antislavery) over the next century. Fullerites avoided the excesses of hyper-Calvinists, who believed there was no point in addressing unconverted people in their preaching and rejected religious agencies outside of local churches, such as missionary societies. But moderate Calvinists also emphasized God's sovereignty over the salvation of the elect in contrast to Arminians such as Wesley and the Methodists, who preached that God offered salvation to all, not just the elect. Calvinists and Arminians feuded bitterly with one another, especially within the ranks of denominations such as the Baptists. But in the "great century" of Christian growth and missions, neither Calvinists nor Arminians had the market cornered on aggressive evangelism. Nineteenth-century Protestant missions and revivals permanently changed the face of world Christianity, exporting historic Christian belief and piety to parts of the globe where it had lagged or been largely unknown.

Andrew Fuller, William Carey, and Protestant Missions

Andrew Fuller (1754–1815) was typical as an evangelical leader and pastor, in the sense that he struggled with the tension (some called it the "modern question") between God's sovereignty and human responsibility in salvation and evangelism. If God had predestined the elect to salvation, why bother to evangelize? Wasn't it inevitable that any elect man or woman would eventually be saved? As he served as a Baptist minister in English churches, Fuller addressed these questions by studying the writings of Jonathan Edwards. Edwards had passed away in 1758 from a smallpox inoculation that inadvertently gave him a full-blown case of the disease just after he became president of the College of New Jersey (Princeton). Edwards's writings on free will and revival continued to have a major effect on evangelical leaders such as Fuller, however. Fuller concluded that only the elect would respond to the offer of salvation, yet all people were held morally accountable for accepting or refusing that offer. The fact that reprobate people were morally incapable of repentance due to the crippling effects of sin was no excuse. (Edwards made a seminal distinction between "natural" and "moral" inability. Only the latter was morally blameworthy.) Moreover, God commanded Christians to proclaim the gospel. They should obey that mandate and let God determine the results.

Fuller's work on Edwards's *Freedom of the Will* (1754) bore fruit in his treatise *The Gospel of Christ Worthy of All Acceptation*, one of the most influential works in the history of evangelicalism. Fuller explained that the lack "of faith in Christ is ascribed in the Scriptures to men's depravity, and is itself there represented as a heinous sin." No man would come to Christ unless the Father drew him [John 6:44], but that reality only highlighted the "ignorance, pride, dishonesty of heart, and aversion to God" that characterized an unregenerate person. Thus, Fuller insisted that preachers should address non-Christians in their sermons, not to seek outward compliance in God's moral law but "to strike at the root . . . to impress them with a sense

> Though believing in Christ is a compliance with a duty, yet it is not as a duty, or by way of reward for a virtuous act, that we are said to be justified by it.
>
> ———
>
> Andrew Fuller. *The Gospel Worthy of All Acceptation*, 1787

of their utter undone condition, and absolute need for Christ." Whitefield would have heartily agreed, but it was left to Fuller to unpack the theological argument for aggressive evangelism and missions by Calvinists.

Fuller's work helped to birth a new, more organized Protestant missionary movement. To be sure, Christianity had been a missionary religion since Christ had made the "Great Commission" to make disciples of all nations (Matt 28:19). But as we have seen, Catholics were often centuries ahead of Protestants in organizing and sending missionaries to the ends of the earth. The Reformers often spoke of the need for missionary activity, but the embattled state of the Protestant churches and their comparative lack of resources delayed the development of a coordinated missionary movement. Protestants who became refugees or immigrants often served as missionaries, however, bringing Reformed Christianity to locations across the Atlantic World. One of the first was a short-lived Huguenot settlement near Rio de Janeiro in Brazil, which probably saw the first Protestant worship service in the New World in 1557.

The Moravians had pioneered one of the first formal Protestant cross-cultural missionary endeavors. The Moravians' work, especially in places like the Caribbean islands, was led by figures such as the remarkable evangelist and organizer Rebecca Protten. Jonathan Edwards had done much for Protestant missions by publishing the diary of his protégé David Brainerd, who worked among the Lenni Lenape (Delaware) Indians of New Jersey in the mid-1740s. Edwards's *Life of David Brainerd* became one of Edwards's most popular works and an inspiration to countless missionaries in the nineteenth century. The Separate Baptists, emerging from the Great Awakening in New England, also traveled to bring the gospel to the American South through Shubal Stearns and the Sandy Creek network of Baptist churches. African American Baptist pastors and evangelists such as George Liele and David George were essential in taking the gospel from the American South to places such as Jamaica, Nova Scotia, and Sierra Leone.

Christian historians, then, should be careful about overstating the precedent set by the formation of the Baptist Missionary Society (1792) or the sending of the missionaries Adoniram and Ann Judson to India and Burma starting in 1812. There were plenty of Protestant missionary antecedents to these developments. Nevertheless, the 1790s saw the advent of a systematic and interdenominational missionary effort by Protestants, which would finally allow them to rival the scale of Catholic missionary work on the global stage. William Carey (1761–1834), an English Baptist pastor, took up Fuller's theme when he promoted overseas missions in his hugely influential *Enquiry into the Obligations of Christians,*

To Use Means for the Conversion of the Heathens (1792). Citing the Great Commission and the example of David Brainerd and Moravian missionaries, Carey argued that world evangelization remained as much of a mandate as it did in the early church. "The work has not been taken up, or prosecuted of late years (except by a few individuals) with that zeal and perseverance with which the primitive [early] Christians went about it," Carey lamented. Noting the great advances in transportation and imperial commerce, Carey insisted that doors were opening for Christians to take the gospel to all corners of the earth.

Like most evangelicals, Carey was not dissuaded by the fact that much of the world was nominally Christian (usually of the Orthodox or Catholic variety). "Most of the members of the Greek church are very ignorant," he surmised, and "papists also are in general ignorant of divine things, and very vicious." Even among Protestants of European background, the gospel was under attack, and "every method that the enemy can invent is employed to undermine the kingdom of our Lord Jesus Christ." The pure gospel and the great tradition of Christian theology remained either unknown or reviled in much of the world. It was time for those of true Protestant faith to rectify that dreadful situation.

Image 13.1. *Serampore College, India*

Carey, Fuller, and others soon founded the Baptist Missionary Society, and in 1793 William and Dorothy Carey and their children went as missionaries to India. During his four decades there, Carey worked with linguists to translate the Bible into a number of local languages. For example, he partnered with the young poet and Sanskrit scholar Madan Mohan Tarkalankar (1817–58) so that Carey could translate the Bible into Sanskrit, the ancient dialect that was the primary language used in Hindu sacred texts. Carey developed such noted linguistic expertise that he became a professor of Indian languages at Fort William College in Calcutta. In 1818, Carey and other missionaries also founded Serampore College, north of Calcutta, as a Protestant training school for Indian minsters. Protestant missionaries left a host of such colleges across their mission fields during the nineteenth century. They saw education as central to the missionary enterprise, especially for training indigenous clergy.

Reform Efforts in the Church of England

Fuller and Carey emerged from English dissenting churches, but a remarkable cast of Church of England evangelicals would also transform British church life, culture, and politics in the late eighteenth and early nineteenth centuries. Arguably the most influential was John Newton (1725–1807), the former slave trader turned evangelical Anglican minister and reformer. Newton grew up with some evangelical influences from his mother, but she died when he was young. By his teens Newton became active in the British seafaring trades. As he descended into immorality and depression, he also got involved with trade in enslaved people on the west coast of Africa. A terrible storm on the Atlantic awakened Newton to his spiritual plight, and he began to read the Bible and devotional books. Finally, he surrendered to Christ. He did not yet see any moral problem with slave trading, however, and he served as a master on several slave trading journeys in the early 1750s. (Whitefield was a slave owner by this point, too, and John Wesley had not yet denounced slavery publicly.) Health problems caused Newton to stop going to sea. Back in London, he became acquainted with the broader evangelical movement, becoming a committed Calvinist as well as an evangelical.

Newton struggled to fulfill his aspiration of becoming an Anglican minister due to his unconventional background and his evangelical associations, which some Anglicans viewed as uncouth. (Many Anglicans still disdained the dissenting denominations as illegitimate.) Nevertheless, after years of failed attempts Newton did get ordained as a priest in 1764. The same year he published his spiritual autobiography, which made him a renowned figure in Anglo-American evangelical circles. It appeared in almost twenty British and American editions by the beginning of the nineteenth century, as well as in several translations. Newton found pastoral work in Olney, England, where he began writing hymns with the English evangelical poet William Cowper (1731–1800). Their collaboration resulted in the *Olney Hymns*, a collection that appeared in dozens of editions after its initial publication in 1779. The hymns included "God Moves in a Mysterious Way," Cowper's ode to God's sovereignty:

> God moves in a mysterious way,
>   His wonders to perform;
> He plants his footsteps in the sea,
>   And rides upon the storm.
> Deep in unfathomable mines
>   Of never failing skill;
> He treasures up his bright designs,
>   And works His sovereign will.

Cowper's collaboration with Newton was tragically cut short by Cowper's severe depression or other mental illness. This often rendered Cowper unable to work and made him occasionally suicidal as he wrestled with terrifying thoughts that he might be damned. The most celebrated product of the *Olney Hymns* was Newton's hymn "Amazing Grace," which became the most popular religious song in the English language.

In 1780, Newton moved to London to minister at the church of St. Mary Woolnoth, supported by his friend and patron, the evangelical merchant shipper John Thornton. In Olney, Newton had been more of a local parish minister, but now he became a renowned preacher and mentor to evangelical clergy and writers in London. Among these was the reformer and philanthropist Hannah More (1745–1833). By the 1770s, More was a socially prominent and sought-after playwright, but she felt that she was spiritually empty. More was moved by reading *Cardiphonia*, Newton's collection of pastoral letters. She believed that Newton understood "vital, experimental religion," or the kind of heart religion that was a signature of evangelical piety. She met and corresponded with Newton in the 1780s, and his counsel helped to turn her into both an Anglican evangelical and a powerful moral reformer, including an activist against the slave trade. One of her best-known tracts, *Thoughts on the Importance of the Manners of the Great to General Society* (1788), appealed to England's upper classes to embrace genuine Christian conviction and to use their resources for godly reform.

The gospel, she wrote, enjoined rigorous disciplines of "renouncing self, of living uncorrupted in the world, of subduing besetting sins, and of not thinking of ourselves more highly than we ought." She urged wealthy English people to move beyond mere profession and to live out their Christian faith in society.

Protestants and the Slave Trade

Newton also began to speak out against the traffic in slaves, prompted by the swelling numbers of evangelical opponents of slavery in England. He also suffered manifest guilt about his former involvement in the trade. In *Thoughts Upon the African Slave Trade* (1788), Newton explained that it was a "subject of humiliating reflection to me, that I was, once, an active instrument, in a business at which my heart now shudders." Newton condemned the wanton physical and sexual abuse that was endemic to the slave system. He knew it was time for the "total suppression of a trade, which, like a poisonous root, diffuses its malignity into every branch." Because he lived a long time, Newton survived to see Britain abolish the empire's slave trade (though not slavery itself). This happened in 1807, the final year of his life. Another disciple of Newton's, William Wilberforce (1759–1833), would carry forward the English antislavery movement, which bore fruit in the Slavery Abolition Act of 1833, passed in Wilberforce's last year of life.

Many British and American evangelicals were becoming sensitized to the immorality of the slave trade. This concern also opened the door for evangelicals of African heritage to enlist in the antislavery movement. For example, the African American poet Phillis Wheatley called proslavery whites "our modern Egyptians" in a widely-reprinted 1774 letter to the Mohegan pastor Samson Occom. She argued that God had given every person a love of freedom. People of African descent shared in humanity's irreducible dignity, which meant that it was wrong to deny Africans their liberty.

The year after John Newton published *Thoughts Upon the African Slave Trade*, the Afro-British Christian Olaudah Equiano (d. 1797) published his fabulously successful *The Interesting*

> I then clearly perceived that by the deeds of the law no flesh living could be justified. I was then convinced that by the first Adam sin came, and by the second Adam (the Lord Jesus Christ) all that are saved must be made alive.
>
> Olaudah Equiano, *The Interesting Narrative of the Life of Olaudah Equiano: Written by Himself*, 1789

Narrative of the Life of Olaudah Equiano (1789). *The Interesting Narrative* became a key text in the movement against the British slave trade. Equiano was probably born in present-day Nigeria, but he was kidnapped and sold as a slave when he was a boy. He journeyed with various masters around the Atlantic World. One of them was a naval officer who served in the Seven Years' War. During the war Equiano experienced Christian conversion and became affiliated with the Methodists. Several years after his conversion, Equiano had the opportunity to hear George Whitefield preach, probably in 1765. Even though Whitefield was growing old and infirm, Equiano was still impressed by his fervor, as people crowded around the windows of the small church where Whitefield was preaching. "I saw this pious man [Whitefield] exhorting the people with the greatest fervor and earnestness and sweating as much as I ever did while in slavery on Montserrat beach." (Montserrat was

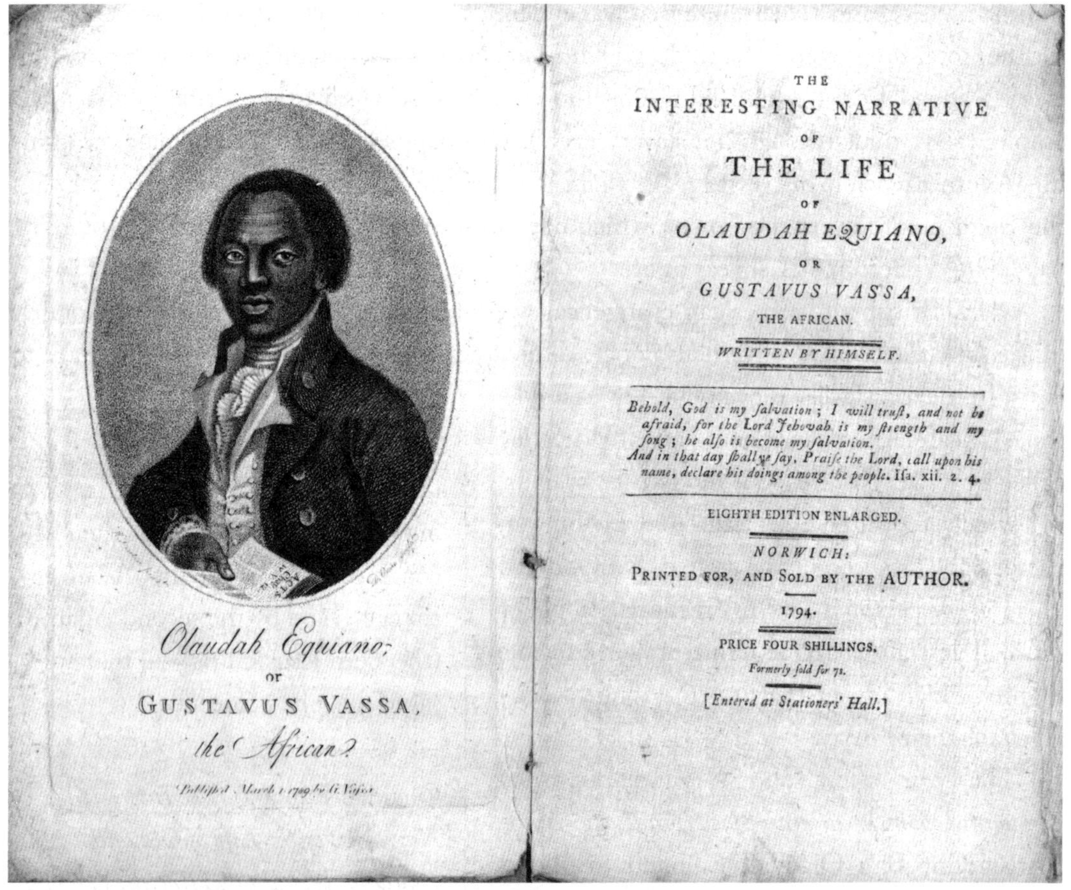

Olaudah Equiano;
or
GUSTAVUS VASSA,
the African.

THE
INTERESTING NARRATIVE
OF
THE LIFE
OF
OLAUDAH EQUIANO,
OR
GUSTAVUS VASSA,
THE AFRICAN.

WRITTEN BY HIMSELF.

Behold, God is my salvation; I will trust, and not be afraid, for the Lord Jehovah is my strength and my song; he also is become my salvation.
And in that day shall ye say, Praise the Lord, call upon his name, declare his doings among the people. Isa. xii. 2. 4.

EIGHTH EDITION ENLARGED.

NORWICH:
PRINTED FOR, AND SOLD BY THE AUTHOR.

1794.

PRICE FOUR SHILLINGS.
Formerly sold for 7s.

[*Entered at Stationers' Hall.*]

Image 13.2. Olaudah Equiano, *The Interesting Narrative*

a Caribbean island where Equiano had labored as a slave until purchasing his freedom.) Equiano wondered why other preachers did not put so much effort into preaching, and he figured this was the reason why their churches often had few attendees. After achieving his freedom, Equiano became involved (via Quaker patrons) in campaigns to alleviate the plight of Britain's free blacks and enslaved people. *The Interesting Narrative* was his key contribution to that cause, giving readers a firsthand account of the brutal nature of Anglo-American slavery and a hopeful view of how Africans could become Christians and help secure their own emancipation.

The growth of Anglo-American antislavery sentiment precipitated a proslavery backlash, especially among merchants and planters involved with the slave trade. As we have seen, many Christian leaders within the British empire, such as Christopher Codrington, a British official in the Caribbean and supporter of the Anglican Society for the Propagation of the Gospel, advocated for a Christianized slave regime. The idea was that since the Bible accepted the existence of slavery, white Christians should cleanse the slave trade of its endemic abuses and evangelize enslaved people. This was also the approach of George Whitefield, who advocated successfully for slavery's introduction in colonial Georgia, where it was originally banned.

Proslavery arguments were hardly restricted to white American southerners, though of course the American South would become the heart of one of the most entrenched and lucrative slave regimes in the world. Whether coming from American or Caribbean planters or from parliamentary defenders of the slave-trading interest in England, the proslavery argument depended on biblical justifications for slavery in addition to economic and racial arguments. As the debate over banning the slave trade in the British empire came to a head in the first decade of the 1800s, proslavery advocates cited verses such as Lev 25:44, which seemed to sanction the buying of "heathen" people as slaves: "Both thy bondmen, and thy bondmaids, which thou shalt have, shall be of the heathen that are round about you; of them shall ye buy bondmen and bondmaids" (KJV). The planter, slave trader, and Parliament member George Hibbert (1757–1837) noted in an 1807 debate that "in the Old Testament, the slave trade, or the sale of men, is spoken of indifferently just as other trades." Moreover, in the book of Philemon, Paul sent the runaway slave Onesimus back to his master: "he sends him back, I say, to resume his station without one word expressive of his disapprobation of slavery, or in vindication of Onesimus," Hibbert asserted. Proslavery Christians often focused on the Bible's lack of explicit condemnation of slavery, whereas antislavery advocates argued that slavery violated the principles of the Bible, such as the Golden Rule:

"as ye would that men should do to you, do ye also to them likewise" (Luke 6:31 KJV). Some also insisted that the Bible did condemn "menstealers," or slave traffickers, who supplied enslaved people from Africa.

The Methodist Church in America

Evangelicals regularly engaged in pro- or anti-slavery advocacy. But for most evangelicals, politics could never be the central concern. Proclaiming the good news about Jesus was too important. The American Revolution had briefly dampened evangelical growth in America, though groups such as Baptists continued to thrive in the South and in New England throughout the war. Wesleyan Methodists had become a factor in the late colonial period in America, but John Wesley's opposition to the patriot cause effectively forced the Methodists in America to go underground, bide their time, and/or return to England. Once the war was over, Methodists gathered themselves for a vigorous program of evangelism and church planting under the leadership of the indefatigable Francis Asbury (1745–1816). Asbury came from an English farming family and experienced Methodist conversion in 1760. Despite his lack of formal education, he began preaching at Methodist meetings when he was eighteen. He accepted John Wesley's call for evangelists to serve in the American colonies and began working as a Methodist "circuit rider" in America in 1771. He took refuge in Delaware during the Revolutionary War, but by 1779 he had already become recognized as the key Methodist leader in America. With John Wesley's blessing, Asbury and the American Methodists effectively declared their independence from English Methodists in 1784 at the Methodist Christmas Conference in Baltimore. The early Methodists were nimble and realized that an independent American church was essential to avoiding the bureaucratic inefficiencies that had bedeviled the Anglican Church in America during the colonial era.

As of 1784, the Wesleyan Methodists were a small segment of the American Protestant population, centered mainly on the east coast from New York to Virginia. Over the next three decades, the Methodists would grow almost tenfold in their number of adherents, and more than thirtyfold in their number of preachers. More than any other Christian group, the Methodists became an almost ubiquitous presence in English-speaking North America, from Canada to the Gulf Coast and from east coast cities to the trans-Mississippi frontier. Thomas Coke (1747–1814) was a key Methodist organizer in North America and the Caribbean, helping to establish Methodist works in the Leeward Islands, especially

Antigua. Coke's travels, if anything, exceeded the scope of George Whitefield's. Coke visited the Caribbean four times in the 1780s and 1790s. By 1804 Coke reported that there were more than 14,000 Methodist adherents in the Caribbean, the vast majority of whom were of African or mixed-race ancestry.

The independence of the Methodist Church in America also placed it firmly in the center of the freewheeling religious environment of the new United States. Outside of the New England states there was a strong move away from official state denominations after the Revolution, so the Methodists (like all churches) needed to become religious entrepreneurs in order to win and maintain adherents. The disestablished, populist environment for American religion also made the Methodists vulnerable to denominational splits. For example, the Virginia Methodist itinerant James O'Kelly (1735–1826) became convinced that Asbury was an autocrat and that the Methodist church needed to repudiate its monarchical tendences, just as the patriots in the American Revolution had done. O'Kelly's agitation led to the formation of the Republican Methodist Church in 1792. That movement would not last long as an independent denomination, however, as many of O'Kelly's followers became affiliated with the new Churches of Christ movement associated with Barton Stone and Alexander Campbell. Such splits became endemic to American denominational life.

Of more enduring significance for the Methodist movement was the formation of the African Methodist Episcopal Church, led by the former slave Richard Allen (1760–1831). As an enslaved man in Delaware, Allen was exposed to the evangelistic preaching of Methodist itinerants. He experienced conversion and "obtained mercy through the blood of Christ." Like the Baptist pastor David George, Allen soon began evangelizing his fellow slaves. Allen was allowed to purchase his freedom and that of his family, partly due to his master's growing doubts about the moral legitimacy of slavery. With Asbury's blessing, Allen began itinerating in Delaware, Maryland, New Jersey, and Pennsylvania in the early 1780s, attracting large crowds of black and white listeners. In 1786 he settled in Philadelphia, ministering chiefly to the African American community there. One of Allen's co-laborers, Absalom Jones (1746–1818), endured an ugly incident at a Philadelphia Methodist church in 1787 in which Jones and other blacks were forced to leave when they tried to pray in a section of the sanctuary reserved for whites. Jones went on to found the city's African Episcopal Church of St. Thomas. Allen remained within the Methodist fold but turned an old blacksmith shop into a church building that in 1794 was dedicated by Asbury as the Bethel Methodist Church. Allen and Jones were engaged in several educational and charitable endeavors among Philadelphia's black community, and they received special commendation for their service amidst an epidemic of yellow fever in 1793. Allen pastored the flourishing congregation and received ordination as a deacon by Asbury in 1799. Yet Allen still found that white Methodists would not grant him full administrative control of the Bethel Church. Thus, in 1816 he and delegates from black-led congregations across several states formed the African Methodist Episcopal Church (AME), the first Protestant denomination led by people of African descent.

Image 13.3. *Rt. Rev. Richard Allen* (1891)

Along with other Baptist and Methodist churches, the A.M.E. spread quickly in the lower South, where the bulk of the African American population lived. Charleston, South Carolina's Emanuel African Methodist Episcopal Church was founded in 1817, but it was a focus of white suspicion from the beginning. When one of the church's founders, Denmark Vesey (1767–1822), was implicated in an alleged slave conspiracy in 1822, vigilantes burned the Emanuel Church. Its members had to meet in secret or in homes until the end of the Civil War. Although their relationship with the white-led Methodist Church was often difficult, the leadership of African American Methodists such as Allen was key to drawing many blacks into Methodist-affiliated churches. For example, Harry Hosier (1750–1806), who was probably a former slave like Allen, became one of the most effective Methodist evangelists in the 1780s and '90s. General consensus held that Hosier was a more skilled preacher than Asbury, and the two traveled together regularly on Asbury's circuits. Thomas Coke wrote that Hosier was "one of the best preachers in the world," yet Hosier never seems to have been granted ordination.

Mission on the African Continent

Due to the labors of Baptists and Methodists, including pioneers such as David George and Richard Allen, by the late eighteenth century Protestant Christianity had advanced among more African-background people in North America and the Caribbean than it had in Africa itself. Protestant imperial nations including Britain often kept chaplains at slave trading ports on the coast of Africa, but these chaplains had little impact on indigenous African populations. There was a trickle of African-born men who received some theological training in Europe and returned to Africa, such as Christian Protten, the husband of Rebecca Protten, who served for a time at the Danish fort of Christiansborg on the Gold Coast. Probably the first African man ordained in Protestant ministry was Jacobus Capitein (1717–47), a native of modern-day Ghana who was enslaved to a Dutch captain as a boy. Capitein was taken to the Netherlands, baptized into the Dutch Reformed Church, and allowed to study at the University of Leiden, beginning in 1737. Perhaps feeling pressure to affirm slavery, Capitein's dissertation at Leiden argued that slavery accorded with biblical morality. He received ordination and returned to West Africa, where he ministered at Elmina, a major slave-trading port. He translated key texts such as the Lord's Prayer and the Ten Commandments into the Fante language.

Philip Quaque (1741–1816) was the first African man to receive ordination in the Church of England and the first African missionary employed in Africa by the Anglican Church. A missionary of the Society for the Propagation of the Gospel (SPG), Thomas Thompson (1708–73), was the first Anglican missionary ever to serve in West Africa. Thompson sent several African children, including Quaque, to study in England, which resulted in Quaque's ordination in London in 1765. The Royal African Company, a London-based trading organization, and the SPG sent Quaque in 1766 to work as a chaplain at Cape Coast Castle, just down the coast from Elmina. Although Quaque would have little success at evangelizing native Africans, his ministry of fifty years established an enduring presence for Protestant Christianity in West Africa. The year 1792 represented a turning point for Protestantism in West Africa, as a major group of blacks from Nova Scotia, including David George, as well as Methodist preachers and leaders in the Countess of Huntingdon's evangelical Connexion, went to establish a new settlement at Freetown, Sierra Leone. This was the same year that Carey published *The Obligations of Christians to Use Means for the Conversion of the Heathens*. English-speaking Protestants were thinking more ambitiously than ever about overseas missions.

The zealous Dutch missionary Johannes Van der Kemp (1747–1811), representing the London Missionary Society (founded 1795, predominantly by Congregationalists), was a far more consequential evangelistic presence in South Africa than Quaque was in West Africa. Van der Kemp was an outspoken critic of the slave trade as well as a motivated evangelist. He was also an organizational whirlwind, helping to form both the Netherlands

Missionary Society and the South African Missionary Society. Van der Kemp had attracted a significant native Khoikhoi congregation at the Cape of Good Hope by 1801, drawing nervous attention from British imperial officials. Van der Kemp was radically committed to identifying with the cultures and languages of southern Africa. He married a young Malagasy slave girl, Sara Janse, whom he had bought and freed. Van der Kemp also did not insist that African Christians should dress in European style for church, as other European leaders had commanded.

Van der Kemp had tried to reach the Xhosa tribe, which was relatively less connected to European powers than were the Khoikhoi. Even though Van der Kemp struggled to sustain his overtures to the Xhosa, one who probably heard him preach became an enormously influential figure in South African Christianity. This was Ntsikana (d. 1821), the son of a Xhosa chief, who in 1815 experienced a visionary conversion which led him to baptize himself in the Ggorha River. Ntsikana repudiated Xhosa rituals, including the smearing of red ochre on his body and the practice of polygamy. But he also refused to receive baptism from British missionaries or to take a European name. He wrote influential hymns with enduring effect on Christian Xhosa worship, including the "Great Hymn." In English, the hymn reads in part,

> He is the Great God, Who is in Heaven;
> Thou art Thou, Shield of Truth . . .
> He, Whose great mantle, we do put it on.
> Those hands of Thine, they are wounded.
> Those feet of Thine, they are wounded.
> Thy blood, why is it streaming?
> Thy blood, it was shed for us.

This hymn and others by Ntsikana became standards in African missionary church hymnals, representing a major step toward the indigenization of African Christianity.

Missions in the South Pacific and Oceania

The evangelical ferment of the 1780s and '90s, finally, led to the expansion of evangelical Protestant faith in the South Pacific and Oceania. The British founded Australia as a colony and penal settlement in 1788, but figures including William Wilberforce and John Newton insisted that the empire appoint a chaplain so that Australia would have godly influences from the start. The first Anglican chaplain there was Richard Johnson (c. 1756–1827), who (as Wilberforce and Newton might have guessed) feuded with secular authorities about the priorities of the Australian colony at New South Wales. Johnson's assistant Samuel Marsden (1765–1838) had a greater impact on Protestantism in the colony and in the wider world of Oceania. Marsden grew up in a modest butcher's family but developed a reputation as a talented preacher, so evangelical sponsors arranged to send him to Cambridge to study. In 1793 he left for the long journey from England to Australia where he mixed the duties of a pastor, magistrate, and commercial farmer in a penal colony. New South Wales leaders gave chaplains such as Marsden quasi-judicial authority, which Marsden used regularly to order the flogging of recalcitrant colonists. This earned him the nickname of the "flogging parson" and an enduring infamy in Australian national memory. Though Marsden had limited success in evangelizing either British convicts or Australian Aborigines, he became the most influential missionary organizer of the early 1800s in Oceania. He was a key advocate for the opening of a London Missionary Society work in Tahiti, as well as stations among aboriginal people in New Zealand and other islands of the South Pacific.

Colonies such as the one in New South Wales (which was in eastern Australia, with Sydney as its capital) usually professed some motivation to reach indigenous people with the Christian gospel. Reality, however, often clashed with evangelicals' desire to proselytize. Such was certainly the case in Australia. British authorities in Australia fought vicious battles with Aboriginal people over the seizure of Aboriginal lands. Politics, money, and land took priority over evangelization in the early decades of Australian colonization. In 1821 the Methodists finally sent William Walker (1799–1855) as a missionary to "the black natives of New South Wales." Even Walker considered the "black" Aborigines to be under the curse of Ham, based on a controversial reading of Gen 9:20–27, which some white Christians used to argue for the inherent inferiority of dark-skinned peoples. Given such notions, Walker assumed Aborigines would be resistant to the gospel and to British civilization. The Australian government in the mid-1820s began setting aside reservations for Aboriginal resettlement and designating missionaries to work on those reservations. Missionaries supported the segregation of Aboriginal settlements from those of whites, believing that unconverted whites would introduce prostitution, violence, alcohol, and generally give Aborigines a terrible model of what "Christian" society should look like. The missionary Lancelot Threlkeld (1788–1859) of the London Missionary Society began outreach to Lake Macquarie natives in 1826, but after seventeen frustrating and under-funded years of work, he concluded that "although much has been done in the way of [Bible] translation, there are now scarcely any Aborigines left to learn to read, and the few who remain appear determined to go on in the broad road to destruction." Andrew Fuller's vision of global evangelism was bracing, and in time it would bear much evangelistic fruit. But in places like Australia and (as we shall see) the American frontier, the clashing priorities and logistical difficulties of missions often led to tragic conflict and few results, at least in the form of indigenous Christian converts.

Selected Bibliography

Carretta, Vincent. *Equiano, the African: Biography of a Self-Made Man*. Athens, GA: University of Georgia Press, 2005.

Dumas, Paula E. *Proslavery Britain: Fighting for Slavery in an Era of Abolition*. New York: Palgrave Macmillan, 2016.

Hastings, Adrian. *The Church in Africa, 1450–1950*. Oxford: Oxford University Press, 1996.

Hindmarsh, D. Bruce. *John Newton and the English Evangelical Tradition Between the Conversions of Wesley and Wilberforce*. Grand Rapids: Eerdmans, 2001.

Morden, Peter J. *Offering Christ to the World: Andrew Fuller (1754–1815) and the Revival of Eighteenth-Century Particular Baptist Life*. Waynesboro, GA: Paternoster, 2003.

Piggin, Stuart. *Evangelical Christianity in Australia: Spirit, Word and World*. Oxford: Oxford University Press, 1996.

Prior, Karen Swallow. *Fierce Convictions: The Extraordinary Life of Hannah More, Poet, Reformer, Abolitionist*. Nashville: Thomas Nelson, 2014.

Smit, Johannes A. "J.T. van der Kemp's Link to the British Anti-slavery Network and his Civil Rights Activism on Behalf of the Khoi (1801–1803)." *Journal for the Study of Religion* 29, no. 2 (2016): 5–28.

Wigger, John. *American Saint: Francis Asbury and the Methodists*. New York: Oxford University Press, 2009.

Yeager, Jonathan M., ed. *Early Evangelicalism: A Reader*. New York: Oxford University Press, 2013.

—— Chapter 14 ——

The Second Great Awakening and a Growing Christian World

When John Wesley died in 1791, the evangelical Protestant world stood at the cusp of massive growth and transformation. The First Great Awakening had inaugurated the evangelical movement, but it clearly descended from the Protestant Reformers in its biblicism and focus on salvation by grace alone. Evangelicals introduced (or reintroduced) an even greater focus on the experience of the "new birth" of salvation, however. They also emphasized the tangible, felt presence of God in the life of a believer. The Great Awakening not only transformed thousands of lives, in places stretching from Continental Europe to the sugar islands of the Caribbean, but it also firmly fixed evangelicals' expectations for revival.

There was no major gap between the "First" and "Second" Great Awakenings. Those are terms more of historical convenience than events with rigid chronological boundaries. There were regional awakenings happening in North America, the Caribbean, and Britain throughout the decades following the Great Awakening. Nevertheless, the 1790s were an essential transition point for evangelicals. Increasingly, evangelicals would see cross-cultural missions as a divine mandate, as reflected in the founding of missionary societies and the publication of William Carey's *Enquiry into the Obligations of Christians, To Use Means for the Conversion of the Heathens*. But the decades following Wesley's death would also see the Methodists—newly independent from the Church of England—and Baptists come to the fore numerically as denominational juggernauts. The numbers of evangelicals in older denominations such as the Anglicans and Congregationalists did not grow as quickly. Such well-connected evangelicals often found themselves in leadership in new missionary organizations, however, and in moral reform movements such as the campaign against slavery.

1791 felt like a turbulent year for anyone following news from Europe and its colonies. The French Revolution had begun to turn more radical. The Revolution had spillover effects in culture and religion outside of France. For example, 1791 saw the publication of the radical writer Thomas Paine's *The Rights of Man* in London. Birmingham, England, saw a rash of anti-dissenter riots that year, focused on the pro-French teachings of the Unitarian pastor and scientist Joseph Priestley (1733–1804). Rioters burned Priestley's home, as well as four dissenting (i.e., non-Anglican) chapels. Priestley subsequently went to America, where he had a major intellectual influence on figures including Thomas Jefferson. Haitians in 1791 started the most successful rebellion by enslaved people in world history. The United States ratified its Bill of Rights. Its First Amendment prohibited Congress from creating an "establishment of religion." This provision banned an established national church. This went against the religious tradition of England, which preserved the Church of England as its national denomination. The First Amendment also guaranteed Americans the "free exercise of religion," promising that the government would not meddle in or persecute anyone for affairs of their faith or their churches.

Decline of Spanish Missions in the New World

Many Catholics would suffer gruesome attacks in the French Revolution's radical phases. In much of the rest of the world, there were signs of quieter change and missionary growth, both among Catholics and Protestants. For example, 1791 saw continued expansion of Spanish Franciscan missions among the native peoples of "Alta California," the far-northern reaches of Spain's aging New World empire. Father Junipero Serra, who died in 1784, had pioneered the Franciscan missions in Alta California in 1769 when he started a mission at San Diego. Serra made his home at Monterey, California, where he founded another mission in 1770. Through Serra and other Franciscan missionaries, thousands of California Indians came into the mission stations, with many of them agreeing to live as sedentary farmers and practicing Catholics. The coming of the Franciscans meant waves of epidemic disease for the California Indians, whose populations suffered and declined accordingly. Fermín de Lasuén

(d. 1803) replaced Serra as the president of the California missions, and in 1791 he founded a new station at Santa Cruz, designed for outreach to local Indian groups such as the Amah Mutsun and the Yakuts peoples. Missions like Santa Cruz often suffered disease, malnutrition, and maltreatment of native converts, who sometimes revolted against the missionaries. In 1812, for example, native proselytes strangled and dismembered the missionary priest Andrés Quintana at Santa Cruz after Quintana had given a vicious whipping to one of them.

Other Catholic missionary works in the vast Spanish empire also struggled through episodes of rebellion, violence, and rebuilding throughout this era. In Peru, a massive anti-missionary rebellion erupted in 1742 (at the same time as the Great Awakening was reaching its apex in Britain and America), prompted by frustrations over the demands of the Spanish religious and political leaders and by the epidemic diseases that the Spaniards' arrival heralded. The rebellion led to the destruction of twenty-one of the twenty-three mission stations affiliated with the Franciscan missionaries of Santa Rosa de Ocopa in the Peruvian Amazon region. An indigenous prophet named Juan Santos (d. c. 1756) spearheaded the 1742 revolt. He allegedly claimed to be a reincarnation of the Inca emperor Atahualpa. Santos combined anticolonial and messianic themes to rouse indigenous rebellion against the Franciscans and Spain's colonial authorities. He was even aided by small numbers of African men who had worked as soldiers or slaves owned by the missionaries.

Santos was familiar enough with intra-Catholic rivalries to play the Jesuits and Franciscans off each other. He promised to force the Franciscans to go back to Spain but to allow the Jesuits to remain, since they were willing to give leadership positions to Peruvians who had both Spanish and indigenous ancestry. Santos's rebellion persisted until he attacked, but then was forced to withdraw from the city of Andamarca in 1752. After this year, he faded from the historical record and died under uncertain circumstances. But his revolt illustrated again the capacity of indigenous people in the Americas to rise up against European colonial and missionary authorities. The Spanish and Franciscan missionaries began to reassert their presence in the region in the 1760s, despite ongoing unrest among indigenous people. (The Spanish expelled the Jesuits from all their territories starting in 1767, seeing them as troublemaking defenders of papal supremacy over Spanish royal authority.) More than a hundred Franciscan missionaries went from Spain to Peru's Santa Rosa de Ocopa from the 1760s to the 1780s. At its height of influence, around 1800, Santa Rosa de Ocopa was arguably the center of the largest missionary enterprise in the western hemisphere, with more than seventy parishes and missionary enclaves covering a vast South American territory of a half a million square miles.

Image 14.1. *The Convent of Santa Rosa de Ocopa, Peru*

The late 1700s saw both Catholics and Protestants seeking major expansion in the Americas with Protestants giving somewhat more attention to eastern North America and the Caribbean and Catholics to Central and South America and to the Catholic-affiliated colonies in the Caribbean. Both sides in the Protestant-Catholic divide were aware of the others' missionary efforts. Sometimes imperial war (such as the Seven Years' War of the 1750s–1760s) made Catholic-Protestant rivalry especially acute. Although Protestants benefitted from the military and commercial might of countries including Britain, the new United States, and other Protestant nations, Catholic missionaries tended to partner more directly with imperial powers such as Spain. This cooperation also caused severe problems for the Catholic Church when a series of Latin American independence movements broke out in the early nineteenth century. Independence leaders such as Simón Bolívar (1783–1830) often viewed churches and missionaries as corrupt enablers of imperial power. Bolívar, for instance, sacked Peru's Santa Rosa de Ocopa convent in 1824 and had many missionaries arrested.

Further Protestant Revivals

In North America and the Caribbean, Protestant missions were especially driven by denominations such as the Baptists and Methodists. After the American Revolution, these denominations operated in an entrepreneurial mode that smoothly adapted to the disestablishment of most state churches in the US. Regardless of whether they faced an established church, however, the Methodists were Protestant expansionists and revivalists par excellence. Methodist growth continued in England after Wesley's death, most notably under the Yorkshire ministry of William Bramwell (1759–1818), probably the most effective Methodist revivalist in England of the era. Bramwell followed Wesley in his emphasis on the believer's potential to achieve "entire sanctification" through God's sanctifying power.

Bramwell was also committed to rigorous prayer for conversions and revival, and he attributed much of the furor of the Yorkshire revival of 1792–96 to the devotion of Ann "Nanny" Cutler, a working-class woman who was one of his early converts and an exemplar of Methodist piety. In his 1796 tract *A Short Account of the Life and Death of Ann Cutler*, Bramwell described her as a "principal instrument" whom God used to bring about the revival. A year before his death, John Wesley told her that there was "something in the dealings of God with your soul which is out of the common way." Cutler seems to have prayed publicly in Methodist meetings, both for revival in general and for individual penitents. Cutler's role drew criticism from some Methodists, as women's speaking roles in Methodist meetings became a divisive matter. But from William Bramwell's perspective, revivals tended to follow wherever Nanny Cutler appeared and prayed: "The Lord made use of her at the beginning of a revival, and the work spread nearly through the circuit. Very often ten or twenty, or more, were saved in a meeting." Cutler died in 1794.

> Her life was a life of prayer. Oh! that I may follow her in this as she followed Christ! . . . I have been in chapel, when suddenly the whole congregation have been deeply affected in answer to her cries. For prayer I never expect to see her equal again.
>
> ---
>
> William Bramwell, *A Short Account of the Life and Death of Ann Cutler*, 1796

Wales also witnessed significant revivals during the 1790s, led by Calvinistic Methodist and Baptist preachers. The Anglican-Methodist preacher and native Welshman Thomas Charles (1755–1814) had experienced conversion in the 1770s under the ministry of the

Welsh Great Awakening evangelist Daniel Rowland. Charles came under the influence of the evangelical Anglican minister John Newton during his studies at Oxford. Marrying a Welsh woman from a Calvinistic Methodist family, Charles moved to Bala, Merioneth, in Wales, where he spent the rest of his ministry. Thomas Charles became familiar with the Welsh language (which had fallen into some disuse in schools) and produced devotional books in Welsh, including a successful evangelical catechism. In 1791, Charles saw the outbreak of revival across the whole town of Bala, with particular successes among children and young adults. The Methodist revival in Wales spread out from Bala and continued for a couple years. Baptists likewise reported revivals in Wales in the mid-1790s; in the south of Wales they reported more than eight hundred baptisms of new converts in the year 1795 alone. As for Thomas Charles, he did not formally break with the Anglican Church until late in life. In 1811, however, he participated in the ordination of lay preachers in the Welsh Calvinistic Methodist denomination.

Befitting the Presbyterian religious culture of Scotland, Methodism played a much smaller role in the Scottish revivals of the 1790s. Still, Scotland was influenced by broader evangelical patterns in England and America. For example, Glasgow and Edinburgh both saw the formation of missionary societies in 1796 and the Society for the Propagation of the Gospel at Home in 1797. The latter organization was the brainchild of the extraordinary Scottish preacher and organizer James Alexander Haldane (1768–1851), a ship captain, independent minister and evangelist. Haldane and his brother Robert, also an evangelical convert, became frustrated with the difficulties of working within existing church structures to pursue ministry in largely unevangelized places such as the Scottish Highlands and the Orkney Islands off Scotland's northern coast. Partnering with a network of evangelical ministers and philanthropists across England and Scotland, James Haldane pioneered evangelistic initiatives in the north of Scotland, even though he was not ordained. Often preaching outdoors, he sometimes saw audiences in the thousands assemble in small villages across northern Scotland. Many of the Church of Scotland clergy saw Haldane as a threat, though some evangelicals in the denomination viewed him as providing a much-needed challenge to the churches' complacency. Haldane figured he would do better without the Church of Scotland's strictures, so he completely broke ties with the denomination in 1799. He began pastoring an independent congregation in Edinburgh, and within a decade he came to Baptist convictions regarding the proper subjects of baptism (meaning persons old enough to repent and believe).

Haldane and other supporters of the Society for the Propagation of the Gospel at Home saw the new evangelistic and missionary efforts as representing an opportunity, perhaps marking the last days, for the rapid expansion of the gospel across the globe. Haldane published his *Journal of a Tour through the Northern Counties of Scotland and the Orkney Isles* in 1798, headed by the popular prophetic verse in Dan 12:4, "many shall run to and fro, and knowledge shall be increased" (KJV). Haldane and his supporters especially endorsed the idea of lay preaching and unlicensed evangelists (such as Haldane) as a counterweight to the corruptions of the established churches. Citing the Enlightenment principles of the great Scottish economist Adam Smith, Haldane endorsed a kind of free market for religion in which biblical truth would beat out its erroneous competitors. "Monopolies are as unfavorable to religion as to trade," he wrote. "Should unfit men engage in the business, their hearers will either leave them, or they will themselves tire of the employment. The chaff will thus be blown away, and the wheat (those who love the Lord Jesus and know the value of immortal souls) will remain." Haldane was implicitly expanding arguments about religious choice, proffered by Great Awakening evangelists such as Gilbert Tennent, to their next logical step. Not only did he advocate that believers should choose a church that taught fully biblical doctrine, but also he de-emphasized the value of ordination and licensing of pastors altogether. Although revivalists had often promoted informal roles for "exhorters," it was extremely unusual to question the value of ordination per se. But to evangelicals such as Haldane, all that mattered was faithful Bible teaching and evangelism, not the educational credentials of the preacher. This kind of flexible, entrepreneurial anti-institutionalism has marked much of the evangelical movement since its inception. This impulse has led many evangelicals to treat the work of the churches as a business: the sacred business of the gospel.

Protestants were spreading across much of the English-speaking world outside of the United Kingdom, too. The African American pastor David George and many in his Nova Scotia Baptist congregation moved to Sierra Leone in 1792. The English minister Samuel Marsden went to Australia in 1793, where he became one of the colony's most influential and controversial religious leaders. The English Baptists William and Dorothy Carey went to India in the same year. Evangelical growth in Canada had burgeoned in the 1770s and 1780s under the leadership of the fiery Nova Scotia evangelist Henry Alline (1748–84), whose revivals set the stage for eastern Canada to become one of the most heavily evangelical areas in the broader British Empire. In 1791, the Nova Scotia Methodist preacher

William Black (1760–1834) helped energize the evangelical movement in the fishing villages of Newfoundland in the far northeast of North America. Black went to Carbonear, on the east coast of Newfoundland, and one of the oldest European settlements in North America. That town had seen revival during Henry Alline's time (Alline had died in 1784). Black found little remaining evidence of evangelical zeal save for some private meetings of devout women. When he preached in the village, however, he saw a great outbreak of fervor, with many crying and asking the way to salvation. "One young woman rose up and declared the loving kindness of the Lord to her soul," he wrote. "She appeared almost carried beyond herself." Within weeks Black offered a communion service to about one hundred thirty people in the village and saw an even more heightened "universal shaking."

Again, the Methodist leader Thomas Coke was arguably the most influential organizer of transatlantic Methodism in this era. Coke bolstered the Methodist movement in places from England and Ireland to the US and the Caribbean. He was one of Wesley's most trusted lieutenants until Wesley's death. Coke and Francis Asbury were the key figures in the establishment of the independent Methodist Episcopal Church in America, which became the greatest source of American evangelical growth during the Second Great Awakening. Starting in 1784, Coke visited the US nine times over the course of twenty years, in addition to four trips to the Caribbean. He also played a role in establishing Methodist missions to India, Sierra Leone, Ireland, and rural areas of Britain not yet evangelized by Methodists. Coke himself left England for a mission to India in late 1813, but during his crossing of the Indian Ocean, he died from an apparent stroke. He was the epitome of the globe-trotting evangelical leaders who followed in the wake of George Whitefield and John Wesley.

Coke and Asbury had a more enduring effect on global Methodism, but probably the most controversial of the Methodist evangelists of the era was Lorenzo Dow (1777–1834), also known as "Crazy Dow." Dow, a native of New England, was converted under Methodist preaching when he was seventeen. He received a series of dreams and visions convincing him that he was called by God as an evangelist. He qualified as a licensed Methodist preacher, but he kept his distance from the Methodist denomination, preferring to remain a relatively independent evangelist. Cultivating an unruly preaching style and appearance, Dow wore his hair much longer than most men of the time, and sometimes wore rough, frontier-style clothing. In 1798 he traveled to Ireland, where some Methodist officials balked at his outlandish reputation. He also made several preaching trips to England over his career. He came back to America in 1801, where he preached in virtually every area of the country populated by whites, from New York to Florida to Louisiana.

Image 14.2. *Lorenzo Dow*

Dow represented a populist, democratized version of evangelicalism that was born in post-Revolutionary America. This style also drew much support from certain segments of the evangelical community in the United Kingdom. Many Methodist leaders, as well as government officials in Ireland and England, looked askance at Crazy Dow. Thomas Coke for one threatened to report Dow to officials in Dublin, Ireland, if he kept preaching without a license. It is easy to overstate the differences in evangelical culture in Britain and America, but Dow certainly represented a democratic insurgent style of ministry that would, at least in stereotype, come to represent the American evangelical ethos itself.

The Second Great Awakening

That ethos was profoundly shaped by the "camp meeting" revivals which began to shake the American frontier starting in the early 1800s. We shouldn't exaggerate the novelty of camp meetings like the one at Cane Ridge, Kentucky, in 1801. Significant revivals kept happening regionally in North America in the decades between the "First" and "Second" Great Awakenings proper. For example, the "New Light Stir" of the early 1780s deeply impacted the Baptist churches of New England and maritime Canada. The New Light Stir fueled sectarian movements such as the Freewill Baptists and the Shakers, the latter of which was led by the English émigré and messianic figure of "Mother" Ann Lee (1736–84). The camp meeting revivals also had deep roots in Scottish and Scots-Irish Presbyterianism and its tradition of "Holy Fairs." More than a century before George Whitefield's great revival at Cambuslang, Scotland, people in Scotland and Ulster (Northern Ireland) had seen great outbreaks of fervor at religious meetings that sometimes lasted for days and culminated in outdoor celebrations of the Lord's Supper. Scots-Irish ministers exported that ministry model to the American frontier, where it took on a rustic cast, but it was no brand-new development in Protestant Christianity. Lorenzo Dow and other evangelical preachers had seen signs of major revival beginning in New England and Canada in the mid-to-late 1790s. Still the revivals of 1800–1801 in Kentucky and Tennessee did strike observers as something new. Those awakenings are useful markers for the beginning of the Second Great Awakening.

The chief instigator of the Kentucky revivals was the evangelical Presbyterian James McGready (1763–1817), the child of Scottish Presbyterian parents in western Pennsylvania. McGready ministered for a time in North Carolina before growing hostility to his provocative preaching led him to decamp for fast-growing Kentucky in 1797. By 1799 he was coordinating Holy Fair-style assemblies in the state with explosive results. An 1800 revival at McGready's Red River church attracted ministers, including some Methodists, from across the region and neighboring Tennessee. The fervor of the meetings led to extraordinary scenes with dozens of penitents "slain in the Spirit" and laying prostrate on the floor. Critics saw such activity as crass enthusiasm, but McGready explained that "it is nothing strange if a man fulfilled with an uncommon sense of terror and divine wrath should fall to the ground and his bodily strength be overcome." As in the First Great Awakening, there were deep divisions among evangelicals regarding propriety in revivalism. In the Second Great Awakening, exuberant and charismatic reactions became more common and accepted, especially among both white and black Methodists and radical Presbyterians.

The open-air communion assemblies across Kentucky and Tennessee became known as "camp meetings." They developed into regional events where people literally camped around the hosting church, sleeping in and under their wagons for a weekend of fellowship. Barton Stone (1772–1844), then the Presbyterian minister at Cane Ridge, Kentucky, was influenced by McGready to bring a camp meeting to his congregation in 1801. In August 1801, the Cane Ridge assembly attracted tens of thousands of Presbyterians, Methodists, and Baptists from across the overwhelmingly rural state. One ambivalent Presbyterian minister, John Lyle, who participated at Cane Ridge, wrote that attendees at one point "got into a singing extacy . . . I went in among a cluster of rejoicers and shook hands with some of them, one stood staring like he saw Christ in the air, I asked him what views he had of Christ. He said he saw a fulness in him for all that come." Lyle vacillated back and forth between participating in the Cane Ridge sessions and talking with other concerned ministers about "disorder" and the "danger of enthusiasm."

Camp meetings spread across North America, especially in rural regions of the South. Methodists in particular sought to export the camp meeting's successes to other places in North America and Britain. In 1805, for example, a camp meeting took place at Hay Bay

Image 14.3. *Old Hay Bay Church, Ontario* (1908)

near Adolphustown, Ontario, in Canada. The Methodists who led the Hay Bay assembly hoped to re-create the scenes at Cane Ridge and were rewarded with astounding reactions of conviction and rejoicing. Though the Hay Bay revival was numerically smaller than Cane Ridge, it still drew masses of people that represented about 5 percent of the whole province of Ontario.

Methodists made the camp meeting a distinctive feature of their movement, while the camp meeting style became more divisive among Presbyterians. Barton Stone and other revivalist Presbyterians became disenchanted with the denomination, and Stone went on to become one of the founders of the restorationist "Christian" or "Disciples" movement, the forerunner of the Churches of Christ and Disciples of Christ denominations. Stone's future restorationist colleague Alexander Campbell (1788–1866) also came out of a Presbyterian upbringing in Northern Ireland. Campbell's father Thomas, and Alexander Campbell himself, founded a "Christian Association" in Pennsylvania in 1809 devoted to restoring the primitive simplicity of the New Testament churches. For a time, Alexander Campbell affiliated with Baptists, convinced that believer's baptism was the original mode practiced by early Christians. In the early 1830s, however, Campbell and Barton Stone brought together an association of "Disciples" and "Christians," forming one of the most influential of the new restorationist churches.

Baptists benefitted from the ongoing revival fervor of the Second Great Awakening, even as they remained somewhat marginal to the camp meeting phenomenon. This was partly due to Baptist scruples about partnering with denominations that continued to practice infant baptism. (Paedobaptists likewise continued to view Baptists with disdain.) Still, Baptists saw massive growth in Kentucky around the time of the Cane Ridge meeting. More than 2,400 people in Kentucky received believer's baptism in one five-month stretch in 1801, which represented more than 1 percent of the state's population. Some Baptist revivals saw the kinds of ecstatic experiences that marked the camp meetings, including penitents laid out on meetinghouse floors. It was not unusual for Baptists to adopt hymns from the camp meetings. They also brought those under conviction of sin to the front of assemblies to receive prayer for conversion, a signature ritual of the camp meetings. Leading Baptist minister Richard Furman (1755–1825) of South Carolina noted that in 1802–1803, Baptist churches in North and South Carolina participated in revival assemblies in the "Kentucky stile."

Elite Presbyterian, Congregationalist, and even Episcopal churches experienced revival during this era, too. Those churches' leaders often prized decorum and sobriety over Pentecost-like fervor, and they tended to attract more well-to-do and politically-connected congregants. This is not to suggest that the religious commitment of these moderate evangelicals did not run deep: their work bore great fruit in terms of conversions, moral reform organizations, and missionary efforts. Arguably the most significant of the Congregationalist revivals transpired at Yale College in 1802, where the Calvinist president Timothy Dwight (1752–1817) presided over the student awakening. As a grandson of Jonathan Edwards, Dwight had deep roots in the New England revivalist tradition. Like Edwards, Dwight was thoroughly conversant with the intellectual trends of the day, but he remained convinced of the debilitating effects of sin on human nature and of all people's need for salvation through Christ. Dwight became Yale president in 1795 and helped to make Yale a leading academic institution, as well as restoring it as a stronghold of evangelical faith. One approving account of the Yale revival attributed to Dwight assured readers of the *Connecticut Evangelical Magazine* that nothing had happened in the revival that would give concern to a "wise and good man, nothing enthusiastic, nothing superstitious, nothing gloomy, morose, or violent." The revival had led to seriousness about Christ and commitment to the "doctrines of grace," or principled Calvinism.

Diversity in the Second Great Awakening

The First Great Awakening had seen deep divisions between moderate and radical revivalists, but now those divisions began to play out between denominations and social classes. Methodists were more comfortable with enthusiastic outbursts of camp meeting revivalism. Along with Baptists, Methodists represented the great engine of evangelical popular growth during the period. But elite, moderate evangelicals such as Timothy Dwight retained disproportionate resources, publishing opportunities, and cultural authority at places such as Yale. Historian Sam Haselby has argued that the Second Great Awakening was riven by a divide between the economically and politically powerful forces of "national evangelism" (such as Dwight's Congregationalists) and "frontier revivalism" (such as Methodists and Baptists). Britain also saw similar divisions among evangelicals, although the religious situation was complicated by the established Church of England, and Church of Scotland. Within both communions, there were significant evangelical strains of belief and practice.

American Christianity had its own diversity, of course, reflected particularly in the growth of Christianity among African Americans. As we have seen, by the early 1800s the growth of black-led Methodist and Baptist churches was under way in the US and the Caribbean. The Baptist leader George Liele had already helped to start African American churches in Savannah, Georgia, and in Kingston, Jamaica, in the 1770s and '80s. Although Congregationalist churches would fall behind Baptists and Methodists in attracting African American adherents, they did produce the extraordinary minister Lemuel Haynes (1753–1833), probably the first ordained African American pastor in a mainstream American denomination. After serving as a soldier on the Patriot side of the Revolutionary War, Haynes was ordained in 1785. In 1788, he began a long tenure as the pastor of a majority white Congregationalist church in Rutland, Vermont. Haynes was a critic of American slavery and liberal theology. For example, his sermon *Universal Salvation* denounced the universalist theology (the idea that all will eventually be saved) of the popular pastor Hosea Ballou as an "ancient devilish doctrine." The tract resulting from Haynes's sermon was reprinted dozens of times over the next few decades, making Haynes one of the best-known opponents of universalism in the American evangelical community.

Haynes was also a product of the "New Divinity," or the broader "New England Theology." The New Divinity was composed of Calvinist theologians and pastors working out the implications of the massive theological legacy of Jonathan Edwards. Not only was the New England Theology the most formidable American doctrinal tradition of the era, but for many whites and blacks it also was a profound resource for antislavery convictions. Even though Jonathan Edwards had been a slaveowner and was reluctant to criticize slave owning per se, many of his disciples, including his son Jonathan Edwards Jr., became outspoken critics of slavery. They advocated an ethical ideal of "disinterested benevolence," or the idea that the greatest acts of Christian charity are those toward people who are incapable of offering anything of value in return, such as slaves. Arguably the most influential promoter of disinterested benevolence was Edwards's disciple Samuel Hopkins (1721–1803). Hopkins pastored in Newport, Rhode Island, a major slave trafficking center, starting in 1770. Disinterested benevolence was epitomized in Christ's death for sinners, "exercised toward those who are not only unworthy and ill deserving, but unreasonable and abusive enemies. This disinterested benevolence he urges Christians to imitate," Hopkins wrote. The realities of the American slave trade helped to turn Hopkins into an opponent of slavery. As we have seen, many of the new missionary advocates in America and Britain, including Andrew Fuller, were inspired by Edwards's writings, as well as by the concept of disinterested benevolence and holy activism for the gospel.

Conclusion

Missions, especially for Catholics, were not new in the 1790s and early 1800s. As seen in Peru, in California, and elsewhere, the scale of Catholic missions remained institutionally ahead of Protestants at the beginning of the Second Great Awakening. Individual Protestant pastors and missionaries, such as George Liele, had already traveled across the seas to do church planting and evangelistic works. The Moravians had paved the way for organized Protestant missions. Yet the ingredients were coming into place for a new British and American Protestant missionary movement which would be one of the most salient factors in nineteenth-century church history. British Protestants were usually ahead of Americans organizationally by a few years, but both Connecticut and Massachusetts had seen the founding of New Divinity missionary societies by the end of the 1790s. Then in 1806, an impromptu rainy-day prayer meeting by Williams College (Massachusetts) students, taking shelter under a haystack, led several of those students to dedicate themselves to foreign missions. These students would help organize the American Board of Commissioners for Foreign Missions (ABCFM) in 1810, the first national missionary organization in the United States. The ABCFM was not officially denominational, but it was dominated by Congregationalists and New Divinity advocates.

Like most of the Protestant missionary boosters of the era, the leaders of the ABCFM believed that the gospel should go out to all nations, eventually hastening the return of Christ. They were inspired by the circulation of missionary accounts from around the globe and stories of people from unfamiliar cultures who accepted salvation through Christ. One of the most unusual cases of such converts was the Hawaiian teenager Opukahaia (1792–1818), or Henry Obookiah, as he became known in the US. Obookiah came from a priestly family of his indigenous religion in Hawaii, but through improbable circumstances he made his way to New England in 1808. In New Haven, Connecticut, he came under the influence and patronage of the Dwight family and went to live in the home of Yale president Timothy Dwight. Obookiah came to believe in Christ and experienced conversion. He became something of a Christian celebrity in the mid-1810s in New England, promoting missions to Hawaii and enrolling in a special missionary school for foreigners and "heathen" that the ABCFM founded in Connecticut. Obookiah began translating parts of the Bible into the Hawaiian language. A great deal of momentum was building for a Hawaii mission, but before Obookiah could depart for his native land, he died of typhus in 1818, at around twenty-six years old. Nevertheless, the ABCFM soon sent missionaries to Hawaii, and *The Memoirs of Henry Obookiah* (1818) became a popular missionary and Sunday school tract. Although the Hawaii missions would be marred by uncritical American attachment to the forces of empire, Obookiah still embodied one of the most powerful impulses in the evangelical movement: the desire to convert the nations to faith in Christ.

Selected Bibliography

Bramwell, William. *A Short Account of the Life and Death of Ann Cutler*. Sheffield, UK, 1796.

Conroy-Krutz, Emily. *Christian Imperialism: Converting the World in the Early American Republic*. Ithaca, NY: Cornell University Press, 2015.

Crisp, Oliver D., and Douglas A. Sweeney, eds. *After Jonathan Edwards: The Courses of the New England Theology*. New York: Oxford University Press, 2012.

Demos, John. *The Heathen School: A Story of Hope and Betrayal in the Age of the Early Republic*. New York: Knopf, 2014.

Haselby, Sam. *The Origins of American Religious Nationalism*. New York: Oxford University Press, 2015.

Jones, Cameron D. *In Service of Two Masters: The Missionaries of Ocopa, Indigenous Resistance, and Spanish Governance in Bourbon Peru*. Stanford, CA: Stanford University Press, 2018.

Rawlyk, George A. *The Canada Fire: Radical Evangelicalism in British North America, 1775–1812*. Kingston, ON: McGill-Queen's University Press, 1994.

Saillant, John. *Black Puritan, Black Republican: The Life and Thought of Lemuel Haynes, 1753–1833*. New York: Oxford University Press, 2002.

Schmidt, Leigh Eric. *Holy Fairs: Scotland and the Making of American Revivalism*. 2nd ed. Grand Rapids: Eerdmans, 2001.

Wolffe, John. *The Expansion of Evangelicalism: The Age of Wilberforce, More, Chalmers and Finney*. Downers Grove: IVP, 2007.

Chapter 15

A New Era of Theological Change and Moral Reform

It would be difficult to overstate the upheavals that the French Revolution and the Napoleonic wars unleashed on European religion. To cite just one example, in 1798 the armies of Napoleon—who had become "First Consul" of France—invaded Italy and arrested Pope Pius VI, who had opposed the French Revolution and its savage abuses against the French Catholic Church. The long-serving pope died in exile in France in 1799. His successor Pius VII sought rapprochement with Napoleon and attended the general's coronation as French emperor in 1804. However, Napoleon invaded Rome once again in 1809, and took Pius VII to France as a prisoner. Pius VII was allowed to return to Rome in 1814, but the point was made. If the papacy was just one more political authority in Europe, then aggressive leaders such as Napoleon might challenge, co-opt, or even humiliate the pope whenever conditions were right. The Napoleonic era undermined the papacy's formidable aura. However, it also energized an "ultramontane" reaction in Europe

> It is better to cherish virtue and humanity, by leaving much to free will, even with some loss to the object, than to attempt to make men mere machines and instruments of a political benevolence.
>
> ---
>
> Edmund Burke, *Reflections on the Revolution in France*, 1790

which encouraged strong fidelity to Catholic authority, especially the pope, in the face of the seeming godlessness of the French Revolution. The duress of the French Revolution left Christians across the nations longing for "revival" of many kinds.

Reviving Catholicism

Protestants were split over the French Revolution, with some rejoicing in the distress of the Catholic Church and the potential for greater liberty for Protestants in Europe. Others, such as the Anglo-Irish conservative writer Edmund Burke, denounced the Revolution for pulling up society by its roots with nothing to replace it but government force. "We know, and, what is better, we feel inwardly, that religion is the basis of civil society, and the source of all good and of all comfort," Burke wrote. A revolutionary assault on the church—even the Catholic Church—was hellish madness. Even many Christians who opposed religious establishments would have agreed with Burke that trying to base a society on anticlerical secularism was a dangerous experiment. Few such observers were surprised when the chaos of the French Revolution was followed by the autocratic Napoleon. He offered order and stability to bleeding France, partly through symbolic support for Christian piety (as long as the Christians in question supported his ambitions). As Napoleon explained, "I closed the gulf of anarchy and cleared the chaos."

The Revolution left many across Europe nostalgic for the stability of pre-Revolutionary religion and society. Few were as eloquent in expressing that nostalgia as François-René de Chateaubriand (1768–1848), a French aristocrat who returned to his Catholic faith after being exiled during the Revolution. In his influential *Genius of Christianity* (1802), Chateaubriand defended Christianity, not so much for its provable truths but for its aesthetic treasures. "Of all religions, the Christian religion is the most poetic, the most humane, the most favorable to liberty and to the arts and literature . . . there is nothing more divine than its morality, nothing more attractive and splendid than its tenets, its doctrines and its forms of worship." Chateaubriand brought a confidence to his defense of Christianity that European Catholics badly needed. "Christianity is perfect; men are imperfect. A perfect outcome cannot follow from an imperfect principle. Therefore, Christianity does not come from men. If it does not come from men, it can only come from God," he argued. Throughout much of Europe, Chateaubriand helped to make Catholicism intellectually defensible again. In some quarters, his type of Catholic traditionalism became downright fashionable.

During the nineteenth century, women increased as a percentage of devout Catholics and Protestants. The reasons for women's predominance are not reducible to social factors alone, but the opportunities for women's fellowship, service, and leadership (though not as priests or pastors) undoubtedly played a role. One American woman who felt the pull of Rome was Elizabeth Ann Seton (1774–1821), who grew up in New York as an Episcopalian in the years following the American Revolution. When her husband developed a terminal case of tuberculosis, the Seton family went to live in Italy for its salubrious climate. He died shortly after their arrival, however, and Elizabeth came under the influence of Italian Catholics who introduced her to the faith. Back in the US, she entered the Catholic Church in 1805. She moved to Maryland and founded the Sisters of Charity, an American religious order. In 1975 she was canonized as a saint by the Vatican, making her the first native-born saint from the US.

In Europe, the number of women in Catholic orders surged in the aftermath of the French Revolution. In France, around four hundred women's Catholic orders were founded or re-established between 1800 and 1880, drawing in about 200,000 women to become religious sisters. Most of these were in outward-facing service roles rather than cloistered and contemplative ones (roles where sisters are usually called "nuns"). Sophie Barat (1779–1865) founded the Society of the Sacred Heart of Jesus in France in 1802, and the order proliferated to more than one hundred convents in Europe, Africa, and North America by the time of her death in 1865. Likewise, the French woman Anne-Marie Javouhey (1779–1851) founded the Sisters of Saint Joseph of Cluny in 1807, which was devoted to ministering to impoverished women and children. Like Barat's order, Javouhey's spread far and wide to mission stations in Africa, South America, and the Caribbean. Javouhey was given the moniker *la mère des noires* ("the mother of the blacks") because the Sisters of Saint Joseph of Cluny became known for their opposition to slavery. Javouhey herself engaged in a remarkable missionary career, working at stations in Africa and South America, among other places. Even in Protestant-dominated England, the number of Catholic convents surged from less than twenty in 1840 to around five hundred in 1900. Most of those convents were affiliated with French or Belgian orders.

European and American Catholicism went through its own forms of revival during the nineteenth century. The piety of Catholic revival was generally quite different from Protestant revivalism. Even American-based Catholic priests who took on quasi-revivalist roles did not so much call on their audience to be born again but to renew their commitment to the church and to holiness. But legions of Catholic women, in particular, devoted themselves to a Catholic vocation. Some went through ecstatic or mystical spiritual experiences that became models for others. Some female saints became the focus of Catholic devotions. For example, the nineteenth century saw increasing claims of stigmata (the miraculous manifestation of the wounds of Christ upon holy persons) and of appearances of Mary. Both phenomena tended to happen to young women, either nuns or laywomen. At the beginning of the nineteenth century, the German nun Anne Catherine Emmerich (1774–1824) reportedly began manifesting wounds on her head and then on her hands, feet, and side, which replicated those of the crucified Jesus. She also received a series of visions and revelations, giving detailed extrabiblical information about the lives of Mary, Jesus, and others. The German Romantic poet Clemens Brentano recorded many of these visions, and after Emmerich's death in 1824 he published the bestselling *Dolorous Passion of Our Lord Jesus Christ*, based on what she told him. Although the reliability of Emmerich's visions and Brentano's records are disputed, the Catholic Church beatified her (giving her the title "Blessed") in 2004. That same year, Mel Gibson released his controversial film *The Passion of the Christ*, which depended heavily on *The Dolorous Passion*.

Marian apparitions had a long history, with Mary's reported appearance to Juan Diego in 1531 in Mexico having arguably the greatest significance for the future of Catholicism in the Western Hemisphere. But the nineteenth and early twentieth century saw several other apparitions, particularly in Europe, that stirred the Catholic faithful. These apparitions sometimes provided guidance and reassurance amid the political upheavals of the century. The era's first such apparition to receive widespread attention and official support from church authorities came in 1830 to Catherine Labouré (1806–76), a French nun in Paris. Labouré received an image of the Virgin Mary and was told to have the image struck on a devotional medal, which would also include the prayer "O Mary, conceived without sin, pray for us who have recourse to thee." The medals began to be minted in 1832, and within a decade a hundred million copies of the "Miraculous Medal" had been created.

The Marian revelations to Catherine Labouré set the stage for the 1854 papal articulation of the Virgin Mary's "immaculate conception." All Christians acknowledge that Mary had a special role as the mother of Jesus. Catholics have typically adopted a stronger view regarding her ongoing assistance to Christians from heaven. (Some Catholics have even posited Mary as a "co-redemptrix" with Christ, but that belief is not officially recognized by the church.) Protestants generally reject prayers to anyone but God himself, but Catholics encourage petitions to saints, including Mary. The prayer "Hail Mary, full of grace" echoed Gabriel's greeting to Mary in Luke 1, and Catholics assumed that Mary was exceptionally holy. But did she have any taint of sin at all? By the 1600s it had become common for Catholics to teach that Mary was born without the curse of original sin, unlike the rest of humanity. This holiness made her a fit vessel for the conception of the Messiah by the Holy Spirit. In 1854, Pope Pius IX stated that "the most blessed Virgin Mary was preserved from all stain of original sin in the first instant of her conception." Protestants reject the immaculate conception as extrabiblical, believing that Mary was subject to original sin and, therefore, was saved via Christ's death and resurrection. Eastern Orthodox Christians give Mary an exalted status as the "Theotokos," or Mother of God, but they, too, have been skeptical about the immaculate conception. Many observers mistakenly assume that the "immaculate conception" refers to the conception of Jesus, but the articulation of this doctrine was actually a key moment in Mary's centrality in Catholic devotion.

Image 15.1. Murillo, *Immaculate Conception of the Choir, the Girl* (ca. 1668–1669)

Perhaps the most influential Marian apparition of the nineteenth century came in 1858 at Lourdes, in southwestern France. A teenage girl named Bernadette Soubirous (1844–79) began receiving messages from a "young lady," subsequently identified as Mary, who told her, "I am the Immaculate Conception." Among other revelations, Mary showed Bernadette an unknown spring of water that possessed healing powers. Church investigations determined that Bernadette was sincere, and in 1933 the church declared Soubirous a saint. The site of the apparitions became associated with healing miracles and Lourdes became one of the most-visited pilgrimage sites in Christendom, with millions of visitors a year going there to pray and to drink the healing waters. Catholics have also built replicas of the Lourdes grotto, the location of the apparitions, all over the world. The most famous replica in the US is on the campus of the University of Notre Dame in South Bend, Indiana.

A complement to the Immaculate Conception was the articulation of papal infallibility at the First Vatican Council in 1869–70. Although some bishops were reluctant to take a strong stance on the matter (partly because it might be seen as undermining the authority of church leaders besides the pope), the majority agreed to affirm the pope's infallibility when "speaking ex cathedra." The council explained that the pope could exercise such authority "when, in the exercise of his office as shepherd and teacher of all Christians, in virtue of his supreme apostolic authority, he defines a doctrine concerning faith or morals to be held by the whole Church." At such times "he possesses, by the divine assistance promised to him in blessed Peter, that infallibility which the divine Redeemer willed his Church to enjoy in defining doctrine concerning faith or morals." Again, papal infallibility has often been misunderstood to mean that the pope is simply incapable of error. But the church considered the pope to be speaking ex cathedra only in unusual situations when he resolved a disputed issue simply by appeal to the authority of his office. In a technical sense, popes have rarely invoked such authority. One of the only modern instances, indeed, was Pius IX's articulation of the Immaculate Conception in 1854. The mere potential for such authoritative statements added to the pope's aura of spiritual power. The claim of infallibility also ran against the tide of rationalist anticlerical sentiment that was a hallmark of the secular Enlightenment. For most of the next century, the Roman Catholic Church would position itself theologically and intellectually as anti-modernist and anti-secular, headed by a powerful pope and, allegedly, visited by an approving Virgin Mary.

The Allure of Rome

As with Elizabeth Ann Seton, certain Protestants found Catholicism's tradition and rootedness compelling. The Anglican priest John Henry Newman (1801–90) had grown up as an evangelical, but along with other high-church clerics known as the "Tractarians," Newman came to defend a Catholic-like vision of the power and grandeur of the Church of England. Indeed, the Tractarians (named for their *Tracts for the Times*) referred to themselves as "Anglo-Catholics." The group was also known as the "Oxford Movement," due to the high number of Oxford clergy among its number. Newman was convinced that modern Protestantism, in both liberal and evangelical forms, was dangerously rootless. Liberal theologians such as Friedrich Schleiermacher were substituting feeling and intuition for historic truth, while evangelicals affirmed biblical truth but made subjective experience the test of true piety. Newman finally determined that the Anglican *via media* was unsustainable. He converted to Catholicism in 1845. In his popular *Apologia pro vita sua* (1864) he explained that "there are but two alternatives, the way to Rome, and the way to Atheism: Anglicanism is the halfway house on the one side, and Liberalism is the halfway house on the other." Trying to hold a moderate position between authority and unbelief was impossible, he argued. He understood that most English Protestants would not follow him to Rome, and he appreciated that Anglicanism was still better than atheism. Yet Newman believed there was only a grim future for mainstream Protestantism due to the inexorable march of liberalism, skepticism, and unbelief.

Newman defended Catholicism by reference to the "development of doctrine," or the idea that some authoritative Christian doctrine (such as beliefs about the Trinity, the nature of Christ, purgatory, or the Immaculate Conception) becomes clearer and more detailed over time, even though it does not depart from the biblical and patristic traditions. Most nineteenth-century Protestants did not agree with Newman about Catholicism being the only alternative to theological liberalism, and they were uncomfortable with his idea that not all authoritative doctrine was clear in Scripture itself. Conservative Protestant theologians and pastors would certainly have agreed with Newman's concern about the liberalism of Schleiermacher and others, however. "Liberalism is the mistake of subjecting to human judgment those revealed doctrines which are in their nature beyond and independent of it," Newman contended. Liberalism took many forms, but its essential tenets after Schleiermacher were that intuition and feeling led to divine truth and that the Bible was a historical document produced by human authors, writing under all the normal limitations common to humanity. Many liberal "higher critics" contended that their real aim was to preserve Christianity, which was at risk when traditionalists insisted upon hidebound "orthodox" interpretations of an errorless Bible.

Liberalism Rising and Rejected

After Schleiermacher (who died in 1834), perhaps the most sensational liberal in the German academy was David Friedrich Strauss (1808–74), University of Tübingen professor and author of *Das Leben Jesu/The Life of Jesus* (1835). Strauss relentlessly depicted the Gospels as full of factual contradictions and undergirded by myths, or fanciful stories used to illustrate timeless principles. He also portrayed Jesus as an unstable zealot. Stung by vociferous denunciations from much of the German theological community, Strauss moderated some of his conclusions about Jesus in subsequent editions, portraying Jesus as a charismatic, insightful religious leader, but still not the unique Christ that orthodox theology embraced. Strauss felt that Schleiermacher was too open to the possibility of supernatural influences in Christianity's beginnings. A more reliable approach would strictly separate the Jesus of history from the Christ of faith. Even many liberal-leaning German theologians registered grave concern about Strauss's radical historicism and anti-supernaturalism. When the English writer and linguist George Eliot (the pen name of Mary Ann Evans) translated *Das Leben Jesu* in 1846, one evangelical leader called it "the most pestilential book ever vomited out of the jaws of Hell." Others were impressed, however, including a young Friedrich Nietzsche (1844–1900), who concluded from Strauss that belief in historic Christianity was intellectually untenable. Nietzsche would go on to become one of the most influential anti-Christian writers in world history.

Strauss's work was so controversial that he was unable to continue teaching as a theology professor. Yet he had taken radical higher criticism to an unprecedented level of notoriety by undermining the veracity of the Gospels themselves. In this sense, Strauss was pathbreaking and shaped much of biblical studies in elite academic settings in lasting ways. However, it is easy to overstate the significance of figures such as Strauss. Historians often tend to give more attention to people who push the boundaries of what is intellectually or theologically possible, such as Strauss (or, in his way, John Henry Newman). Yet most Protestant theologians and pastors in the 1830s remained convinced of the Bible's authority and divine origins and had no difficulty in rejecting the work of radical critics such as Strauss.

One of the most influential of the traditionalist Protestant German theologians was Ernst Wilhelm Hengstenberg (1802–69), a long-serving theology professor at the University of Berlin. His work especially focused on the divine inspiration and historical reliability of the Old Testament. In his most famous work, *Christology of the Old Testament* (publication began in 1829), Hengstenberg made a powerful case, against Schleiermacher, for the divine inspiration and theological unity of the Old and New Testaments. Do "genuine prophecies of the Messiah really exist in the Old Testament[?]," he asked. "This Schleiermacher denies." Yet Hengstenberg insisted that "whoever truly believes Christ and the Apostles, must acknowledge the divine authority of the Old Testament, to which they give so clear and definite testimony." There is considerably less scholarship on Hengstenberg, especially in non-German sources, than on Schleiermacher. Some would undoubtedly claim that this disproportionate attention has to do with the relative brilliance or significance of their theological writings, but it may also result from the penchant for innovators among historians. Schleiermacher was an innovator; Ernst Wilhelm Hengstenberg was not. Yet in his time, Hengstenberg was a far more representative figure. Even a critic of Hengstenberg like Philip Schaff, the Swiss-born theology professor of Mercersburg, Pennsylvania, admitted that Hengstenberg was "one of the most important and influential men in the kingdom of Prussia. He leads the extreme right wing of the orthodox party in the Established [Lutheran] Church, and is the uncompromising opponent of all rationalists and semi-rationalists, all latitudinarians and liberals." Schaff also conceded that Hengstenberg was probably the most revered German theologian in England and America in the mid-nineteenth century.

Indeed, many traditional American Protestants who studied theology in Germany found it a relatively congenial environment in the mid-nineteenth century because of "awakened" (i.e., pietistic and biblicist) scholars such as Hengstenberg. These included Hengstenberg's Berlin colleague and convert from Judaism, Johann August Neander (1789–1850), and August Tholuck (1799–1877) of the University of Halle. Tholuck was representative of the "mediating theology" among many German theologians of the time. They believed that the challenge of theological education was both to inform the head and touch the heart. Tholuck was more supportive of Schleiermacher's work than many traditional theologians were, partly because he felt that Schleiermacher's emphasis on interior experience would keep theology from becoming coldly rationalistic. Likewise, Tholuck was opposed to any kind of coercive use of creeds, such as the Augsburg Confession (1530), which remained foundational for Lutherans such as Hengstenberg. Yet Tholuck prized the writings of the Reformers, especially Calvin. Any observer could see that Tholuck's learning was prodigious, as he was an expert in fifteen languages by the beginning of his teaching career at Halle. In 1827, Charles Hodge (1797–1878) of Princeton Seminary visited Halle as part of a longer European tour, and he and Tholuck became lifelong friends, despite Tholuck's greater tolerance for Romantic-influenced theology. Reformed traditionalists such as Hodge found Tholuck to be an encouraging example of warm Christian faith amidst the disturbing patterns of speculative and higher critical German theology.

Hodge himself represented arguably the most enduring source of biblicist Protestant theology in nineteenth century America: Reformed Presbyterianism. Hodge taught at Presbyterians' leading theological school, Princeton Seminary. Princeton, or the College of New Jersey, had been founded in 1746 by evangelical Presbyterians, growing out of the Great Awakening. Jonathan Edwards was briefly the president of Princeton before his untimely death in 1758. As noted earlier, John Witherspoon's tenure at Princeton kept the school firmly within the Reformed theological tradition, even if Princeton became somewhat more optimistic about the power of unaided human reason to understand truth. In 1812, Princeton Theological Seminary was founded as an independent Presbyterian institution. It was the second standalone seminary in America after Andover Theological Seminary in Massachusetts. Andover was founded in 1807 as a conservative counterweight to the Unitarian drift then happening at Harvard. Particularly in the US, Harvard and Andover set a recurring pattern of liberalism in the theological academy prompting the creation of conservative alternatives. The pattern of drift and renewal rarely saw the rise of conservative theology at seminaries inspiring new liberal alternatives: the trend was usually leftward in the existing institutions.

Princeton Seminary, however, was not so much a conservative alternative as a means for better theological training of "a learned, orthodox, pious, and evangelical ministry" than what Princeton College could provide. Archibald Alexander (1772–1851) became the seminary's first principal and professor, and he served there for thirty-nine years. In his inaugural address, Alexander insisted that the essential task of Bible scholars and students was "to ascertain that the scriptures contain the truths of GOD" and "to ascertain what these truths are." The operative assumption was that the Bible was the unique revelation of God's truth.

One might think that the establishment of the independent seminary signaled Princeton College's departure from orthodox evangelical belief, but that was not yet the case. The key development in Princeton College's spiritual alignments, in addition to the 1812 creation of the seminary, was the appointment of Ashbel Green (1762–1848) as college president the same year. Green was a committed Presbyterian evangelical, and he introduced required study of the Bible into the college curriculum. In 1814–15, Green also presided over a major revival at Princeton. Like other elite Presbyterian and Congregationalist revivalists of the Second Great Awakening, Green was adamant that the Princeton revival proceeded "without noise" or any extreme precipitants, such as overly emotional preaching. "The divine influence seemed to descend like the silent dew of heaven; and in about four weeks there were very few individuals in the college edifice who were not deeply impressed with a sense of the importance of spiritual and eternal things." One of those who was converted and mobilized for Christian ministry in the revival was Charles Hodge, who had planned to become a medical doctor. One of Hodge's friends noted that he had "enlisted under the banner of King Jesus." In 1816, Hodge entered Princeton Seminary where he would become a full-time professor in 1822. As we saw above, Hodge traveled in Europe in the late 1820s to finish his education. His exposure to Tholuck, Hengstenberg, and other Continental scholars solidified Hodge's conviction that there was no contradiction between world-class biblical scholarship and warm Christian piety.

As seen at Princeton and the German universities, traditional Christians retained positions of elite intellectual and theological influence in the American and European academy throughout the nineteenth century, despite the increasingly prominent role for theological liberals and skeptical versions of biblical criticism. With more than three thousand students training under him, Hodge likely taught more divinity students (or graduate students in any field) than any other professor in nineteenth-century America.

Among Baptists, Brown University in Providence, Rhode Island, also remained a bastion of traditional belief through the Civil War era. Brown president and Baptist minister Francis Wayland (1796–1865) wrote textbooks on moral philosophy and political economy in the 1830s that became standards at American colleges (not just Baptist institutions) for decades to come. Wayland believed that science, economics, and other fields operated on immutable rules reflecting God's created order. Therefore, Wayland and his fellow evangelical educators tended to be optimistic that higher education, scientific study, and technological progress would all complement biblical revelation. In retrospect, Wayland's optimism looks somewhat naïve. By the late 1800s, it was easy for European and American intellectuals to conceive of a secularized world of science detached from the providential work of the creator. Yet Wayland's representativeness in American higher education suggests the pervasive hold that Christian—or at least theistic—belief held in western intellectual life through the first half of the 1800s.

Divisions within Denominations

Partly because of their de facto, or de jure (e.g., in Britain) established status, Christian intellectuals often battled against one another with as much zeal as against their skeptical or heterodox rivals. Who would control the religious and theological establishment(s) and institutions, and who would be regarded as beyond the pale? Rival versions of Presbyterianism clashed fatefully in the devastating Presbyterian schism of 1837–38 in America, the first of several major denominational splits over the next seven years. As we will see, the Baptists and Methodists in America substantially divided over the issue of slavery, an issue that was involved in the New School/Old School Presbyterian split, too. But the Presbyterians' struggle was more complex, involving questions about revivalism, social agendas such as temperance (anti-alcohol), and the status of traditional Calvinist beliefs. Some of the New

England theology, especially the brand promoted by Andover Theological Seminary and Yale Divinity School, was pro-revival and anti-Unitarian. It downplayed the effects of original sin and magnified the role of human choice in salvation. Thus, to Old School Presbyterians, it was a dangerous departure from the faith articulated in the Westminster Confession. Such concerns became even more amplified with the publication of revivalist Charles Finney's *Lectures on Revivals of Religion* (1835), which blamed Calvinist beliefs about God's sovereignty for American Christians' complacency about revival. The tensions over revivalism and traditional Calvinism finally erupted in an ugly, chaotic Presbyterian assembly in 1838, resulting in the creation of a separate New School assembly. Within a few decades the two sides would reunite, but by then American Presbyterians had also divided into competing sectional denominations fueled by the struggle over slavery.

The slavery question was a distinctively American one, but Scottish Presbyterians (the cultural origin of much of American Presbyterianism) also endured a schism at around the same time. The key figure in the 1843 "Disruption" in the Scottish church was Thomas Chalmers (1780–1847). Chalmers had been a bright but negligent Church of Scotland minister until he experienced a dramatic conversion in 1811 through reading the works of ministers and reformers such as the English abolitionist William Wilberforce. Chalmers transformed into a fiery Calvinist preacher, as well as a formidable pastor-scholar, and soon began ministering in Glasgow, Scotland's largest city. There he developed innovative programs of urban ministry and poor relief before becoming a professor at the University of St. Andrews and then the University of Edinburgh. In the late 1830s, Chalmers became embroiled in a controversy over cases where the British government and elite church patrons imposed unpopular ministers on churches over the opposition of the congregation. Chalmers did not object to government involvement with religion per se, but he saw these impositions as the functional subservience of church to state. Chalmers found no relief in appeals to London, so in 1843 he and almost five hundred Scottish Presbyterian ministers—a little less than half of all the establishment's ministers—left the Church of Scotland to form the Free Church of Scotland. This was a grievous blow to the established church and a strong challenge to the traditional union of church and state in Britain.

Charles Finney and the Mechanics of Revival

The United States did not have an official national church, of course, though Congregationalists and Presbyterians often saw themselves as having a custodial relationship with

American culture. Congregationalists retained established churches in New England states (except for Rhode Island) well after the adoption of the US Constitution. The last established church, in Massachusetts, fell to the forces of religious diversity in 1833. Revivalism, not establishment, was the defining religious force for most antebellum American Protestants. And no one played a more definitive role in shaping revivalism than Charles Finney (1792–1875). Indeed, Finney played such an outsized role in the later Second Great Awakening in the North (and to an extent in Britain) that for a time he became the face of the American evangelical movement. Despite liberal Christians' reluctance about the focus on sin and conversion, and despite traditionalists' (such as the Old School Presbyterians) concerns about the theological novelties emerging from Finneyite revivalism, his teachings on revival and his "new measures" in meetings became widely accepted across evangelical denominations. Finney grew up in the "Burned-Over District" of upstate New York. That region was known for successive revivals and spawning of numerous sectarian groups. These included the Shakers, the intensely eschatological Millerites, and the Mormons. Finney, then working as a lawyer, experienced conversion in 1821 and soon became a Presbyterian preacher. But he turned away from the Presbyterian and Calvinist theological heritage toward zealous, pragmatic advocacy of revival. He believed preachers should promote revival by virtually any means necessary, as long as it was not forbidden in Scripture.

Indeed, Finney was convinced that God had already given the church the means of revival: prayer, hard work, and clear gospel preaching. If those were practiced, the church should expect revival. Only erroneous beliefs, confused preachers, or stiff-necked people could hinder God's means to see sinners saved. Finney's new measures focused on getting the unconverted man or woman to make a decision to accept God's forgiveness and to be born again. Perhaps the most famous innovation (though it was not entirely novel) was the "anxious seat," in which people struggling for assurance would be placed in a seat at the front of an assembly and receive lengthy, personal prayers for their conversion. Following the pattern of the camp meetings, Finney would also schedule revivals to last several days in a row, thus adding to the intensity and focus of the assembly. Some New England revivalists balked at Finney's flamboyant methods, though they shared his concerns about the tension between orthodox Calvinism and zealous revivalism. (Again, this concern would have perplexed many in the First Great Awakening when the most zealous revivalists, especially in America, were committed Calvinists.) The height of Finney's success came in a months-long campaign in Rochester, New York, in 1830–31. Rochester was one of the cities of western New York transformed by the Erie Canal, which in the 1820s had connected the Great

Lakes to the Hudson River and New York City. Rochester and the rest of the Burned-Over District was growing fast. Many new settlers came from New England. They might have experienced revivalist Christianity in their past, but they felt rootless and disconnected in their new environs. Finney's preaching perfectly matched the spiritual and cultural mood of Rochester and the Erie Canal corridor.

Finney's sensational revivals were consolidated in his internationally popular and controversial *Lectures on Revivals of Religion* (1835). In this work, Finney put far more responsibility on man for generating revival than previous revivalists would have allowed. The question was not whether God would send revival, but whether man would obey the mandate of revival that God had already sent. "Religion is the work of man," Finney stated baldly. "It is something for man to do. It consists in obeying God." Finney rejected the older Calvinist conviction that God sovereignly sent or withheld revival according to his will. Revival, to Finney, was mechanistic, in the sense that the church's obedience to pray and clearly preach the gospel would almost automatically lead to revival. God had instituted the means of revival as a virtual law of nature and man's duty was to obey and seek the conversion of sinners. A revival was not a miracle, then, but a "right exercise of the powers of nature" and the "right use of constituted means." Finney took this message personally to Britain in 1849–51, but his triumphs there were somewhat limited by the power of the Anglican Church and by English Methodism, which was England's primary source of revivalism. Most of Finney's work in England was among Baptists and Independents.

Finney would never replicate his phenomenal results in the Burned-Over District of the early 1830s. But by the end of his life, he had put a deep imprint on revivalism in the English-speaking world. Whereas the First Great Awakening in America had largely been a Calvinist affair, Finney's revivalism turned away from an emphasis on God's sovereign control to a mechanistic view that made Christian obedience the key to revival. It was a form of revivalism attuned to the spirit of an unsettled, emerging modern world hungry for predictability and assurance. From the 1830s forward, however, even many defenders of evangelical revival criticized Finney's views as theologically aberrant and methodologically suspect. Charles Hodge, for one, commissioned a review of *Lectures on Revivals* in Princeton Seminary's *Biblical Repertory and Theological Review*. It warned readers that Finney's theology was full of "exploded errors and condemned heresies" and that it was shockingly "hostile to divine sovereignty." Finney would reject such charges, of course, but there can be little doubt that much of Anglo-American revivalism after Finney became routinized, pragmatic, and more concerned with the duty of man than with the mysterious sovereignty of God.

Selected Bibliography

Aubert, Annette G. *The German Roots of Nineteenth-Century American Theology*. New York: Oxford University Press, 2013.

Carwardine, Richard. *Transatlantic Revivalism: Popular Evangelicalism in Britain and America, 1790–1865*. Westport, CT: Greenwood, 1978.

Clark, Linda L. *Women and Achievement in Nineteenth-Century Europe*. New York: Cambridge University Press, 2008.

Hambrick-Stowe, Charles. *Charles G. Finney and the Spirit of American Evangelicalism*. Grand Rapids: Eerdmans, 1996.

Harris, Ruth. *Lourdes: Body and Spirit in the Secular Age*. New York: Viking, 1999.

Iliff, Joel R. "The Great Communion of Scholars: The American South, Germany, and the Creation of Modernity in the Nineteenth Century." PhD dissertation, Baylor University, 2020.

Jennings, Jeremy. *Revolution and the Republic: A History of Political Thought in France since the Eighteenth Century*. New York: Oxford University Press, 2011.

O'Malley, John W. "A Movie, a Mystic, a Spiritual Tradition." *America: The Jesuit Review*. March 15, 2004.

Schwarz, Hans. *Theology in a Global Context: The Last Two Hundred Years*. Grand Rapids: Eerdmans, 2005.

Zimdars-Swartz, Sandra L. *Encountering Mary: From La Salette to Medjugorje*. Princeton, NJ: Princeton University Press, 1991.

—— Chapter 16 ——

Missionaries, the Benevolent Empire, and Global Christian Growth

By the early 1800s, Protestants committed to a dizzying array of missionary and reform efforts that would, in time, dramatically change the shape of world Christianity. Protestants had a long-standing sense that they had fallen behind Catholics in world evangelization. New avenues of global trade and empire also helped Protestants conceive of world evangelization in new ways. The missionary vision crossed racial, national, and geographic lines. To cite just one example, in 1811 an African American sea captain, the Quaker and moral reformer Paul Cuffee (1759–1817), went to Sierra Leone in West Africa. Sierra Leone had become a British crown colony in 1806, and Cuffee hoped to spread Christian knowledge and to establish commercial connections with native African people there. Cuffee, whose father was of African descent and mother was a Wampanoag Indian, attended a meeting of Baptists in Sierra Leone. Its members listened with "good satisfaction" to an edifying letter written by Christianized American Indians. Cuffee delivered a copy of the same letter to a Methodist Church in Sierra Leone. Cuffee may not technically have been a missionary, but he did regard himself as an agent of Christian and commercial expansion. He relished spreading the word about indigenous Christians in America, hoping that their example might inspire the progress of Christian knowledge among indigenous

Africans. Through countless encounters like Cuffee's in Africa, Protestants envisioned a global Christian movement.

Expanding Protestant Missions

The 1790s had seen the formation of new Protestant missionary organizations. They were inspired, to varying degrees, by William Carey's *Enquiry into the Obligations of Christians, To Use Means for the Conversion of the Heathens* (1792), the theology of Jonathan Edwards, and the Christian mandate of "disinterested benevolence." But cross-cultural Protestant missions had been growing more common since the Great Awakening in the 1740s, led by groups such as the Moravians and by individual missionaries and church planters such as the African American Baptists David George, who relocated to Nova Scotia and Sierra Leone, and George Liele, who became one of the key early Protestant leaders in Jamaica.

Still, the 1790s represented a turning point toward a more organized Protestant missionary movement. This was part of a broader turn toward a whole array of Christian reform endeavors that would focus on bringing the gospel to unreached people groups, distributing Bibles, curtailing alcohol abuse, and perhaps most controversially, opposing slavery. Historians have sometimes called these international Christian initiatives the "benevolent empire." As seen in Cuffee's example, such endeavors were often more complex than they seem at first glance, tied up as they were with issues of commerce, freedom, and clashing notions of cultural superiority. Nevertheless, the nineteenth century saw great Protestant gains in matters such as the mass availability of the Bible, the presentation of the gospel to non-Christians, and the abolition of slavery and the slave trade. The campaign against slavery owed much to British evangelical activists. In America, white evangelicals' record on slavery varied widely, and in 1865, the same year the Civil War ended, legislation was ratified to make slavery illegal.

The colonial experiment in Sierra Leone encapsulated many of the overlapping priorities of Christian mission, antislavery activism, empire, and commerce. English evangelical abolitionists such as brothers Thomas and John Clarkson, and Granville Sharp, envisioned Sierra Leone as a free English colony for Loyalist refugees such as David George's Nova Scotia congregation. Organizers also figured the colony could relieve London of its growing population of free, indigent blacks. (The *Somerset* decision of 1772 in England, in which Sharp played a key role, had effectively banned slaveholding in England itself but not in England's colonies.) Englishmen including Clarkson and Sharp founded the Sierra Leone Company in 1792 to facilitate the emigration of black settlers to the new colony. Other black Nova Scotia refugees, including Methodists led by minister Moses Wilkinson, a blind and crippled former slave and veteran of the British army, joined the exodus to Sierra Lone.

The English abolitionist William Wilberforce imagined that the black Christians settling Sierra Leone would teach native Africans "language and religion, the habits of industry, the mode of cultivating lands, and the mechanical arts." Such combining of civilization and Christianity was commonplace in nineteenth-century Protestant ideas of missions. White organizers also assumed that settlers of African heritage would be able to thrive better in the hot African climate. Tragically, this proved false, as a high percentage of the early black migrants to Sierra Leone died shortly after they arrived due to disease and lack of medical care. Arguments between the settlers and British imperial authorities over trade made Sierra Leone chronically unstable, a far cry from the founders' vision of a thriving black Christian society. Some of the black Methodists told John Clarkson that although the colony's capital was named "Freetown," they had reason by the mid-1790s to "call it a town of slavery."

Figures such as Granville Sharp and William Wilberforce were members of England's "Clapham Sect," a group of Anglican evangelical reformers associated with the campaign against the slave trade. But the Clapham Sect's priorities also drew upon the older Protestant ideal of the "reformation of manners." Wilberforce himself proclaimed in the 1780s that the "suppression of the slave trade and the reformation of manners" were the two great goals that God had commissioned him to pursue. Wilberforce and the Clapham Sect believed that wealthy Christians in particular had a duty to reform society in alignment with Christian virtue. Slavery and the slave trade entailed grievous sin, so Wilberforce and his allies felt called to combat it. This zeal did not always guarantee success or even synchronization with goals of former slaves, of course. One of the members of the Clapham Sect, Zachary Macaulay (1768–1838), served as British governor of the Sierra Leone colony in the 1790s and was despised by many of the black Christian settlers there. Nevertheless, Macaulay spent much of the rest of his life advocating

> Infidelity is not the result of sober inquiry and deliberate preference. It is rather a slow production of a careless and irreligious life, operating together with prejudices and erroneous conceptions concerning the nature of the leading doctrines and fundamental tenets of Christianity.
>
> ---
>
> William Wilberforce, *A Practical View of the Prevailing Religious System of Professed Christians, in the Middle and Higher Classes in this Country, Contrasted with Real Christianity*, 1797

against slavery and promoting causes such as the reformation of manners and Bible distribution.

Wilberforce set the tone for much of the Clapham Sect's work with his 1797 book *A Practical View of the Prevailing Religious System of Professed Christians, in the Middle and Higher Classes in this Country, Contrasted with Real Christianity*. "Real Christianity" was a watchword of the evangelical movement. Wilberforce believed that a return to heartfelt Christian commitment, especially among English elites, was essential to the moral transformation of society. "Our dependence on our blessed Saviour," he warned, "as alone the meritorious cause of our acceptance with God . . . must be not merely formal and nominal, but real and substantial." English aristocrats, he insisted, must use their political influence and financial resources to promote Christian virtue and to war against vices endemic to the slave trade, the prison system, the alcohol business, and more. He was careful to note, however, that moral reform would be ephemeral if not rooted in the "prevalence of Evangelical Christianity." *A Practical View* was a huge publishing success in both Britain and America and was translated into other major European languages.

The Sunday School Movement

Sunday schools were one of the most important components of the reformation of manners among English-speaking Protestants. Churchgoers today are familiar with Sunday school as a program of local churches. Initially, however, they were parachurch initiatives promoted by figures such as the Clapham Sect's Hannah More. Many evangelical leaders were pleased with the advent of the schools. An aging John Wesley wrote in 1784, "I find these schools spring up wherever I go; perhaps God may have a deeper end therein." The Sunday School Society in Britain was founded in 1785. It was supplanted by the London Sunday School Union, starting in 1803. Sunday schools took off quickly in England, enrolling some 41,000 students by 1789. The Sunday schools were particularly targeted at uneducated, poor children in England's cities. They sought to inculcate literacy so that all children could read the Bible. They also promoted Christian virtues with a big dose of English manners, including cleanliness, promptness, and truth-telling. Marxist scholars have viewed the Sunday schools as tools of elites for indoctrinating the working classes. More recent scholarship has noted that working-class people, including women, played decisive roles in organizing many Sunday schools. Sunday schools soon began appearing in Continental Europe, Canada, Australia, and the US. The Sunday School Union introduced the model in missions to countries such as Japan, China, and India. Methodists and Baptists participated in the interdenominational Sunday school movement at first but then began forming their own denominational schools. Liberal denominations joined in, with Unitarians forming a Sunday School Society in Boston in 1827.

In the US, Sunday schools followed the English model, beginning with an Episcopal-led program in Philadelphia in the early 1790s to encourage literacy and improve the "morals of the common people." The early iteration of the American Sunday school initiative focused more on fostering the virtue of republican citizens than on piety or evangelism. But the Second Great Awakening gave the Sunday schools a more evangelistic bent. Organizers worried that they needed to meet the burgeoning youth population of early national America with efforts to convert children to personal faith in Christ. Leaders of revivals in the early 1800s often noted that awakenings took hold primarily among young people and teenagers, and the evangelical Sunday schools fit this model of youth-driven revivalism. Early Sunday schools often welcomed poor adults as well. By the 1820s, however, the schools tended to focus exclusively on children and teenagers, as organizers believed that youth represented a time of relative innocence and receptivity to the gospel that would fade as people entered adulthood. The primary exception to this child-centric vision was the inclusion of African American adults, many of whom were illiterate. Some white organizers and teachers believed that no group of adults exhibited "so much debasement and wretchedness, as that of the free blacks," as one sponsor of a Pennsylvania Sunday school put it. For many Sunday school leaders, adult blacks were objects of pity.

Conversely, the Sunday schools commonly gave white teens and young adults prominent teaching roles and levels of authority that were rarely paralleled elsewhere in early national America. As with Hannah More in England, women routinely served as founders and superintendents of Sunday schools in America. The founding of the American Sunday School Union in 1824 marked the maturation of Sunday schools in the US. By the early 1830s around 10 percent of all white children, and significant numbers of Native American and African American children, attended a Sunday school. But the percentage of children in England attending Sunday school in the 1830s was even more impressive, perhaps around 45 percent.

British Missionary Efforts

As broadly influential as Sunday schools were, missionary agencies were more significant in shaping the future of world Christianity. As of 1800, the vast majority of the world's

Protestants still lived in Europe and North America. Catholics had more of a global presence, but its power centers remained in Europe. Orthodox Christians dominated in the eastern reaches of Christendom, including Russia, Greece, and the Middle East. Yet there were enormous parts of the globe that, from a Protestant perspective, had little Christian witness at all. If explorers such as Captain James Cook were unveiling parts of the globe hitherto unknown in Europe, then missions advocates such as William Carey figured that it was time for Protestants to take the gospel to those distant lands, too. Protestant missions proliferated in the 1790s and early 1800s, resulting in organizations such as Carey's Baptist Missionary Society (1792), the London Missionary Society (1795), the Connecticut Missionary Society (1798), the British and Foreign Bible Society (1804), and the American Board of Commissioners for Foreign Missions (1810). Over time, virtually every Christian denomination in the English-speaking world established its own missionary society, such as the General Missionary Convention of the Baptist Denomination in the United States of America for Foreign Missions (1814), conventionally known as the Triennial Convention.

As seen in cases such as Johannes Van der Kemp's labors for the London Missionary Society (LMS) in South Africa, missionary work could create dazzling new opportunities for cross-cultural interactions and presenting the gospel. Empire and commerce were almost always part of the picture, too, and so it was no coincidence that the founding of the LMS and British occupation of the Cape of Good Hope (from the Dutch) both transpired in 1795. South Africa became a primary focus of the LMS after 1795. Some eight years after Van der Kemp's death, the Scottish Congregational minister John Philip (1775–1851) became the LMS's director in South Africa. In 1815 Britain had taken over South Africa, where the white population was overwhelmingly composed of Afrikaners of Dutch ancestry. The Khoi people were the dominant indigenous population. The colony had many African slaves, but even the free people among the Khoi were treated poorly by Europeans. Black Africans were legally assumed to be servants or dependents of white people. To the chagrin of many Afrikaners and British settlers, the LMS's John Philip became active in antislavery and civil rights causes on behalf of indigenous South Africans. Indeed, he saw such activism as an essential precedent to the gospel. "Let the advocates of religion and humanity use their efforts to put a period to the slavery of the Aborigines . . . and they will, by that single act, do more for the promulgation of the gospel in South Africa, than all the funds of the London Missionary Society could effect while things continue in that colony as they now are." Philip also pushed for missionary societies to engage in works in different parts of South Africa, successfully persuading groups such as the Rhenish Missionary

Society (Germany) and the Paris Evangelical Missionary Society (of the Reformed Church in France) to open stations there.

Easily the most famous (and controversial) of the LMS missionaries in Africa was the Scottish doctor-explorer David Livingstone (1813–73). His family had lived in the Glasgow area and became affiliated with an Independent (Congregational) church there, and after his conversion he devoted his life "to the alleviation of human misery." In 1841 he went to South Africa to begin his long career as a missionary. Livingstone explored much of southern and central Africa and wrote about his experiences in books such as the enormously popular *Missionary Travels and Researches in South Africa*.

Like many missionaries, Livingstone combined Christian outreach with empire and commerce, believing that the key to finally eliminating slavery and the slave trade in Africa was the development of thriving free commerce. Livingstone was less a "discoverer" of African geography than a popularizer of it, and he actually did little in the way of personal evangelism. In the mid-1860s, he engaged in a long but futile search for the source of the Nile River, leading to rumors that he had died somewhere in the African interior. This

Image 16.1. *Stanley Meets Livingstone* (1872)

led to a celebrated search for Livingstone, ending in late 1871 with the journalist Henry Stanley finding him at Lake Tanganyika (in Tanzania), and asking the iconic question, "Dr. Livingstone, I presume?"

Livingstone only made one known convert: King Sechele (d. 1892) of the Bakwena people in modern-day Botswana. In order to convert, Sechele overcame intense hostility to Christianity among his tribesmen. Indeed, when Sechele declared in 1848 that he was becoming a Christian, he told his people that they should kill him immediately if they were going to do so. Livingstone and Sechele confronted a problem that missionary observers have often called syncretism, or how much native practices conflicted with Christian faith. (It is always easier to observe syncretism in a person from another culture than to see your own cultural compromises, of course.) The most immediate such problems for Sechele were his multiple wives, and his traditional role as a rainmaker, or one who could summon rain by incantation.

As for polygamy, most western Christians (with the exception of sectarian groups such as early Mormons) had rejected the practice, although patriarchs in the Hebrew Bible had kept multiple wives. Polygamy was common in African tribal cultures, including among the Bakwenas, but Livingstone was uncertain if he could baptize Sechele if he did not reject his multiple wives. Right until Sechele's baptism, however, his fellow Bakwenas tried to dissuade him from going through with the ritual. Some spread a rumor that baptism was actually a satanic observance which required drinking "men's brains." Others complained that if Sechele could not summon rain after becoming a Christian, he should have at least delayed his baptism until the rains fell. Sechele ultimately returned to polygamy and rainmaking, which gravely disappointed Livingstone, who excommunicated him from the missionary church. However, there seems little doubt about the earnestness of Sechele's conversion, as he faced enormous hostility for becoming a Christian. He went on to become a sort of king-preacher-rainmaker for the Bakwenas, regularly preaching from the Bible to them on Sundays.

Another top LMS priority were the islands of the Pacific Ocean. Tahiti became the LMS's first mission field in 1796, a year after the society's founding, and they soon expanded to places such as Tonga and the Marquesas Islands. When the missionaries encountered trouble in the islands, they often retreated to New South Wales in Australia. Eleven LMS missionaries went to Sydney in 1798, fleeing Tahiti for fear of their lives. The LMS and other English-speaking missionaries eventually made major inroads in the Pacific islands, with the conversion of leaders such as the Tahitian chief Pomare II (1774–1821), who went on to formally make Tahiti a Christian kingdom in 1815. The LMS understood Tahiti to be exclusively Protestant, of course, which generated friction when French Catholic missionaries appeared on the island in 1836. In 1842, Tahiti became a French protectorate, and France guaranteed Catholics there the right to practice their faith freely. France also realized that many Tahitians were already Protestants, however. Officials encouraged the French Protestant Society for Evangelical Missions (1822) to send ministers to the island.

British Protestants had relatively less geographic room for "home" missions than did American Protestants, although evangelicals such as James and Robert Haldane were concerned with reaching the Scottish Highlands and the Orkney Islands with the gospel. One of the problems with reaching the Highlands was the prevalence of Gaelic speakers there. Evangelical leaders such as the Methodist Thomas Coke made halting efforts over several decades to have a Gaelic-speaking Methodist missionary assigned to the Highlands. Other denominations, including Baptists and Congregationalists, also made overtures in the Highlands, and they managed to appoint dozens of Gaelic-speaking missionaries over the first half of the nineteenth century. Interdenominational Gaelic mission schools taught literacy and Bible reading, both in English and in Gaelic. The small but growing Highland evangelical movement developed a deep attachment to the Gaelic Bible, a translation which had only been completed in 1801. At a London meeting of the Baptist Home Missionary Society for the Highlands and Islands of Scotland, a minister explained that "preaching the gospel in the Gaelic language" was essential to the mission's success. He contrasted this trend with "Popery," which depended upon Latin in the mass and could never be adequately understood by Catholic laypeople.

Missions in America

American Protestants, of course, had a broader field for "home" missions, especially after President Thomas Jefferson's 1803 Louisiana Purchase effectively doubled the size of the US, absorbing large numbers of additional Native American groups under nominal American authority. Thus, the American Board of Commissioners for Foreign Missions (ABCFM), despite its "foreign" name, gave half its attention in the 1810s to missions among Native Americans. But those missions often struggled even more than overseas ones. Relatively few Native Americans had converted to Protestantism in the first two centuries of English settlement in America. Missionaries to Native Americans such as John Eliot and David Brainerd received much attention in the missionary community, but the Moravians probably had the most success in bringing Indians to Christian faith among Protestants. The Moravian missionary David Zeisberger (1721–1808) served from the 1750s to the early 1800s among the Delaware/Lenni Lenape Indians of Pennsylvania and Ohio. Even though he had comparatively significant success in his work, it was arduous, and Zeisberger conceded its small impact on the Indian population generally. "There are so many other places where God's word ought to be preached," he said, "and so many Indians who have not yet heard that their Maker is their Redeemer." Zeisberger was jailed by the British during the Revolutionary War, and during his absence in 1782 American militiamen massacred almost one hundred Christian Lenapes, many of them women and children, at the Moravian mission village of Gnadenhütten, Ohio.

Like many British counterparts, American missionaries in the early 1800s combined evangelism with "civilization" in their outreach to Native Americans. Missionary schools were essential to the evangelistic strategy, and the schools' aims in some ways overlapped with the work of Sunday schools among poor whites and blacks in American cities. As one missionary explained, the schoolteachers hoped to inculcate in Indian pupils "habits of sobriety, cleanliness, economy, and industry, so essential to civilized life." Most missionaries would see such aims as incomplete without basic instruction in Christian doctrine and appeals for students to put their faith in Christ. Yet in retrospect, it is clear that some of the missionaries injected a dose of 1800s Anglo-American culture into the historic essentials of Christianity.

The Cherokee Indians became a special focus of the ABCFM and other Protestant organizations. A major tribe in the American southeast, the Cherokees were relatively accessible geographically, and its leaders were often some of the most culturally Anglicized among all Native Americans. Cherokees realized that Anglo politicians and settlers coveted their lands, which were centered in Georgia. Cherokees figured that adapting to the culture and language of whites would help them thrive and maintain tribal autonomy. The white missionary community was somewhat divided over the land rights of eastern Indians, with some supporting Indians' removal beyond the Mississippi River and others defending the Indians' land claims. One of the ABCFM missionaries who defended Indian legal rights, Samuel Worcester (1798–1859), lent his name to one of the key Supreme Court decisions over the Cherokees' sovereignty, the 1832 case of *Worcester v. Georgia*. Ultimately the Cherokees' appeals to stay on their land were futile, and in 1838 government officials removed them to the Indian Territory in Oklahoma via the infamous "Trail of Tears."

Still, the ABCFM mission to the Cherokees bore considerable fruit in evangelism and "civilization," as Worcester and other missionaries were involved in promoting the written

Cherokee language developed by the Cherokee linguist Sequoya in 1819. Worcester translated parts of the Bible into the Cherokee language, and he raised money to open the *Cherokee Phoenix*, the first Native American-language newspaper. Worcester's primary Cherokee collaborator was Galagina (d. 1839), who took the Anglo name Elias Boudinot (the name of a prominent American Founder and president of the American Bible Society). Galagina became the editor of the *Phoenix*. Galagina began his education at a Moravian school in Georgia, but in the late 1810s he began attending an ABCFM school in Cornwall, Connecticut. In 1820 he became a Christian, and in 1826 he married Harriet Gold, a white woman from Cornwall, despite the outraged protests of many whites in Connecticut.

Galagina actively raised money for Cherokee education and evangelism. He saw the Cherokee language as a bridge for the gospel, much as people in Britain touted the importance of Gaelic for reaching Highlanders. Cherokees "may now read the precepts of the Almighty in their own language," he said in an 1826 address in Philadelphia. Galagina believed in the inexorable spread of the gospel among Indians as part of the rising glory of Christ's millennial Kingdom. "Already do we see the morning star, forerunner of approaching dawn, rising over the tops of deep forests in which for ages have echoed the warrior's whoop. But has not God said it, and will he not do it?" Galagina became convinced that the Cherokees should accept removal to the western Indian Territory, where they could ostensibly live in peace, away from the influence of corrupt alcohol-peddling whites. Shortly after the Trail of Tears, Galagina was murdered by a group of anti-removal Cherokees in the Indian Territory.

The Baptist Board of Foreign Missions, operated by the Triennial Convention, also focused on Native Americans generally, and Cherokees in particular. During the first half of the nineteenth century, a considerable majority of Indian converts for Baptists came from the Cherokees. The Baptists' work demonstrated a tendency which was repeated globally: missionary work enjoyed the most success when cross-cultural missionaries gave leadership roles to indigenous evangelists and clergy. Yet ethnic and cultural prejudice often made it difficult for missionaries to apply this principle and relinquish power in the missions. The most influential white Baptist missionary among the Cherokees was Evan Jones (1788–1872), who in the 1820s ran a missionary school for Cherokees in western North Carolina. Jones worked with several Cherokee men who became Baptist preachers.

Arguably the most successful of these Cherokee ministers was Tastheghetehee (1804–44), who took the Anglicized name Jesse Bushyhead. Bushyhead had experienced Christian conversion at an ABCFM school, but he had adopted Baptist principles by the late 1820s. In 1833, Bushyhead received ordination as a Baptist minister and became employed by the

Baptist missions board. Bushyhead and other Cherokee Baptist ministers saw considerable gains among the Cherokees in the early 1830s, including (atypically) among Cherokees who did not speak English. Unlike Galagina and some other white Baptist missionaries, Jones and Bushyhead opposed the Cherokees' forced removal. Jones and Bushyhead kept preaching to Cherokees even as American forces began detaining them in preparation for the long march to Oklahoma in 1838. They baptized dozens of Cherokee converts in the detention camps and then accompanied the Cherokees on the Trail of Tears, during which about a quarter of the sixteen thousand Cherokee deportees died.

The Challenge of Islam

As troubled as Native American missions were, Islam was perhaps the greatest world challenge as the era of major Protestant missions began to unfold. Indeed, the nineteenth century was not so much a time of missionary breakthroughs among Muslims, but the time when European and American missionaries began to grasp the enormous difficulties involved in reaching Muslims with the gospel. These difficulties included the Ottoman Empire's legal prohibitions against proselytizing, cultural and legal hostility toward any Muslims "apostatizing" from their religion, language barriers, and the fact that Muslims had a long theological tradition of apologetics against Christianity. Muslims rejected Christian doctrines such as the Trinity, which they saw as polytheistic. Muslims also had a clear place in their theology for Jesus, but as a prophet, not as the Son of God. All these issues presented major obstacles to Muslim evangelization. Many of the missionary efforts in Muslim lands ended up focusing on Orthodox Christians instead.

Still, key Protestant scholars and missionaries began to establish beachheads for Muslim evangelization in the Middle East and South Asia. One of the most significant leaders was Henry Martyn (1781–1812), a linguist and chaplain to the British East India Company (EIC). As a student at Cambridge, Martyn came under the tutelage of Anglican minister Charles Simeon (1759–1836), who was one of the key evangelical Anglicans at the beginning of the nineteenth century. Simeon spent most of his ministerial career at Holy Trinity Church, Cambridge, a strategic educational post in the Anglican communion. Martyn had illustrious academic success at Cambridge, but through Simeon's urging and through reading the works of William Carey and David Brainerd, Martyn became convinced that God was calling him to the mission field. Martyn opted to become a chaplain for the EIC, the trading behemoth that ruled imperial India until 1858. (Again, the connections between missions, trade, and empire were ever-present.) When Martyn arrived in Calcutta in 1806, his missionary exemplar William Carey was there to greet him, and the two joyfully prayed together in the Bengali language. Despite their denominational differences as an Anglican and a Baptist, Martyn and Carey were both evangelicals, meeting on an overseas mission field. These factors were often (though not always) enough to mute differences between Protestants who might have been unable to cooperate back home.

Martyn first imagined that his evangelistic priority would be Indian Hindus. Soon he found his (short) life's work in Bible translation, however, especially in languages common among Muslims. He translated the New Testament and the Book of Common Prayer into Urdu, the chief language of northern India (especially in the Muslim-majority region that became Pakistan in 1947). He also produced New Testament translations in Persian and Arabic. Martyn was assisted by an Arab Christian convert named Sabat, with whom Martyn developed a tempestuous but productive relationship. Sabat's conversion testimony "The Star in the East" (1809) was recorded by another EIC chaplain, Claudius Buchanan (1766–1815). Sabat's testimony became ubiquitous in the English-speaking world, with editions of it published from New York to London as well as in small towns like Greenock, Scotland, and Chillicothe, Ohio. Sabat's story helped to inspire Adoniram Judson to go to Burma as a missionary. The real-life Sabat was brilliant yet erratic, however, and within a decade of the publication of "The Star in the East," Sabat had repudiated Christianity. After four years, Martyn left India with the intention of taking a circuitous route back to England via Iran and Arabia. He was terminally ill with tuberculosis, but in Iran he still managed to get approval from the ruling Shah for the production of his New Testament in Persian. On his journey Martyn made it as far as Tokat, in modern Turkey, where he died in 1812. Martyn had once written in his journal of his desire to be a "light burning out for God," and like David Brainerd before him, he got his wish. Martyn died at age thirty-one, leaving a monumental record of Bible translation for the Muslim world.

Martyn also left a major legacy in his apologetical debates with Muslim scholars, debates which were translated and published in 1824 as *Controversial Tracts on Christianity and Mohammedanism*. Martyn was hardly the first Protestant apologist to argue against Islam, but he was one of the first Protestant scholars who had engaged deeply with Islamic teachers and languages. Prior to this point, knowledge about Islam tended to be based on caricatures of the Qur'an or Muhammad, or derived from what Christian readers learned in stories about the "Barbary pirates" of North Africa. Even Martyn's apologetical methods tended to depend upon conventional Protestant polemics against Islam, which often described Muhammad as demon-inspired and an "impostor." But Martyn heralded a more intellectually sophisticated and knowledgeable evangelical approach to the Muslim religion and toward actual Muslim people. Martyn also realized the limits of purely rationalistic apologetics, which could at most clear an intellectual path for Muslims' conversion to Christianity. As Martyn put it in one of his published addresses to Muslim professors, if his arguments did not produce conviction leading to conversion, "my prayer is, that God himself may instruct you." He prayed that the Muslim scholars would become teachers of the truth as revealed in the Bible, and that God would transform them into teachers about "Jesus Christ, who had loved and washed us in his own blood." As a Christian apologist, Martyn had strong reasons for hope. Yet the Muslim world has remained arguably the most intractable challenge for Christian missions through the present day.

Selected Bibliography

Bennett, Clinton. "The Legacy of Henry Martyn." *International Bulletin of Missionary Research* 16, no. 1 (January 1992): 10–15.

Jeal, Tim. *Livingstone*. New Haven, CT: Yale University Press, 2013.

Kidd, Thomas S. *American Christians and Islam: Evangelical Culture and Muslims from the Colonial Period to the Age of Terrorism*. Princeton: Princeton University Press, 2009.

Leal, K. Elise. "'All Our Children May be Taught of God': Sunday Schools and the Roles of Childhood and Youth in Creating Evangelical Benevolence." *Church History* 87, no 4 (December 2018): 1056–1090.

Neill, Stephen. *A History of Christian Missions*. 2nd ed. New York: Penguin, 1986.

Perdue, Theda, ed. *Cherokee Editor: The Writings of Elias Boudinot*. Athens: University of Georgia Press, 1996.

Powell, Avril A. *Muslims and Missionaries in Pre-Mutiny India*. New York: Routledge, 2013.

Ross, Andrew C. *John Philip (1775–1851): Missions, Race and Politics in South Africa*. Aberdeen, Scotland: Aberdeen University Press, 1986.

Sanneh, Lamin. *Abolitionists Abroad: American Blacks and the Making of Modern West Africa*. Cambridge: Harvard University Press, 1999.

Sidbury, James. *Becoming African in America: Race and Nation in the Early Black Atlantic, 1760–1830*. New York: Oxford University Press, 2007.

Stott, Anne. *Hannah More: The First Victorian*. New York: Oxford University Press, 2003.

—— Chapter 17 ——

The Age of Societies

British politician and abolitionist James Stephen wrote in 1844 that Britons were living in an "age of societies." As seen in the previous chapter, dozens of new missionary organizations appeared in the early 1800s, signaling an unprecedented Protestant commitment to the systematic spread of the gospel. They were determined to take the Bible and the great tradition of Christian theology to "all nations, and kindreds, and people, and tongues" (Rev 7:9 KJV). Missionary societies were just the beginning, however, as Europe and America were deluged with moral reform organizations of every stripe. They sought the "reformation of manners" and spiritual transformation of their own nations and those of peoples living in every corner of the globe.

Orthodox and Catholic Missions

It was not just Protestants who invested in missions. Catholic missions continued to offer an alternative to the surge in Protestant activism. But the Catholic Church suffered terribly from internal feuds and political antagonism during the French Revolution and Napoleonic era. Secular animosity toward the Jesuits had led to their complete suppression, a move confirmed by a politically-compliant Vatican in 1773. Pope Pius VII reversed the abolition of the Jesuit order in 1814, but the crackdown on the Jesuits was devastating for overseas Catholic ambitions. Still, the post-1814 period saw major new developments in Catholic missions.

One of the most notable was the Catholic return to Japan, where the Catholic Church had suffered murderous persecution and expulsion in the early 1600s. Catholic missionaries returned in 1859 (Protestant missionaries were first allowed into the formerly-closed nation that same year) and were shocked to discover some remaining Japanese Catholics. Their ancestors had preserved the faith by meeting in secret for hundreds of years. The Japanese parishes were entirely cut off from the world Catholic community, however, and seemed to have virtually no access to external sources of Christian doctrine, including the Bible. The new Japanese publicity for Catholicism unfortunately led to another round of anti-Catholic persecution, with thousands of Japanese Catholics arrested, tortured, and exiled in the 1860s. By the late 1800s, Japan began opening itself more fully to western influences and ended much of the repression of Christians. Christianity has struggled to become an indigenous Japanese movement, however, in contrast to Christianity's rootedness in neighboring China or Korea.

The Orthodox Church, particularly in Russia, was also buffeted by change and challenges in the age of revolutions. In 1773, Catherine the Great issued an edict guaranteeing religious freedom in Russia. This led to a proliferation of western Christian groups in the Russian Empire, and Russia even got its own Bible society in 1812, though Nicholas I banned the society in 1826. The society helped to coordinate the effort to finally translate the whole Bible into Russian, but it took another half century, partly due to persecution and suppression of the translations. Still, the Orthodox churches produced influential scholars and zealous missionaries of their own. One of these was Macaire Gloukharev. Gloukharev, an up-and-coming scholar and priest in the early 1800s, became convinced that God was calling him to a monastic vocation. Taking inspiration from the Desert Fathers, Gloukharev worked in isolated monasteries and translated devotional classics of the Orthodox tradition, as well as texts by non-Orthodox figures such as the Catholic mystic Teresa of Ávila and the Catholic mathematician and apologist Blaise Pascal. In 1828, Gloukharev responded to a call for missionaries from the Russian Orthodox Church, going to work in the Altai Mountains of Mongolia. He learned native dialects and preached to indigenous people of the desolate region but to little avail. He did not give up, however, musing "who am I to judge a people's unreadiness to receive the universal faith in Jesus Christ, who shed His blood on the Cross and tasted death for all men and for their salvation?" Gloukharev kept teaching the people of Altai about Christ, while also offering medical help and other services, including simply sweeping out people's homes. Over his fourteen years of work in the mountains, he eventually saw more than 600 people baptized.

Protestant Missions

Protestants maintained the most dynamic missions in the nineteenth century, however. These were often most effective when the Scriptures became available in native languages and mission leadership transferred to indigenous people and preachers. For example, Adoniram Judson's (1788–1850) work in Burma continued after 1813, following his conversion from paedobaptist to Baptist principles. But Judson suffered terribly when he was jailed during the Anglo-Burmese War in the mid-1820s. Ann Hasseltine Judson, his wife, died shortly after the war ended, but the intrepid Judson kept working. He finally helped produced a Burmese translation of the whole Bible in 1834.

Judson's associate George Boardman (1801–31) saw the first major evangelistic breakthrough in the Baptists' Burma mission. In particular, the Baptists made great inroads among the Karen people, a persecuted ethnic minority in Burma. In 1828, Ko Tha Byu (d. 1840) became the first known Christian convert among the Karens. Judson wrote that as a nonbeliever Tha Byu had a "diabolical temper" and lived for many years as a hardened criminal, so his conversion was quite dramatic. Tha Byu was probably about fifty years old when he became a Christian. He served as a zealous evangelist and itinerant, helping to draw thousands of Karens into the Christian fold. Age and illness seemed to be the only limitations on his ministry, as he died in 1840. Virtually all Protestant converts among the Karens became Baptists, and by the mid-1850s tens of thousands of Karens were affiliated with Baptist churches.

Baptists would experience even greater success in the state of Nagaland, in northeast India. Baptists began work in Nagaland in the 1830s. After the formation of the Southern Baptist Convention in 1845, American (northern) Baptists took the lead in the region. Naga Baptists went through waves of revival and awakening starting in the 1890s, turning Nagaland into an overwhelmingly Christian state. Demographically, Nagaland became the place in the world with the highest percentage of Baptists. At more than 75 percent, Nagaland far exceeded even Mississippi (which, even in the center of the US "Bible Belt" only had 55 percent) in the percentage of people identifying as Baptists. Baptists were a comparatively small factor in the global expansion of Christianity in the nineteenth and twentieth centuries, however, with groups such as Anglicans, Methodists, and Congregationalists generally taking a more prominent role. Baptists exceeded all groups but the Methodists in American expansion in the 1800s. This fact had enduring significance for American Christianity and later for world missions.

No Protestant work was more significant for the future of world Christianity than the spread of the gospel into sub-Saharan Africa. It made sense that Christian influence in Africa often began with Christian missionaries, officials, and traders, who congregated in port cities such as Cape Town, South Africa, or Freetown, Sierra Leone. But western Christian influence often extended little beyond those cities. This is partly why David Livingstone's journeys generated such excitement: it seemed as if the African interior was finally opening to Christianity.

But travel narratives could only stir interest. Missionaries had to do the actual work of bringing the gospel into the vast African interior. One of the most significant workers was Thomas Birch Freeman (1809–90). Freeman was a pioneer for Methodist evangelism in sub-Saharan Africa, which by the early twenty-first century would become the most dynamic region of world Methodism. Freeman was born in poverty in England, to an African father and an English mother. His mixed-race background made him a liminal figure in England and Africa, but also seems to have prepared him to become an effective cultural and Christian intermediary between English and African cultures. He became involved with the Wesleyan Methodist movement as a young man, and in the mid-1830s he went to West Africa as a Methodist missionary. He preached among major tribes of Nigeria and the Gold Coast (Ghana), including the powerful Asante Empire. In his popular *Journal of Two Visits to the Kingdom of Ashanti, in Western Africa* (1843), Freeman described preaching in one Asante town. "The sublime truths concerning the mysterious plan of human redemption—God becoming incarnate and dying to save his rebellious creatures, to bring them to eternal glory—made such an impression on the minds of the chief and his captains, that they could not contain themselves; but spreading abroad their hands, and lifting up their voices, they acknowledged the lovingkindness of God, and declared before many of their people who were present, that they would worship Him." Eternal verities such as the incarnation and Christ's redeeming death could, for preachers like Freeman, precipitate revival anywhere in the world.

Freeman knew, however, that such initial bursts of revival excitement often did not last, so he worked feverishly to establish Methodist churches. His eagerness to appoint native Africans as Methodist lay preachers and ministers meant that there were nine African Methodist ministers working in his ministry region by 1858. Freeman enjoyed an unusually long career in West Africa, though he struggled to manage the breakneck growth of Ghanaian Methodism and spent long years in the mid-1800s in disfavor with critical English Methodist authorities. Though removed from ministry for a time, he resumed his work in 1873. Freeman was even able to preach a fiftieth anniversary sermon at the Wesley Methodist Church in Cape Coast. He died in Accra, Ghana, in 1890.

For the Anglican Church, the most important West African leader of the 1800s was Bishop Samuel Ajayi Crowther. Born around 1807, Crowther came from a Yoruba family in southwestern Nigeria. He narrowly avoided enslavement to Portuguese traders as a boy when the British navy saved him and took him to Freetown, Sierra Leone. There he received an education from the Anglican Church Missionary Society, or CMS (founded in 1799 by William Wilberforce and other evangelical Anglicans). Upon his baptism in 1825, he took the Anglicized name Samuel Crowther. Shortly thereafter Crowther went to England for further study, then returned to Sierra Leone to enroll at the CMS-run Fourah Bay College in Freetown. Crowther became an accomplished scholar-missionary, with particular expertise in West African languages. In the early 1840s Crowther went back to England for yet more education with the CMS. Before returning to Nigeria, he received ordination as an Anglican minister. In Africa he produced landmark grammatical studies of African languages as well as Yoruba translations of the Bible and the Book of Common Prayer. His Bible translation was apparently the first in an African language composed by a native African.

> It is the faithful preaching of the Gospel, which is the power of God unto salvation to every one that believeth; it is that alone which can work a change in hearts both at home and abroad.
>
> ---
>
> Samuel Crowther, *A Charge Delivered on the Banks of the River Niger in West Africa*, 1866

In 1864, Crowther became the first African Anglican bishop, assigned to oversee "Western Africa beyond the limits of our dominions." This effectively divided the Anglican hierarchy into white clergy in cities under the authority of the bishop of Sierra Leone and African indigenous clergy under the supervision of Crowther. "I know that my new position sets me up as a kind of landmark, which both the Church and the Heathen World must needs behold," Crowther said upon his consecration as a bishop. "I am aware that any false step taken by me will be injurious to all the Native Churches." Despite the segregated arrangement in West African Anglicanism, the Anglican Church in the Niger delta of southern Nigeria grew swiftly. In areas such as Brass and Nembe, major revivals broke out. Crowther and the African Anglican mission confronted the usual problems of syncretism, facing dilemmas such as whether to require men to give up polygamous marriages before receiving baptism. Some converts took their own initiative on such questions. Upon conversion, one of the kings in the area threw many of his ritual fetishes into the river, and he gave the rest of them to Crowther. (A fetish is an object, such as a carved image, which is believed to contain supernatural powers.) The king also ended the polygamous relationships with his twenty-five wives.

Image 17.1. *Samuel Adjai Crowther, D.D.* (1899)

In the 1880s and '90s, Crowther and the CMS suffered many reverses in the Niger delta due to conflicts within the Anglican hierarchy and with the leaders of the cruelly imperialist British Royal Niger Company. The Company cut out all African middlemen in its trade in the region, and the CMS partnered with the Company in the suppression of the lucrative (but debilitating) gin trade. Mass frustration among the Christians of the delta led to defections from the churches and from Christianity itself. In Brass, Nigeria, a young king named Frederick Koko (1853–98) had once been a Sunday school teacher but apostatized in his rage against the Niger Company and British imperial power. Koko returned to his original tribal religion, took a second wife, and started a brutal war with the Company. During the same period, white Anglican critics began to push for Crowther's removal as bishop. By the time of Crowther's death in 1891, the Niger delta churches had broken with the CMS and declared themselves collectively as a self-governing unit within the Anglican Communion. Colonial authority and African independence would remain major political and religious concerns for decades to come.

The Power of Print

As seen in the case of Crowther, missions were usually connected with a desire to translate and distribute the Bible and other devotional literature into vernacular languages. For Protestants, the Bible remained the chief textual source of the great tradition. The Protestant

Bible and tract societies that proliferated in the early 1800s were following broader trends in publishing. Printers, periodicals, and peddlers of print were becoming ubiquitous in Europe and America. Religious publishing was a lucrative part of the print business, making it difficult to discern whether profit or evangelism was the key priority. (Sometimes it was both.) In the 1740s, the evangelist George Whitefield had made Ben Franklin his lead publisher in America, not because Franklin was an evangelical, but because Franklin was the most innovative printer in the colonies. But few would have questioned Whitefield's basically spiritual motivations for the print sensation that he and Franklin generated.

England set the pace in interdenominational Protestant publishing with the creation of the Religious Tract Society (1799) and the British and Foreign Bible Society (1804). The work of the Religious Tract Society (RTS) followed the enormous popularity of evangelical reformer Hannah More's *Cheap Repository Tracts.* She designed these to supply reliable Christian options in the "chapbook" market, which often provided farmers and working-class people with ribald ballads and superstitious tales of ghosts and witches. More's tracts offered godly stories of "striking Conversions, Holy Lives, Happy Deaths, Providential Deliverances, Judgments on the Breakers of Commandments, Stories of Good and Wicked Apprentices, Hardened Sinners, Pious Servants &c." When the tracts began to appear in 1795, they met with insatiable demand, especially among middle-class Christian readers and pastors, who often passed the tracts on to neighbors and family. Millions of copies of these tracts had already been distributed by the end of 1795.

The RTS seized on this kind of potential to generate an unprecedented supply of pietistic and evangelistic literature, especially for children and poor people. In a twentieth anniversary reflection, the RTS explained that it wanted its tracts to convey "PURE TRUTH." Christian truth was pure not only when it came from the Bible but also when it reflected "those evangelical principles of the Reformation, in which Luther, Calvin, and Cranmer were agreed." Salvation by grace, the authority of the Bible, and the mandate of Christian holiness were included in such principles. Interdenominational societies like the RTS steered clear of dogmatic or sectarian controversies related to church government, baptism, or Calvinist theology. They were motivated by the new possibilities in printing and tract distribution for the sake of the gospel. "This is the age of ingenuity," the RTS proclaimed. "Let it now appear that we are busied in discovering every way of access for divine truth into the human heart; and that we are resolved to employ every means we can think of as conducive to that end." By the mid-nineteenth century the RTS had distributed around 500 million tracts. Fervent evangelical activism was a hallmark of the era.

Image 17.2. *Cottage of the Dairyman's daughter* (1866)

The RTS and similar organizations such as the American Tract Society (1825) often published editions of Christian classics by authors such as John Bunyan and Richard Baxter. Among the newer publications, however, none was more popular than Anglican minister Legh Richmond's spiritual biography *The Dairyman's Daughter* (1809). Similar to More's writings, *The Dairyman's Daughter* celebrated and idealized the simple but enduring faith of poor Christians, namely the Wallbridge family and their daughter Elizabeth. Modern scholars often criticize the overwrought sentimentalism of such writings, but the early 1800s was a time in which writers took seriously the power of holy sentiment to generate virtuous action. Elizabeth Wallbridge had neglected religion until she was converted in her mid-twenties, after which she became a model of faith until her untimely death in 1801, at age thirty-one. In Richmond's account, Wallbridge herself became an embodiment of the spiritual effects that groups such as the RTS hoped to have on common English people. Her faith was "of a highly spiritual character, and of no ordinary attainment. Her views of the divine plan in saving the sinner, were clear and scriptural . . . She had but few books beside her Bible; but these few were excellent in their kind." They included English Reformed classics like Bunyan's *Pilgrim's Progress*, Richard Baxter's *The Saint's Everlasting Rest*, and Philip Doddridge's *The Rise and Progress of Religion in the Soul.* Wallbridge's holiness only increased as death approached. Richmond concluded with an admonition to the poor readers whom he hoped would read the story. "Dost thou resemble her, as she resembled Christ? Art thou made rich by faith? . . . Is thine heart set upon heavenly riches? If not, read this story once more, and then pray earnestly for like precious faith." The "dairyman's cottage" on the Isle of Wight and Wallbridge's grave became popular pilgrimage sites for decades to come.

Protestant Outreach to Jews

Many Protestant societies were designed with outreach to specific vocations (such as sailors), or to particular ethnic or religious groups. This was the case with the London Society for Promoting Christianity Amongst the Jews (1809). Christians had a natural historic and theological interest in Jews and the Hebrew Bible, of course. But many Christians in the eighteenth and nineteenth centuries had a fascination with Jewish conversions and the last days, prompted by Bible passages such as Paul's assertion in Romans 11 that "all Israel will be saved." One early supporter of the London Society explained that it aimed to hasten the prophesied conversion of the Jews, "by the most disinterested benevolence to win their esteem and soften their prejudices; by reason and argument to convince their understandings; [and] by putting into their hands the Christian Scriptures, translated into their own sacred and original language [Hebrew]." Accordingly, the society distributed many thousands of Hebrew New Testaments and other tracts in Hebrew.

The German Jewish convert Joseph Samuel Frey (1771–1850) took a leading role in the formation of the London Society for Promoting Christianity Amongst the Jews. Frey had thought of going on mission to Africa with the London Missionary Society (LMS), but instead LMS officials encouraged him to minister to the Jewish community in London. He served with the LMS until 1808, but he clashed with its leaders over an apparent lack of conversions resulting from his ministry. Thus in 1809 Frey and his supporters banded together to form the independent London Society for Promoting Christianity Amongst the Jews. By 1817 Britain had some forty-five auxiliaries of the group, including many outside

London. The number of actual Jews living in England was fairly small, so by the mid-1840s the society had sent missionaries to centers of Jewish life in Europe and the Middle East, including Berlin, Warsaw, Jerusalem, and Baghdad. Among the Society's chief promoters were William Wilberforce; Charles Simeon, the evangelical Anglican and mentor of Henry Martyn; and Legh Richmond, author of *The Dairyman's Daughter*.

Christian millennial belief undergirded many of the new evangelical reform and missionary societies. Anticipation of the return of Christ and the millennial era derived from Scripture, including passages such as Revelation 20. The era of the French Revolution and the rise of Napoleon stoked a new fascination with prophetic interpretation. This is not the place to review all the varieties of end times belief in the early 1800s. Suffice it to say that many optimistic Christian observers believed that a massive expansion of global revival, activism, and evangelism was a necessary precedent for Christ's return. Scholars often label such a view as "post-millennial," but that term did not come into widespread use until the 1830s. Postmillennialism was a reaction to the "pre-millennial" beliefs promoted by British writer John Nelson Darby and others.

Missions and Millennial Expectations

Missions to the Jews were among the most obvious Christian works rooted in millennial belief. Many interpreted Scripture passages such as Rom 11:26 as indicating a major ingathering of the Jews to Christ in the last days. Since Christianity itself began as a Jewish messianic movement, evangelism to Jews carried a special interest for many Christians, especially those with a more eschatological bent. Typical of such beliefs were those expressed by the evangelical Anglican minister George Stanley Faber (1773–1854), who addressed the London Society for Promoting Christianity Amongst the Jews in 1822. Faber saw evangelism to the Jews and the global work of missions to the Gentile nations as inextricably connected. Indeed, he expected mass conversion of the Jews to happen first. Then the new Jewish converts would lead a great evangelistic campaign among remaining unconverted Gentile nations in the last days. Faber saw growing British support for the "Hebrew cause" and "the very existence and increase of a society whose special object is to evangelize the house of Judah in every quarter of the globe" as evidences that "the hand of God is now specially stretched forth upon the earth." Such sentiments would also undergird Christian support for a Jewish homeland in Palestine, a cause which Britain would formally endorse in the 1917 Balfour Declaration.

Among the most influential British exponents of millennialism was John Nelson Darby (1800–1882). Darby was one of the chief articulators of "dispensational" theology. He also helped found the primitivist Plymouth Brethren movement in Britain and Ireland. Though ordained as an Anglican minister in the mid-1820s, Darby became increasingly disaffected from the church as he ministered in Ireland and England. By the mid-1830s Darby became affiliated with a Brethren assembly in Plymouth, a group which sought to radically manifest the practices of the New Testament churches. One of their distinctive rituals was their weekly, lay-led "breaking of bread" services, or a simplified version of the Lord's Supper. Darby extended his ministry to the European Continent, helping to form Brethren assemblies in Switzerland and France. Ultimately, he traveled as an itinerant teacher across the world from New Zealand to Canada and to the United States. The Plymouth Brethren remained a relatively small denomination worldwide, but Darby's teachings became enormously influential in evangelical and fundamentalist theology more broadly.

In particular, Darby advocated a dispensational view of Scripture, in which God dealt with humanity in different ways at different times. To Darby, it was essential to understand which dispensation was in effect at any given moment in Scripture. Darby also developed an exceedingly negative view of denominations, including the Church of England, believing that a general apostasy would afflict the visible church until just before Christ's return. Darby shifted the fulfillment of biblical prophecy to an almost entirely "futurist" mode. This was opposed to the "historicist" view, common in Britain and America in the 1700s, which had seen many of the prophecies in books such as Daniel and Revelation as already fulfilled in history. For Darby, the inaugural event of prophecy fulfillment in the last days was the "rapture" of God's saints from earth (based on passages including 1 Thess 4:13–17), after which the earth would endure the Great Tribulation and reign of the Antichrist. Finally, Christ would return in conquering glory, to establish the millennial kingdom.

The Bible Societies

Darby's popularity depended upon many of the same trends in global transportation, print, and commerce that facilitated the great evangelical reform and missionary causes of the era. Yet Darby's view of the true church as a beleaguered remnant was far different from many of the evangelical reformers' idea of the church as a triumphant host preparing the way for Christ's return. Perhaps the most representative of the latter movements were the Bible societies, which became ubiquitous across the Protestant world by the 1820s. These included behemoths like the British and Foreign Bible Society (1804) and the American Bible Society (1816), as well as a host of auxiliaries and other denominational and national Bible societies, including ones in Calcutta (1811), Nova Scotia (1813), and Sydney (1817), which followed paths cut by the British Empire. The Bible societies combined the impulses of biblicism, evangelism, and reform. They epitomized the Reformation principle of *sola scriptura*, or the Bible as the final, perfect authority for Christian belief and practice. How could anyone fully live a Christian life without access to the Bible? The societies believed that the Bible itself was one of the most effective tools of evangelism. Who knew what work that the Holy Spirit might do in a person's heart, as he or she read the unmediated words of Scripture, translated in their own language? Finally, there was a pervasive Christian assumption (one hardly restricted to evangelicals) that the Bible was the essential text of Western civilization. Law, morality, and culture depended upon familiarity with and adherence to the principles of the Bible, especially passages such as the Ten Commandments and the Golden Rule (Matt 7:12). Even theological skeptics such as American founder Thomas Jefferson conceded that families would be better off morally and intellectually if they had access to a Bible at home.

Making cheap Bibles widely available would seem to be a unifying Protestant cause, but the BFBS and ABS encountered major controversies throughout their founding decades. Among the most pressing questions were what counted as "the Bible," and how broad their "non-denominational" character should be. Protestant Bibles, especially on the Continent, often included the Apocrypha, or the non-canonical books of the Hebrew Bible. Many Protestants regarded these texts (such as 1 and 2 Maccabees) as useful for the church, but they did not believe they had the same inspired status as the canonical books. Critics balked at their misleading presence in the Bible alongside the inspired Scriptures. The question of whether to include the Apocrypha became enormously controversial for the BFBS in the 1820s. Moreover, while the Bible societies were generally non-denominational, they were also broadly committed to the orthodoxy of the great tradition, including Trinitarianism. Thus it was dismaying to many supporters when Unitarians, who denied the Trinity, became key participating members in the societies. The inclusion of Unitarians led to a breakaway Trinitarian Bible Society in England, formed in 1831.

It was typical for women to play a major role in Bible societies, Sunday schools, missions, and other evangelical initiatives. Their roles are often obscured because women tended not to have formal leadership offices in such organizations, especially before the twentieth century. Middle-class married white women were typically expected to have little engagement with the world of business. That assumption could be modified or overlooked when women engaged in moral reform, education, or evangelism, however. On the local level, the Bible societies expected recipients of their Bibles to pay a small fee, on the assumption that families would value their Bible more if they had a stake in purchasing them. This practice effectively turned legions of evangelical women into Bible vendors. They would take subscriptions (typically from poorer families) for a copy of the Bible, deliver the Bible, and keep returning to the home for installment payments, routinely one penny a week, until the book was paid for. In the case of the BFBS, the women typically passed on the collected funds to male Bible agents, who then sent the money to the London headquarters of the society. Women often did the bulk of such work on the local level. One male philanthropist and supporter of the BFBS exulted in 1818 about the proliferation of Ladies Bible Associations in English towns and the "moral benefit resulting from the weekly visits of the Ladies at the cottages of the poor." But both male and female evangelicals believed that the women's work should remain "unostentatious," and that their roles in the Bible transactions should not become a point of contention in the societies.

Groups such as the BFBS were interested in global Bible distribution as well. For the BFBS, this worldwide vision included places bereft of Bibles in the British Isles and out to the entire globe—especially in places encompassed by the growing British empire. In its first fifty years, the BFBS would print and sell a stunning 250 million copies of the Bible, New Testament, or Gospels. Following the vernacular ideal of the Reformation, they sought to make the Bible available in as many languages as possible. This resulted in some 125 new translations of the Bible in the society's first half century into languages that had not previously had a printed edition of the Scriptures. The society's first printed translation was an edition of the Gospel of John into the Mohawk language for the benefit of the Mohawk Indian nation in North America. The Bible societies assiduously sought to avoid denominational or doctrinal squabbles in their work of Bible translation. Yet such a massive undertaking inevitably drew criticisms, often related to the vast sums of money that the societies were gathering from donors and purchasers of the Bibles. Bible translation and distribution also raised perennial issues about the reliability of the translations themselves. For example, some questioned the BFBS's Mohawk New Testament project because it depended upon the work of just one Mohawk convert, a man named Teyoninhokarawen (c. 1770–1831). Moreover, Teyoninhokarawen's New Testament was a translation of the English King James text, not the Greek, into Mohawk. Nevertheless, critics could not effectively slow the massive expansion of Bible translation and distribution that marked the nineteenth century.

Groups such as the BFBS partnered with denominational missionaries and Bible translation projects, such as William Carey's Baptist mission in Serampore, India. In 1813 Baptists received an encouraging report from Serampore that illustrated the great confidence that evangelicals had in the power of Scripture, enabled by the Holy Spirit, to convert readers. A number of high-caste Brahmins had been converted and received baptism. The report noted that several of them had "obtained knowledge of the truth, and met for Christian worship on the Lord's days, before they had any [interaction] with the missionaries, simply by reading the Scriptures." While missionaries, as well as promising native converts, also preached to interested Indian people, a certain tension remained in the Protestant missionary impulse. Evangelicals put such a premium on *sola scriptura* that the missionaries seemed to inordinately value conversion testimonies of those who received the gospel with no aid besides the Bible. Taking a missionary or a preacher out of the equation seemed to guarantee the purity of Scripture-only conversion. Many were the "instances of conversion," the Serampore station reported, "by means of the Scriptures alone, without the intervention of the missionary." Similarly, the missionaries were pleased that almost every Indian station had church services performed "by natives alone, without the presence or assistance of Europeans." Even at this early date, evangelical missionaries realized that cultivating a church led by indigenous people who focused on vernacular Bible reading and teaching was the ultimate goal. They would have done their job if the local churches became self-sustaining, self-replicating, and tutored in the Scriptures. But achieving that ideal was complicated by almost innumerable factors, including linguistic challenges, the difficulty of trusting indigenous leaders to carry on the work in a satisfactory manner, and the ongoing danger of non-Christian faiths and (in the view of the American and European missionaries) indigenous people's corrupted versions of Christianity.

Protestant missionaries and Bible translators in the Middle East and southern Europe often found themselves working primarily with people of Roman Catholic or Orthodox background. Protestants classically criticized such people as being largely ignorant of correct Christian doctrine and of the Bible in the vernacular. Missionary reports from outside of Christendom often related difficulties with indigenous non-Christian shamans, imams, or priests. Those from the wider lands of Christendom often echoed themes dating to the Reformation. Catholic or Orthodox clergy, missionaries reported, resisted efforts to make the Scriptures available to the people. One unnamed American missionary in Crete (a large

Image 17.3. *The Monastery Hodegetria Gonias, Crete*

island in southern Greece) told the story of a monk (presumably Orthodox) who made rounds in the villages soliciting donations by carrying around the supposed "relics of some saint" and offering blessings to the people in exchange for money. But the monk increasingly found that the Cretans "had learned better than to worship saints and their relics, since they had had the Bible introduced among them." The monk angrily "began to cry out against . . . the distribution of the Bible."

This missionary further reported that at the Orthodox monastery of Gonia monks requested copies of the Bible in modern Greek since all they possessed was the ancient Greek version, which they found difficult to understand. The missionary readily complied with their request, but the Orthodox exarch (bishop) reportedly found out about the monks' Protestant Bible translations and had them burned. We may take such polemical accounts with a grain of salt. Yet there can be no doubt that the new societies' campaigns for missions and the Bible were undergirded by classic Protestant convictions about the authority and availability of a vernacular Bible, which God could use in surprising ways.

Selected Bibliography

Browne, George. *The History of the British and Foreign Bible Society*. 2 vols. London, 1859.

Case, Jay Riley. *An Unpredictable Gospel: American Evangelicals and World Christianity, 1812–1920.* New York: Oxford University Press, 2011.

Howsam, Leslie. *Cheap Bibles: Nineteenth-Century Publishing and the British and Foreign Bible Society*. Cambridge: Cambridge University Press, 2002.

Jagodzińska, Agnieszka. "'For Zion's Sake I Will Not Rest': The London Society for Promoting Christianity among the Jews and its Nineteenth-Century Missionary Periodicals." *Church History* 82, no. 2 (June 2013): 381–87.

Stubenrauch, Joseph. *The Evangelical Age of Ingenuity in Industrial Britain*. Oxford: Oxford University Press, 2016.

Struve, Nikita. "Macaire Gloukharev: A Prophet of Orthodox Mission." *International Review of Mission* 54, no. 215 (July 1965): 273–80.

Ucerler, M. Antoni J, S.J. "The Christian Missions in Japan in the Early Modern Period." In *A Companion to the Early Modern Catholic Global Missions*, edited by Ronnie Po-Chia Hsia, 303–43. Boston: Brill, 2018.

Walls, Andrew F. "The Legacy of Samuel Ajayi Crowther." *International Bulletin of Missionary Research* 16, no. 1 (Jan. 1992): 15–21.

Zemka, Sue. "The Holy Books of Empire: Translations of the British and Foreign Bible Society." In *Macropolitics of Nineteenth-Century Literature: Nationalism, Exoticism, Imperialism*, edited by Jonathan Arac and Harriet Ritvo, 102–37. Philadelphia: University of Pennsylvania Press, 1991.

Chapter 18

An Era of Theological Innovation

Unprecedented doctrinal change is usually troubling, from the perspective of the great tradition of Christian theology. Fidelity to the great tradition, defined primarily by the Bible and secondarily by the creeds and confessions of the early church, suggests the need for constant preservation and renewal of orthodox theology and practice. "Renewal" was most obviously manifested in the Reformation, one of the most jarring but warranted episodes in church history. In light of the great tradition paradigm, however, we wouldn't technically say that the Reformation entailed "change" so much as theological recovery.

Given this view of theological change, the first half of the nineteenth century can seem like an unsettling era for adherents of the great tradition. Innovators such as Friedrich Schleiermacher and a host of scholars who came in his wake posited that truth was more individual and interior than the church had traditionally believed. Religious truth, they argued, was not to be found primarily in historic statements of faith or classical Christian texts but in one's own heart and mind. The Bible (or parts of it) remained a valuable guide, but the creeds of the early church became viewed more as tools of institutional power than as authoritative guides to doctrines such as the Trinity.

Many Protestant liberals heralded virtually any theological change as being faithful to the spirit of the Reformation, however. They were not persuaded by those who distinguished between theological recovery and theological novelty. Catholics, too, endured debilitating battles over rising modernist theology in their ranks, often as byproducts of secularizing and anticlerical tendencies emerging from the French Revolution. In 1864, Pope Pius IX issued the *Syllabus of Errors*, an extraordinary indictment of the theological and political threats facing the church. This was mostly a collection of anathemas that popes had already pronounced in the preceding decades, but it was still breathtakingly bold and comprehensive. The *Syllabus* condemned pantheism, socialism, Protestant Bible societies, the separation of church and state, liberalism in all its forms, and much more. The document concluded by condemning the notion, put forward by Catholic liberals, that the pope should "reconcile and harmonize himself with progress, with liberalism, and with modern civilization." The *Syllabus* got a warm reception from Catholic traditionalists. But it drew howls of derision from liberals and many Protestants who (among other criticisms) said that it proved Catholicism was incompatible with the type of republican government pioneered by the United States. The Catholic condemnation of "modernism" per se was reaffirmed in Pope Pius X's 1907 encyclical on the "doctrines of the modernists." In it, he attacked the notion that religious truth was to be found in the "experience of the individual." Catholic and Protestant traditionalists were often reacting to the same threats, especially those expressing skepticism about objective, historic theological truth. Conservatives typically offered quite different responses to those threats, however, with Protestants emphasizing the Bible and the Reformation's renewal of *sola scriptura*, and Catholics emphasizing church tradition and the authority of the Vatican.

We can observe change in virtually any era of church history, even in times of relative stability. The church's perception of change is equally pervasive. As a historical rule, people see their own era as a time of tumultuous transformation, even when retrospect would suggest that the changes were relatively minor. But there seems no doubt that the early nineteenth century was one of the most profound eras of change in modern church history. Some of those transformations were theological, with the rising prominence of liberal, Romantic, and higher critical beliefs. Others were not so much theological as methodological, such as in the advent of global Protestant missions and print/Bible distribution, or the Second Great Awakening's institutionalization of revival techniques such as the camp meeting and the anxious bench. Other changes were even deeper, such as the modern era's focus on individuals instead of communities. This rising individualism was shared by movements as varied as democratic revolutions in the US, France, and elsewhere, and in evangelical piety and its renewed emphasis on individual conversion and salvation.

The age of democratic revolutions, impacting places from France to the US, Haiti, and Latin America, often produced anticlericalism and the disestablishment of many state churches. It also made the early nineteenth century seem like a time of unparalleled change in churches and states. The period was a time of startling Protestant growth, especially in the US, but it was also an era of exceptional sectarian ferment and secularization. The disestablishment of the state churches also made this a booming period for religious entrepreneurs. Preachers, organizers, and itinerants as diverse as Charles Finney, the Baptist pastor and itinerant George Liele (in the American South and Jamaica), the Methodist Thomas Coke, and the Plymouth Brethren leader and dispensationalist pioneer John Nelson Darby, effected enormous change. They felt themselves limited only by how hard they could work.

The number of new sects and theological innovations during the era—especially in global perspective—is nearly impossible to capture in the composite. But their growth was massive and often disturbing to outsiders. Some of the new trends, such as the anti-Calvinist bent of the Methodists, Freewill Baptists, and the disciples of Finney, started out controversial but became broadly accepted in the evangelical movement. Other trends featured new prophets and visionaries, predictions of the last days, and even new authoritative religious texts, ones that few adherents of the great tradition could countenance. Many of these groups and leaders, though not all, emerged in the relatively free religious climate of the independent United States.

The Shakers

One messianic figure who bridged the age of revolutions in Britain and America was "Mother" Ann Lee, the key figure in the Shaker movement. Lee was born into poverty in Manchester, England, in 1736. (This was the same year of George Whitefield's first public sermon.) By the late 1750s, Lee became associated with an intense sectarian group near Manchester. The charismatic scenes of dancing, trembling, and screaming in their meetings led critics to call them Shakers. (This is the same derisive way in which Quakers got their name a century earlier.) Lee and other Shakers suffered terrible persecution and occasional imprisonment in England, even as she began to make bold claims about her prophetic authority. For example, she reportedly could speak in dozens of languages of which she had no prior knowledge.

Lee, her husband, and a small group of her followers departed for America in 1774. As they struggled to make a living in New York City, Lee's religious views became more extreme. She became convinced that all sexual activity, even within marriage, was fleshly and sinful. Her husband disagreed. They became estranged. Around the beginning of the

Revolutionary War, Lee left her husband and moved with other Shakers to a farming village in upstate New York. The sect remained isolated there until 1780, when a couple events turned the Shakers into a sectarian destination for some radical evangelicals emerging from the "New Light Stir" of the Revolutionary years in New England. One event was the so-called Dark Day of May 1780, when smoke from forest fires cast heavy darkness over the whole region. Many believed that the Dark Day was a portent of God's wrath, if not the second coming of Christ. Lee proclaimed that the occasion marked the "first opening of the gospel in America." The Dark Day also led to many conversions and recommitments in New England and New York's more conventional evangelical churches.

The second crucial development for the Shakers in 1780 was the decision by New Light Baptist preacher Joseph Meacham (1742–96) to affiliate with the group. Meacham had worked as a Baptist itinerant in the 1770s, but he became increasingly radical, partly due to his disillusionment with the violence of the Revolutionary War. He sought a pure, called-out community of believers and thought that he found it in the Shakers. He believed that Mother Ann Lee was "the Bride, the lamb's wife." What exactly Lee taught on these matters

Image 18.1. *Shaker worship* (ca. 1830)

is not clear, but she certainly claimed special prophetic authority. The Shakers' radicalism, including their pacifism, drew many critics. The group continued to suffer persecution, even as they drew more radical evangelical adherents into the fold. Lee died in 1784, the year after the Treaty of Paris secured American independence from Britain.

By the early nineteenth century, Shakers began to assert that Lee was in fact the second coming of Christ in female form. Shaker evangelists and missionaries continued to attract converts out of evangelical churches during the Second Great Awakening. Their evangelistic impulse waned after the Civil War, however. Their opposition to marital sex made it impossible to sustain the movement via fertility, the essential source for sustaining virtually every religious movement. By the early twenty-first century, the Shakers had nearly vanished. The Shakers established no enduring presence outside the US, but they did attract comment from European observers including Charles Dickens, who described their worship practices as "unspeakably absurd." The writer Friedrich Engels (coauthor with Karl Marx of *The Communist Manifesto*) took a more positive view, however, regarding them as one of the first socialist experiments in world history.

Edward Irving and the Catholic Apostolic Church

Countless preachers, theologians, or laypeople in church history have started roughly within orthodox belief and then burst the bounds of orthodoxy altogether, either through liberal innovation or exotic, unbiblical charisma. The latter was the case with the Scottish minister Edward Irving (1792–1834), one of the most fascinating figures of British church history. As a young man Irving became assistant pastor to the formidable Thomas Chalmers, then serving a Glasgow parish in the Church of Scotland. Chalmers was far more famous than Irving, and the two big personalities did not complement each other. In 1822 Irving relocated to London, where at a chapel affiliated with the Church of Scotland he soon became one of the most sensational preachers the city had known since George Whitefield.

> [Ministers] must discover new vehicles for conveying the truth as it is in Jesus into the minds of the people; poetical, historical, scientific, political, and sentimental vehicles.
>
> Edward Irving, *The Oracles of God and The Judgment to Come*, 1823

Irving was unusually tall, with long, black hair, and preached with eloquence, urgency, and biblical learning. Like Whitefield, Irving had crossed eyes, which to some seemed to enhance his aura of spiritual power. He combined the evangelical Calvinism of his Scottish background with up-to-date learning and literature. Irving befriended leading figures of the Romantic movement such as the theologian and poet Samuel Taylor Coleridge (1772–1834). Coleridge was the author of works such as the opium-fueled poem *Kubla Khan*, with its immortal first line, "In Xanadu did Kubla Khan a stately pleasure-dome decree." Once a Unitarian, Coleridge had returned to the Church of England by the time he befriended Irving. Despite Irving's cosmopolitan influences, he unhesitatingly preached the wrath of God against sinners. The unrepentant sinner was "a groveling, lustful creature, whom heaven would not be polluted with for an instant," Irving wrote in his popular *The Oracles of God and The Judgment to Come* (1823). Irving bemoaned the masses of damned people languishing in London, "perishing under the mortal disease of sinfulness. . . . Oh, for the spirit of a Luther . . . that a reformation might come about, which would not need to be reformed," he proclaimed. Soon Irving's supporters began building a large Gothic church for him in London to contain the huge crowds waiting to hear him preach.

Irving's initial popularity waned as he offended wealthy would-be supporters with attacks on the theater (even the plays of Shakespeare), as well as on groups such as the London Missionary Society and the British and Foreign Bible Society. He particularly lambasted the latter for including the Apocrypha in editions of the Bible. His sermons were marathon sessions, sometimes lasting over three hours. Irving had briefly hoped that he could restore rigorous Christian commitment to the ruling classes in the United Kingdom, but many elite Anglicans who had supported him now found him tiresome and extreme.

Irving's declining popularity fed his growing penchant for apocalyptic speculation. The French Revolution had spawned a generation of intensified eschatology in Europe and America. Irving joined the ranks of the end-times writers, even suggesting that he had calculated the date of Christ's return as the year 1868. (Jonathan Edwards had speculated that the downfall of Roman Catholic power would occur in 1866, based on similar reckonings from Daniel and Revelation.) Other more ambitious prophets in his movement named the date as 1835 or thereabouts. Irving also began studying the work of a renegade Chilean Jesuit named Manuel de Lacunza (1731–1801), who wrote on prophetic interpretation under the pseudonym Juan Josafat Ben-Ezra. Lacunza began publishing on biblical prophecy after the suppression of the Jesuit order in 1773, resulting in his *The Coming of the Messiah in Glory and Majesty*, which appeared in various editions across Europe. Its unusual conclusions led the Spanish Inquisition to condemn Lacunza's book. Irving was captivated by it, even though he was just starting to learn Spanish. In 1827 he produced an

English-language translation of Lacunza's work. Reading Lacunza helped finalize Irving's conviction that Christ's return was imminent and that it would inaugurate the millennium. Irving's appropriation of the beliefs of a Chilean Jesuit was an example of the sometimes porous boundaries between Catholic and Protestant theological cultures.

Irving became a leading spokesman of the emerging Anglo-Irish premillennial movement, along with John Nelson Darby. But unlike Darby, Irving delved into more and more speculative theology of all types, ultimately leading former allies to charge him with heresy. Perhaps via Coleridge's influence, Irving began to emphasize Jesus's full humanity and ability to sin, though Irving insisted that the Holy Spirit had protected Jesus from actually sinning. Theologians such as Jonathan Edwards had taught that although the incarnate Christ was fully God and fully man, it was morally impossible that he could have sinned. The presbytery of London found Irving guilty of heresy in 1830, leading him to secede from the Church of Scotland.

In the late 1820s, Irving also became involved with prophecy conferences at the Albury Park estate of the English evangelical banker and philanthropist Henry Drummond (1786–1860). These meetings became one of the engines of English premillennial belief. Then Irving began hearing reports of an extraordinary revival happening in Rhu, Scotland, in the parish of one of Irving's friends, John Macleod Campbell (1800–72). The revival was unusual in two respects: one was that it was Arminian, emphasizing that Christ had died for all humankind, not just the elect. (This put Campbell at odds with the Church of Scotland and its adherence to the Calvinism of the Westminster Confession.) Second, in the spring of 1830 the Rhu parish saw an outbreak of prophesying, instant healings, and speaking in tongues. Tongues had heretofore appeared only occasionally among radical sectarian movements such as the French Prophets or the Shakers. At almost exactly the same time as the Rhu revival, tongues also surfaced in the new Mormon movement in America. It was quite unusual for tongues to be manifested in a mainstream denominational setting. Observers such as Irving were intrigued. Irving and his associates began to surmise that as the return of Christ drew near, they were also seeing the renewal of the miraculous gifts of the Spirit, ones that had marked the church in the Book of Acts. Irving identified this renewal of tongues and healings with the "latter rain" referenced in Joel 2:23. Whereas premillennialists such as John Nelson Darby rejected the reappearance of tongues and other "sign gifts," Irving helped to pioneer a charismatic strain of premillennialism.

As with many later advocates of tongues-speaking, Irving discovered that it was easier to affirm the validity of tongues than to know how to handle manifestations of tongues in church services. Guidelines such as those in 1 Corinthians 14 gave no sanction for people to start speaking in tongues whenever they liked in public assemblies. Parishioners did begin speaking in tongues and offering interpretations in small-group meetings associated with Irving's church, but he was reluctant to permit tongues in his regular services. The tongues speakers began interrupting meetings, however. After initially trying to suppress them, Irving reversed course and began trying to integrate tongues and interpretations into church services.

In 1833 Irving became the pastor of a new independent congregation in London. He took the office of "angel," following terminology used in Revelation 2 and 3. For the "Irvingites," "angel" basically meant head pastor. The church became the flagship congregation of the new Catholic Apostolic Church, a movement which embraced Irving's Pentecostal premillennialism. By this time, however, Irving's health was declining fast, probably from consumption or tuberculosis. He died on a visit to Glasgow in 1834. Some of his followers kept vigil at his grave, expecting him to rise from the dead. The Catholic Apostolic Church continued to grow and expand geographically after Irving's death. It became a major movement in subsequent decades in Germany, for example. Repeated schisms and differing national versions led to multiple descendant denominations of the Irvingites. The New Apostolic Church, which grew out of divisions within the German Irvingite movement, is the largest of these descendant groups. In a typical global pattern, the New Apostolic Church grew quickly in Africa in the twentieth century. Today a strong majority of the New Apostolic Church's adherents are African, not European. Despite the common assumption that most of the fast-growing African denominations must be Pentecostal, however, the New Apostolic Church has shed almost all the original charismatic distinctives of the Irvingite movement. It is a major denomination in countries such as Ghana, Zambia, and the Democratic Republic of the Congo.

The Rise of Mormonism

Although Britain, Germany, and other European countries were not immune, America seemed especially susceptible to radical religious movements in the early 1800s. Some of them sprang up quickly and expired just as fast. One example was the New York cult led by the would-be prophet Robert Matthews (1778–1841) in the 1830s. Matthews spent time in a mental hospital and died in near-total obscurity. Eventually Matthews was largely forgotten, his fame surpassed by his housekeeper, the former slave Isabella Baumfree, who changed her name to Sojourner Truth (d. 1883) in 1843. Sojourner Truth became one of the mid-nineteenth century's most powerful advocates for women's rights and the abolition of slavery. Matthews's group reflected a remarkable openness to sectarian religion in New York, especially in the Burned-Over District of the upstate. The Shakers made numerous converts in New York even before the Second Great Awakening began.

Perhaps the new movement there of the most enduring consequence, however, was the Church of Jesus Christ of Latter-day Saints (LDS), or the Mormons, led by Robert Matthews's contemporary Joseph Smith (1805–44). Mormonism may be the most uniquely American religion. Its history and beliefs are inextricably tied to the United States, though it has hardly remained a religion exclusive to America's boundaries.

Mormons made major departures from the great tradition of Christian theology, especially regarding the biblical canon, Christ's nature, and the Trinity. But it grew out of the fertile milieu of the Second Great Awakening in New York. Joseph Smith was born in 1805 while the Second Great Awakening was well under way. His parents moved from Vermont to Palmyra, New York, a region marked by regular camp meetings, revivals, and vociferous arguments about Christian doctrines. In his early teens Smith claimed that he began to receive a series of visitations from heavenly beings who assured him that none of the bickering churches in America reflected God's truth. In 1823 an angel identified as Moroni (not a name recorded in the Bible) directed Smith to the location of buried golden tablets. Using a seer stone he had found at the site of a well, Smith translated the "Reformed Egyptian" writing on the tablets. This translation became the Book of Mormon, first published in 1830.

The Book of Mormon purports to record, in language strongly reminiscent of the King James Bible, ancient conflicts in the Americas between Hebrew tribes known as the Nephites and Lamanites. (The Book of Mormon routinely quotes the KJV directly, and large portions of Isaiah in particular are reproduced in it.) Jesus allegedly appeared to these groups following his resurrection, making the book "another testament of Jesus Christ," as recent LDS imprints have phrased it. Moroni was one of the only survivors from the Nephites, a group whom the Lamanites destroyed. Moroni's father, Mormon, preserved the history of these tribes' struggles on the golden plates. Moroni transformed into an angel after his death. He began appearing to Smith in the 1820s to have Smith rediscover ancient America's place in redemptive history and restore the true church (the LDS).

Anyone possessing basic familiarity with Christian orthodoxy, and with the Protestant principle of *sola scriptura*, would immediately recognize how troubling Smith's claims were. The early Christian church had, of course, debated what to include in the canon of Scripture.

Indeed, contemporaries of Smith were still arguing about whether to include the Apocrypha in editions produced by Bible societies. But for a mostly uneducated man in upstate New York to claim that he had discovered lost scriptures possessing the same (or more) authoritative status as the Bible itself was, to critics, outlandish and offensive. The Bible was easily the most influential book in Western culture and the cornerstone of Christian belief. How could God possibly allow another divine revelation to suddenly appear, dug out of a hill in rural New York? To Smith's opponents, the answer was that God was not behind the Book of Mormon. It was a product of Smith's overactive imagination, at best.

Indignation at Smith and the LDS became more intense as the Mormons aggressively evangelized for their new faith. In addition to claiming the gift of tongues, Mormon beliefs included other unconventional ideas about God and about social relations, including marriage. They denied that the persons of the Godhead—Father, Son, and Holy Spirit—were three persons and one God. Instead, they argued that each member of the Godhead was a separate being. Mormon doctrine about Jesus has developed over time, but Christ clearly plays a subordinate role to the Father in Mormon Christology. As Mormon leader Brigham Young (1801–77) put it in 1865, "God is our Father, Jesus is our Elder Brother, and we are all brethren." Humans were similar to Jesus, according to Mormon authorities, in their potential for divinity.

However Smith and his followers developed these new beliefs about the Trinity (or the non-Trinity, to be precise), we should note that their ideas were not unprecedented. Unitarians, of course, had given Jesus a secondary role to the one, unitary God (the Father). They viewed the doctrine of the Trinity as logically absurd. John Adams and Thomas Jefferson, who by the 1810s had both become Unitarians, discussed the Trinity in extensive correspondence in retirement. Adams assured Jefferson in 1813 that "had you and I, been forty days with Moses on Mount Sinai . . . and there told that one was three and three, one: We might not have had courage to deny it; but we could not have believed it." Transcendentalist Theodore Parker (1810–60) in an 1841 address described Jesus as the best of all men, yet basically still like us: "was he not our brother; the son of man, as we are; the Son of God, like ourselves?" More broadly, liberal European theologians such as Schleiermacher did not necessarily deny the Trinity, yet they saw the doctrine as largely irrelevant to the nature of true religion, which was experiential and ethical.

Casual observers might not grasp Mormonism's distinct departure from historic Trinitarian orthodoxy. But it was not hard to appreciate the novelty of Joseph Smith's teachings on marriage and his approval of men marrying multiple wives. Polygamy occurred in the Hebrew Bible, of course, and people of European descent knew that many Native American and African peoples still practiced plural marriage. Though it was unusual for anyone in modern church history to endorse polygamy, Joseph Smith contended that plural marriage was a feature of God's restored church, just as it had been for the Old Testament patriarchs. Indeed, Smith married dozens of women aside from his first wife Emma, though Emma vociferously opposed polygamy and naively denied that Smith was a polygamist. The LDS did not publicly acknowledge Smith's plural marriages until eight years after his death. Brigham Young made polygamy a fixture of Mormon religion, marrying fifty-five women.

Image 18.2. *Mormon temple at Kirtland, OH*

Due to Smith's exotic beliefs and sometimes belligerent advocacy of Mormon faith, he and his followers found themselves subjected to vicious persecution. They moved to various places throughout the Midwest, fleeing hostile government officials and extrajudicial mobs. Smith and his brother Hyrum were finally jailed and murdered by anti-Mormon zealots in Illinois in 1844. The Mormons could have easily vanished like so many other radical sectarian groups were it not for the decisive and controversial leadership of Brigham Young. He famously led many of his followers to the Great Salt Lake in Utah, founding Salt Lake City in 1847. Mormons continued to face challenges over polygamy, however, resulting in the 1879 Supreme Court case of *Reynolds v. United States*. This landmark case tested the validity of US laws prohibiting polygamy and concluded that the free exercise clause of the First Amendment did not give people permission to disobey otherwise valid laws in the name of religion. The Mormons accordingly agreed to stop openly violating American laws against polygamy, and Utah became a US state in 1896. Utah has remained the center of world Mormonism, but the religion has also developed a major global missionary presence with strong communities in places such as Mexico, Brazil, and the islands of Oceania.

William Miller and the Millerites

Like his younger contemporary Joseph Smith, the Adventist leader William Miller (1782–1849) grew up in the luxuriant but unstable religious atmosphere of upstate New York. He was reared in a Baptist family in the border region between Vermont and New York. By the early 1800s, Miller had been exposed to skeptical writings by Thomas Paine and David Hume and went through a phase as a deist. Military service in the War of 1812 and the death of his father apparently helped convince Miller to return to the biblicist faith of his childhood. As we have seen, there was an intense flowering of eschatological speculation in the early decades of the nineteenth century. Miller studied Daniel, Revelation, and other passages related to the end times. Drawing on calculations based on passages such as Dan 12:7's "time, times, and a half," Miller figured that the Second Coming of Christ, or the Second Advent, would occur around the year 1843 to inaugurate the millennial kingdom on earth. His views became popular among local Baptists and other evangelicals in New York and Vermont. His *Evidences from Scripture and History of the Second Coming of Christ about the Year A.D. 1843, and of His Personal Reign of 1000 Years* (1833) gave him broader fame. Miller began preaching across the northern states. Miller's work attracted the attention of Joshua Himes (1805–95), a Boston minister affiliated with the restorationist Christian Church movement. Himes became Miller's lead publicist, providing him access to pulpits and venues in major cities of the East and Midwest. Himes arranged for the construction of a "great tent" for Miller's outdoor speaking events. It was reportedly the largest tent in the nation, capable of seating three thousand people under its canopy.

Himes's promotional work also made Miller a figure of international renown. His ideas influenced millions of people throughout North America and Britain. Miller was undoubtedly sincere in his prognostications, but his movement also took on a magnitude that Miller could not have anticipated. He surely felt pressure from supporters to get as specific as possible about the timing of the Second Advent. By the beginning of 1843, Miller declared that he expected Christ to return to earth sometime in the twelve months following March 21 of that year. Some popularizers of eschatology (such as Edward Irving) had suggested dates for

Christ's return, or for the beginning of the millennium, in the not-too-distant future. Few had ever made such a bold and imminent prediction as Miller, however, and doing so generated massive notoriety. Until this point, most Millerites had remained within established churches, but now some followers (with little support from Miller) called for the establishment of Adventist, or "come-outer" congregations, focused on Christ's imminent return.

The conflicted Miller had always reminded his adherents that his predicted dates might not be accurate. He did not profess infallibility as a Bible interpreter. So it was not entirely devastating to the Millerites when March 21, 1844 came and went without any visible event related to Christ's return. His followers regrouped, and Miller readily admitted that his initial calculation had been off. Many Millerites seized upon October 22, 1844, as the corrected date for the Second Advent. When that date similarly passed without Christ's appearing, the episode became known as the "great disappointment." Miller's Baptist church in New York expelled him and his supporters. His followers fell into factions about how to interpret Christ's apparent "tarrying." Some suggested that Christ's return happened but that it was not perceptible on earth. Others argued that it remained imminent.

The largest group to emerge from the splintering of the Millerites was the Seventh-day Adventists, led by the visionary writer Ellen White (1827–1915). White had come under Miller's influence in 1840. After the great disappointment, she claimed that she began receiving visions and prophetic knowledge related to the true church and the Second Advent. Among her emphases were a Saturday Sabbath (thus "Seventh-day") and strict dietary practices, including vegetarianism. She wrote more than one hundred books and pamphlets, including the wildly popular *Steps to Christ* (1892). In a familiar story across a number of Christian denominations, Adventism became a fully global religion in the twentieth century. Already by the 1920s, Adventist foreign membership equaled that of North America. In the second half of the twentieth century Adventists saw massive expansions in Africa, the Caribbean, Latin America, and South Asia. Brazil, India, and Zambia now have larger Adventist populations than the US does.

The Heavenly Kingdom

We have focused on sectarian movements originating in Britain and the US, but such movements have hardly been limited to the English-speaking Christian world. One of the most tragically consequential sects of the mid-nineteenth century was led by China's Hong Xiuquan (1814–64). Hong challenged China's Qing dynasty in the devastating Taiping

Rebellion of 1850–64. In the 1830s, Hong came under the influence of American and British evangelical missionaries. He consulted Christian pamphlets written by Liang Fa, the first Chinese Protestant convert ordained as a pastor. But Hong went well beyond the teachings of the missionary community and began to experience visions of heaven in which God anointed him to destroy demons on earth. Hong became convinced that he was a messiah figure, the Son of God, and the younger sibling of Jesus. He began preaching against Confucianism and Buddhism and studied briefly in 1847 with a Southern Baptist missionary in Guangzhou. Soon he founded a series of militia-like religious communities, the Society of God Worshippers, which attracted tens of thousands of followers. China's Qing government was alarmed by the growing movement's militancy and moved to crush it. In 1851, Hong proclaimed that he was the king of the Heavenly Kingdom of Great Peace, or the *Taiping Tianguo*.

Hong's followers fought a brutal civil war against the Qing dynasty. With tens of millions of Chinese people dying during the long conflict, many regard the Taiping Rebellion as the deadliest civil war in world history (it certainly killed far more people than the contemporaneous American Civil War). Terrible battles and mass executions were rampant, and many died from disease and famine. The Heavenly Kingdom's leaders, headquartered at Nanjing, instituted Christian-themed prohibitions on opium smoking, prostitution, and other immoral practices. They also practiced forms of land and property redistribution that led later observers to suggest they were proto-communists. Hong Xiuquan died during the siege of Nanjing, and Qing forces conquered the city in 1864. It may have had less enduring religious significance than Mormonism or Adventism, but in terms of social upheaval and military impact, Hong's Heavenly Kingdom was arguably the most cataclysmic sectarian movement of the nineteenth century.

Select Bibliography

Appleby, R. Scott. *Church and Age Unite: The Modernist Impulse in American Catholicism*. Notre Dame, IN: University of Notre Dame Press, 1992.

Bushman, Richard Lyman. *Joseph Smith: Rough Stone Rolling*. New York: Knopf, 2005.

Carter, Grayson. *Anglican Evangelicals: Protestant Secessions from the* Via Media, *c. 1800–1850*. Oxford: Oxford University Press, 2001.

Dallimore, Arnold. *Forerunner of the Charismatic Movement: The Life of Edward Irving*. Chicago: Moody, 1983.

Givens, Terryl L. *By the Hand of Mormon: The American Scripture that Launched a New World Religion*. New York: Oxford University Press, 2002.

Johnson, Paul E., and Sean Wilentz. *Kingdom of Matthias: A Story of Sex and Salvation in 19th-Century America*. New York: Oxford University Press, 1994.

Prothero, Stephen. *American Jesus: How the Son of God Became a National Icon*. New York: Farrar, Straus and Giroux, 2003.

Rowe, David L. *God's Strange Work: William Miller and the End of the World*. Grand Rapids: Eerdmans, 2008.

Spence, Jonathan D. *God's Chinese Son: The Taiping Heavenly Kingdom of Hong Xiuquan*. New York: Norton, 1996.

Stein, Stephen J. *The Shaker Experience in America*. New Haven, CT: Yale University Press, 1992.

Turner, John. *Brigham Young: Pioneer Prophet*. Cambridge: Harvard University Press, 2012.

Chapter 19

Christians and the "Heinous Sin" of Slavery

In 1833, when Britain abolished slavery in its colonies, white Christians remained divided on what the Bible taught about slavery. Evangelicals such as William Wilberforce and John Newton championed abolition, but many other English-speaking Christians, especially in the American South, saw abolitionism as anti-Christian madness. Some observers sought to take a middling position: during the parliamentary debate over abolition in 1833, the Tory politician Richard Vyvyan (1800–79) admitted that he was "not one of those who think that Christianity and slavery are incompatible. Let the Gospel be searched, and nothing will be found which can lead to a supposition that slavery, in the abstract, is prohibited by the revealed word of God." Slavery "in the abstract" was discussed constantly in such debates. Few white Christians would openly defend the rampant sexual and physical abuse that was widespread in the chattel slavery regime. Many conceded that the "manstealing" responsible for much of the supply of African slaves was condemned repeatedly in the Bible. Fewer would countenance a blanket condemnation of slavery itself, however. They could not find an outright prohibition on slavery in the Bible, and both Britain and the US depended heavily on slave-grown crops, especially cotton. Black Christians who bore the brunt of slavery saw the question differently, of course. Slavery was not "abstract" for them. They knew firsthand the cruelty of the indiscriminate beatings, breakup of families, and sexual exploitation of women and children that was endemic to the system.

Drumbeat of Reform

In any case, Richard Vyvyan and others like him in Britain did find the actual conditions and risks of legalized slavery troubling enough to support abolishing it. The fact that missionaries had taught the Bible to enslaved people admittedly exacerbated the tension over slavery, according to Vyvyan. What slave could read the Bible and not see it as affirming human dignity and freedom? For enslaved people, the spirit of the Scriptures would be more compelling than the letter. "It would be fruitless to attempt to perpetuate a system under which discontent and hopelessness of their condition must be productive of the worst feelings of human nature," Vyvyan concluded. Such concerns about the fruitlessness of perpetuating slavery were not theoretical. Slave rebellions, undergirded by Christian conviction, happened more frequently in the early 1800s. In 1822, an alleged conspiracy in Charleston, South Carolina, was led by Denmark Vesey and other enslaved people affiliated with the African Methodist Episcopal Church. An 1823 rebellion in the British colony of Demerara (Guyana), on the northern coast of South America, was directed by enslaved men inspired by the abolitionist pastor and London Missionary Society affiliate John Smith. In 1831, the British colony of Jamaica was convulsed by the "Baptist War," a slave rebellion led by the Jamaican Baptist preacher Samuel Sharpe. Again in 1831, white Virginians were terrified by the murderous uprising led by the Baptist preacher and slave visionary Nat Turner. The drumbeat to end slavery was growing louder.

As Thomas Jefferson had written in 1820, slaveowners had the "wolf by the ear, and we can neither hold him, nor safely let him go." Governments across Europe and the Americas responded variously to this dilemma. Britons grudgingly decided to let go of the proverbial "wolf." For Catholics, Pope Gregory XVI in 1839 gave his blessing to the abolitionist cause—or at least to the end of the slave trade—in an encyclical which insisted that no Christian should "dare to vex anyone, despoil him of his possessions, reduce to servitude, or lend aid and favour to those who give themselves up to these practices, or exercise that inhuman traffic by which the Blacks, as if they were not men but rather animals . . . in contempt of the rights of justice and humanity, bought, sold, and devoted sometimes to the hardest labour." Certain Catholic and Protestant-dominated nations held out longer, however. The

United States banned its international slave trade in 1808, but not slavery itself until the Thirteenth Amendment to the Constitution in 1865. Despite the pope's injunction, Cuba and Brazil were the last holdouts in the Western Hemisphere, keeping slavery legal until 1886 and 1888, respectively.

The nineteenth century saw a host of reform movements challenging unfree labor systems, as well as new forms of worker exploitation associated with the factories of the Industrial Revolution. These reforms, including antislavery, reflected a combination of humanitarian or democratic ideals emerging from Enlightenment thought and more traditional Christian belief in the *imago dei* and the inherent dignity of every human being. Christian authorities often found themselves uncertain whether to support labor reform and antislavery movements, especially when such reforms seemed associated with French-style radicalism. In Russia, for example, the Orthodox Church was divided about whether to back the abolition of serfdom. This traditional agricultural labor system had made peasant workers into feudal dependents, permanently attached to the lands and lords for whom they worked. Serfdom was not the same as "chattel" slavery in the Americas, in the sense that the workers were not technically property, and it did not have the racial dynamic that New World slavery possessed. Serfs were often of the same ethnicity as the feudal lord. Nevertheless, serfdom was still galling to liberal proponents of democratic equality and human rights.

Filaret Drozdov (1782–1867), the Orthodox Metropolitan (archbishop) of Moscow, was a relatively liberal figure on such matters amidst a widely conservative Orthodox leadership. (Filaret was also a key advocate for the translation of the whole Bible into modern Russian language.) Yet Filaret was still hesitant about abolishing serfdom until Tsar Alexander II's officials apparently convinced him to draft the emancipation edict of 1861. The edict used traditionalist Christian language to bless a relatively radical reform. Much of it commended the nobles' (presumed) willingness to comply with the edict, and it enjoined the freed peasants to manifest hard work and responsibility. Citing Paul's letter to the Romans, Filaret declared that "every individual who enjoys freely the benefits of society owes it in return certain positive obligations; according to Christian law every individual is subject to higher authority; everyone must fulfill his obligations, and, above all, render tribute, dues, respect, and honor." Like Britain, Russia chose legislative emancipation of unfree workers rather than risk violent revolution. Such revolution would come to Russia anyway, a half century later. Still, it was striking that Russia accomplished this massive reform starting in 1861, the same year that the American Civil War began.

Pushing toward Reform in America

The Civil War in America capped decades of political and religious struggle over slavery's future. Until the invention of the cotton gin in 1793, it seemed that America might gradually phase out slave owning, as the northern US states had begun doing during the Revolutionary era. The Constitution of the US (ratified 1788) also permitted the termination of new slave importations as early as 1808. Congress, with the encouragement of President Jefferson, had approved this prohibition at the appointed time. Yet the cotton boom of the early 1800s, paired with a slave population growing rapidly by natural increase, made the "Cotton Kingdom" the most powerful economic interest in the US in the period between 1800 and 1860.

Many southern slaveholders, including traditional Christians such as the Episcopalian Patrick Henry of Virginia, readily admitted that slavery was indefensible according to Christian principles. Thomas Jefferson, normally skeptical about the providential workings of God, mused in *Notes on the State of Virginia* that slavery was so offensive it would likely lead to the outpouring of God's wrath on slaveowners. This reluctance to defend slavery transformed by the 1820s into a paternalistic Christian ideology of slavery as a God-ordained good. Now many white Christians, even those without a direct financial stake in slavery, argued that the Bible endorsed slave owning. Slaves, the paternalists said, fit into the broader system of household responsibilities of Christian patriarchs. They cited passages such as Ephesians 5 and 6 and Colossians 3 and 4, which enjoined slaves ("servants" in the King James Version) to work hard and to obey their masters, and for masters to treat slaves fairly. The emergence of a more radical abolitionist movement led by figures such as the New Englander William Lloyd Garrison, Nat Turner's revolt in Virginia, the Baptist War in Jamaica, and Britain's abolition of slavery in its Caribbean colonies all made slavery's defenders anxious to craft a biblicist defense of the institution in the 1830s.

The advent of a more vehement white proslavery Christian ideology ran parallel to a maturing African American church in the US, Canada, and the Caribbean, as well as the beginnings of black American missions and immigration to West Africa. In the American Revolutionary era figures such as Richard Allen of the African Methodist Episcopal Church and the Baptist pastors David George and George Liele had begun to pioneer African American churches in places from Jamaica to Philadelphia to Sierra Leone. Black-pastored congregations became more numerous in the early 1800s, although unrest and controversy often put such churches' existence at risk. In Georgia, George Liele left the black Baptist movement in good hands in the person of Andrew Bryan (b. 1737), who organized an African American Baptist church in Savannah in 1788. In Boston, Massachusetts, Thomas Paul (1773–1831) became the pastor of the city's first black Baptist church in 1806. Paul went on to itinerate widely in the United States and the Caribbean, helping to establish such churches as New York's influential Abyssinian Baptist in 1809. By 1830, there were about a dozen independent African American Baptist churches in the North and three times as many of them in the South.

One of the most impactful black congregations in the South was Richmond's African Baptist Church, pastored by the dynamic Lott Cary (c. 1780–1828). Cary was a former slave, but he worked with supporters in Richmond's First Baptist Church to gain his freedom and obtain a preaching license. Like many pioneering African American leaders, Cary was not satisfied to restrict his influence just to one church and town. Accordingly, he founded the African Baptist Missionary Society in 1815. Leaders of the Baptists' Triennial Convention (founded 1814) were delighted with Cary's organization, speculating that it might be a sign that the "unoffending Africans" who had come to America as slaves might providentially return to the "land of Ham" (Africa) to spread the gospel there. In 1821 Cary himself went as a missionary to Liberia, a West African colony identified by the American Colonization Society as a promising destination for freed slaves.

> I am an African, and in this country, however meritorious my conduct, and respectable my character, I cannot receive the credit due to either. I wish to go to a country where I shall be estimated by my merits, not by my complexion; and I feel bound to labor for my suffering race.
>
> ---
>
> Lott Cary, *Sketch of the Life of the Rev. Lott Cary*, 1835

Churches such as Richmond's African Baptist congregation routinely fell under suspicion for alleged complicity in slave unrest or rebellion. We have seen how the Emanuel African Methodist Episcopal Church in Charleston was destroyed in the aftermath of the Denmark Vesey plot in 1822. White authorities placed severe restrictions on Richmond's African Baptist Church after Nat Turner's rebellion in Virginia in 1831. After Turner's revolt, the independent black Baptist church in Williamsburg, Virginia, was closed entirely after four decades of operation. Indeed, 1831 was a turning point for slavery and Christianity in North America and the Caribbean, with the twin episodes of Turner's revolt and Jamaica's "Baptist War" forcing white leaders to either move forward with abolition or to make slavery more entrenched. Turner, a Virginia slave and lay Baptist preacher, had begun to experience apocalyptic visions by the mid-1820s. He believed that God was raising him up as a prophet and avenger and that he was to take up Christ's yoke and "fight against the Serpent, for the time was fast approaching when the first should be last and the last should be first." By 1831 he watched earnestly for signs that he should initiate a rebellion against slave masters. Confirmation came in August, with a total eclipse of the sun. Turner and his followers murdered dozens of white men, women, and children in Southampton County, Virginia. Virginia authorities and white vigilantes murdered hundreds of African Americans in reprisals. Turner was captured, tried, and convicted. After his execution by hanging he was dismembered. There was some talk in Virginia of adopting a plan for gradual emancipation after Turner's revolt, but the majority of white politicians remained protective of slavery.

Image 19.1. *Discovery of Nat Turner*

Challenges to Slavery in the Caribbean

The situation in Britain's Caribbean colonies was different from Virginia. Britain and America had outlawed the transatlantic slave trade around the same time (1807–08), but the proslavery interest in the United States (including influential pastors and theologians) was more entrenched than in Britain. Thus, by the 1820s many of the British missionaries in the Caribbean had already become convinced that slavery needed to be abolished. Revolts in Demerara and Jamaica only reinforced that conviction. In Jamaica, independent black churches ("Native Baptists") descended from the work of George Liele had become centers for black gospel preaching as well as social organization. Even white missionaries such as the English Baptist William Knibb (1803–45), who came to Jamaica in 1824, routinely appealed to allies to help bring down the "cursed blast of slavery" in the British colonies.

The key leader of the Baptist War of 1831, however, was the slave and Baptist minister Samuel Sharpe (c. 1801–32). Sharpe had extensive connections to the Native Baptist churches, as well as to British missionaries such as Knibb. Sharpe and his associates planned a series of sit-down strikes to begin shortly after Christmas in 1831, but antislavery missionaries proved less enthusiastic about the plans than Sharpe had hoped. Knibb warned his followers to not be deluded by "wicked persons" and to go on with their work as usual. Indignant slaves began burning plantation buildings and crops in the region of Montego Bay, on the northern coast of Jamaica. By the beginning of 1832, much of the Montego Bay area was under the control of the enslaved rebels. The Jamaican government and militia eventually regained control of the whole island, executing dozens of conspirators, including Sharpe. Even though most white missionaries had balked at outright rebellion, many of them, including Knibb, were arrested for their alleged role in instigating the revolt. Angry whites also destroyed many of the island's chapels that had provided ministry to enslaved people. Knibb soon returned to England and insisted that if Christian missions were to continue in the Caribbean, it would require the "entire and immediate abolition of slavery." All the momentum in British politics was on the side of abolition, and Parliament enacted a program of gradual emancipation for the Caribbean colonies in 1833. Unlike in the United

Image 19.2. *Roehampton estate, Jamaica* (1833)

States, the religiously-inspired slave rebellion in Jamaica hastened the end of slavery itself through legislative reforms that English leaders such as William Wilberforce had been advocating for decades.

The Divisive Issue of Slavery in America

In the United States, factors including the Nat Turner rebellion and the advent of the militant abolitionist movement made the slavery issue more intractable than ever in the 1830s and '40s. The troubles over slavery had periodically affected individual congregations at least since the 1780s. Churches with enslaved members and slave masters routinely had to confront issues raised by the institution's practices. For example, could enslaved members who had been sold away from their spouses get remarried? Some church members wanted their congregation to take strong stances for or against slavery. Others wanted the churches to leave the slavery issue to civil authorities. It was not just men who were involved in such local church struggles. Rhoda Bement found herself in an 1843 disciplinary proceeding at the First Presbyterian Church of Seneca Falls, New York, for confronting the pastor and demanding that he publicize abolitionist lectures in town. The "ultraist" evangelical Bement was also known for refusing to drink from the cup in communion because she opposed consumption of alcoholic beverages under any circumstances.

Bement's confrontation reflected the larger clashes in the national Protestant denominations. The first of the major denominational splits came in Bement's Presbyterian denomination, which in 1837 divided into "Old School" and "New School" factions. That division related more to differing views of revivalism, especially concerning the theology of revival preachers such as Charles Finney, than to slavery per se. But New School Presbyterians were more supportive of national reform movements of all kinds, including antislavery, than Old Schoolers were. Princeton Seminary, home of theologian Charles Hodge, took criticism both from staunch Old School and New School advocates, but by the time of the 1837 split, most observers considered Princeton a bastion of moderate Old School sentiment. This led New School Presbyterians to found Union Theological Seminary in 1836 in New York City. As the New School and Old School denominational split loomed, Hodge wrote in his book *Slavery* that while he found the institution of slavery less than ideal, he did not approve of Christians forbidding other Christians from owning people as slaves. The Bible never forbade it, so how could Christians enforce extrabiblical moral mandates on the matter?

The Old School/New School controversy began to come to a head in 1836 as Old School Presbyterians tried Albert Barnes (1798–1870), pastor of First Presbyterian Philadelphia, for heresy. He was accused of functionally denying basic precepts of the Westminster Confession of Faith, including original sin, innate human depravity, and justification by faith alone. The Presbyterian General Assembly, with a majority of New School delegates, repudiated the Old School's concerns about Barnes and returned him to his pulpit in Philadelphia. An indignant Old School faction regained the majority at the 1837 General Assembly and put forward a "Testimony and Memorial" against the pervasive theological errors of the New Schoolers, as they saw them. "We contend especially and above all for *the truth*, as it is made known to us of God, for the salvation of men," they wrote. "It is against *error* that we emphatically bear our testimony; error, dangerous to the souls of men, dishonoring to Jesus Christ, contrary to his revealed truth, and utterly at variance with our standards." Not surprisingly, New School delegates did not warm to the "Testimony and Memorial," so Old Schoolers used procedural moves to expel many of the New School congregations and more than five hundred ministers from the denomination. Hodge, for his part, thought such a split was inevitable, but he worried that the Old School tactics were ruthless and unchristian in spirit. The next General Assembly was marked by wild scenes of the factions literally fighting over access to seats closest to the assembly's moderator, and Old Schoolers strategically locking doors to keep New Schoolers away from the choicest seats. Even though the 1837 split was not primarily about slavery, both the Old School and New School wings would split again on the eve of the Civil War—this time into sectional northern and southern branches of the New School and Old School divisions.

When the American Methodists divided in 1844, the rift was more transparently precipitated by the question of owning slaves. The Methodist Episcopal Church was itself founded as a geographic breakaway from British administrative control in 1784. The denomination had also seen the formation of separate, black-led denominations, including Richard Allen's African Methodist Episcopal Church (1816). Still, by the 1840s, the Methodist Church was the nation's largest denomination and was in some ways the most pervasive organization of any kind in the United States. John Wesley, the founder of Methodism, had taken a firm stance against slavery in the 1770s, but in the early 1800s the views of slavery among white Methodists divided largely along sectional lines. Some staunch antislavery northern Methodists had already begun abandoning the national denomination in the early 1840s. Controversy crested in 1844 when a majority of Methodist General Conference delegates asked for the resignation of a Georgia bishop who owned slaves. This led southern representatives to withdraw from the assembly, forming the Methodist Episcopal Church, South. The divide in the Methodist Church would persist until a reunion of the denomination's sectional branches in 1939.

After 1833, many English Baptists pled with their American brethren to stand against slavery. They found a receptive audience among some northern Baptists but not among the white Baptists of the South. The Triennial Convention had dealt in the 1820s and '30s with a major outbreak of opposition to national missionary and reform organizations, producing a powerful Primitive Baptist movement, especially in the South and Midwest. The pro-missionary Baptists who led the Triennial Convention into the 1830s were not eager to allow slavery to become the denomination's next polarizing issue. The Convention had long-standing experience with having slaveholders serve as the denomination's president. The influence of radical abolitionism, and the growing alarm among the proslavery interest in the South, made a clash over slavery unavoidable among Baptists, however.

In the 1830s, antislavery radicals began to insist that slavery was a "heinous sin" that Baptists should not tolerate. Proslavery apologists responded by characterizing the radicals as "fanatics" and "ultraists" who intended to disrupt the unity of the nation's Baptists and to damage their common missionary cause. Some northern Baptist associations began adopting resolutions condemning Baptists who owned slaves and refusing to maintain fellowship with them. Antislavery activists founded the American Baptist Anti-Slavery Convention in 1840, which was committed to pushing forward the Baptist movement without the taint of slaveholders' sins. Like Charles Hodge, many Baptist moderates and conservatives noted that there was seemingly no prohibition on slavery in Scripture. Therefore, Baptists should not make one's view of slave owning a test of fellowship. South Carolina Baptist pastor and slaveowner Richard Fuller said that antislavery activism was "a most unnecessary agitation" on a topic that lay outside the purview of the Baptist missionary agencies.

It remained uncertain whether organizations such as the Baptist Home Mission Society were willing to keep appointing slaveholders as missionaries. Georgia Baptists turned the appointment of one of its missionary candidates into a test case over slavery. The Home Mission Society declined to act on the slaveholder's nomination. Alabama Baptists similarly pushed the issue of slaveholders as foreign missionaries. The Triennial Convention responded ambiguously to their queries, but the Convention's leaders seemed to indicate they were no longer comfortable with appointing slaveholders as foreign missionaries, either. These moves by the national Baptist denomination led to an 1845 meeting of (mostly southern) Baptists in Augusta, Georgia. They formed the Southern Baptist Convention

(SBC) as an alternative to the Triennial Convention. Organizers insisted that the SBC was not formally proslavery, but its organizers opposed making one's opinion of slaveholding a divisive issue. They believed they should focus on the gospel and missions alone. Unlike the Methodists and Presbyterians (whose Old School/New School and sectional divisions were abolished through a series of mergers over more than a century), the Baptists would never have a sectional reunion, remaining in separate Northern (American) and Southern Baptist denominations into the twenty-first century.

The Catholic Response to Slavery

The breakup of Protestant denominations over slavery was an ominous prelude to southern secession and the American Civil War (1861–65). Only the Union military in the Civil War, aided by massive numbers of slave runaways and black enlistees, could force the end of the slave regime in America. As we have seen, 1865 did not represent the end of slavery in the Western Hemisphere; it lingered in certain enclaves in the Caribbean and South America. Puerto Rico, Cuba, and Brazil were all traditionally Catholic colonies of Spain and Portugal (Brazil had declared independence from Portugal in 1822). Nineteenth-century Catholic opinion of slavery was divided, as was Protestant opinion. Although the role of the pope made a decisive Catholic theological pronouncement on slavery more feasible than it was among the scattered Protestant denominations, no such pronouncement was forthcoming. Pope Gregory XVI's 1839 encyclical had just inveighed against the slave trade. Part of the Catholic Church's hesitancy emerged from the common association of radical abolitionism with anti-Christian Jacobinism and the extreme phases of the French Revolution.

In Brazil, the Catholic Church was deeply invested in slavery, too, making it an unlikely source of abolitionism. Nevertheless, certain orders such as the Benedictines began gradually emancipating and freeing thousands of Brazilian slaves in the 1860s and '70s. Joaquim Nabuco (1849–1910), the leading antislavery politician in Brazil, attempted to mobilize the Catholic Church for abolition. He even met personally with Pope Leo XIII in 1888 but failed to get the church to enlist for abolition in a forceful way. Nabuco said that "our clergy's desertion of the role which the Gospel assigned to it was as shameful as it could possibly be." For his part, Nabuco cited British and American antislavery writers, including William Wilberforce and Harriet Beecher Stowe (author of the Christian antislavery bestseller *Uncle Tom's Cabin*), as significant shapers of his own convictions. Like other Brazilian abolitionists, Nabuco was profoundly influenced by the writings of Castro Alves (1847–71), whom

Image 19.3. *Abolition in Brazil*

many scholars regard as Brazil's greatest poet and most powerful antislavery writer. Alves manifested a reformist Catholic spirit in his poetry. Speaking as the "Voice of Africa," one of his poems cried "God! O God! Where are you that you do not answer!"

> Today my blood feeds America . . .
> Enough, Lord! Send forth your potent arm . . .
> Listen to my protest from your everlasting throne,
> My God! Lord, My God!

Alves and Nabuco reflected a long-standing reformist Catholic sentiment that was used to criticize the oppression of slaves and the abuses of corrupt governments in Latin America.

War and Theology

In America, the Civil War wrecked slavery and the southern economy, but it also represented a "theological crisis," in the words of historian Mark Noll. American evangelicals were enormously confident about an individual believer's ability to interpret the text of Scripture. Yet Christians in America simply could not agree upon the Bible's message about slavery. Both sides in the pro- and anti-slavery debate accused the other of dishonesty and bad exegesis of Scripture. Confederates presented secession and the defense of slavery as a godly cause. Untold numbers found themselves wondering what had gone wrong, as the last hopes of the Confederacy failed in April 1865, when Robert E. Lee surrendered the last remnants of his Confederate army in Virginia. South Carolinian Grace Brown Elmore wrote candidly that "hard thoughts against my God" troubled her mind after the South's loss. "Questions of his justice, of his mercy arise, and refuse to be silenced." Many northerners rejoiced at the end of the war, of course, believing that the outcome had proven God was on their side. Abraham Lincoln (1809–65) took a more complex view of the war's providential significance, suggesting in his Second Inaugural Address that God had given "both North and South this terrible war" as the means to remove the sinful institution of slavery.

The Thirteenth Amendment (1865) to the US Constitution formally ended slavery, a legal process begun by the Emancipation Proclamation in 1863. The war's end and the emancipation of enslaved people led to one of the most dramatic shifts in American church history: the advent of countless new African American-led churches. The number of African American converts had been growing steadily in the first half of the nineteenth century, but many of those converts attended white-pastored congregations. After 1865, there was a great parting of ways, particularly in Baptist churches. Many white and black Baptists alike were content to allow the freed people to open their own churches. In Montgomery, Alabama, for example, almost all the black members of First Baptist Church left in 1867 and started their own congregation. Such departures were repeated all over the country, but especially in the South. African Americans were ready to be free, not only of slavery, but also of white paternalism. One black pastor explained that he intended to keep relating to white Christians as "brethren, but never again shall we let them rule us as masters."

Among Methodists, the war's end led to the dramatic return of African Methodist Episcopal bishop, Daniel Alexander Payne (1811–93), to Charleston, South Carolina. Three decades earlier, Payne had left the city of his birth, despairing of ever advancing black education and sustaining black church life. But a new day dawned in 1865. One of Payne's key associates was Richard Harvey Cain (1825–87), who became the minister of the restored Emanuel A.M.E. Church in Charleston. In 1873, Cain would become a member of the US House of Representatives, one of a number of black church leaders who would briefly serve in state and national politics from the South in the 1870s. Cain explained in

1865 that "God's providence had leveled the barriers, and rolled away tyranny's mountain." Cain and other black church leaders would find their highest hopes for the Reconstruction South dashed, with black political rights severely curtailed by the late 1870s. Yet 1865 was a moment of relief and optimism for many African Americans, who regarded emancipation as a long-awaited Jubilee.

Mid-Nineteenth-Century Revivals

Even as the American nation stood on the precipice of civil war, however, one could see signs of massive revivals that would change the face of Protestant Christianity in the English-speaking world. The period from 1857 to 1859 saw an intense series of awakenings stretching from America to Britain and Australia. The awakenings known as the 1857–58 "Businessmen's Revival" in America, and intense revivals in Wales and Ulster in 1859, are probably the best known of these. In London, there was also growing excitement around the preaching ministry of a young Charles Spurgeon (1834–92), who in October 1857 spoke to a reported crowd of more than 23,000 people at London's Crystal Palace. Spurgeon had been converted as a fifteen-year-old in 1850 under the preaching of a Primitive Methodist (a revivalist breakaway from the Wesleyan Methodists) minister in Colchester, England. Spurgeon also came to Baptist convictions and received believer's baptism. By 1850 he began preaching. In 1854 Spurgeon took his first full-time preaching job as an unordained nineteen-year-old at London's New Park Street Chapel. His forceful evangelical sermons and roughhewn style resonated powerfully with average Londoners. Spurgeon's enormous crowds soon drew comparisons to George Whitefield's ministry in London, more than a century earlier.

Deep intellectual changes were afoot, however, at the same time that Spurgeon's fame was cresting. Trends associated with revival and skepticism often grew simultaneously; they were not necessarily a zero-sum game. For example, in the mid-1850s, scientist Charles Darwin (1809–82) was preparing to publish his theory of natural selection. Darwin's research and travels had already led him to develop a naturalistic theory of evolution two decades earlier. He was hesitant to make his views known lest he jeopardize his status in English academic circles at Oxford and Cambridge, which remained deeply connected to the Anglican Church. Finally, Darwin published his theory in the book *On the Origin of Species* (1859). In it, he argued that differences between species occurred through nature's selection of beneficial characteristics over long periods of time. "If variations useful to any organic being do occur, assuredly individuals thus characterised will have the best chance of being preserved in the struggle for life; and from the strong principle of inheritance they will tend to produce offspring similarly characterised. This principle of preservation, I have called, for the sake of brevity, Natural Selection." As presented, Darwin's theory was not overtly antagonistic toward traditional Christian belief. Followers such as Thomas Huxley (1825–95) would eagerly draw out the anti-Christian implications of evolutionary theory, however. Darwin himself was apparently more of a deist than an atheist; he seems to have believed in a distant God who somehow structured the created order. But in practice, Darwin was positing a purposeless, purely naturalistic view of animal life, including that of humans. God was functionally absent in Darwin's scheme. Species changed and evolved over eons in a remorseless "survival of the fittest."

Advancing a master scientific theory without God, Darwin's book enjoyed notable success among intellectuals and an international public audience. Its popularity made *On the Origin of Species* a watershed moment in the world history of belief and unbelief. Skepticism, materialism, and even atheism were not new, of course. Darwin did represent a major point of departure in *secularism*, meaning here the absence of religion from intellectual trends. After Darwin, it became increasingly common for scientists to argue that their field had nothing to do with religion. Providential claims about the causes of natural phenomena became passé in many academic fields, especially the natural sciences. As seen in the new black churches, Spurgeon's ministry, and the upsurge in revivals in the late 1850s, traditional belief was hardly in decline. But traditional belief was increasingly treated as separate from or antagonistic toward elite academic knowledge. This transition heralded a new, more secular modernity. It placed the adherents of the great tradition of Christian theology into a different, and often embattled, cultural stance in the coming decades.

Selected Bibliography

Altschuler, Glenn C., and Jan M. Saltzgaber. *Revivalism, Social Conscience, and Community in the Burned-Over District: The Trial of Rhoda Bement*. Ithaca, NY: Cornell University Press, 1983.

Desmond, Adrian, and James Moore. *Darwin*. London: Michael Joseph, 1991.

Ford, Lacy K. *Deliver Us from Evil: The Slavery Question in the Old South*. New York: Oxford University Press, 2009.

Gutjahr, Paul C. *Charles Hodge: Guardian of American Orthodoxy*. New York: Oxford University Press, 2011.

Hildebrand, Reginald F. *The Times Were Strange and Stirring: Methodist Preachers and the Crisis of Emancipation*. Durham, NC: Duke University Press, 1995.

Lynch, John. *New Worlds: A Religious History of Latin America*. New Haven, CT: Yale University Press, 2012.

Moon, David. *The Abolition of Serfdom in Russia, 1762–1907*. New York: Routledge, 2014.

Nettles, Tom J. *Living by Revealed Truth: The Life and Pastoral Theology of Charles Haddon Spurgeon*. Fearn, Scotland: Christian Focus, 2013.

Turner, Mary. *Slaves and Missionaries: The Disintegration of Jamaican Slave Society, 1787–1834*. Urbana, IL: University of Illinois Press, 1982.

Weitz, Eric D. *A World Divided: The Global Struggle for Human Rights in the Age of Nation-States*. Princeton, NJ: Princeton University Press, 2019.

Chapter 20

A New Era of Biblical Criticism

Before Charles Darwin, a number of skeptical or materialist figures had attacked basic Christian doctrines. These included David Hume's criticism of belief in miracles. Darwin's popularity, and his scientific approach, undermined the Christian and theistic worldview at a more fundamental level than most of his predecessors, however. After Darwin it became common for academics to conceive of humanity's origins without reference to God or to any providential plan. Yet Darwin was also a culmination of trends that had been developing for decades. Repeated blows from Romantic and Enlightened sources had raised troubling questions about humanity's basis for belief, the reliability of the Bible, and the nature of religious authority.

The Influence of Samuel Taylor Coleridge

In England, many traditionalist believers produced popular defenses of Christianity, such as Joseph Butler's *Analogy of Religion* (1736) or William Paley's *A View of the Evidences of Christianity* (1794). Many still found such arguments compelling in the early nineteenth century. But some such as the poet and theologian Samuel Taylor Coleridge found rationalist arguments for belief inadequate, if not damaging, to faith. Coleridge, associate of the charismatic preacher Edward Irving, had his life shortened by a debilitating dependence on opium as a painkiller. (This addiction was common in the era.) Intellectually,

Coleridge was bothered by what struck him as the cold rationalism of the Anglican Church of his time. To Church of England authorities, being a Christian seemed to require only baptism and assent to Anglican doctrine. Professing Anglican belief also brought access to education and political power. (Oxford and Cambridge functionally started to open to non-Anglicans only in the 1850s.) Like many dissenters and evangelicals, Coleridge felt that this type of Anglican nominalism was an impoverished, politicized, and corrupt religion.

Image 20.1. *Samuel Taylor Coleridge* (1854)

Coleridge, like the German theologian Friedrich Schleiermacher, believed that true faith must engage the heart and the affections. Coleridge remained more committed to the primacy of revelation in Scripture than did Schleiermacher. But Coleridge sought to balance his relatively high view of the Bible with a rejection of its "infallibility," or the idea that God had "dictated" word-by-word what the biblical authors were to say. "In the Bible there is more that *finds* me than I have experienced in all other books put together," Coleridge wrote. "The words of the Bible find me at greater depths of my being; and . . . whatever finds me brings with it an irresistible evidence of its having proceeded from the Holy Spirit." Despite its uniquely divine qualities, however, the notion of "plenary inspiration" (which Coleridge seems to have equated with a robotic dictation) struck him as "superstitious and unscriptural."

Samuel Taylor Coleridge had an enormous impact on British and American belief and theology, partly because he did not just write technical metaphysics. He composed more popular poetry and theological reflections, such as *Aids to Reflection* (1825) and the posthumously-published *Confessions of an Inquiring Spirit* (1840). In the United States, Coleridge's emphasis on Scripture and on personal experience gave him an audience among some evangelical Calvinists, such as James Marsh (1794–1842), president of the University of Vermont. In 1829, Marsh produced the first American edition of Coleridge's *Aids to Reflection*, including an introduction in which Marsh recommended Coleridge to evangelical

Americans. Marsh believed that Coleridge was a powerful corrective to the dominance of Lockean thought and Scottish Common Sense rationality in Anglo-American theology. Too often, theologians seemed to functionally put their faith in theological systems and their own rationality rather than the "substantial being, and the living energy of the WORD," Marsh cautioned. Too many Christians were "fed with the lifeless and starveling products of human understanding, instead of that 'living bread which came down from heaven.'" Coleridge offered a path out of the cul-de-sac of bare human rationality. Many Americans agreed with Marsh's assessment, and they eagerly read Coleridge for decades. Many of them, however, including Transcendentalists such as Ralph Waldo Emerson (1803–82) and Theodore Parker had no use for Coleridge's balance of the heart's intuitions and dependence on Scripture. They jettisoned the latter for radical individualism alone, or what Emerson would call "Self-Reliance."

More typical than Emerson was Horace Bushnell (1802–76), who like Marsh came from an evangelical Calvinist background. After a conversion experience in 1831, Bushnell studied under Nathaniel William Taylor (1786–1858) at Yale Divinity School. Taylor was a key advocate of the "New Haven Theology," which remained structurally Calvinist, while it blunted most of the controversial elements in Calvinist theology. For example, Taylor taught that Adam's sin was not imputed to his descendants. Instead, all people sinned the same way Adam had, as an act of free will. Thus, Bushnell and many of his admirers rejected the traditional belief in original sin. Unlike Taylor, Bushnell eventually repudiated the whole revivalist tradition of the Second Great Awakening. Bushnell embraced a radically intuitive understanding of religious truth, based in part on his reading of Coleridge. "The teachings of Christ," Bushnell wrote in *God in Christ* (1849), "are mere utterances of truth, not argumentations over it. . . . Truth is that which shines in its own evidence, that which *finds* us, to use an admirable expression of Coleridge, and thus enters into us." The Bible was no mere catalog of doctrinal propositions, but "inspirations and poetic forms of life, requiring, also, divine inbreathings and exaltations in us, that we may ascend into their meaning." Conservative theologians were not impressed with Bushnell's exuberant individualism. Charles Hodge saw Bushnell's theology as a product of "spiritual inebriation."

Hodge was concerned that Bushnell and Coleridge's dependence on interior feeling was, like Schleiermacher's, damaging to orthodoxy and the great tradition of Christian theology. As soon as one's feelings did not confirm a teaching of Scripture, Hodge and other traditionalists warned, Scripture and orthodox tradition was jettisoned. Hodge argued that Coleridge effectively changed "the whole system of the gospel as it has been commonly understood. That instead of the sinner's depending on what Christ had done [especially in the atonement], as the ground of his acceptance; he is taught to look to himself—to a change wrought in his own heart."

Reformed theologians such as Hodge were concerned about the emphasis on internal feelings promoted by theologians such as Schleiermacher, Coleridge, and Bushnell, but also by the emphasis placed on religious experience by evangelicals and preachers of the new birth. These overlapping concerns help explain why certain evangelicals have always had a penchant for individualistic, politicized, or ahistorical readings of Scripture. In some cases, such readings have rejected the plain meaning historically given to Scripture passages, despite evangelicals' stated commitment to the Bible as the sole guide to belief.

Theological Influence of Germany

After the death of Schleiermacher, Germany remained a source of influential liberal theology in the mid-nineteenth century. Key figures included David Friedrich Strauss, author of *The Life of Jesus* (1835). Strauss helped make the German universities, at least by reputation, strongholds of skepticism about biblical authority and factual access to the "historical Jesus." This was despite the work of conservative theologians such as Ernst Wilhelm Hengstenberg, who defended a historic view of Scripture's inspiration. Albrecht Ritschl (1822–89), theologian at the University of Göttingen, extended the legacy of Strauss and other German higher critics into the later nineteenth century. Ritschl was also one of several German theologians who imported the ideas of German philosopher Georg Wilhelm Friedrich Hegel (1770–1831) into his work. Hegel, a colleague of Schleiermacher's at the University of Berlin, was known for his dialectical view of the unfolding of history. Virtually everything in Hegel's thought proceeds according to the dialectical principle. A thesis is always met by an antithesis, and their resolution produces a synthesis, leading to a higher plane of development. Hegel was highly theoretical and often difficult to understand. But his dialectical principle accorded well with Darwinian evolution, as well as the (anti-Christian) philosophy of Karl Marx (1818–83).

Ritschl applied the philosophy of Hegel to Lutheran theology. Extending and modifying Luther's conclusions, Ritschl posited that the essence of the Christian experience was Christ's historic work of justification meeting human corruption. Christ's work resulted in the Christian's reconciliation with God. Ritschl was less interested than Pietist theologians in a person's experience with God. He believed that reconciliation with God inevitably led to Christian practice and moral living. Ethics, for Ritschl, was the heart of Christianity, rather than doctrinal belief. God purposed to establish his kingdom on earth, as opposed to the earthly kingdom of sin, or the "world." Ritschl took an optimistic view of human capacity for good. Christ made the way for humanity's justification, and Christians possessed all they needed to enlist in the work of the kingdom. Ritschl's moderate Lutheran modernism was not as pathbreaking as Schleiermacher's theology. But it was broadly influential, not least because his students included German theological luminaries including Adolf von Harnack (1851–1930) and Ernst Troeltsch (1865–1923).

Ritschl's work primarily focused on Christian ethics, yet he also represented a growing mainstream academic comfort with types of higher biblical criticism that would have once been seen as radical. By the late nineteenth century, German scholars and other higher critics routinely suggested that the books of the Bible, especially in the Old Testament, were simply not what they appeared to be. They were not written at the time they purported to be written, critics argued, nor were they written either by the authors claimed by the text or those identified in Christian or Jewish antiquity. The German orientalist and Hebrew Bible scholar Julius Wellhausen (1844–1918), for example, became known in the 1870s and '80s for a version of the "documentary hypothesis." This was the idea that the Pentateuch was the product of earlier documents, some of which were composed much later than the events traditionally believed to have been recorded by Moses.

Wellhausen admitted that, as a young scholar, he had relished the historical and prophetic writings far more than the Torah, or the Jewish law. He learned from Albrecht Ritschl about an emerging scholarly view that dated the composition of the Hebrew law after the prophets, not before them, as the Bible presented it. Wellhausen recalled that "without knowing his reasons for the hypothesis, I was prepared to accept it; I readily acknowledged to myself the possibility of understanding Hebrew antiquity without the book of the Torah." Wellhausen's bold articulation of a theory of four independent Hebrew source documents, dating from the tenth to the fifth centuries BC, dominated the field of Pentateuch source studies for a century. There was no way to prove Wellhausen's hypothesis because the documents in question (as well as ancient copies of the Pentateuch itself) were long since lost. Yet Wellhausen and others made radical doubt about the dating, sources, and authorship of the Mosaic books commonplace in academic study and elite denominational circles. Conservative defenders of biblical authority were increasingly forced to accommodate the conclusions of the higher critics or to be academically marginalized. Many elite scholars no longer regarded conservatives as legitimate biblical scholars or theologians.

The New Testament also fell under heightened scrutiny. Probably the pinnacle of German higher criticism of the New Testament came in the work of Ritschl's student Adolf von Harnack. Harnack made a sharp distinction between the Jesus of history and the dogmatic teachings of the Christian church. "The claim of the Church that the dogmas are simply the exposition of the Christian revelation, because deduced from the Holy Scriptures, is not confirmed by historical investigation," he asserted. Again, Harnack's work represented more of a culmination of long-standing trends than a dramatic departure. For example, American president Thomas Jefferson had reached similar conclusions almost a century before Harnack. Jefferson believed that later Christians, ones influenced by Platonic Greek philosophy, made damaging changes to Jesus's original teachings. These changes allegedly corrupted much of the New Testament. Jefferson, of course, had neither the time nor the scholarly resources to develop this theory to the extent that Harnack did.

Adolf von Harnack's most popular work was *What is Christianity?* (1900), which would go through many editions and translations in Europe and America. In it, Harnack argued that Jesus only intended to have his followers believe in his commandments, not to worship him as a divine person. Harnack further contended that Jesus's self-description as the "Son of God" did not carry the divine significance that dogmatists assigned to it. By Son of God, Jesus was simply signaling that he knew God as Father in a special but not unique way. "The name of Son means nothing but the knowledge of God," Harnack concluded. For Harnack, following Ritschl, the essence of Jesus's teachings was the value that God placed on humans and the divine mandate to love one another. The Gospels contained the kernel of those teachings, even if they might not be entirely reliable in all respects. Jesus also may not always have been sincere, especially in his teachings about hell and judgment. Harnack represented a cresting of German higher criticism and ethics-centered Christian teaching which fueled the social gospel in Europe and America. Social gospel advocates commonly de-centered doctrine and focused on Christian love manifested in service to one's neighbor. Yet there was also a sense, even among those sympathetic to higher criticism, that Harnack's faith was too man-centered. Did his skepticism risk eviscerating the majesty and power of the Christian faith? This would be the critique adopted by Harnack's most famous student, Karl Barth (1886–1968). Even Harnack's father, a Lutheran traditionalist, worried that Harnack's theology had become non-Christian.

The Reception of German Higher Criticism

Germans pioneered much of the most radical higher criticism of the Bible, but their influence extended to other parts of Europe, and to North America. The influence flowed from theology graduates who studied in Germany and imbibed higher criticism. (Certainly not all foreigners who studied in Germany came back doubting the fundamental reliability of the Bible, however.) More broadly, the influence of higher critics flowed through translations of popular books such as Harnack's *What is Christianity?* By the late nineteenth century, the legitimacy of higher criticism became a recurring flashpoint of controversy in many theological schools and denominations internationally. In some of the most liberal denominations, higher criticism was received with little controversy. Conversely, higher criticism made hardly any mark in some traditionalist denominations. Ironically, the new critical approaches to the Bible attracted almost no adherents among Lutherans in America, despite their heavy contingent of German-background immigrants. Lutheran denominations in America such as the Missouri Synod (founded 1847) were known for their traditionalism and defense of classic Lutheran beliefs, including *sola scriptura*.

Denominations with a relatively conservative laity but liberal seminary professors were most likely to see fireworks over higher criticism. For example, the Southern Baptist Convention pastorate and laity remained overwhelmingly conservative as of the 1870s, three decades after its founding. The denomination had opened the Southern Baptist Theological Seminary in Greenville, South Carolina, in 1859 (later relocated to Louisville, Kentucky). In 1869, the seminary hired Crawford Toy (1836–1919), a native of Virginia and doctoral graduate of the University of Berlin. Toy was an adherent of biblical criticism advanced by figures such as Schleiermacher and Julius Wellhausen. Following Wellhausen's theory of the documentary sources of the Pentateuch and Darwin's work on evolution, Toy concluded that while Scripture was reliable spiritually, it was not reliable on a scientific and historical basis. He advised students that the New Testament authors were wrenching the Hebrew Bible out of context when they interpreted it as making messianic predictions about Jesus. Moreover, he registered doubts about the authorship of certain books, suggesting for example that Isaiah was composed by three authors, not one.

After teaching at Southern Seminary for a decade, Crawford Toy resigned under pressure from administrators and took a position at Harvard. He also adopted Unitarian principles. Toy characteristically wrote in *The History of the Religion of Israel* (1882), published for Sunday schools by the American Unitarian Association, that contrary to the Old Testament's account, the "law grew up gradually, and hundreds of years after Moses, when pious prophets and priests gathered together the religious uses of the times, they thought that it must all have been revealed in the beginning by the God of Israel, and so they came to believe that their great deliverer from Egyptian bondage had received it all at once. But . . . history does not bear this out." For higher critics such as Toy, much of the message of Scripture was profitable. An astute reader needed to understand that a plain reading of the Bible, however, did not reveal the text's true nature, or its historical origin.

A range of American denominations, from the Episcopal Church to the Disciples of Christ, experienced controversies as akin to the Southern Baptists' fracas over Toy. Probably the most sensational doctrinal controversy of the era, however, resulted from the Presbyterian trial of the combative Union Theological Seminary professor Charles A. Briggs (1841–1913), a colleague of Toy's from their student days in Berlin. The Presbyterian General Assembly removed Briggs from the Presbyterian ministry in 1893. Briggs had taught that theology was a science and that doctrinal standards such as the Westminster Confession of Faith were obstacles to the object of that science, namely understanding what the books of the Bible were saying in their original context and what that message meant for the contemporary world. As scholars' understanding of the Bible changed, the Scriptures would effectively become new in every generation. "The Bible gives us the *material* for all ages," Briggs wrote, "and leaves to man the noble task of shaping the material so as to suit the wants of his own time." Like many higher critics, Briggs was comfortable using terms like "infallible" to describe the Bible's meaning, but he employed such terms toward radically relativistic purposes. To Briggs, the message of the infallible Bible changed as cultures changed.

The publication of Charles Briggs's *The Authority of Holy Scripture* (1891) restated the theologian's convictions about higher criticism. Its popularity forced traditionalist Presbyterians to act against him. They charged him with rejecting the Westminster standards. Briggs again responded by affirming the Bible as the infallible rule for Christians. Modernists and conservatives sometimes used the same words, but their meanings were radically different. Briggs's presbytery in New York initially dismissed the charges against him, but after some procedural maneuverings the national assembly overwhelmingly voted to suspend him from the ministry. Briggs left his denomination, receiving ordination in the Episcopal Church. The disciplinary measures against Briggs convinced leaders of Union Theological Seminary to abandon the Presbyterian Church. Union went independent and became a bastion of liberal and social gospel thought. Some of the faculty at Union, including Briggs's colleague Arthur McGiffert (1861–1933), were too liberal even for Briggs's taste, however. Briggs was uncomfortable with McGiffert questioning Christ's physical resurrection and denying the virgin birth. Once having cast doubt upon aspects of the great tradition, some higher critics like Briggs found it difficult to reset doctrinal limits. Were there any traditional doctrines that professors at institutions such as Union could *not* question? The answer was generally "no."

Responding to Higher Criticism

In reaction to controversies related to higher criticism, Christian traditionalists began to articulate and expand upon the doctrine of biblical inerrancy. Belief in the perfection and full authority of the Bible was an ancient doctrine, of course. Catholics and Orthodox Christians might quibble with Protestants about the individual believer's role in interpreting the Bible, or which books counted as Scripture. Most Christians of all confessions affirmed that the Bible was wholly truthful, however, in both facts and morals. *Sola scriptura* was an essential principle animating the Reformers, and that doctrine assumed the Bible's perfection and total reliability. The Westminster Confession of Faith, for example, had spoken of the "infallible truth and divine authority" of the Bible. That did not quite solve the problems of the late nineteenth century, however, as figures such as Briggs affirmed infallibility, after a fashion. The framing of higher criticism as a scientific matter led conservatives to speak more commonly of the Bible being "without error" in the original manuscripts. No matter how conservative the interpreter, few believed that the Bible could be without error in transcriptions or translations. Much less did careful students of the Bible believe that human interpretation of Scripture was infallible. But biblical traditionalists insisted that God had indeed inspired the authors of the Bible. God preserved those authors from introducing mistakes or false assumptions related to chronology, narrative, cosmology, or similar matters. Accordingly, the use of the term

> [If Christ has risen] the Bible is true from Genesis to Revelation. The kingdom of darkness has been overthrown. Satan has fallen like lightning from heaven; and the triumph of truth over error, of good over evil, of happiness over misery, is forever secured.
>
> Charles Hodge, *Systematic Theology*, 1871

"inerrant" or "without error" as applied to the Bible became vastly more common in American conservative circles in the late 1800s.

In the United States, Princeton Seminary professors were the chief articulators of the doctrines of inspiration and inerrancy. In 1857, Charles Hodge defended the concept of the "plenary inspiration" of the Scriptures, meaning that the whole Bible was the product not of the "fallible intellect of man, but of the infallible intellect of God." Scripture was not partly inspired—inspired only in its moral or spiritual meaning—but wholly inspired. God has "used the sacred writers as his organs of communication," Hodge explained. "The Bible is the product of one mind." Inspiration did not mean that the biblical authors were perfect or omniscient in their everyday lives. But when the Holy Spirit inspired them to write the books of the Bible, the Spirit also preserved them from mistakes, making the Scriptures themselves "absolutely free from error."

Higher critics countered that the Bible was subject to chronological and scientific errors and that the books were often composed by authors other than those the church had traditionally taught. Traditionalists responded by arguing that the Bible was fully inspired and, indeed, inerrant. A plain reading of the text would supply any honest Christian with an accurate view of what the Bible meant and what God meant to communicate through its words. Hodge's son Archibald (1823–86), who also taught at Princeton Seminary, joined the eminent Presbyterian theologian (and student of Charles Hodge) Benjamin Breckinridge Warfield (1851–1921) in publishing a landmark article in 1881 on "Inspiration." Archibald Hodge and Warfield were confident that faithful biblical scholarship would bolster the church's belief in the divine authority of the Bible. Hodge and Warfield explained that the doctrine of inspiration asserted the "absolute infallibility of the record in which the revelation, once generated, appears in the original autograph." They argued that when the biblical authors composed their books, "the Holy Spirit was present, causing His energies to flow into the spontaneous exercises of the writer's faculties, elevating and directing where need be, and everywhere securing the errorless expression in language of the thought designed by God. This last element is what we call Inspiration."

While they utterly rejected the notion of an erroneous Bible, both Archibald Hodge and B.B. Warfield believed that scientific theories like evolution could fit within traditional Christian belief, as long as evolution did not entail materialism or a rejection of God's superintending role. Charles Hodge had been more dubious about Darwinian evolution, contending that it philosophically amounted to atheism. Charles Hodge's type of anti-Darwinian view became more common among the emerging "fundamentalist" cohort in North America.

Many fundamentalists connected a literal reading of the opening chapters of Genesis to anti-evolution and to inerrancy. The newer Princeton seminarians tended to focus on inspiration and inerrancy alone and to treat evolution as a separate and secondary issue.

Roman Catholics engaged in equally vitriolic debates over higher criticism as Protestants. As we have seen, the papacy had been wary of liberal Catholic trends since the mid-1800s. Pope Leo XIII addressed higher criticism directly in an 1893 encyclical, *Providentissimus Deus*. While the pope conceded that there could be errors in transcription, and that certain Bible passages were ambiguous and could be clarified by sound scholarship, it was nevertheless "absolutely wrong and forbidden, either to narrow inspiration to certain parts only of Holy Scripture, or to admit that the sacred writer has erred." The Bible was inspired by God, the pope argued, and therefore it was logically impossible for it to err. The pope connected the higher critics with the Reformers of the sixteenth century, however. Both trusted too much in individual conscience and rationality as arbiters of biblical truth. But while the Reformers cast doubt on the spiritual integrity of the Catholic Church, higher critics undermined the authority of the Bible. They presented the Scriptures as "only the forgeries and the falsehoods of men; they set down the Scripture narratives as stupid fables and lying stories." These were "detestable errors" posturing as objective science, according to Leo XIII.

Despite the church's warnings about the dangers of new scholarship on the Bible, some Catholic professors and priests did engage in radical forms of higher critical teaching. For example, the French priest and theologian Alfred Loisy (1857–1940), under the influence of Adolf von Harnack and other higher critics, questioned whether the historical Jesus was conscious of his own divinity and whether the Pentateuch was accurate as history. In 1907, the Catholic traditionalist Pope Pius X issued an encyclical, *Pascendi Dominici gregis*, which condemned modernist thought such as that promoted by Loisy, whom the church excommunicated in 1908. Loisy came to realize that reconciling his views with those of the Catholic hierarchy was impossible. He even admitted privately that he had little attachment to Christ, and that he would describe his religious beliefs as "more pantheist-positivist-humanitarian than Christian."

The Irish-born Jesuit priest George Tyrrell (1861–1909) likewise ran afoul of Catholic authorities for promoting higher criticism generally, and the writings of Loisy specifically. Tyrrell knew his modernist convictions would not please church officials, so for a time he published his work under pseudonyms. He helped to promote Loisy's controversial book *The Gospel and the Church* by writing the introduction to the text's English translation. Like many higher critics, Tyrrell was convinced that the essence of Christianity lay in ethics, not doctrinal affirmations. When the encyclical *Pascendi* appeared in 1907, Tyrrell immediately recognized that it was designed to silence Catholic modernists such as Loisy and himself, and he vociferously attacked it. Like Loisy, Tyrrell was excommunicated; though unlike Loisy, Tyrrell never doubted that he was still a believing Catholic.

Committed to eliminating modernism in the church, Pope Pius X prepared an antimodernist oath in 1910. The church required all clergy and church-affiliated professors to take the oath. It condemned the notion of doctrinal evolution and progress and insisted that there was no place in the church for teachers who affirmed dogma they did not believe was true in a historic or scientific sense. The oath committed Catholic clergy to reject the "heretical misrepresentation that dogmas evolve and change from one meaning to another different from what the Church held previously." Moreover, the pledge rejected the "error of those who say that the faith held by the Church can contradict history, and that Catholic dogmas, in the sense in which they are now understood, are irreconcilable with a more realistic view of the origins of the Christian religion." This oath remained obligatory for Catholic teachers and clergy until 1967 when the Catholic Church repealed it in the wake of the Second Vatican Council (Vatican II).

Protestants outside Germany dealt with similar controversies over higher criticism. In Scotland, the Free Church pastor and professor William Robertson Smith (1846–94) came under the influence of Albrecht Ritschl and Julius Wellhausen in the early 1870s. Smith wrote an article on the Bible for the *Encyclopedia Britannica* in 1875, outlining his higher critical views for a general audience. The article landed him in trouble with Free Church of Scotland authorities and earned him scorn from evangelical and Reformed critics. London pastor C.J. Whitmore, for example, concluded that Smith's article was "simply a resumé of destructive objections of the farthest advanced school of unbelievers in the inspiration and authority of the Word of God." Whitmore asserted that many of Smith's conclusions about the sources of the Old Testament were just warmed-over versions of arguments made by deists such as Voltaire and Thomas Paine. Smith was indignant about the accusations made against him and demanded that the Free Church try him for his supposed heresy. They did. After a convoluted series of hearings, the Free Church general assembly voted to remove him as a denominational professor.

In England, perhaps the height of popular controversy over biblical authority came in the "Downgrade Controversy" of 1887–88, led by the celebrated evangelical pastor Charles Spurgeon. Spurgeon had long been concerned about evangelicals' de-emphasizing of traditional doctrines, such as the substitutionary atonement of Christ for sinners and the reality of hell's eternal torments. But by the mid-1880s, Spurgeon had become convinced that most of the vague and watered-down theology he saw in British evangelical and Baptist life, including in the Baptist Union of Great Britain, was due to the erosion of biblical authority. A growing refrain in his teaching was that the Scriptures were "free from error, certain, enduring, [and] infallible."

Image 20.2. *Charles Spurgeon* (c. 1859–1870)

Spurgeon began to question whether evangelicals could remain in fellowship with "those who deny plenary inspiration." For Spurgeon and many traditionalists, this was not a secondary theological issue. In his magazine *The Sword and the Trowel*, Spurgeon declared "A new religion has been initiated, which is no more Christianity than chalk is cheese; and this religion, being destitute of moral honesty, palms itself off as the old faith with slight improvements. . . . The Atonement is scouted, the inspiration of Scripture is derided, the Holy Spirit is degraded into an influence, the punishment of sin is turned into fiction, and the resurrection into a myth, and yet these enemies of our faith expect us to call them brethren, and maintain a confederacy with them!" This rhetoric left little doubt as to what Spurgeon believed conservative Protestants should do. Spurgeon resigned from the Baptist Union by the end of 1887. Liberal Baptists criticized Spurgeon for a failure to name names in his criticisms, and the Baptist Union censured Spurgeon for withdrawing. They lamented his perceived lack of interest in giving the Union a chance to seek reconciliation between the liberal and Spurgeonite factions. Although Spurgeon's departure was a terrible blow to the Baptist Union, Spurgeon found comfort in relationships with British and American evangelicals who shared his view of the Bible's authority, such as the prominent American pastor and missions advocate A. T. Pierson (1837–1911). Pierson gave a popular series of sermons at Spurgeon's Metropolitan Tabernacle shortly after the Downgrade Controversy ended. The ailing Spurgeon died in

1892 at the age of fifty-seven, depriving the Anglo-American world of one of its most powerful evangelical voices. The advent of higher criticism had given evangelicals and fundamentalists such as Spurgeon and Pierson a strong sense of trans-denominational, transnational unity, however. The evangelical and traditional biblicist segments of Protestantism may have felt embattled, but they were not in decline.

Selected Bibliography

Breimeier, Thomas. *Tethered to the Cross: The Life and Preaching of C.H. Spurgeon*. Downers Grove: IVP Academic, 2020.

Hopkins, Mark. *Nonconformity's Romantic Generation: Evangelical and Liberal Theologies in Victorian England*. Eugene, OR: Wipf and Stock, 2007.

Hutchison, William R. *The Modernist Impulse in American Protestantism*. Durham, NC: Duke University Press, 1992.

Jodock, Darrell, ed. *Catholicism Contending with Modernity: Roman Catholic Modernism and Anti-Modernism in Historical Context*. New York: Cambridge University Press, 2000.

Massa, Mark S. *Charles Augustus Briggs and the Crisis of Historical Criticism*. Minneapolis: Fortress, 1990.

Noll, Mark A. *America's God: From Jonathan Edwards to Abraham Lincoln*. New York: Oxford University Press, 2002.

———. *Between Faith and Criticism: Evangelicals, Scholarship, and the Bible in America*. San Francisco: Harper & Row, 1986.

Rogerson, John. "History and the Bible," in *The Cambridge History of Christianity*, vol. 8, *World Christianities c.1815–c.1914*, edited by Sheridan Gilley and Brian Stanley, 181–96. Cambridge: Cambridge University Press, 2005.

Schwarz, Hans. *Theology in a Global Context: The Last Two Hundred Years*. Grand Rapids: Eerdmans, 2005.

Zaspel, Fred G. *The Theology of B. B. Warfield: A Systematic Summary*. Wheaton, IL: Crossway, 2010.

—— Chapter 21 ——

Sources of Christian Recovery and Renewal

Depending on how you look at it, the story of modern Christian history can appear as a tale of decline or revival. From the perspective of the great tradition of Christian theology, there is much reason for concern regarding intellectual developments in the European and American academy during the second half of the nineteenth century. Germany was the source of much of the new higher criticism of the Bible and questioning of traditional Christian belief. But even in Germany there were indications of revival, missions, and gospel activism at the same time as the new skeptical trends in academia. For example, the German missionary Ingwer Ludwig Nommensen (1834–1918) was deeply impressed by the scholarly pietism of German theologians such as Johann August Neander and August Tholuck. To them, Christianity entailed much more than doctrinal propositions: it was an entire way of holy living. Serving with the Rheinish Missionary Society (founded 1828), Nommensen devoted his career to spreading the "New Life" of Christianity to the Batak people of Sumatra in the Dutch East Indies. He is generally regarded as one of the most consequential missionaries ever. Nommensen was rigorously committed to raising up native leaders and clergy in the Batak church, simply requiring that they commit themselves to biblical orthodoxy as guided by standards such as the Heidelberg Catechism. Between his arrival among the Bataks in 1864 and his death in 1918, Nommensen saw the Batak church

Image 21.1. *Christian Batak Church on Sumatra's East Coast* (c. 1935)

grow from less than one hundred Christians total to some 180,000 church members, with hundreds of native pastors and teachers serving the congregations in Sumatra.

The Existentialist Response

In the mid- to late nineteenth century, the European nations' nominal religious culture also generated a powerful Christian backlash. These critics were not always inspired directly by the great tradition of Christian theology, but they did sense that the modern world was cut off from the spiritual and cultural riches of the Christian tradition. In northern Europe, arguably the most formidable antagonist of cultural Christianity was Denmark's Søren Kierkegaard (1813–55). In his powerful yet troubled writings, Kierkegaard raged against his culturally conformist Danish Christian society. A Christianity that was worldly and indistinct was hardly Christianity at all, Kierkegaard warned. The death of Kierkegaard's father and a broken engagement seem to have sent Kierkegaard into a period of tormented self-examination and prodigious literary output. Starting with 1843's *Either/Or*, Kierkegaard produced a series of philosophical and theological classics, including *Fear and Trembling*, *The Concept of Dread*, *The Sickness unto Death*, and *Training in Christianity*. Kierkegaard's dense yet searching philosophy had a massive impact on both theistic and secular existentialism, or the philosophy of human action in the face of life's apparent meaninglessness or absurdity.

Kierkegaard was depressive and intellectually tormented, but he also went through major conversion-like experiences that solidified his Christian convictions and his experience of God's grace. One such conversion came in his mid-twenties when a sublime sense of "indescribable joy" persuaded him of Christianity's truth after having gone through a skeptical phase as a young man. A decade later, during Easter week of 1848, Kierkegaard experienced a deeper conviction of God's forgiveness of his sins. "My whole nature is changed," he proclaimed. Of course, his doubts and struggles were not entirely finished. Still, the writings of Kierkegaard's final years of life were informed by a profound sense of Christianity as a radically different code from that offered by the world or by worldly churches. "Christendom has done away with Christianity, without being quite aware of it," he lamented in *Training in Christianity*. "The consequence is that, if anything is to be done, one must try again to introduce Christianity into Christendom." Christianity was a "breach" with the world, not a harmonizing with it. Kierkegaard's criticisms of the Danish state church carried echoes of the Reformers' denunciations of the Roman Catholic Church's worldliness. His emphasis on the "endless yawning difference between God and man" would also exercise a major influence on the "neo-orthodox" theology of the twentieth century, especially the work of Karl Barth.

Russia's Fyodor Dostoevsky (1821–81) also served as a Christian progenitor of existential thought, but from an Orthodox perspective. Dostoevsky has retained an even broader international influence than Kierkegaard, however, because of the enduring popularity of his novels, including *Crime and Punishment* (1866) and *The Brothers Karamazov* (1879–80). In the modern era, Christian writers such as Dostoevsky or England's C. S. Lewis have often found a wider audience for literary fiction than for formal theology or philosophy, attracting readers who might not be interested in direct apologetic defenses of Christian belief. As a young man, Dostoevsky was influenced by socialist and utopian thought, leading eventually to his arrest for subversion by Russian authorities. In a scarring experience that would shape much of his writing, Dostoevsky was sentenced to death. Just minutes before the execution, his sentence was commuted to hard labor in Siberia. Themes of chance, suffering, irrationality, and the paradoxes of human free will (or lack thereof) subsequently marked his fiction.

In the last decade of his life, Dostoevsky became deeply committed to the Orthodox tradition and the Christian ethical ideal. He also became increasingly critical of western

Europe's skepticism and secularism. These commitments informed *The Brothers Karamazov*, arguably his greatest novel, which he completed the year before he died. By the time of his death Dostoevsky had become one of the most celebrated writers in Russia, with tens of thousands of mourners attending his funeral. He was buried at the Alexander Nevsky Monastery in St. Petersburg, the resting place of other Russian luminaries, including the composer Pyotr Ilyich Tchaikovsky. Although the Communist revolution in Russia would turn the state into a vicious persecutor of Christians and other religious groups, figures such as Dostoevsky helped to cement the historic connection between Orthodox faith and traditional Russian culture.

Dutch Calvinists

During the late nineteenth century, the Dutch Reformed tradition similarly produced a renewal of orthodox Protestantism. This theological renaissance was on par with intellectual developments in American Presbyterianism (at Princeton Seminary in particular) during the same period. Theological modernism had a powerful presence within Dutch churches. Dutch modernists claimed that if higher criticism was true, then acknowledging the myths and errors within the Bible was the only way to redeem Scripture's transcendent truths for the modern world. One modernist Mennonite claimed in 1878 that "Jesus without miracles is more magnificent than with miracles." Certain notable modernist ministers became so gripped with doubt that they stepped down as pastors. A few abandoned Christianity altogether, which seemed to confirm traditionalists' warnings that modernism was a slippery slope toward unbelief. As in other nations, the modernists' novel views of Scripture led to a conservative counter-reaction, spearheaded by the Dutch Calvinist luminaries Abraham Kuyper (1837–1920) and Herman Bavinck (1854–1921).

As a theologian and political leader, Kuyper has exercised profound influence on the shape of international Reformed Protestantism. In 1862, Kuyper received a doctorate in theology at the University of Leiden and showed sympathy for modernist thought during his early career. But Kuyper's pastorate in the Dutch town of Beesd introduced him to the sturdy, everyday Calvinist belief of many parishioners. He began to see their faith as preferable to the shifting fashions of elite modernist thought. Calvin's writings, and traditional biblicism more generally, became to him "that shelter in the rocks which, being founded on the rock and being hewn from the rock of thought, laughs at every storm." As Kuyper moved on to Utrecht and then Amsterdam, he became a rising star in Reformed theology and Dutch politics. He eventually served as Dutch prime minister from 1901 to 1905. Kuyper advocated a robust Calvinist theology in the churches but appealed for a Christian democratic pluralism that befitted the realities of diverse Dutch society. In particular, he fought for the right of conservative Reformed Christians to operate their own schools as part of the broader Dutch educational system. His theological conservatism and political pluralism led to a split with the Dutch Reformed Church in 1886. Kuyper's departure led to the formation of the Reformed Churches in the Netherlands, a denomination whose leaders recommitted themselves to the Calvinist Canons of Dort, the classic Reformed statement of faith of 1618–19. The Reformed Churches in the Netherlands had a counterpart in North America's Christian Reformed Church, a denomination which drew heavily on Dutch Reformed immigrants to western Michigan.

In 1898, Abraham Kuyper gave the Stone Lectures at Princeton Seminary. In them he sought to bolster the international Calvinist network, especially its connections between the Netherlands and the US, where so many Dutch Calvinists had immigrated over the past century. Although J. Gresham Machen had not yet begun his studies at Princeton Seminary at the time of Kuyper's lectures, Kuyper's comments on modernism were similar to Machen's views, articulated in his landmark book *Christianity and Liberalism* (1923). "In deadly opposition to [Christianity], against the very Christian name, and against its salutiferous influence in every sphere of life," Kuyper declared, "the storm of Modernism has now arisen with violent intensity." The "turning point" in which modernism began to battle against the Christian tradition, Kuyper explained, was the French Revolution. The great struggle in Europe and America was between those who wished to replace the Christian tradition with rigid naturalism and materialism, or "to construct man himself from the data of nature." Kuyper argued that the best place from which to combat the modernist menace was not the Christian tradition in general, but Calvinism in particular. "In Calvinism my heart has found rest," he proclaimed. Calvinist belief was "the only decisive, lawful, and consistent defense for Protestant nations against encroaching, and overwhelming Modernism."

> The world-view of Modernism, with its starting-point in the French Revolution, can claim no higher privilege than that of presenting an atheistic imitation of the brilliant ideal proclaimed by Calvinism, therefore being unqualified for the honor of leading us higher on.
>
> ---
>
> Abraham Kuyper, *Lectures on Calvinism* , 1898

Of course, Kuyper also understood Calvinism as standing within the longer great tradition of Christian theology. "In its deepest logic Calvinism had already been apprehended by Augustine; [and] had, long before Augustine, been proclaimed to the city of the seven hills by the Apostle in his Epistle to the Romans," he said. For Kuyper, the great tradition was extended and elaborated for new generations in the great clashes between Protestantism and Catholicism in the sixteenth century, and between orthodox Christian belief and modernism in the nineteenth. Kuyper became perhaps best known for the concept of "worldview," or the idea that your perspective on a given issue will differ dramatically depending on whether you possess Christian philosophical presuppositions or not. Amidst the opposing beliefs of the modern world, the church could not take Christian presuppositions for granted, even among people who were nominally Christian.

Kuyper influenced many subsequent Reformed thinkers, including his theological protégé Herman Bavinck. Like Kuyper, Bavinck studied theology at Leiden, where Bavinck kept a poster of Kuyper tacked on the wall of his bedroom. They would not always agree theologically, but Bavinck and Kuyper represented a titanic renaissance in Dutch Reformed thought at the beginning of the twentieth century. Like many European graduate students in divinity, Bavinck wrestled with the tensions between the Dutch Reformed piety of his youth and the modernist liberalism of his schooling. The ethics-focused liberal Christianity of Albrecht Ritschl was especially prominent in his graduate training. Bavinck saw his own Pietist heritage as fundamentally otherworldly, while Ritschl's teachings were equally this-worldly. Bavinck struggled to reconcile the two, but he was convinced that orthodox Christian belief would have to contend with both Pietism and liberalism. After receiving his doctorate and briefly pastoring in the Dutch province of Friesland, Bavinck taught for two decades at the Theological School at Kampen in the Netherlands. After repeatedly turning down offers to teach at Kuyper's Free University in Amsterdam, Bavinck finally relocated there in 1902. Shortly before making this switch, Bavinck finished the first version of his magnum opus, the four-volume *Reformed Dogmatics*.

Bavinck's studies at Leiden exposed him to the influential Bible professor and higher critic Abraham Kuenen (1828–91). Kuenen rejected the idea that the Bible itself was supernatural revelation, or the possibility that the Old Testament spoke prophetically about Jesus Christ. Kuenen taught Leiden students that the Pentateuch was composed and compiled from a variety of sources, many of which dated much later than the events the Pentateuch allegedly described. Kuenen's views received wide acclaim in the Netherlands and attracted international attention from figures such as Crawford Toy, the modernist professor at

Southern Baptist Theological Seminary in Louisville, Kentucky. Toy credited Kuenen's work as an influence on his own higher critical beliefs and teaching. Bavinck did acknowledge how his modernist professors helped to mature his view of Scripture. The Bible was a more complex book than his Pietist upbringing had perhaps suggested. Yet Bavinck, similar to Kuyper, found that the practical experiences of pastoring in the Christian Reformed Church and teaching in the Kampen seminary revealed the practical deficiencies of modernist theology. After Leiden, Bavinck reclaimed great confidence in the Scripture as revelation, and the value of traditional Reformed dogmatics for understanding truth about God, humanity, and the plan of redemption. Bavinck put special weight on the doctrine of the Trinity, which modernists had long derided as an extrabiblical, philosophical invention. Bavinck not only saw the Trinity as the true way to understand God's nature but also as the key to correct Christian thought. "The Christian mind remains unsatisfied until all of existence is referred back to the triune God," he wrote. Modernists believed that Christianity needed updating to survive. Bavinck countered that the modern world—including its theologians—needed Christianizing or it would become mired in misery and moral chaos.

Further Concerns in East Asia

By 1900, higher criticism of the Bible and skepticism about the great tradition of Christian belief was ascendant in elite academic and denominational circles. But around the globe, traditionalist Christians also had many other concerns at the dawn of the twentieth century. These included the monumental challenge of world evangelization by Protestants and looming threats of war, rebellion, and violence against a host of Christian groups and missionaries. In some ways, the twin concerns about missions and violent disruption were related. This became especially evident in China in the last years of the nineteenth century. Chinese nativists became increasingly hostile toward foreign influence, an influence represented by Western missionaries and their Chinese Christian compatriots. Foreign missionaries, both Catholic and Protestant, as well as the Chinese Christian community, fell under suspicion and sometimes outright attack. The anti-foreigner crusade in China came to a head in the so-called Boxer Movement of 1900.

The Chinese anti-foreigner sentiment found a champion in the Empress Dowager Cixi (1835–1908), effectively the ruler of China from 1861 until 1908. In 1900, she gave open support to the violent nativists known as the "Righteous Harmony Fists," or the "Boxers." In Peking (Beijing) and other parts of the country, diplomats, missionaries, and Chinese

Christians—especially Catholics—came under attack. The Boxers, operating under the slogan "exterminate the foreigners," killed tens of thousands of people in China, including almost two hundred men, women, and children associated with Protestant missions. Eastern Orthodox Christians perished by the hundreds as well, including Chi Sung Metrophanes (1855–1900), the first known Chinese Orthodox priest to suffer martyrdom.

The China Inland Mission (CIM), led by the legendary missionary J. Hudson Taylor (1832–1905), suffered among the worst losses in the Boxer attacks. The English-born Taylor struggled to make headway in his first missionary assignment in China in the mid-1850s. His experiences led him back to England, where Taylor founded the independent mission agency CIM. The CIM was interdenominational but committed to traditional theological orthodoxy. It focused more exclusively on evangelism than on church- or institution-building. As opposed to many denominational missionary societies, which had a tendency toward elitism, the CIM was open to theologically-sound missionary candidates regardless of education. Taylor was committed to basing the CIM's administration in China, not England. There he would run the CIM as a sort of benevolent autocrat. Taylor insisted that he and all CIM staff would dress in Chinese style, not European attire. By virtually any standard, the CIM became a wild success, and it vastly increased the Protestant witness to the "unreached" segments of the diverse Chinese population.

Many Chinese people resonated with the gospel as presented by CIM missionaries. The Methodist-affiliated David Hill (1840–96) of the CIM witnessed to a Confucian scholar named Xi Shengmo (later called "Pastor Hsi" by the English missionaries) in 1879. Xi was an opium addict, a tragically common affliction in nineteenth-century China. He had tried many foreign and Chinese medical remedies to stop smoking opium, but to no avail. After Hill introduced Xi to the Bible, he came to realize that "there was a Holy Spirit who could help men. I prayed to God to give me his Holy Spirit. He did what man and medicine could not do; He enabled me to break off opium-smoking. So, my friends," Xi concluded, "if you would break off opium, don't rely on medicine, don't lean on man, but trust in God." Soon Xi not only experienced freedom from addiction but also spiritual deliverance in Christ. Xi Shengmo (c. 1836–96) became the best-documented Chinese Protestant believer of the 1800s, due to an enduringly popular biography of him written by Hudson Taylor's daughter-in-law, Geraldine (Guinness) Taylor (c. 1862–1949). Geraldine Guinness was one of the children of the great Irish evangelical preacher Henry Grattan Guinness. She married Howard Taylor in 1894 and became the author of books including missionary classics such as (with Howard Taylor) *Hudson Taylor's Spiritual Secret* (1932). Another Irish evangelical,

Amy Carmichael (1867–1951), was inspired by Taylor to devote her life to missions. She served for much of the first half of the twentieth century in India, especially among destitute women and girls. Carmichael's fame has endured due to the dozens of books she wrote about missions and to works written about her, including Elisabeth Elliot's popular biography *A Chance to Die: The Life and Legacy of Amy Carmichael* (1987).

As we have seen, Japan opened to Christian missionaries once again in the mid-1800s after centuries of prohibition on foreign evangelistic overtures. Japan saw considerable growth in Protestant missions by the late 1800s, but Christianity has never sunk deep roots in Japan the way it has in China and Korea. The reasons for Christianity's lack of popular influence in any cultural setting can be difficult to diagnose. In Japan, widespread adherence to Shintoism has clearly been an obstacle to Christian conversion. Shintoism is the Japanese spiritual tradition that involves veneration rituals at shrines across the island nation. Many Japanese Christians regarded Shintoism as polytheistic and therefore incompatible with their faith.

Like Japan, Korea had been closed to Western missionaries for much of the 1800s. It opened its doors to more Western influence in 1882, following a treaty with the United States. One of the key figures in the introduction of Protestant faith in Korea was John Nevius (1829–93), who was called to the foreign mission field while studying at Princeton Theological Seminary in the early 1850s. He went with the Presbyterian Board of Foreign Missions to China in 1853. He spent most of the next four decades in China, but in terms of missionary philosophy and tactics he made his deepest impact by training Presbyterian missionaries in Korea, starting in 1889. Based on long experience in China, Nevius developed a new approach to missions that came to be known as the "Nevius Plan." Nevius focused on ministering to people's spiritual and physical needs, the priority of individualized evangelism and mentoring, and the desire to turn the work of the church over to local people as soon as possible. Nevius took a high view of Scripture, but he was less keen on simple Bible distribution than other missionaries and Bible societies were. Missionaries and churches must emphasize in-person Bible teaching, he said, as well as Bible study, catechesis, and memorization for new believers. Indigenous converts were expected to take on the discipling and teaching work of the church, not to be passive recipients of the missionaries' instruction. The Nevius method made a mark on the ethos of many Korean Protestant churches, which grew quickly, with tens of thousands of adherents by 1910.

Korean churches were galvanized by a massive revival which crested in Pyongyang in early 1907. The revival was marked by widespread public repentance from sin and emotional prayers for forgiveness, holiness, and a fresh outpouring of the Holy Spirit. One missionary described a revival meeting in 1907 as "a vast harmony of sound and spirit, a mingling together of souls moved by an irresistible impulse of prayer. The prayer sounded to me like the falling of many waters, an ocean of prayer beating against God's throne. It was not many, but one, born of one Spirit, lifted to one Father above." The missionary thought the episode had distinct similarities to the day of Pentecost in the Book of Acts. For a time, Pyongyang seemed like a showcase of missionary success, with thriving churches and a number of supporting Christian institutions, including the Pyongyang Chosun Jesus Presbyterian Seminary (founded in 1901). When Korea was divided into North and South after World War II, North Korea fell under Soviet influence. It birthed an especially virulent form of atheistic communist rule, one that remains viciously intolerant of Christianity today. Many North Korean Christians were murdered or sent to detention camps; others fled for China or South Korea as they had opportunity. After the Korean War of 1950–53, South Korea emerged as having one of the most dynamic and missions-oriented Christian populations in Asia. After having only a tiny Christian presence before the 1890s, Protestantism became the most common religion in South Korea by the beginning of the twenty-first century.

Women in Protestant Missions

Missionary work gave female Protestants special latitude, especially in the second half of the nineteenth century. Only a small number of denominations questioned the traditional biblical interpretation of a male-only pastorate or priesthood. But there seemed to be few if any biblical restrictions on women as missionaries. Also, missionaries were regularly involved in nursing or medical service, or in teaching children, and these were widely approved cultural roles for women in Europe or America at the time. As more women became well-known missionaries, they created a template for women in the Christian West to emulate. One of the best-known British missionaries was the Scotswoman Mary Slessor (1848–1915). Slessor was a devout Presbyterian who was inspired in the 1870s to carry on the legacy of the celebrity missionary-explorer David Livingstone, who died in 1874. In 1876, Slessor traveled to the southern Nigerian coast and settled at Duke Town, on the Calabar River. She struggled terribly with illness and homesickness in the early years of her missionary labors, but she also developed a conviction that Christianity could bring salvation and civilizational reform to the indigenous people of the Calabar region. She was especially repulsed by the Nigerian practices of twin-murder and the abandonment of orphans. She became a zealous rescuer and protector of at-risk infants, taking many of them into her home. Like Hudson Taylor, Slessor was committed to living in indigenous style, allowing herself only tea as a European luxury. In 1888 she moved further inland to minister to the Okoyong territory, whose people were largely unreached with the gospel and had a terrible reputation for violence. She worked among the people of the Okoyong territory for fifteen years, becoming known for her fearlessness and formidable spiritual power. One visitor called her a "veritable white chief" in the district. Along with missions advocates such as Hudson Taylor and John Nevius, Slessor represented western missionaries' growing attentiveness to indigenous culture and indigenous leadership.

Image 21.2. *Mary Slessor*

Charlotte "Lottie" Moon (1840–1912) played a similar role to Slessor's in her missionary work but has left an even deeper imprint on her Baptist denomination's culture. Moon has become arguably the best-known missionary in Baptist history, due to the Christmas missions offering that is named for her. Moon studied at a woman's college in Charlottesville, Virginia, where one of her professors was the modernist biblical scholar Crawford Toy. She and Toy remained in contact and may have nearly gotten engaged in 1881. Moon had her faith energized in an 1858 student revival in Charlottesville and was baptized. In 1873, Moon received an appointment to serve as a Southern Baptist missionary to China, one of the first single women so chosen. She went to Tengzhou in Shandong Province, a few hundred miles south of Beijing. Tengzhou would remain her primary base of operations for four decades. She learned Chinese and took up Chinese dress and customs, taught at a girls' school, and engaged in personal evangelism, especially with Chinese women.

Baptist missions in China were riven by personality clashes, disputes over governance, and theological tensions, including the modernism represented by Baptists such as Crawford Toy. Lottie Moon seemed able to hover above the fray, however, and to expand the Baptist work in China. In 1888, she wrote a fateful letter asking that Southern Baptists in America raise money to support a Baptist work in Pingdu. This turned into the concept of the Lottie Moon Christmas offering, which historian Catherine Allen has called "the most magnetic collection plate in mission history." One of Moon's students in Pingdu, Li Shouting, became the most influential Baptist pastor in China in the first quarter of the twentieth century, baptizing thousands of converts. For her part, Moon endured in her missionary work despite threats posed by the Boxer Movement and by the Sino-Japanese War of 1894–95, during which her house was bombed by the Japanese. At the end of her life, Shandong Province was devastated by plague and famine. Moon stopped eating to identify with the suffering of the Chinese and to share her food with others. Shockingly emaciated, she finally left China in 1912, dying onboard her ship at Kobe, Japan.

> How many there are among our women, alas! alas! who imagine that because Jesus paid it all, they need pay nothing, forgetting that the prime object of their salvation was that they should follow in the footsteps of Jesus Christ in bringing back a lost world to God.
>
> ———
>
> Lottie Moon, "Letter to the *Foreign Mission Journal* from Miss Lottie Moon, September 15, 1887"

Cooperation in Missions

For all the success stories of evangelistic progress, Protestants still had a nagging sense that their missions were uncoordinated and ineffective in light of the massive numbers of unreached people around the globe. This concern led to the creation of new interdenominational missionary organizations, including the Student Volunteer Movement for Foreign Missions (SVM), and the meeting of the 1910 World Missionary Conference in Edinburgh, Scotland. Missionary advocates knew that they could not control results and conversions, but there was a new urgency for coordinating missions to reach as much of the world as possible, as soon as possible, with the gospel. The SVM's A. T. Pierson coined the phrase "the evangelization of the world in this generation" as the "watchword" of the new generation of missions. Although the Edinburgh 1910 conference was theoretically open to all Protestants, evangelicals such as the American Methodist leader John R. Mott (1865–1955) dominated the proceedings. Mott, arguably the most influential missions advocate of the early twentieth century, embodied in his career the emerging tensions between evangelism and social work in the Western missionary community. Mott would later turn most of his focus to Christian peacemaking and ecumenical relations, winning the Nobel Peace Prize in 1946 and helping to organize the World Council of Churches in 1948. But as of 1910 he remained more of a conversionist evangelical. He wrote stirringly about the unprecedented prospects for world evangelization, bolstered primarily by the church's "superhuman resources," namely the "dynamic power of the Gospel of Christ; the unrealized possibilities of intercession; the triumphant power of holy lives," and "the presence of Christ Himself in His Church by His Spirit, the One Who is able to subdue all things unto Himself." Mott remained comfortable with talk of "subduing" and "conquering" non-Christian peoples with the gospel, but even traditionalist missionary advocates became queasy about employing such rhetoric in the coming decades. Missionaries reckoned increasingly with the problematic connections between missions and empire.

Although the Edinburgh conference is often called "ecumenical," it was so only in a limited sense. The assembly sought to downplay theological differences among Protestants and to encourage interdenominational coordination of missionary efforts. But like most such missions efforts, the Edinburgh conference was limited by sharp disagreement about issues such as the evangelization of global Catholics and Orthodox Christians, most of whom appeared to be unconverted in evangelicals' estimation. The delegates tended to represent voluntary missionary societies only, not denominations. The relationship between groups like the SVM and individual denominations was complicated at best. Most importantly, Edinburgh's twelve hundred delegates were mostly Westerners, with only about twenty representatives from the rest of the world. There was just one representative from Africa, despite the fact that sub-Saharan Africa would become the world's greatest engine of Christian growth over the next century. For better or worse, missionary work would always be controlled by individual denominations and by entrepreneurial voluntary agencies such as the SVM. The dream of broader denominational and interagency cooperation often availed few practical results or ran into theological or denominational tensions. As seen in Lottie Moon's experiences, denominations had plenty of difficulties in sustaining internal cooperation. Interdenominational partnership in missions was likely to be even more problematic.

Still, figures such as A. T. Pierson reflected an evangelical penchant for interdenominational cooperation since evangelicals could (usually) agree at least on the basic gospel message, the priority of individual conversion, and the reality of judgment for all those who did not respond to Christ's offer of forgiveness. Pierson grew up in a Presbyterian context in New York, was converted in a Methodist meeting, and took his first pastorate at a Congregational church. Pierson increasingly came under the influence of American evangelist Dwight Moody (1837–99) and of British evangelical leaders such as Charles Spurgeon. Ordained a Presbyterian, Pierson eventually received believer's baptism from James Spurgeon, Charles's brother, leading to the revocation of Pierson's Presbyterian credentials. By the 1880s, Pierson was far more comfortable with his transatlantic network of evangelists and missionaries than with any one denomination. His exposure to the Keswick, or "higher life" movement, centered on annual interdenominational conferences in Keswick, England, enhanced Pierson's interdenominational proclivities. Evangelicals such as Pierson often found themselves attending conventional Sunday services at a denominational church but advocating for causes such as holiness (Keswick) or missions (SVM) by entrepreneurial means outside of traditional denominational contexts.

As Pierson began to call for a massive, student-led campaign for world evangelization in the mid-1880s, he made clear that the imminent return of Jesus Christ to earth was a primary impetus. At an 1886 prophecy conference in Chicago, Pierson gave one of his signature addresses, "Our Lord's Second Coming, a Motive to World-wide Evangelism." Belief in the Lord's return was a biblical theme and a core tenet of the great tradition. But beginning in the mid-nineteenth century there was a sharper focus on the "imminence" of Christ's second coming, drawing from the increased prominence of dispensational premillennialism as taught by John Nelson Darby and others. Christ's imminent return was a defining belief of the emerging Anglo-American Fundamentalist movement, too. Pierson explained that "imminence" was not synonymous with "impending," emphasizing that Christians must live with a constant expectation that Christ could return at any moment. This gave compelling urgency to missions. Pierson had no illusion that evangelicals would "convert" the world, for the individual results of gospel proclamation were up to God. "We go forth to work out the decreed, declared plan of God to every land, in His name to call his sheep into the folds, looking for the chief Shepherd to appear and gather all into one flock," Pierson declared.

Pierson heralded the prospects for the gospel in places including Hawaii, Polynesia, China, Korea, Madagascar, and more. Pierson's SVM sent out some eight thousand male and female missionaries between 1886 and 1920. That was just part of the legions of new Protestant missionaries like the Rheinish Missionary Society's Ingwer Ludwig Nommensen entering the global mission field during the era. These missionaries would first and foremost take with them the message of salvation through Christ. They also carried with them a trust in a divinely-inspired Bible translated into vernacular languages, a determination to serve the "least of these" through education and health care, and a confidence in the tenets of the great tradition and the beliefs of the Reformation, including salvation by grace alone. Pierson's assurance about the spread of the gospel was warranted. If the nineteenth century was the "Great Century" of missions sending, in the words of Yale historian Kenneth Latourette (himself a veteran of the SVM), the twentieth was arguably a greater century of Christian growth. But that growth would happen in surprising ways, often via indigenous leaders, ones that many in the Western missionary community might not have imagined.

Selected Bibliography

Allen, Charlotte. "The Legacy of Lottie Moon." *International Bulletin of Missionary Research* 17, no. 4 (October 1993): 146–52.

Carlisle, Clare. *Philosopher of the Heart: The Restless Life of Søren Kierkegaard*. New York: Farrar, Straus, and Giroux, 2020.

Eglinton, James. *Bavinck: A Critical Biography*. Grand Rapids: Baker Academic, 2020.

Heslam, Peter S. *Creating a Christian Worldview: Abraham Kuyper's Lectures on Calvinism*. Grand Rapids: Eerdmans, 1998.

Hunt, Everett. "The Legacy of John Livingston Nevius." *International Bulletin of Missionary Research* 15, no. 3 (July 1991): 120–24.

Krijger, Tom-Eric. *The Eclipse of Liberal Protestantism in the Netherlands: Religious, Social, and International Perspectives on the Dutch Modernist Movement (1870–1940)*. Boston: Brill, 2019.

Lehmann, Martin E. *A Biographical Study of Ingwer Ludwig Nommensen (1834–1918): Pioneer Missionary to the Bataks of Sumatra*. Lewiston, NY: Mellen, 1996.

Mott, John R. *The Decisive Hour of Christian Missions*. New York: Board of Foreign Missions of the Presbyterian Church in the USA, 1910.

Robert, Dana L. *Occupy Until I Come: A. T. Pierson and the Evangelization of the World*. Grand Rapids: Eerdmans, 2003.

Schreiner, Lothar. "The Legacy of Ingwer Ludwig Nommensen." *International Bulletin of Missionary Research* 24, no. 2 (April 2000): 81–84.

Stanley, Brian. *The World Missionary Conference, Edinburgh 1910*. Grand Rapids: Eerdmans, 2009.

—— Chapter 22 ——

Revival, Revivalists, and the Coming of Pentecostalism

Missions advocates such as A. T. Pierson had a great supporter in Dwight Moody, the most influential American revivalist of the late 1800s. As standard-bearers for traditionalist and conversionist theology, Moody and his English contemporary Charles Spurgeon exercised outsized sway among the evangelical Protestant community. From their respective bases in Chicago and London, Moody and Spurgeon renewed and expanded existing evangelical networks, reaching massive numbers of people in Britain and America with the gospel. Since the 1740s, the evangelical movement was never exclusively Anglo-American, but Anglo-America did often dominate the movement financially and strategically. Britain and America also raised up an extraordinary series of evangelical preachers from Whitefield and Finney to Spurgeon and Moody.

> Every man and woman who loves the Lord Jesus Christ must wake up to the fact that he or she has a mission in the world, in this work of reaching the lost.
>
> ———
>
> Dwight Moody, *To the Work*, 1884

D. L. Moody

Moody was originally a shoe salesman, first in Boston and then in Chicago. But joining the Young Men's Christian Association energized his faith and gave him a vision for nondenominational cooperation in evangelism, education, and missions. The YMCA, originally founded in London in 1844, reflected a combination of zeal for the gospel and the Christian ideal of bodily health and athleticism. Historians regard the YMCA as an embodiment of "muscular Christianity," or the idea that sports, physical health, and Christian devotion had a complementary relationship. The Young Women's Christian Association, which coalesced as a single organization by the mid-1880s, operated on similar principles. Both the YMCA and YWCA would eventually turn to Christian modernism. Eventually both would retain only vestiges of their Christian mission. But that was certainly not the case with Moody's evangelistic YMCA of the 1860s.

After becoming president of the Chicago YMCA in 1866, Moody began traveling and preaching widely, first in the Midwest, then nationally, and then in the UK. Moody had experienced conversion in the 1850s, but he received an intense consecrating experience in 1871 that some observers, such as the Holiness preacher and author Reuben A. Torrey (1856–1928), a close colleague of Moody's, regarded as the baptism with the Holy Spirit. Such writers saw the baptism of the Spirit as a post-conversion moment when the believer received new power and anointing. Other evangelicals believed that a Christian received the baptism of the Holy Spirit fully at conversion, but that he or she needed continual refreshing to be filled with the Spirit. As Moody put it, "we are leaky vessels." Christians needed constant renewal in the Spirit to remain obedient and energized in holiness.

In any case, after 1871, Moody's boldness and effectiveness soared, and he emerged as the dominant Anglo-American revivalist of the era. Indeed, his introduction as a full-time popular evangelist came in a two-year campaign, starting in 1873, in England and Scotland. American independence in 1776 had broken the political bond between Britain and the United States, and traditionalist Christians found themselves in deeply different situations in the two nations. In particular, Britain maintained its official Anglican establishment while the US was committed to church-state separation and religious freedom, per the First Amendment to the US Constitution. Nevertheless, Moody's enormous successes in Britain reflected the ongoing ties between the evangelical communities in both nations, as well as in Canada, where Moody and Reuben Torrey both regularly preached. Although a few Canadian critics regarded Moody's style as "offensively American," for the most part Canadian Protestants received him warmly. Moody preached in Toronto for the first time in late 1884, drawing a total attendance of some 45,000 over three days in a city of about 100,000 people.

Even more than Charles Finney, Moody exemplified the populist dynamic within Anglo-American revivalism. Unlike college-educated predecessors such as Whitefield and Edwards, Moody only had a grammar school education. Spurgeon likewise never went to college. This hardly meant that they were ignorant or anti-education, but both had a kind of autodidactic training and homespun style that fueled their popularity. Calvinist critics, such as the dispensationalist writer John Nelson Darby, lambasted Moody for what they regarded as an Arminian tinge to his preaching. To Moody, there was no point dwelling on the mysteries of election or predestination. He simply believed he was called to preach the gospel, and he assumed anyone in his audience was capable of responding to Christ's call. Moody wrote that "if a man preaches the Gospel, and preaches it faithfully, he ought to expect results then and there." Although he was no systematic dispensationalist like Darby, Moody did adhere generally to Darby's type of premillennial belief. He was not optimistic about the potential of Christian reform movements being able to introduce an epoch of Christian virtue in the world. By the 1880s, Moody had begun hosting annual summer conferences in Northfield, Massachusetts, his hometown. These conferences drew many college YMCA students, including future missionary leaders such as John Mott. The 1886 Northfield meeting saw the beginning of what became the Student Volunteer Movement for Foreign Missions.

Revival in Africa

Viewed from a global perspective, Moody and Spurgeon were hardly the only preachers of historic note during the era. The late nineteenth and the early twentieth century saw the emergence of patterns of growth that would profoundly shape world Christianity. Globally, this proliferation often entailed dynamic independent Christian movements and Pentecostal churches across the "global South." Sub-Saharan Africa began to see the development of African independent, or African initiated churches (AIC), which either challenged or operated independently from Western missionary control. Normally the first step in the Africanization of Christianity was the establishment of indigenous leaders in missionary churches. Among these leaders was the great African Anglican bishop Samuel Ajayi Crowther, who had died in 1891.

The leading Liberian preacher William Wadé Harris (c. 1860–1929) represented a step beyond Crowther in African Christian independence, however. Harris was from the Grebo tribe of Liberia. For decades Liberia had been seen as a destination for freed American slaves. It became an independent republic in 1847. Harris was converted to Christianity under Methodist preaching, but he joined the Episcopal Church. He also became involved in rebellious actions by the Grebo against the Liberian government, which landed Harris in jail in 1909. While in prison, Harris received a transformative vision of the angel Gabriel, who convinced Harris that he was being raised up as a prophet. He was to call on Africans to believe in Christ and to reject African tribal religions, including their pagan altars, ceremonial masks, and fetishes. When he was released from prison, Harris began preaching and baptizing in the Ivory Coast, east of Liberia.

Soon William Wadé Harris was baptizing extraordinary numbers of people. Astounded colonial officials estimated he may have baptized as many as 120,000 people in just one year. These vast numbers may not have been entirely accurate, but they did suggest Harris's popularity and his relative willingness to baptize people based simply on their profession of faith and willingness to abandon animistic religion. Harris exhorted these converts to learn from missionaries in the region, whether Catholic or Protestant. Disdaining the traditional divide between Catholics and Protestants, missionaries from both sides were overwhelmed with Africans who converted under Harris's preaching. The Methodists were the most welcoming to Harris's converts, and by 1926 the Methodist Church in the Ivory Coast had grown to some 32,000 congregants in hundreds of churches. Harris died in 1929. In the 1930s, one of Harris's disciples, Jonas Ahui, founded an independent church, the *Eglise Harriste*, which became one of the leading AICs throughout the region.

Even African figures associated with Western denominations, such as Crowther, had to face concerns from white officials about the indigenous leaders' alleged heterodoxy and other indiscretions. Fair or not, the further Africans moved toward independence, the more likely they were to attract charges of "syncretism." This was usually what Western leaders saw as an unhealthy mixing of animistic traditions with orthodox Christianity. Over the twentieth century, missiologists became far more comfortable than earlier Western leaders with forms of Christian cultural indigenization and the mandate of indigenous leadership. Still, some of the AICs unquestionably departed from the great tradition of Christian theology. Not that such movements had a unique problem with theological waywardness. As we have seen, elite theological modernists in Europe and America were also leaving the great tradition behind for very different reasons than heterodox AIC leaders. Nevertheless, the independent African church leaders sometimes struggled to assert institutional independence while also keeping their teachings within the bounds of historic Christian belief.

For example, Simon Kimbangu (1887–1951) came out of a Baptist background in the Belgian Congo, or what now is the Democratic Republic of Congo. The Baptist churches in the area were fruits of the British Baptist Missionary Society. Kimbangu received a visionary call to preach in the late 1910s, but church authorities were not convinced that he had sufficient education or gifting to become a pastor. As a rift opened between Kimbangu and Baptist church officials, he became convinced that he was called to an apostolic role of preaching and healing. Only months after establishing an independent apostolic ministry, alarmed Belgian officials had Kimbangu arrested for seditious activities that allegedly threatened the stability of the colony. He received a life sentence and died in prison in 1951.

Kimbangu's short public ministry caused huge divisions among European and African-background Baptists in Congo, some of whom believed he had a special anointing for healing. Others regarded him as a charlatan. His supporters resented the Belgian authorities' suppression of Kimbangu's ministry, as well as Baptist missionaries' apparent cooperation or deference to the authorities. After his death, Kimbangu's movement became an AIC, the *Église du Jésus Christ sur la Terre par le Prophète Simon Kimbangu*. Kimbangu's sons and grandsons took the movement in differing directions in the following decades, with some trying to establish the new denomination as a respected, mainstream Christian denomination. Others attached cultic significance to Kimbangu and his descendants. In the early 2000s, for example, one of Kimbangu's grandsons claimed that Kimbangu himself was the Holy Spirit. By that point the Kimbanguist church had more than ten million members.

The Gifts of Pentecost

The controversy over Kimbangu was exceptional theologically as it revolved around the increasingly extravagant claims he and his family made about his spiritual authority. In another sense, however, the initial clash over Kimbangu was typical of emerging debates over healings and other miraculous works in the modern church age. All branches of Christendom have had saints, prophets, and healers through the centuries. These figures claimed that their miraculous power was simply continuing the "greater works" that Jesus had promised the church would do, in verses such as John 14:12.

Yet the beginning of the twentieth century saw an unprecedented outburst of healings, speaking in tongues, and other charismatic gifts. These were associated with AICs, the early Pentecostal movement, and other sectarian groups around the world. We tend to assume that fundamentalist Christianity was the Protestant church's primary reaction against modernism. But the new Pentecostal movement also responded to growing naturalism and skepticism in modern culture, and within many Christian denominations. If the modern world offered unprecedented ways of being secular, the surging supernaturalism across many Christian movements and nations offered a different way of being modern.

One of the most extraordinary healing ministries of the late nineteenth century was led by John Alexander Dowie (1847–1907), a Scot whose family moved to Australia in the 1860s. Dowie first worked as a Congregationalist minister in Australia, but his practices and beliefs became increasingly eccentric. He was briefly jailed for financial improprieties, but in the early 1880s he opened a tabernacle in a suburb of Melbourne. There he began to develop a reputation as a faith healer. After reportedly healing tens of thousands of people in Australia, he began preaching in North America. In 1893 he founded Zion's Tabernacle in Chicago, which became his primary base of ministry. Soon he also established the Christian Catholic Church in Zion, with a hierarchy of leaders and himself as "general overseer." The community relocated north of Chicago to Zion City, Illinois, where Dowie built Zion Temple. He increasingly cast himself as a new Elijah figure. Dowie and his movement soon descended into controversies over finances and governance, and by the time of his death in 1907, Dowie was beset by financial, mental, and physical maladies.

Dowie might have become just one more eccentric prophet in church history. But like Simon Kimbangu, his movement took on a powerful life after the prophet's death. Dowie's Zionist Church was exported to South Africa by missionaries from the US. In South Africa, a former Dutch Reformed missionary named P. L. Le Roux (1865–1943) adopted and championed the Zionist movement. Le Roux carried on the work, now called the Apostolic Faith Mission, which emphasized faith healings, baptisms in rivers, and speaking in tongues. As we have seen, tongues-speaking (or glossolalia) was not unknown in the long post-Pentecost history of the church. But outbreaks of tongues were rare in most of Christendom until the beginning of the twentieth century.

From Le Roux's Apostolic Faith Mission, a great succession of Zionist and Apostolic AICs followed, led by charismatic African preachers and healers. The most successful of these was the Zion Christian Church (ZCC), founded in 1924 by Engenas Lekganyane (c. 1885–1948), a former evangelist for the Free Church of Scotland. Lekganyane himself reportedly received physical healing when he was baptized into the Apostolic Faith Mission. He began to develop a reputation for prophecy and healing powers, too, and fell out with Apostolic Faith Mission leaders over issues including polygamy (Lekganyane had married a second wife). This break led to the formation of the ZCC. Lekganyane built a headquarters for the movement at Zion City, Moria, in South Africa. The ZCC assembly ground attracts hundreds of thousands, even millions, of members annually for Easter celebrations. Engenas Lekganyane became such a sought-after healer that in his later career he began putting his blessing on all manner of goods, from strips of cloth to walking sticks. Followers obtained these for healing and protection. Again, critics have argued that the rituals of groups like the ZCC are uncomfortably similar to traditional animistic African practices. The proper boundary between Christian inculturation and syncretism is not always clear. However, there can be no doubt regarding the popularity of the ZCC, which stood at some five million South African members at the beginning of the twenty-first century. Yet the ZCC was only the largest of many other Apostolic and Zionist movements and denominations in Africa.

Many of the new charismatic and Pentecostal groups had roots in the Holiness movement of the mid- to late 1800s. Methodist and Finneyite revivalists emphasized the complete sanctification that a fully-surrendered believer might achieve in this life. The Holiness movement in American and Canadian Methodism found perhaps its most influential champion in Phoebe Palmer (1807–74). Palmer became a popular Methodist revival speaker and advocate of "entire sanctification." In 1850 she founded the Five Points mission in the slums of New York City. Five Points was an innovative evangelistic, educational, and social mission, demonstrating the connections between Holiness and broad-based social reforms. The emphasis on the power of the Holy Spirit for obedience and effective ministry also filtered into the Anglo-American work of figures such as Dwight Moody and Reuben Torrey.

Holiness took a definite turn, however, at the beginning of the twentieth century, when increasing numbers of Christians began to argue that tongues were a sign of the Spirit's purifying work. Some argued that speaking in tongues was confirmation of the post-conversion "baptism of the Spirit." Pentecostals traditionally look to events at Bethel Bible College in Topeka, Kansas, as a great new outpouring of the Spirit and of the miraculous gifts. In 1901, at a service marking the beginning of the twentieth century, a Bethel student named Agnes Ozman (1870–1937) began speaking in a language she did not know. Some believed the language was Chinese. Indeed, Ozman found that she was unable to speak in English for three days and could only speak in her newfound dialect. The Holiness minister Charles Fox Parham (1873–1929), who had just founded Bethel Bible College the previous year, began teaching Holiness audiences across the country about the gift of tongues as the fruit of the baptism of the Spirit.

The outbreak of tongues in Topeka connected to an even larger and more momentous episode at Los Angeles's Azusa Street Revival of 1906. Charles Fox Parham mentored the African American Holiness preacher William J. Seymour (1870–1922) in the gifts of the Spirit, and Seymour headlined the astonishing revival meetings in Los Angeles. The expectation of tongues as a sign of the Spirit rocketed through the Holiness community. For example, Charles H. Mason (1866–1961) was a child of enslaved parents and a founder of the Holiness-centered Church of God in Christ (1897), which went on to become one of the largest African-American denominations in the US. Mason went to the Azusa Street revival, seeking the baptism of the Spirit and the gift of tongues. Like Ozman, Mason for a time not only spoke in tongues, but he also found he could not speak English. He returned to his church in Mississippi, telling them about his experience. Many white and black Holiness advocates in the US also accepted glossolalia. Others rejected tongues as the fruit of overzealous minds.

The Global Revival

The US-focused account of Bethel Bible College and Azusa Street has tended to obscure a whole series of Holiness and Pentecostal revivals breaking out globally between 1900 and 1910. Indeed, one of the early historians of Azusa Street claimed that the "revival was rocked in the cradle of little Wales . . . [and] 'brought up' in India," only to become "full grown" in Los Angeles. The spread of the gifts of the Spirit was transpiring so quickly that some Pentecostals regarded the movement as the fulfillment of the "latter rain" promised in passages such as Joel 2:23.

The tension between advocates of the great tradition of Christian theology and its various modernizers and skeptical opponents, is the key theme of this volume. Yet the divide between Pentecostal and "cessationist" Christians became a major theme in modern church history, too. In a numerical sense, this is a more consequential story even than the rivalry between liberals and the traditional biblicists. World Christian growth over the past century has been due largely to the vast increases in charismatic and Pentecostal Christianity. This has included charismatic growth among Catholics and among traditionally "mainline" or established Protestant groups, such as the Anglican Church. With few exceptions, denominations dominated by modernist thought have struggled to sustain their membership numbers over the past hundred years. But during the same period, Pentecostals have often exceeded the growth of those traditionalist Christians who steered away from exuberant supernaturalism and the gift of tongues. Areas in Latin America, Africa, and Asia have experienced massive Christian growth, much of it driven by Pentecostal spirituality.

The aforementioned Holiness/Pentecostal revival in India of the early twentieth century was led primarily by a young woman named Pandita Ramabai (1858–1922). Ramabai grew up in a Hindu family but encountered Anglican missionaries. She became a Christian when she visited England in the mid-1880s. Upon returning to India, Ramabai began numerous charitable works in and around the city of Pune in western India. She also began to read Holiness works of piety and to attend Holiness revival meetings, where she said that she was baptized in the Spirit. At her Mukti school in 1905, she and her female students began praying for revival, and some of the girls reported experiencing powerful feelings of burning and tingling while they were praying. The students concluded that this was a sign of the baptism of the Holy Spirit. The Mukti school in 1905–6 became a major center of charismatic revival, with reports of tongues, exorcisms, healings (including survivals of poisonous snake bites), and more than a thousand new converts.

Her Anglican mentors were delighted with Ramabai's conversion, but her meteoric ascent as a Holiness leader and preacher baffled many of them. Reserved Anglicans cautioned her about spiritual extremism (though she herself did not speak in tongues) and about biblical restrictions on women publicly teaching men. But the new Pentecostals, like a number of radical evangelicals before them, tended to handle issues about women's roles in preaching—as well as interracial cooperation in ministry—more flexibly than did more established denominations and their missionaries. It was also not unusual in the early Pentecostal context to find that the workers at Ramabai's Mukti center included forty-five Indians, plus twenty-five missionaries from America, England, and Sweden. Accounts of the mission implied that these workers held relatively equal status within the mission. The role of women and of speaking in tongues led observers such as A.T. Pierson to worry that much of what was happening at Mutki was indecent, superstitious, and syncretistic. Ramabai pushed back, saying that such critiques reflected Western missionary snobbishness and male suspicion of women's piety.

The early Holiness and Pentecostal networks were thoroughly international, as the charismatic devout eagerly followed news of spiritual outpourings of the "latter rain." One of the revivals that attracted the most attention happened in Wales from late 1904 to early 1906. Wales had a deep tradition of evangelical Calvinism dating to the Great Awakening of the mid-1700s. The key figure in the new Welsh revival was the miner and Calvinistic Methodist preacher Evan Roberts (1878–1951). Roberts, one of fourteen children in a Welsh coal-mining family, had already begun preaching when he received a sanctifying experience in the Spirit in a Calvinistic Methodist meeting. He immediately began preaching that a great outpouring of the Spirit was available to believers when they radically repented of sin and pursued total sanctification. Newly-composed Welsh-language hymns electrified the overflow meetings Roberts held across the principality, and he published a hymnal in 1905 titled *Emynau wedi eu cyfansoddi gan Mr Evan Roberts (Y Diwygiwr)* ["Hymns composed by Mr. Evan Roberts (the revivalist)"]. Following Dwight Moody's revival techniques in America and England, Roberts used talented soloists and enthusiastic congregational singing to stir the hearts of his Welsh audiences. The intense services went on for as many as eight hours, with tens of thousands of Welsh people confessing new faith in Christ. There is some debate about just how Pentecostal the Welsh revivals were, particularly with regard to tongues. There were certainly reports that young English-speaking people who had never known the Welsh language suddenly became fluent in it during revival meetings.

The news of global revivals and Holiness and Pentecostal cross-currents became dizzying by 1909. In addition to those at Azusa Street in Los Angeles, in Wales, and in India, there were reports of major revivals that had transpired in Korea (Pyongyang and Seoul), Zimbabwe, China, Norway, Denmark, Sweden, and Germany. The devout traveled great distances (with travel time shortened by the power of modern steamboats) to participate in the revivals. Then they took word of the Spirit's movements back to their home countries. The surge in Pentecostal publications and missionary works was as momentous as the revivals themselves. By 1910, Pentecostals had established newsletters and magazines in indigenous languages on most of the world's continents. They had also opened missionary works in dozens of countries.

One of the countries impacted by the work in India was Chile. A Mukti missionary from America, Minnie Abrams (1859–1912), sent her booklet *The Baptism of the Holy Ghost & Fire* to a missionary friend named May Hoover, an American Methodist working in Chile. May and her husband Willis Hoover began praying for Holy Spirit revival in their working-class church in Valparaiso, Chile. When it came, the revival was marked by exorcisms, visions, words of knowledge, holy laughter, and tongues. Several local Methodist officials were troubled by what they saw as enthusiastic excesses, and they encouraged the couple to go back to the United States. Instead, the Hoovers and their Chilean supporters broke from the missionary Methodist church and founded the Iglesia Metodista Pentecostal. This was one of many independent Pentecostal denominations that would emerge in Central and South America over the next century.

Missionaries such as the Hoovers often represented a bridge to indigenous leadership. The most successful evangelists were generally those who worked among people of the same ethnic group. In the southwestern United States and Mexico, one of the most accomplished Hispanic revivalists of the era was the Holiness-Pentecostal preacher Francisco Olazábal (1886–1937). Olazábal grew up Catholic in Mexico, but his mother became a Methodist in 1898 and soon began working as a lay evangelist. On a visit to the US, Olazábal dedicated his life to Christ and the ministry. He began preaching in the US-Mexico borderland region, taking a Methodist pastorate in El Paso, Texas, in 1911. The same year he went to Chicago to study at Moody Bible Institute. There he encountered the Holiness leader Reuben Torrey, who taught Olazábal about the baptism of the Spirit. In the mid-1910s, Olazábal relocated to California where he came under the influence of Pentecostals. They insisted that the baptism of the Spirit was a discernible experience after conversion and they taught of the availability of spiritual gifts such as healing and tongues. Soon Olazábal became a Pentecostal and broke with the Methodist denomination. He joined the Assemblies of God, a Pentecostal denomination founded in 1914 which would go on to become the world's largest Pentecostal group.

By the early 1920s, however, Olazábal fell into conflict with white Assemblies of God leaders in California, leading him to found his own Pentecostal organization, the Interdenominational Mexican Council of Christian Churches. By the 1920s, the denomination had dozens of congregations across the US and Mexico. Francisco Olazábal's massive evangelistic and healing campaigns culminated in a series of huge assemblies in Spanish Harlem, New York City, in 1931. As many as one hundred thousand people, calling Olazábal "El Azteca," attended in Spanish Harlem and other New York City revival meetings. Many attendees were recent immigrants from Puerto Rico or Italy, or African American migrants from the southern US.

The Holiness and Pentecostal revival preachers often came from traditional Protestant backgrounds. Their innovations typically did not entail challenges to foundational doctrines of the great tradition, such as salvation through Christ. Instead, their novel practices and beliefs touched on themes such as radical holiness and discernible works of the Spirit. These controversies went back at least to the Reformation. Tongues was arguably the most distinctive departure in new Pentecostal movements, although Pentecostals would characterize tongues as a recovery of a biblical practice long absent from most churches. Pentecostals also veered from evangelical tradition in their insistence that the baptism of the Spirit was a post-conversion experience. They showed relative comfort with women teaching audiences that included adult men, contrary to most traditional Christians' view that Scripture prohibited the practice. Small numbers of liberal churches had begun ordaining women as pastors, too, by the late 1800s. But liberal Protestants did not represent as much of a demographic force for twentieth-century Christian growth as did Pentecostals. For Pentecostals, anyone filled with the Spirit was better qualified to preach than the seminary-trained men who were often filled, they thought, only with worldly learning.

Suffering and Renewal around the World

It was not just Protestants who seemed to long for spiritual power and assurance in the early twentieth century. In 1917, the town of Fátima, Portugal, witnessed arguably the most celebrated Marian apparition among Catholics in the twentieth century. In the rural, agricultural region north of the city of Lisbon, Portuguese Catholics retained a robust system of parishes and devotional shrines into the early twentieth century. But Portugal endured a republican, anti-monarchical revolution in 1910 that was intensely secular and anticlerical. Although it would not reach the murderous heights of the French Revolution, Portuguese republican authorities seized church property, expelled bishops from their dioceses, and shut down many Catholic seminaries. Pope Pius X was appalled at what he called the "incredible series of excesses and crimes which has been enacted in Portugal for the oppression of the Church."

These events, plus the turmoil of World War I, cast Portugal and the rest of Europe into deep cultural turmoil by 1917. In that year, young shepherds in Fátima, including one named Lúcia dos Santos (1907–2005), began reporting seeing "a Lady more brilliant than the sun." The interest of Portuguese Catholics was piqued by the children's statement that the lady (Mary) had revealed spiritual visions and secrets to them and promised to show them more in follow-up visits. Many devout Catholics waited eagerly for each new revelation, while secular critics scoffed at the apparitions as mere superstition. The visions culminated in an extraordinary scene at Fátima in October 1917, when tens of thousands of people gathered to witness (or to mock) the next alleged miracle or revelation. Many of those in attendance, including some who had previously been skeptical, claimed to see extraordinary signs in the sun. The "dancing" sun reportedly lurched toward the earth and sent out rainbow flashes of color before returning to its normal position. Many Catholics saw this phenomenon as a fulfillment of John's vision of "a woman clothed with the sun" in Rev 12:1 (KJV). The fame and controversy surrounding the Fátima revelations increased during the twentieth century,

Image 22.1. *Miracle of the sun photo* (1917)

due to memoirs written by Lúcia dos Santos and the continued revelations of the Fátima "secrets," including one that seemed to prophesy the 1981 assassination attempt on Pope John Paul II.

The beginning of the rabidly anti-Christian Russian Revolution just weeks after the "miracle of the sun" seemed to confirm, for many of the devout in Europe, that the end of the world was near. The Russian communist leader Vladimir Lenin (1870–1924) gestured at religious freedom, but in fact the regimes of Lenin and Josef Stalin (1878–1953) virtually destroyed the Russian Orthodox Church and most other forms of Russian Christianity, save for small cells of believers who met in secret. By 1930, the Russian Orthodox Church was a shell of its former self, as Stalin (a former seminarian) closed church-affiliated schools, monasteries, religious presses, and more. A few churches managed to remain open, but Orthodox clergy were required either to profess absolute loyalty to the state or to suffer extreme consequences, often execution. The Metropolitan Veniamin of St. Petersburg (the city renamed Petrograd by the Soviets) refused to take a loyalty oath to the Soviet regime and Lenin had him executed in 1922. The Orthodox Patriarch Tikhon died in the mid-1920s, likely at the hands of Stalin's executioners. Surviving Orthodox officials faced a choice between martyrdom and obsequious devotion to the state. For much of the communist period, the beleaguered remnants of the church became Soviet tools for propaganda and gaining intelligence on Russian citizens.

While the virtual destruction of the Russian Orthodox Church was extreme, its experience sadly reflected the travails of Christian churches under many absolutist regimes in the twentieth century. Such persecuting governments included those in Nazi Germany, communist China, and Soviet satellite states in Eastern Europe and Cuba. Small numbers of Christians living under these conditions did organize in secret resistance cells. But lest we be nostalgic about churches thriving under persecution, it is important to remember just how devastating a totalitarian, anti-Christian regime can be for churches and Christians faced with the choice of utter compliance, or prison, exile, and death. It was a lesson that too many churches would learn in the coming decades.

Selected Bibliography

Anderson, Allan. "Pandita Ramabai, the Mukti Revival, and Global Pentecostalism." *Transformation* 23, no. 1 (January 2006): 37–48.

Bennett, Jeffrey S. *When the Sun Danced: Myth, Miracles, and Modernity in Early Twentieth-Century Portugal.* Charlottesville: University of Virginia Press, 2012.

Bourdeaux, Michael, and Alexandru Popescu. "The Orthodox Church and Communism." In *The Cambridge History of Christianity, vol. 5: Eastern Christianity*, edited by Michael Angold, 558–79. New York: Cambridge University Press, 2006.

Case, Jay R. *An Unpredictable Gospel: American Evangelicals and World Christianity, 1812–1920.* New York: Oxford University Press, 2012.

Crouse, Eric R. *Revival in the City: The Impact of American Evangelists in Canada, 1884–1914.* Montreal, QC: McGill-Queen's University Press, 2005.

Espinosa, Gastón. "*El Azteca*: Francisco Olazábal and Latino Pentecostal Charisma, Power, and Faith Healing in the Borderlands." *Journal of the American Academy of Religion* 67, no. 3 (September 1999): 597–616.

McGee, Gary B. "'Latter Rain' Falling in the East: Early-Twentieth-Century Pentecostalism in India and the Debate over Speaking in Tongues." *Church History* 68, no. 3 (September 1999): 648–65.

Roberts, Dyfed Wyn, ed. *Revival, Renewal, and the Holy Spirit: Remembering Revivals in Wales and Beyond.* Milton Keynes, UK: Paternoster, 2009.

Stanley, Brian. *Christianity in the Twentieth Century: A World History*. Princeton, NJ: Princeton University Press, 2018.

Walker, Sheila S. *The Religious Revolution in the Ivory Coast: The Prophet Harris and the Harris Church*. Chapel Hill: University of North Carolina Press, 1983.

—— Chapter 23 ——

Theological Divisions and the Era of the World Wars

The horrors of World War I fatally damaged the optimism of theological modernism and postmillennial reform of the late nineteenth century. American president Woodrow Wilson (1856–1924), a moderate Presbyterian, proclaimed that America's entry into the war represented a crusade to "make the world safe for democracy." But from the perspective of many Christians, much of the carnage in Europe's trenches seemed revoltingly pointless, not noble. The slaughter in the Ottoman Empire's killing fields, moreover, seemed manifestly evil. Before American entry into the war, Britain had suffered terrible stalemate and defeat against Ottoman forces at Gallipoli in modern Turkey and in Mesopotamia (modern Iraq). British attacks further emboldened the Muslim Turks to launch a genocidal campaign against Armenian (Orthodox) Christians within its empire. Under the cover of a mass deportation campaign, ethnic Armenians were starved, poisoned, slaughtered, raped, and tortured in scenes that anticipated Nazi campaigns against Europe's Jews three decades later. As one American diplomat explained in 1915, "The Mohammedans in their fanaticism seemed determined not only to exterminate the Christian population but to remove all traces of their religion."

Historians have debated how much of the murderous hatred for the Armenians was religious in nature or how much of it just reflected a modernizing state cracking down on a potentially subversive group, using religion as an excuse. In any case, despite their theological and denominational differences from the Armenian Apostolic Church, many western Christian observers sympathized with the plight of this Orthodox community and other Christians of the Middle East. By the end of World War I, perhaps a million Armenians had died. The Ottoman Empire's Armenian population dropped by as much as 90 percent.

Image 23.1. *Allenby enters Jerusalem*

The grim realities of World War I and the genocide in the Ottoman Empire seemed to hold faint glimmers of hope, too, at least in the eyes of some evangelical Christians. In particular, the British conquest of Jerusalem in 1917 and the issuance of the Balfour Declaration in favor of a Jewish homeland in Palestine seemed pregnant with prophetic significance. At the beginning of World War I, Palestine was part of the struggling Ottoman Empire. Figures such as the Hungarian Jewish leader Theodor Herzl (1860–1904) had promoted the establishment of a Jewish national refuge in Palestine since the late 1800s. To critics (even among Jews) the Zionist idea seemed far-fetched and counterproductive, given the struggles that many Jewish diaspora communities faced in the Middle East, Europe, and America. However, after General Robert Allenby (1861–1936) took control of the British war effort in the Middle East in 1917, he began scoring victories across the historic lands of the Bible. His successes emboldened Britain to issue the Balfour Declaration in November 1917, a major diplomatic coup for the Zionist cause. A month later, the Ottomans evacuated Jerusalem before Allenby's advancing army, giving up the holy city they had controlled since 1517, the year the Protestant Reformation began.

In 1918, Allenby's campaign culminated with a stunning victory over the Ottomans at Megiddo, which many Christians saw as the prophesied site of the Battle of Armageddon in Revelation 16. These events led to a surge in eschatological speculation. George Jeffreys (1889–1962), a prominent Welsh Pentecostal evangelist, echoed many Protestants when he claimed that Allenby's victories related to prophecies in Luke 21. Jerusalem, he said, was no longer "trodden down of the Gentiles." Jeffreys suggested that the British victories marked the beginning of the final countdown to the return of Christ. Many evangelicals and Pentecostals became heavily committed to the Zionist cause during this era. Following the establishment of the state of Israel in 1948, they also became committed to the diplomatic and military defense of the modern Jewish nation.

The events of 1917–18 emboldened many traditional Christians, who saw evidence that Scripture prophecy was being fulfilled before their eyes. Many biblicists also rejoiced at the defeat of Germany in World War I, since they regarded Germany as the progenitor of higher biblical criticism, modernism, and skepticism. The barnstorming American evangelist Billy Sunday (1862–1935) declared that if you turned hell upside down, you would find "'Made in Germany' stamped on the bottom." Once America entered World War I, Sunday became an exuberantly patriotic preacher, effectively equating American loyalty with the Christian faith. This blending of patriotism and piety was a template that many preachers across denominations would follow over the next century, especially during times of war.

Challenging Modernism

World War I brought the progressive optimism of much of European and American Christianity into question. The war also set the stage for some of the most influential examples of fundamentalist and neoorthodox writings of the era. Even before the war, conservatives and fundamentalists were producing theological and biblical writings of enduring significance. Princeton theologians such as Charles Hodge and Benjamin Warfield, and the Dutch theologian Herman Bavinck, had renewed an intellectually formidable argument for Reformed and biblically traditionalist views. Among dispensational thinkers, no development was more important than the 1909 printing of C. I. Scofield's (1843–1921) massively popular reference Bible, published by Oxford University Press. Scofield's Bible would become the most widely-circulated study Bible of the twentieth century.

In 1910, North American and European conservatives sought to articulate a unified response to modernism in *The Fundamentals*, a twelve-volume series of articles edited by Reuben Torrey and A. C. Dixon (1854–1925), pastor of the Moody Church in Chicago. The essays combatted higher criticism, defended historic Christian doctrines, and explained an orthodox Protestant view of other religious groups such as Catholics, Mormons, and Jehovah's Witnesses. (The latter had been founded in the 1870s by Charles Taze Russell (1852–1916). Among their controversial beliefs were a rejection of trinitarian doctrine and opposition to the observance of virtually any holidays and anniversaries, including birthdays.) But arguably the most essential purpose of *The Fundamentals* was defending the authority of the Bible.

James Gray (1851–1935) of Moody Bible Institute wrote one of the key essays on the "definition, extent, and proof" of the Bible's divine inspiration. He asserted that the Bible's character, "the unity of its parts, the fulfillment of its prophecies, the miracles wrought in its attestation, the effects it has accomplished in the lives of nations and of men, all these go to show that it is divine, and if so, that it may be believed in what it says about itself." To Gray and other inerrantists, God conveyed the themes and the words of Scripture to the human authors. Gray admitted that while the means God used in working with the biblical authors were mysterious, they reflected "miraculous control" by God. The result was "an absolute transcript" of God's mind, in the fully inspired Word of God. Gray and other authors regularly cited the great tradition of theology to bolster their point, quoting sources including Clement of Alexandria, Augustine, Calvin, and the Westminster Confession of Faith.

The Fundamentals helped to give shape to the emerging "fundamentalist" cohort in North America and Britain. For a time, this anti-modernist movement almost became synonymous with "evangelical," at least in the English-speaking world. Although they were united in their opposition to modernist theology, "fundamentalists" were otherwise never in lockstep culturally or doctrinally. All fundamentalists defended the reliability of the Bible, but they were not all committed to the doctrine of inerrancy. Even Curtis Lee Laws, the northern Baptist who coined the term fundamentalist in 1920, was not persuaded by the concept of inerrancy. He did not believe in insisting upon the Bible's factual, scientific accuracy in every detail. Laws figured that the Scriptures testified to their entire truth through a believer's experience and common sense. Many other fundamentalists eagerly embraced inerrancy, both because they thought it was the correct way to describe the Bible's perfection, and because they believed that an objective reading of Scripture would sort out any apparent discrepancies in matters such as chronology or potentially conflicting narratives.

Some fundamentalists, like the prominent Democratic politician William Jennings Bryan (1860–1925), wished to make anti-evolution a central commitment of the Fundamentalist movement. Others saw evolution as a secondary concern, especially as it related to public school instruction. Similarly, some fundamentalists invested heavily in the crusade to ban the production and sale of alcohol, which resulted in the ill-fated prohibition amendment to the US Constitution in 1919. Other fundamentalists saw prohibition of alcohol as an extrabiblical, moralistic distraction. Finally, some fundamentalists wanted to make premillennialism a test of faith for the movement, while others saw premillennialism, especially in its Darbyite dispensationalist form, as theologically debatable, if not aberrant. For such fundamentalists, there was danger in adding novel concerns to the historic repertoire of the great tradition.

The US was the heart of the Fundamentalist movement, which tended not to take root as deeply in other English-speaking countries such as Australia or England. Fundamentalists in those countries did found a series of Bible colleges and institutes, such as Australia's Sydney Missionary and Bible College (1916) and the Melbourne Bible Institute (1920), the latter of which wholeheartedly accepted "the entire sacred volume of the Old and New Testaments as from God." In England, a series of conflicts harking back to Charles Spurgeon's "Downgrade Controversy" of the 1880s roiled denominations, missionary societies, and the Keswick Convention (one of the great sources of Anglo-American Holiness teaching), usually due to debates over including modernists as officeholders in Christian organizations or schools. For example, the election of a modernist as the vice-president of the Baptist Union led Baptist minister James Mountain (1844–1933) to form the Bible Baptist Union in 1923. Mountain encouraged Bible-believing Baptist churches to leave the Baptist Union of Great Britain and to unite around the total authority of the Scriptures.

> The great redemptive religion which has always been known as Christianity is battling against a totally diverse type of religious belief, which is only the more destructive of the Christian faith because it makes use of traditional Christian terminology. This modern non-redemptive religion is called "modernism" or "liberalism."
>
> J. Gresham Machen, *Christianity and Liberalism*, 1923

Fundamentalists (and evangelicals more generally) had a fraught relationship with elite educational institutions. On one hand, much of the impetus of fundamentalism was anti-modernist and anti-institutional. Fundamentalists reacted against the fact that most of the elite theological schools in Europe and America had become dominated by modernist scholars. Evangelists with relatively little formal education such as Billy Sunday deliberately cultivated a folksy, homespun style that resonated with working-class audiences. On the other hand, fundamentalists were always happy to have allies in elite academic circles and would often cooperate with such scholars, even if their core fundamentalist *bona fides* were not entirely certain. Such was the case with J. Gresham Machen (1881–1937), arguably the last of the great Reformed traditionalist scholars to teach at Princeton Theological Seminary. Machen came from an affluent family in Baltimore and graduated from the city's Johns Hopkins University, widely considered America's first full-fledged research university. Machen also studied at Princeton Seminary, Princeton University, and in Germany at Marburg and Göttingen. At Marburg, Machen learned from the modernist scholar Wilhelm Herrmann (1846–1922), who also taught the major Swiss theologian Karl Barth.

Machen wrestled over the trajectory of his theological convictions, but in 1906 he accepted an instructor's position at Princeton Seminary. At Princeton, established professors such as Benjamin Warfield and the New Testament scholar William Park Armstrong (1874–1944) helped convince Machen that one could be fully conversant with biblical higher criticism while remaining committed to traditional Reformed beliefs and retaining a warm Christian piety. In 1914, Machen received ordination in the northern Presbyterian Church and became a professor of New Testament at Princeton. Much of his scholarly work focused on the narratives of Jesus's birth in the New Testament. Machen demonstrated that belief in the virgin birth was a central tenet of the early Christian community, not a myth tacked onto the Christian tradition in later decades, as many modernists argued. Similarly, Machen sought to show the continuity between Paul's teachings and those of the rest of the New Testament, including the Gospels. Although Machen's scholarly work was generally well-received in the biblical studies community, that work would not define his career. Instead, Machen enlisted against the threat of modernism in the Presbyterian Church and at Princeton. His argument against modernism was encapsulated in his most famous book, *Christianity and Liberalism* (1923).

Following his Princeton predecessor Charles Hodge, Machen defended the "plenary inspiration" of the Bible, which ruled out the possibility of error:

> The doctrine of plenary inspiration does not deny the individuality of the Biblical writers; it does not ignore their use of ordinary means for acquiring information;

> it does not involve any lack of interest in the historical situations which gave rise to the Biblical books. What it does deny is the presence of error in the Bible. It supposes that the Holy Spirit so informed the minds of the Biblical writers that they were kept from falling into the errors that mar all other books. The Bible might contain an account of a genuine revelation of God, and yet not contain a true account. But according to the doctrine of inspiration, the account is as a matter of fact a true account; the Bible is an "infallible rule of faith and practice."

Machen's characterization of the Bible as the "infallible rule of faith and practice" employed a common phrase in traditional Christian sources, including the Presbyterian Church's own confession of faith.

Had Machen left his argument as a defense of fundamentalist doctrines such as plenary inspiration, *Christianity and Liberalism* would have garnered less notice. But Machen memorably concluded that the conflict between modernists and fundamentalists was not actually an intra-Christian feud. It was a clash of different religions. Machen admitted that this was a provocative argument, but he believed it was time to illuminate the utter dissimilarity of modernism from the Christianity of the great tradition. Modernists talked as if they adhered to Christianity, but in fact they were just hijacking Christian rhetoric in defense of another religion. "The great redemptive religion which has always been known as Christianity is battling against a totally diverse type of religious belief, which is only the more destructive of the Christian faith because it makes use of traditional Christian terminology." Modernism or liberalism was ultimately rooted in "naturalism," or the "denial of any entrance of the creative power of God . . . in connection with the origin of Christianity." The modernists interpreted Christ's birth, the inspiration of the Bible, and other essential Christian beliefs, in naturalistic categories. The exclusion of the supernatural, to Machen, meant the evisceration of the Christian faith.

Modernists were outraged by Machen's claims. Yet *Christianity and Liberalism* received praise even from decidedly nonfundamentalist writers such as the journalist H. L. Mencken (1880–1956), who fondly called Machen "Doctor Fundamentalis." But in a time when many of the most established American denominations were exalting the value of ecumenical relations, Machen's approach was easy to deride in moderate and liberal Presbyterian circles. Instead of confronting the substance of his charges against the modernists, Machen's critics increasingly cast him as a bitter troublemaker. Liberal Presbyterians contended that they were willing to remain in fellowship with traditionalists, but they declared that conservative insistence on doctrines such as inerrancy, the virgin birth, and the resurrection was mean-spirited. Such strictures disrupted the unity of the church. Christian harmony and loving service were essential, said the modernists. Controversial doctrines were not.

Liberals could be quite strident in their denunciations of fundamentalists, too. Among the most notorious of the modernist preachers was New York's Harry Emerson Fosdick (1878–1969). Fosdick was ordained as a Baptist minister, but in 1918 he became pastor of New York's First Presbyterian Church. Fosdick became best known for his widely-distributed 1922 sermon "Shall the Fundamentalists Win?" He condemned fundamentalists such as his fellow Presbyterian Machen for insisting "that we must all believe in the historicity of certain special miracles, preeminently the virgin birth of our Lord; that we must believe in a special theory of inspiration—that the original documents of the Scripture, which of course we no longer possess, were inerrantly dictated to men a good deal as a man might dictate to a stenographer; that we must believe in a special theory of the Atonement—that the blood of our Lord, shed in a substitutionary death, placates an alienated Deity and makes possible welcome for the returning sinner; and that we must believe in the second coming of our Lord upon the clouds of heaven to set up a millennium here, as the only way in which God can bring history to a worthy denouement." Machen replied that such "caricature and vilification" of basic Christian doctrines only demonstrated that the modernists and fundamentalists did not share the same religion.

J. Gresham Machen and his conservative allies were ultimately unable to win control of Princeton Seminary. Moderates and liberals outmaneuvered the fundamentalists and reorganized Princeton in a way that permanently secured a place for modernist thought. Ultimately, this guaranteed that traditional Reformed scholars would be excluded at the seminary, which had been the most important center of orthodox Reformed belief in America. This brought Machen to a crisis of conscience. Could he stay at Princeton if he knew the seminary would continue to promote views he regarded as hostile to Christianity? He decided he could not stay. In 1929, he and other conservative Presbyterians founded Westminster Theological Seminary in Philadelphia. Machen called the triumph of modernism at Princeton the "end of an epoch in the history of the modern church." This was certainly the case, at least in the context of American theology and Presbyterian life. Continuing fights within the Presbyterian Church led Machen to cut ties with the historic denomination itself. In 1936 he founded what became the Orthodox Presbyterian Church, one of several conservative Presbyterian breakaways in twentieth-century America.

Resistance in the Baptist Tradition

As significant as the fundamentalist-modernist split was, it did not account for all the variety of commitments among Protestants in America and the broader English-speaking world. Indeed, despite his conservatism, Machen registered concerns about evangelical revivalism, experientialism, and pragmatism, concerns that harked back to the Old School/New School Presbyterian split of the 1800s. Machen was critical of the work of moderate evangelical theologians at Princeton, as well as those in other denominations, including the Southern Baptist leader E. Y. Mullins (1860–1928). Although Mullins believed that Christian experience would complement historic doctrines, such as the divinity of Christ and the resurrection, Machen still worried that evangelicals such as Mullins put too much emphasis on subjective experience. In particular, they gave too much weight to feelings associated with the new birth of conversion. According to Machen and other traditionalists, the primacy of religious feeling was indebted to Romantic figures such as Friedrich Schleiermacher, one of Mullins's influences.

Mullins was arguably the most impactful Baptist leader in America in the early twentieth century. He certainly represented a moderate evangelical trend within Southern Baptist life. The Southern Baptist Convention weathered storms in the late nineteenth and early twentieth century over "Landmarkism," a sectarian historical theology that argued for the continuity of Baptist belief and practice throughout church history. The SBC also endured a version of the fundamentalist-modernist controversy. Baptists certainly had their representative fundamentalists, such as the Fort Worth, Texas pastor J. Frank Norris (1877–1952). They also had key liberals, such as Fosdick and the New York social gospel pastor and professor Walter Rauschenbusch (1861–1918). But Mullins represented a broad middle ground of Baptists in America, particularly in the South. These moderates wanted to maintain Baptist unity around conversion, missions, and the mere fact of being Baptist. Mullins became the president of his alma mater, Southern Baptist Theological Seminary in Louisville, in 1899. He stabilized the seminary after a horrible conflict over Landmarkism nearly capsized it under his predecessor, William Whitsitt (1841–1911). Mullins would go on to serve as president of the Southern Baptist Convention, the Baptist World Alliance (founded in London in 1905), and a framer of the Baptist Faith and Message (1925). Although it has gone through several revisions, the Baptist Faith and Message has served as the definitive statement of Southern Baptist beliefs through the present day.

In works such as *Christian Religion in Its Doctrinal Expression* (1917), Mullins placed experience at the center of Christian faith. He assumed that authentic experience would always confirm the truth of Scripture. Experience was rooted in knowledge of God through the Bible. Still, theology was ultimately derived from faithful experience, according to Mullins. True religious experience was a "fact," not just a subjective phenomenon. Christian experience was rooted in the dynamics of a relationship to the one true God, including repentance, conversion, and sanctification. "Religion has to do with the facts about God and man," Mullins wrote, "and the relations between God and man. Doctrines are simply the expression of the meaning of those facts and relations." Ultimately, doctrine was secondary to the human experience of God's saving power. For critics such as Machen, this was a slippery slope. Mullins undoubtedly affirmed the supernatural authority of Scripture. What would keep other Baptists, however, from jettisoning objectionable parts of Scripture if those parts seemed not to accord with experience? Even Mullins drifted away from a traditional understanding of Christ's substitutionary atonement. The atonement was typically one of the first historic Christian doctrines modernists dismissed due to its uncomfortable emphasis on sin, wrath, and the blood of Christ.

As with evangelical principles, fundamentalists were also not in agreement about the relative priority of the anti-evolution crusade. Most of them followed figures such as Charles Hodge, who argued that Darwinian evolution was essentially anti-Christian when it functioned as an explanation for the origins of human life. But was it acceptable for fundamentalists to leave evolution as a secondary concern? As of the mid-1910s, evolution was one among many fundamentalist priorities. Maintaining firm commitments to doctrines such as the virgin birth and the resurrection of Christ garnered more general consensus. Machen seemed to have been intentionally elusive regarding evolution, preferring to stick to doctrines with a longer track record as essential points of orthodox belief. Some fundamentalists were also uncomfortable with extending their agenda beyond denominations and seminaries into fighting over what was taught about evolution in public schools.

Fundamentalism on Trial

The great anti-evolution advocate William Jennings Bryan tried to recruit Machen to serve as an expert witness at the Scopes Trial in Tennessee in 1925. Machen declined, apparently believing that evolution was becoming too central to the fundamentalist cause. The Scopes Trial, for reasons partly out of Bryan's control, became a public relations debacle for the Fundamentalist movement. Like other southern states, Tennessee had passed a law forbidding instruction in evolutionary theory in public schools. Although the era of formal religious establishments had long passed away in America, many public-school systems were functionally Protestant and gave a prominent role to the King James Bible and at least generic Christian beliefs and morals. Some state legislatures concluded that evolution was effectively anti-Christian and, therefore, had no place in public education. In Dayton, Tennessee, the science teacher John Scopes (1900–1970) agreed to work with pro-evolution activists, breaking the law against teaching evolution in hopes of creating a test case about the issue. The publicity effort succeeded beyond anyone's expectations, as the Scopes "Monkey Trial" became a national media sensation.

There was no question about the outcome of the trial because Scopes readily admitted that he had broken the anti-evolution law. The trial's main event was the debate between Scopes's lawyer, the skeptic and civil rights attorney Clarence Darrow (1857–1938), and the ailing Bryan, who assisted the prosecution. Bryan was a brilliant public speaker, but he was no Bible scholar. He was also desperately sick at the trial, suffering from an illness that would lead to his death just days after Scopes's conviction. Yet Bryan took the stand in defense of the Bible, and Darrow humiliated the addled politician with standard higher critical questions about the plausibility of Bible stories, such as the fish that swallowed Jonah. It is easy to overstate the significance of Scopes in the actual history of fundamentalism, however. Conservative Protestantism was hardly derailed by Scopes and fights over orthodox doctrine and evolution continued for decades afterward. The dramatization of the Scopes trial in the anti-fundamentalist play and 1960 movie *Inherit the Wind* probably had more enduring popular impact than the trial itself. The movie portrayed Bryan as a classic demagogue, who seemed charming at first, but was ultimately exposed as unhinged and pathetic. In American popular memory, the Scopes trial helped to cement the stereotype of conservative Protestants as anti-science and anti-intellectual, despite abundant historical evidence to the contrary.

Varieties of Fundamentalism

As seen in Machen's example, even the American Fundamentalist movement was quite varied in its priorities. This variety becomes even clearer when you include the burgeoning Pentecostal movement of the same era. Pentecostals were supportive of signature fundamentalist doctrines such as inerrancy and the virgin birth, but they did not agree with mainstream fundamentalists on the role of the gifts of the Spirit, particularly tongues. Other divisions also played a role in the fundamentalist cohort. Many scholars of fundamentalism have assumed that African Americans did not participate in the movement. Many traditionalist African American pastors and theologians did in fact call themselves "fundamentalists," however. Despite social tensions with white leaders and the post-Civil War advent of African American-led denominations such as the National Baptist Convention (1895), many African American Protestants resonated with the fundamentalist defense of orthodox doctrines. African American fundamentalists defended these doctrines out of the same base of theological conviction as white fundamentalists. In the case of evolution, they had special reasons for concern, as evolutionary theory was often used to explain the alleged differences between whites and people of color. African Americans had their own divides between modernists and fundamentalists, too. The prominent African American Baptist leader J. H. Frank, for example, identified himself and the majority of African American believers as "fundamentalists," in opposition to the "so-called 'Intellectuals' of our race." This alluded to figures such as the modernist African American intellectual and activist W. E. B. Du Bois (1868–1963), the first black person to earn a PhD from Harvard.

Many African American traditionalist Christians of the fundamentalist era found themselves torn between grave concern over racial prejudice and the threat to belief posed by higher criticism and modernism. Of course, few African Americans saw any inherent tension between action on these issues. Yet relatively few white fundamentalists spoke out as vehemently against lynching as they did against modernism. In some cases, white Christian leaders seemed to justify episodes of extralegal violence against black men. Perhaps the most articulate example of a traditionalist African American pastor and civil rights activist of the period was the Presbyterian minister Francis Grimké (1850–1937). The son of a South Carolina plantation master and an enslaved woman, Grimké was able

Image 23.2. *Francis Grimké*

to study in the North after the Civil War, completing a degree at Princeton Seminary in 1878. He was assisted in his education by his white aunts, the antislavery activists Angelina and Sarah Grimké. Grimké spent much of his long pastoral career at Fifteenth Street Presbyterian Church in Washington, DC. Unlike more angular black fundamentalists, Grimké admired the civil rights activism of W. E. B. Du Bois. Grimké used his pulpit and publications to speak out against lynching and the legally-mandated segregation enshrined in "Jim Crow" laws.

Yet Grimké was adamant that black Christian social concern should remain rooted in the perfectly inspired Word of God. He was contemptuous toward the skeptical lawyer Clarence Darrow, for example, reviling him as a "scoffing infidel and atheist—the man who ridicules the Bible, who makes light of prayer, who looks upon religion as a dope for taking advantage of the ignorant." And he warned black pastors about the temptation of neglecting the Bible in order to win the approval of modernists and skeptical civil rights activists. Too many pastors, Grimké declared, "for the sake of a little cheap popularity, pass over the word of God and substitute other things in the place of it. And the result is a weak, sickly, namby-pamby set of [professing Christians], that can't be depended upon in any moral crisis."

The Rise of Neoorthodoxy

By the early 1900s, there was a growing sense, even among some nonfundamentalists, that modernist theology had become decadent and feckless. Modernism seemingly humanized and politicized the Christian faith while threatening the church's historic confidence in the Bible. Especially after the shocks of World War I, a domesticated religion of feelings, rationalistic natural theology, and/or humanistic social service hardly seemed adequate to the grave challenges of the time. The neoorthodox reaction to liberal Christianity affected many denominations, seminaries, and countries, but its undisputed leader was the Swiss theologian Karl Barth. At least in academic circles, Barth became the most influential theologian of the twentieth century. Like virtually all Continental theologians of his era, Barth was impacted by his early reading of Schleiermacher, but he concluded that Schleiermacher had put too much emphasis on religious experience as a guide to divine truth. Barth was hardly a fundamentalist or inerrantist, but he still believed that God revealed himself in the person of Christ, as attested by the Bible. To critics who charged him with rejecting higher criticism of the Bible, he fully conceded the value of critical-historical approaches to Scripture. Yet he admitted to his "prejudice that the Bible is a good book and that it is worthwhile for someone to take its thoughts at the very least as seriously as their own." Taking the Bible seriously was one of Barth's chief ways to retain a sense, echoing Søren Kierkegaard, of the "infinite qualitative difference" between God and man. True religion was based on knowledge of a God, who differed fundamentally from humanity in his grandeur and holiness.

After Barth's theological studies, including a semester with Adolf von Harnack in Berlin, he took a pastorate at Safenwil, Switzerland in 1911. World War I sobered Barth about the state of theology in the German and Swiss churches, especially after Harnack and other intellectuals injudiciously backed the German government's wartime policies under Kaiser Wilhelm II. Again, following Kierkegaard, Barth was convinced that the churches had become captive to culture, politics, and nationalism. The kingdom of God did indeed have political and social implications, but God himself was deeply, shockingly unfamiliar to the dominant systems of this world. In his commentary on Romans (first edition 1919), Barth exploded what he saw as the human-centric complacency of the European churches and theologians. "The Gospel is not a religious message to inform mankind of their divinity or to tell them how they may become divine," he wrote. "The Gospel proclaims a God utterly distinct from men. Salvation comes to them from Him, because they are, as men, incapable of knowing Him, and because they have no right to claim anything from Him." The Gospel is "not an event, nor an experience, nor an emotion—however delicate! Rather, it is the clear and objective perception of what eye hath not seen nor ear heard." Barth's bracing style and timely rejection of liberal excess is what made the commentary on Romans a "bombshell in the playground of the theologians," as one observer put it.

> The Gospel is not a truth among other truths. Rather, it sets a question-mark against all truths.
>
> ---
>
> Karl Barth, *The Epistle to the Romans*, 1919

Having been concerned about the cultural captivity of theologians in Germany in the 1910s, Barth was even more disturbed by the rise of Adolf Hitler (1889–1945) and the Nazis in the early 1930s. He was horrified by many German churches' embrace of Nazism and its radical racialist and nationalist agenda. Barth had held several university positions in the 1920s and '30s, but he was fired from the University of Bonn in 1935 because he refused to affirm a loyalty oath to Hitler. Barth was also the primary author of the Barmen Declaration of 1934, in which a select group of German Protestant leaders rejected the totalizing claims of the Nazis over the German church. After his dismissal from Bonn, Barth returned to Switzerland and took a position in Basel, where he would serve as a professor for the rest of his life. Barth's opposition to the Third Reich marked him as one of the most politically courageous theological figures of the twentieth century. Yet a number of traditionalists still regarded Karl Barth's work as inadequate at best. Cornelius Van Til (1895–1987), one of the founders of Westminster Seminary in Philadelphia, saw Barth's theology as warmed-over modernism and "destructive of the gospel." Barth also led a conflicted and troubled personal life. Recent scholarship has confirmed that Barth maintained an amorous relationship with his colleague and assistant, Charlotte von Kirschbaum, who lived for decades with Barth in the same home as Barth's wife Nelly.

Its effects amplified by the world wars, Barth's theology effectively ended a century of Continental theological liberalism which had begun with Schleiermacher. Barth likewise became the one theologian that scholars in Europe and North America had to contend with, even if they ultimately reached different conclusions about God's nature or the Bible. Barth also had an immediate impact on neoorthodox theologians and pastors such as Dietrich Bonhoeffer (1906–45). The pastor and dissident Bonhoeffer was another courageous opponent of Hitler, but his agitation against the Nazis ultimately cost him his life in a death camp at the very end of World War II. Bonhoeffer became best known for his classic work *The Cost of Discipleship* (first German edition 1937). In it, he argued that God's grace called and empowered the believer to a life of radical devotion to Christ. This was Bonhoeffer's idea of "costly grace," and his execution at the hands of the Nazis seemed to exemplify the lengths to which a Christian might go to obey the Lord. To fundamentalists and neoorthodox critics, the liberal theological tradition had become ineffective, individualistic, and overly experiential. Barth's theology, and the radical devotion of disciples such as Bonhoeffer, offered a different way.

Selected Bibliography

Bare, Daniel R. *Black Fundamentalists: Conservative Christianity and Racial Identity in the Segregation Era.* New York: New York University Press, 2021.

Bebbington, David. *Evangelicalism in Modern Britain: A History from the 1730s to the 1980s.* Grand Rapids: Baker, 1992.

DeJonge, Michael P. *Bonhoeffer's Theological Formation: Berlin, Barth, and Protestant Theology.* New York: Oxford University Press, 2018.

Hart, D. G. *Defending the Faith: J. Gresham Machen and the Crisis of Conservative Protestantism in Modern America.* Grand Rapids: Baker, 1995.

Jenkins, Philip. *The Great and Holy War: How World War I Became a Religious Crusade*. New York: HarperOne, 2014.

Kelly, Geffrey B. and F. Burton Nelson, eds. *A Testament to Freedom: The Essential Writings of Dietrich Bonhoeffer*. San Francisco: HarperSanFrancisco, 1995.

Larson, Edward J., *Summer for The Gods: The Scopes Trial and America's Continuing Debate Over Science And Religion*. New York: Basic Books, 1997.

Machen, J. Gresham. *Christianity and Liberalism*. New York: Macmillan, 1923. Reprint, Grand Rapids: Eerdmans, 1987.

Marsden, George M. *Fundamentalism and American Culture*. 2nd ed. New York: Oxford University Press, 2006.

Tietz, Christiane. *Karl Barth: A Life in Conflict*. Oxford: Oxford University Press, 2021.

Wills, Gregory A. *Southern Baptist Theological Seminary, 1859–2009*. New York: Oxford University Press, 2010.

—— Chapter 24 ——

Resistance and Realism in the Mid-Twentieth Century

As seen in the martyrdom of Dietrich Bonhoeffer, the twentieth century turned into an era of unprecedented violence against Christians and other religious groups by totalitarian regimes in Germany, Russia, and China. The Ottoman Empire had seen the century's first mass extermination campaign against the Armenian Christian population, culminating in the Armenian Genocide of the 1910s. Soon thereafter, Russia's communist revolution unleashed almost a century of persecution against Russia's Christians and Jews. China's communist revolution similarly led to violence and repression against Christians and Muslims which continues to present day. The twentieth century tragically demonstrated the unchecked power of modern states to persecute, murder, and destroy whole people groups. Such unchecked power climaxed in the Nazis' "final solution," the campaign to exterminate Europe's Jews during World War II.

Western Christians have sometimes tended to romanticize persecution, often quoting Tertullian's statement that the "blood of the martyrs is the seed of the church." Persecution has sometimes led to the near-annihilation of historic Christian communities, however, such as those in the broader Middle East in the late twentieth and early twenty-first centuries. Nevertheless, as in the case of Bonhoeffer, persecution has almost always raised up courageous dissidents. Repression sometimes has given churches a dose of theological realism and recourse to the harder truths of the great tradition. Persecution is a fulfillment of Christ's promise to his followers: "You will have suffering in this world. Be courageous! I have conquered the world" (John 16:33).

Marxism, Communism, and Christianity

The Soviet crackdown on the Orthodox Church, as well as on Jews and non-Orthodox Christians, was perhaps the longest-lasting campaign of religious persecution of the twentieth century. Although Karl Marx occasionally said good things about communal Christian movements such as the Shakers, overall the Marxist-communist tradition was firmly anti-Christian. Classically, Marxists regarded religion as the "opiate of the masses." At best, religion was an understandable refuge for the oppressed proletariat, or the working classes. Marx was primarily focused on the oppression of working classes, but others have applied the Marxist view to religion and racial oppression. Nation of Islam leader Malcolm X, for example, argued that Christianity was the white man's religion, designed to keep blacks under the thumb of whites. Christianity made blacks "keep our eyes fixed on the pie in the sky and heaven in the hereafter" while the white man "enjoys his heaven right here . . . on this earth . . . in this life." Malcolm X believed that the Nation of Islam, an unorthodox form of Islam founded in America's urban Midwest, was far preferable to Christianity as a black nationalist religion.

When Vladimir Lenin inaugurated the communist revolution in Russia in 1917, he aimed to marginalize and eviscerate the Orthodox Church, the long-standing center of Russian religious and cultural identity. By the end of 1917, Lenin decreed that all church property was to be confiscated. In 1918 he followed up with a radical program of church-state separation and the abolition of church-run schools. As we have seen, Orthodox leaders faced a choice of absolute obedience to the Soviet state or the threat of exile, jail, or execution. "Sectarian" groups, which included virtually all non-Orthodox communities, were subjected to particular scrutiny by Soviet intelligence services. The Ukrainian Communist Party wrote, in a typical edict of 1923, that "the activity of sectarians reveals enemy elements against the Soviet state."

The remorseless attacks on Orthodoxy and other religious groups lessened slightly during World War II. The dictator Josef Stalin realized that the devastating Nazi invasion of Russia required the mobilization of churches to encourage patriotism and the sort of sacrifice that the war required. A number of clergy whom Lenin and Stalin had jailed or exiled were released, provided they took a loyalty oath to the Soviet state. The Orthodox Church was allowed to re-establish its diocesan system and to reopen some schools and monasteries. It was an enormous relief to Orthodox leaders after the bitter early decades of the Russian Revolution and Soviet persecution. But the church still only operated with the permission of the state.

All manner of Russian people, as well as Ukrainians and other groups, fell victim to the Stalinist Terror of the 1930s, including many of the small number of Protestants in Russia and the Soviet satellite states. As with the Orthodox, Russian Protestants found some new freedoms to practice during World War II, and in 1944 Russian "evangelicals" (many of whom were influenced by England's Plymouth Brethren) and Baptists achieved a formal union which conveyed some legal recognition to the groups and permitted them to fitfully publish religious periodicals. But these privileges were understood to depend entirely on the patience of the atheistic state. Typical articles written by the evangelical-Baptist union journal praised the beneficence of the Soviet authorities and heralded the heroes of the "Great Patriotic War," as Russians called World War II. Limited contact with western Protestant leaders was permitted after World War II. In 1946, Louie Newton (1892–1986), a future president of the Southern Baptist Convention, visited Russia at Stalin's invitation and reported favorably (if naively) on the freedoms of Protestants in the Soviet Union. The late 1950s and early 1960s saw another burst of persecution under Soviet first secretary Nikita Khrushchev (1894–1971) against virtually all religious groups in the empire. Across the Soviet Union, the Orthodox Church saw 40 percent of its churches closed. Twenty percent of Baptist congregations were shut down. More than four thousand churches were closed in Ukraine alone.

> But if I were asked today to formulate as concisely as possible the main cause of the ruinous revolution that swallowed up some 60 million of our people, I could not put it more accurately than to repeat: "Men have forgotten God; that's why all this has happened."
>
> ---
>
> Aleksandr Solzhenitsyn, "Templeton Prize Acceptance Address by Mr. Aleksandr Solzhenitsyn", 1983

It is difficult to quantify the range of Christian responses to these waves of persecution. Leaders and congregants confronted a seemingly impossible choice between cooperation with the atheistic state or severe punishment. But the Russian and eastern European persecutions undoubtedly produced courageous Christian dissidents, many of whose stories were never told. The surviving stories include that of the Russian Baptist pastor Gennadi Kryuchkov (1926–2007). Kryuchkov grew up in a Russian Baptist family in Stalingrad (today's Volgograd). His father had suffered persecution and imprisonment by the Soviet state, and Kryuchkov would follow in his steps. When Kryuchkov became a leader of the evangelical/Baptist union in the early 1960s, the group was divided over how much to accommodate Soviet demands in order to survive. For example, some argued that the union's churches should accept state restrictions on baptisms for people under eighteen years old and limits on their pastors' ability to preach anywhere but inside their churches. Kryuchkov and other "reform" Baptist leaders thought accepting the restrictions was a mistake and a grave violation of a believer's conscience. His advocacy for religious freedom led to his arrest, torture, and a show trial in 1966, ending in Kryuchkov's sentencing to three years in a labor camp. Upon his release, Kryuchkov went straight back to advocacy and resistance work, coordinating reform churches and working to get word to Western supporters about the duress of the churches under Soviet rule. Gennadi Kryuchkov managed to avoid detection and arrest for two decades before the collapse of the Soviet Union in 1991.

Arguably the most influential Christian voice in twentieth century Russia was the Orthodox dissident Aleksandr Solzhenitsyn (1918–2008). In classic works such as *The Gulag Archipelago* (1958–68) and *One Day in the Life of Ivan Denisovich* (1962), Solzhenitsyn depicted the horrors of the Soviet prison camps, like the one to which he was sentenced in 1945 for criticizing Josef Stalin. Early in life, Solzhenitsyn had become an atheist and Marxist, but as a dissident he became convinced that Russians should return to the spiritual riches of the Orthodox tradition. The fundamental problem with communism was a spiritual one. In *One Day in the Life*, Solzhenitsyn drew a favorable portrait of a Baptist character, Alyosha, in contrast to the chief protagonist, Ivan Denisovich Shukov, who is something of an agnostic. Shukov is angry and consumed with political injustice. Alyosha receives his imprisonment with grace and patience, believing that God will use prison to make him more Christlike. Although Alyosha is not Orthodox, he embodies the spiritual and moral resources that Solzhenitsyn believed Christian dissidents could draw upon to stand against the communist state. Solzhenitsyn was highly critical of the compromises that the Orthodox church made with the Soviet authorities, such as remaining silent about church closings and the removal of dissident priests from the ministry. "A church dictatorially directed by atheists is a sight not seen in 2,000 years," he told the Patriarch of Moscow in 1972.

Image 24.1. *Aleksandr Solzhenitsyn*

Solzhenitsyn's work was wildly popular in the West, and he won the 1970 Nobel Prize for literature. But Solzhenitsyn, who moved to Vermont in 1976 following his expulsion from the Soviet Union, was almost as critical of Western culture as he was of Russian communism. Both cultures had become deeply materialistic, despite their dissimilar political systems. In 1978 he was granted an honorary degree at Harvard. Some may have regretted allowing him to speak to the graduating class, regarding his commencement speech as reactionary and out-of-touch with elite Western institutions. He indicted Western secular culture as decadent and suffering from a "lack of manhood." Western elites had forgotten that true liberty was not the freedom to do whatever you please, Solzhenitsyn chided, but the freedom to do what is right. Consumer culture fed all of humanity's base inclinations. "The human soul longs for things higher, warmer, and purer than those offered by today's mass living habits," he told the Harvard audience, deploring the "revolting invasion of commercial advertising," "TV stupor," and "intolerable music."

Solzhenitsyn concluded with a stunning indictment of the loss of spiritual direction in America. America was born in 1776 with the understanding that

> all individual human rights were granted on the ground that man is God's creature. That is, freedom was given to the individual conditionally, in the assumption of his constant religious responsibility. Such was the heritage of the preceding one thousand years. Two hundred or even fifty years ago, it would have seemed quite impossible, in America, that an individual be granted boundless freedom with no purpose, simply for the satisfaction of his whims. Subsequently, however, all such limitations were eroded everywhere in the West; a total emancipation occurred from the moral heritage of Christian centuries with their great reserves of mercy and sacrifice . . .

> The West has finally achieved the rights of man, and even to excess, but man's sense of responsibility to God and society has grown dimmer and dimmer.

Solzhenitsyn, carrying on the Russian Orthodox literary tradition of Dostoevsky, used his writing to show the emptiness of individualistic consumerism and the dangers of abandoning the Christian cultural tradition, whether in America or Russia.

Although Russia and China came from vastly different religious trajectories, their stories converged in the ways that churches came under terrible persecution under communist rule in the twentieth century. (Their story would repeat wherever communists took control, including in North Korea, once one of the great Christian centers of the East.) No Christian church ever had the kind of dominance in China that Orthodoxy did in Russia, Ukraine, and other Soviet republics. Both Catholics and Protestants had made significant inroads in China prior to the creation of the communistic People's Republic of China in 1949, despite occasional outbursts of anti-missionary violence such as the Boxer Rebellion of 1899–1901. Evangelical missionaries like J. Hudson Taylor and Lottie Moon had helped to transition Protestant Christianity into an indigenous Chinese faith. By the early twentieth century, Chinese church leaders began to come increasingly to the fore. Native Chinese preachers led revivals in Manchuria that were influenced by the great Pyongyang awakening in Korea in 1907. One estimate holds that the number of Protestant adherents in China rose from 37,000 to 178,000 between 1889 and 1906. There was a growing sensitivity among Chinese Protestants, however, that they needed to move beyond the organizational dominance of Westerners and become fully indigenized and independent.

Some of the new Chinese church leaders were influenced by international trends in missions and charismatic renewal, but they wanted to manifest fully Chinese leadership in their churches. Wang Ming-dao (1900–91) was a clear example of this trend: he attended a school sponsored by the London Missionary Society and received baptism as a Christian. But in 1920, the twenty-year-old Wang was exposed to the emerging charismatic movement. He received baptism again, this time by immersion. Wang became a powerful preacher, focused on evangelical and charismatic themes of salvation through Christ alone, the authority of the Bible, the mandate of holy living, and walking in the Holy Spirit. He became suspicious of the creeping modernism affecting Western missionary organizations and drew a clear line about the priority of the Bible in all his teaching. "I believe all the Truth that is written in the Scriptures and am unwilling to accept any reasoning that are not found in Scripture," Wang declared. In Wang's model, biblical traditionalism became associated with indigenous independence from Western authorities. Wang's "Christian Tabernacle" began in Beijing and spread as a self-propagating network of house churches. The house church movement would become evermore important as a means to maintain independence once Chinese communists came into power.

The Chinese indigenous church that became best known in the West was the "Little Flock" founded by Tousheng Ni, whose Anglicized name was Watchman Nee (1903–72). Like Wang, Nee studied at a Western missionary school, but he experienced conversion at an evangelistic meeting led by a Chinese Methodist preacher named Dora Yu (1873–1931). Later Nee came under the tutelage of an English evangelical missionary named Margaret Barber (1866–1929), who was affiliated with the Plymouth Brethren. Barber taught Nee the doctrines of premillennial dispensationalism and the ideal of Christian holiness. Like most of the Chinese independent church leaders, Nee took a high view of the inspiration of the Bible, the composition of which was directed by the Holy Spirit. "The Spirit behind the words of the Scripture is complete and strong. The Spirit cannot be wrong. The Spirit is inerrant," Nee explained. Nee built a network of churches that came to be known as Assembly Halls, or the Little Flock. He thought that denominational divisions departed from Christ's plan for a single Christian church in every town. Nee personally resisted any denominational-sounding name for his movement's congregations, preferring to call them by the New Testament's simple terminology of "the Church in [name of town]." By the 1940s, there were more than 700 Nee-affiliated churches in China.

Nee's best-known work globally is his book *The Normal Christian Life*, first given as a series of talks to missionaries meeting in Denmark in the late 1930s and then published serially in a British evangelical magazine starting in 1940. Nee argued that because of the pervasive neglect of the Holy Spirit in believers' lives, the average Christian's existence fell far short of the biblical, "normal" (or normative) Christian life. Drawing on Western sources including John Bunyan, Reuben Torrey, and his mentor Margaret Barber, Nee took readers through a study of Romans to explain the biblical vision for a devout and holy life. "God makes it quite clear in His Word that He has only one answer to every human need—His Son, Jesus Christ," Nee declared. "In all His dealings with us He works by taking us out of the way and substituting Christ in our place. The Son of God died instead of us for our forgiveness: He lives instead of us for our deliverance. So we can speak of two substitutions—a Substitute on the Cross who secures our forgiveness and a Substitute within who secures our victory." Like many of the leaders of indigenous Chinese Christian movements, Watchman Nee attracted attention from communist authorities, and in 1952 they arrested him on a host of charges. Eventually he was sentenced to fifteen years in prison. Partly due to Nee's widespread and enduring popularity (he has been cited as an influence by Bono, the lead singer of the Irish rock band U2, for instance), the Little Flock also became a source of controversy among some Western Christians who accused it of cultlike beliefs and behavior.

Watchman Nee and countless other Chinese Christians fell victim to the communist Chinese government's "Three-Self Patriotic Movement." This communist-sponsored philosophy drew on older missionary rhetoric but was now intended to turn churches into tools of the state. The three "selves" of the movement were "self-governance, self-support, and self-propagation" of the Chinese churches, all with the aim of removing "imperialist" (i.e. foreign and non-communist) influences from among Chinese Christians. Similar to the experience of churches under the dictatorial governments of Nazi Germany and Soviet Russia, the Chinese churches faced a choice of accommodation or resistance. Many chose accommodation and supported the Three-Self Movement. The churches that did not comply became known, variously, as "house" or "unregistered" congregations.

As one of the key house church leaders, Wang Ming-dao emerged as arguably the most influential of the Chinese Christian dissidents. Wang already had practical experience of resistance when he refused to cooperate with occupying Japanese authorities in Beijing during the 1940s. Then he stood against the Three-Self Patriotic Movement in the 1950s, believing that the churches must remain independent of government control and insisting that his church never had any "imperialist" influences anyway. Communist authorities imprisoned Wang for sedition in 1955. They briefly released him after he signed a confession of his political sins, a nearly universal demand Chinese communist authorities made against dissidents of all kinds. But Wang quickly recanted his confession and went back to prison, where he remained until 1979.

Wang's theology was deeply influenced by the Fundamentalist movement in the West of the early twentieth century. He adopted a commonsense approach to the plain truth of the whole Bible. "Whatever the Bible says, I will accept," Wang contended. "Whatever the Bible does not say, I will not take them even a little bit. My faith and my message are fully back to the Bible. No matter how many people subtract some truths from the Bible, and no matter how many people add some traditions other than the Bible, I always believe in everything in the Bible, no less and no more." Drawing on the older Reformation principle of *sola scriptura*, this type of common-sense biblicism and suspicion of modernistic compromise characterized much of the Chinese house church movement. Wang was critical of the Chinese churches that compromised with communists as well as those under Western denominational influence that compromised with modernist thought.

Catholics in Communist China dealt with similar pressures as Protestants did, confronting hard choices between compromise and repression. As of 1949, the Catholic community in China was far older and larger than the Protestant movement. Its direct connection to a foreign authority, the pope, made the Chinese Catholic Church an organization of acute concern to Chinese authorities, a concern that has persisted through present day. Pope Pius XI had already rejected communism in 1937 as "intrinsically hostile to religion." While many Protestants in China could seemingly justify support for the anti-imperialist ethos of the Three-Self Patriotic Movement, it was vastly more problematic for Catholics to abandon their connection to the Vatican. Thus in 1951 Chinese authorities initiated a massive crackdown on Catholics, especially in Beijing and Shanghai. More than a thousand Catholic leaders and dissidents were executed. By 1953, Chinese communists had expelled most foreign priests from the country, leading Chinese Catholics to scramble to ordain more indigenous clergy. Control over appointment of Chinese Catholic priests remained a major point of contention between the Vatican and the Chinese government. The nadir of communist repression of Christian worship came during the vicious "Cultural Revolution" (1966–76) under party chairman and Chinese dictator Mao Zedong (1893–1976). Communist authorities achieved total suppression of public Christian worship of all kinds by 1967. At that point, the only Christian meetings that continued in China were held in secret, at great risk to the Christians involved. After Mao's death, China haltingly entered a new phase of greater religious tolerance combined with state surveillance. House churches in particular began to grow steadily once again.

Higher Criticism and Neoorthodoxy

The repeating horrors of world wars, the Holocaust, and the mass killings under communist regimes made Karl Barth and other theologians' reactions against humanistic, optimistic, and modernist theology seem increasingly warranted. Not that liberal theology was at an end. Higher criticism of the Bible, in particular, was by the early twentieth century a permanent fixture of elite theological schools in North America and Europe. Indeed, doubt about the inspiration of Scripture had almost become a creedal test for employment at many such institutions. The twentieth century also saw a vast new output of scholarly work on the "historical Jesus," much of which assumed that the Gospels did not offer a complete or accurate view of the historical person of Jesus of Nazareth. The German physician and New Testament scholar Albert Schweitzer (1875–1965) published arguably the most influential and sensational of these works in his 1906 *The Quest for the Historical Jesus*. Liberals welcomed Schweitzer's contention that there was a difference between the Jesus of history and the Jesus of the Bible. Many liberals recoiled, however, at Schweitzer's argument that even Jesus's ethics were transitory and unreliable. Jesus himself had preached in anticipation of a kingdom that did not arrive, Schweitzer claimed. Jesus may have been heroic, Schweitzer contended, but he was tragically mistaken about eschatology and his own role in inaugurating the kingdom of God.

As seen in Schweitzer, Germany kept producing theological luminaries, including the Lutheran existentialist scholar Rudolf Bultmann (1884–1976). While Schweitzer and others researched what we could know about the historical Jesus, the Jesus of history became virtually irrelevant for Bultmann and his disciples. The power of Christianity lay in the "kerygma," or proclamation, of the New Testament. Influenced by the existential philosophy of Martin Heidegger (1889–1976) and by the Lutheran pietist tradition, Bultmann insisted that the grounding of faith was not in the historical record of Jesus's life but in acting upon the church's historic proclamation of faith in Christ and his work on the cross. In his analysis of the Synoptic Gospels, Bultmann concluded that there was little in them that one might regard as "historical" at all. Trying to measure the literal accuracy of the Gospels was almost beside the point. What the New Testament really revealed was what the early Christian community believed and proclaimed about their faith. Many of those beliefs were no longer tenable according to the precepts of modern science. They were more properly regarded as myths, Bultmann explained. For scientifically-minded modern people, it was no use to "repristinate" the "mythical world picture" of the New Testament. Nevertheless, through stories of the cross and resurrection, God had made salvation and an "authentic" existence available to the believing Christian.

Bultmann's radical "demythologizing" of the Gospels did not go unanswered, even in elite academic circles. The New Testament scholar C. H. Dodd (1884–1973) finished his teaching career at the University of Cambridge, becoming the first non-Anglican (as a Congregationalist) to hold a chair of divinity at Oxford or Cambridge since the mid-1600s. Dodd defended the historicity of the Gospels in many books, including his magisterial *Historical Tradition in the Fourth Gospel* (1963). To Dodd, the Gospel accounts were largely based on early, reliable historical information. He also countered Schweitzer's view of Jesus's failed eschatology with the concept of "realized eschatology," a term coined by Dodd. Much of Jesus's eschatological teaching, encapsulated in the phrase "the kingdom of God is at hand," was fulfilled in his own person and ministry, Dodd suggested. Dodd was no inerrantist, but he reflected a more neoorthodox or conservative trend in British theological schools than those in Germany. British culture was secularizing in many of the same ways as countries on the European Continent, but it was also heavily seeded by traditional Christian popularizers and novelists. These included the writers and academics affiliated with the "Inklings," the informal literary group based at Oxford that attracted major Protestant and Catholic figures including C. S. Lewis, Dorothy Sayers, and J. R. R. Tolkien.

The United States, with its sprawling denominational character and vital evangelical movement, was more institutionally diverse in theological commitments. Losses in the fundamentalist/modernist wars had led to secessions from modernist-led schools, and the creation of new academic outlets, such as J. Gresham Machen's Westminster Seminary in Philadelphia (1929). Dispensationalists founded a stronghold at Dallas Theological Seminary, established by the brothers Rollin T. (1868–1940) and Lewis Sperry Chafer (1871–1952) in 1924. Baptists in Texas had opened Southwestern Baptist Theological Seminary (1908) as a reflection of the desire to offer theological education to Baptists in the growing Southwest. Overall, the first half of the twentieth century saw a burst of traditionalist Protestant institution-building in America.

But not all academic theological institutions had become decidedly modernist or traditional. The Southern Baptist Theological Seminary remained the flagship school for the Southern Baptist Convention. Its theological moderation was representative of a trend across much of American denominational life: academic theologians were familiar with higher criticism and liberal perspectives, but they knew that their students and sponsoring churches would have limited patience for questioning the Bible's essential historicity. In the mid-twentieth century, Harold Tribble (1899–1986) occupied Southern Seminary's chair of theology, succeeding the formidable E. Y. Mullins. Tribble cautiously familiarized students with European liberal and existentialist theology. Like all academic theologians, he had to contend with Karl Barth. Like others at Southern, Tribble preferred the neoorthodox theology of Emil Brunner (1889–1966), who seemed to take a mediating position between Barth's stark neoorthodoxy and the humanistic predilections of the modernists. Brunner was a Swiss theologian, heavily influenced by his countryman Barth, but Brunner made more room than Barth for the possibility of natural revelation and for humanity's natural ability to know God. Barth saw Brunner as fatally compromising with modernism, but Brunner's relative moderation made him a popular choice among teachers at schools such as Southern

Seminary. During the World War II era, Southern repeatedly endured controversies when faculty or visiting speakers pushed the limits of acceptable theology, demonstrating the gulf between the seminary faculty and rank-and-file Southern Baptist pastors. For the next half century, Southern Baptist seminaries would struggle to find the balance between outright liberalism and accountability to its largely conservative constituency.

Northern Baptists produced perhaps the most consequential American evangelical institution-builder of the mid-twentieth century: Carl F. H. Henry (1913–2003). After experiencing conversion in 1933, Henry took degrees at Wheaton College and Northern Baptist Theological Seminary, both in the Chicago area, before completing a PhD at Boston University in 1949. Well-connected in evangelical academic and missionary circles, Henry participated in the forming of the National Association of Evangelicals (NAE) in 1942, an organization intended to engage in public advocacy on matters of concern to the broad "neo-evangelical" movement. "Neo-evangelical" was a term that Henry and others proposed as a successor to the somewhat tarnished word "fundamentalist." Henry published his classic work *The Uneasy Conscience of Modern Fundamentalism* in 1947, in which he argued that fundamentalists should maintain their unwavering commitment to biblical authority while also engaging with cultural concerns such as poverty and racism that had seemingly become the purview of modernists and of those associated with the "social gospel." Henry also took part in the 1949 formation of the Evangelical Theological Society (ETS), an organization of biblical scholars and theologians united around the doctrine of inerrancy, a belief that remained decidedly unfashionable in many academic schools of theology.

> A Christianity without a passion to turn the world upside down is not reflective of apostolic Christianity.
>
> ---
>
> Carl F.H. Henry, *The Uneasy Conscience of Modern Fundamentalism*, 1947

Henry and his allies were convinced that evangelicals in America needed to establish topflight academic outlets for biblical studies and theology, since so many premier graduate programs and faculties were functionally closed to people with traditional views of the Bible's inspiration and authority. Therefore, in addition to the founding of the NAE and ETS, Henry was one of the charter faculty members at Fuller Theological Seminary (1947) in Pasadena, California. Henry partnered with Charles Fuller (1887–1968), the popular Baptist radio evangelist, and Harold John Ockenga (1905–85), pastor of the venerable Park

Image 24.2. *Payton Hall, Fuller Theological Seminary*

Street Church in Boston, who served as Fuller's first president. In 1956, Henry left Fuller to become the founding editor of *Christianity Today*, a magazine and theological journal created by Billy Graham, by then the most celebrated American evangelist. Graham and Henry wanted *Christianity Today* to project cultural and academic sophistication paired with conservative theology. As editor, Henry remained engaged with theological trends in North America and Europe, publishing occasional interviews and columns from neoorthodox figures such as Karl Barth and Emil Brunner. Henry's brand of evangelicalism reflected a cosmopolitan, learned spirit, as well as the fundamentalist penchant for building institutions free from modernist control. Henry assumed that scholars with a strong view of divine revelation would not be welcome at top-tier divinity schools, so the best thing for traditionalists to do was to create their own publications and institutions devoted to outstanding biblicist scholarship. In the best case, such scholarship might open doors for more traditionalists at elite schools. At a minimum it would give bright conservative students reliable places to go and solid resources to study.

Despite Henry and others' attempts to forge a neo-evangelical cohort, probably the best-known Christian intellectual in America in the mid-twentieth century was the liberal realist theologian Reinhold Niebuhr (1892–1971). Although Niebuhr was more of an ethicist than a biblical scholar, he played a similar cultural role in America to that of Barth in Europe. Niebuhr called on American Christians, pastors, and theologians to return to the Reformed understanding of human sin and frailty, which would foster a neoorthodox sense of Christian realism. This philosophy was well-suited to the era of the world wars, the Holocaust, and communism. Niebuhr advised caution about idealistic plans for ushering in a kingdom of God on earth. Such plans, even well-intentioned ones, often produce "ironic" outcomes (ones out of sync with stated goals), and tragic results.

Niebuhr grew up in a German immigrant family in Missouri, and his father was a pastor in the German Evangelical Synod. His family was extraordinary in its academic achievements. His sister Hulda taught at McCormick Theological Seminary in Chicago. His brother H. Richard Niebuhr taught at Yale Divinity School and wrote books including the classic *Christ and Culture* (1951), which considered historic stances of churches toward the dominant culture. Reinhold Niebuhr graduated with a master's degree from Yale in 1915. He pastored a German-American church in Detroit until 1928, during which time he became attracted to the ideals of the social gospel, especially as articulated by Walter Rauschenbusch. The young pastor Niebuhr also became convinced by the philosophy of socialism. Troubles in the burgeoning automobile industry in Detroit sensitized Niebuhr to the need for churches to speak on issues of capitalism, class conflict, and the suffering of industrial workers.

In 1928, Niebuhr accepted a position at Union Theological Seminary in New York City, which since the controversy over the liberal teachings of Charles A. Briggs in the 1890s had become a center of liberal and social gospel thought. In the early 1930s, as the nation sank into the Great Depression, Niebuhr became involved with the Socialist Party, including running for office on the Socialist ticket. Niebuhr was also a pacifist, but the advent of Nazism in Germany began to erode his idealistic liberal convictions. By the outbreak of World War II, Niebuhr had become disillusioned with the Socialist Party and with pacifism, and he actively promoted the Allies' fight against the Axis powers. He promoted a version of Christian "just war" theory, however, believing that nations must attend to the ethical limits of war-making. He objected to the firebombing of German and Japanese cities and to the use of the atomic bomb, both of which indiscriminately targeted civilians.

For his views on foreign policy, war, and statecraft, Niebuhr became a trusted adviser to the Harry Truman administration of the late 1940s. Niebuhr had become the nation's best-known advocate of Christian Realism. Theologically and ethically, Niebuhr insisted that sin tainted the perspective of individuals, but even more so it clouded the vision of social groups and nations. As he explained in *Moral Man and Immoral Society* (1932), individuals "may be moral in the sense that they are able to consider interests other than their own in determining problems of conduct." But in groups, "there is less reason to guide and check impulse, less capacity for self-transcendence, less ability to comprehend the needs of others and therefore more unrestrained egoism than the individuals, who compose the group, reveal in their personal relationships." It was exceedingly difficult for governments to anticipate the consequences of far-reaching policies. Thus, the best political policies were marked by caution, humility, and acceptance of less-than-perfect scenarios. Utopian schemes (such as communism) might sound like they are motivated by moral ideals, but they were actually prideful and destined to cause unanticipated harm or possibly descend into unchecked evil. Niebuhr won the admiration of a host of American academics, including a group of prominent secular scholars who whimsically called themselves "Atheists for Niebuhr." They liked his moral philosophy, despite their rejection of his theology. Niebuhr's fame proved enduring, as he has been cited as a major influence by figures including Martin Luther King Jr., Barack Obama, and many others.

In another sense, however, Niebuhr was an artefact of a time that passed with the coming of the Vietnam War. His 1948 appearance on the cover of the twenty-fifth anniversary issue of *TIME* magazine may have represented one of the high-water marks of the influence of "mainline" Protestantism in America. When he was awarded the Presidential Medal of Freedom in 1964, few could have imagined that America's mainline Protestant churches—Presbyterian, Lutheran, Episcopalian, Methodist, and American Baptist—were entering a period of precipitous decline. Even though some politicians, both Democrat and Republican, still cite Niebuhr as an influence, it would be hard to imagine any Christian academic theologian commanding the kind of cultural and political attention today in America that Niebuhr did in the mid-twentieth century. Barth and Niebuhr's respective turns to versions of "neoorthodoxy" (though Niebuhr rejected that label, as well as associations with Barth) were brilliantly suited to the cultural crises of their age, when the menace of evils such as Nazism and communism seemed stark and immediate. In retrospect, the neoorthodox moment seemed less well-suited to the turbulence of the 1960s and beyond.

Selected Bibliography

Caird, George B. "Charles Harold Dodd, 1884–1973." *Proceedings of the British Academy* 60 (1975): 497–510.

Dowling, Maurice. "Soviet Baptists and the Cold War." In *Baptists and War: Essays on Baptists and Military Conflict, 1640s-1990s*, edited by Gordon L. Heath and Michael A. G. Haykin, 169–202. Cambridge: Lutterworth, 2015.

Froese, Paul. *The Plot to Kill God: Findings from the Soviet Experiment in Secularization.* Berkeley: University of California Press, 2008.

Kwok, Wai Luen. "*Sola Scriptura*'s and the Chinese *Union Version* Bible's Impact upon Conservative Christian Leaders: The Case of Watchman Nee and Wang Mingdao." *Journal of the Royal Asiatic Society* 30, no. 1 (January 2020): 93–103.

NG, Peter Tze Ming. "Dissenting Traditions and Indigenous Christianity: The Case in China." In *The Oxford History of Protestant Dissenting Traditions, Volume IV: The Twentieth Century: Traditions in a Global Context*, edited by Jehu J. Hanciles, 127–44. Oxford: Oxford University Press, 2019.

Inboden, William. *Religion and American Foreign Policy, 1945–1960: The Soul of Containment.* New York: Cambridge University Press, 2008.

Pearce, Joseph. *Solzhenitsyn: A Soul in Exile.* Grand Rapids: Baker, 2001.

Wanner, Catherine. *Communities of the Converted: Ukrainians and Global Evangelism.* Ithaca, NY: Cornell University Press, 2007.

Warren, Heather A. *Theologians of a New World Order: Reinhold Niebuhr and the Christian Realists, 1920–1948.* New York: Oxford University Press, 1997.

Xi, Lian. *Redeemed by Fire: The Rise of Popular Christianity in Modern China.* New Haven, CT: Yale University Press, 2010.

Chapter 25

Global Christian Growth in the Age of Billy Graham

As we enter the post-World War II era of church history, it becomes more difficult than ever to tell a linear, or comprehensive story. During this period, Christianity became globally decentered in ways that the faith had perhaps never been before in history. This was especially true of the faith's evangelical and Pentecostal expressions. Unless one produced a much lengthier account than this one, there is no way to account adequately for the incredible flourishing of biblicist, Spirit-filled faith in nations from Argentina to Zimbabwe.

Still, there are overarching patterns to note in our final chapters. One is the sheer vibrancy of evangelical and Pentecostal faith, especially as compared to "mainline" traditions. Mainline leadership largely set aside the great tradition of Christian belief in favor of modernist theology and liberal politics. In some ways, Catholicism fell victim to the same trends as the mainline Protestant denominations, especially after the Vatican II assembly of the 1960s. Even among mainline Protestants and Catholics, there was also a global conservative renewal movement, however, often fueled by burgeoning numbers of adherents in sub-Saharan Africa. Catholics suffered terrible losses in Latin America to evangelical and Pentecostal churches. Vatican II was followed by massive declines in Catholic clergy in many parts of the world. Yet as we will see in our final chapters, the dynamic papacy of John

Paul II (1920–2005), beginning in 1978, bolstered a renewed Catholicism that was both traditionalist and global.

Another theme has been the relationship between global growth and the continuing power and influence of the West, in both Protestant and Catholic communities. There can be no disputing the enormous influence of Billy Graham (1918–2018) on American and global evangelicalism in the second half of the twentieth century, for example. Graham made important visits to Africa, including 1960 crusades in Ghana, Nigeria, and Kenya. But from an African perspective, Graham was something of a secondary influence compared to African Independent Church leaders such as Josiah Olufemi Akindayomi (1909–80), the founder in 1952 of the Redeemed Christian Church of God, one of the most dynamic global Pentecostal denominations. Graham's direct influence in Africa likewise paled in comparison to the German Pentecostal evangelist Reinhard Bonnke (1940–2019), whose evangelistic and healing crusades across Africa spanned four decades and reached tens of millions of people. One million six hundred thousand people reportedly attended just one Bonnke meeting in 2000 in Lagos, Nigeria. Lagos, a megacity with a metropolitan area of some 24 million people, has become one of the most vibrant centers of evangelical and Pentecostal growth in the twenty-first century, along with other megacities such as São Paulo, Brazil. None of this is meant to imply that figures such as Billy Graham were less influential than Western Christians have assumed. Instead, it suggests that there is a much larger story of Christian growth over the past seven decades than many American Christians realize.

New Traditionalist Leaders and Billy Graham

Despite the accelerating pace of Christian global growth, the 1950s still saw the emergence of an extraordinary new set of evangelical leaders in the English-speaking world. They helped to re-energize the evangelical movement after some decades of defensiveness and fundamentalist separatism. These leaders included Graham and Carl Henry in America, John Stott (1921–2011) and Martyn Lloyd-Jones (1899–1981) in Britain, and J. I. Packer (1926–2020) in Britain and Canada. By the 1950s, Graham was the most famous evangelist in the world, following in a long line of evangelical preachers from George Whitefield to Dwight Moody whose ministries caused an international sensation and brought untold thousands to faith in Christ. Graham was ordained to the ministry in the Southern Baptist Convention and maintained important institutional ties to the Baptist world. But his undergraduate studies at Florida Bible Institute and Wheaton College introduced Graham to a broader spectrum of American evangelicalism. His marriage to Ruth Graham, daughter of Presbyterian missionaries to China, further secured Graham's pan-evangelical and international focus. He became associated with the Youth for Christ parachurch movement, which gave him abundant preaching opportunities across North America and Europe. Finally, his 1949 crusade in Los Angeles secured Graham's fame as a media superstar, partly through newspaper coverage in publications owned by the magnate William Randolph Hearst (1863–1951).

Image 25.1. *Graham speaking in Norway, 1955*

From Whitefield to Graham, effective use of media was essential to the emergence of celebrity preachers. Graham and Whitefield both depended on print coverage of their revival meetings, but Graham was a preacher par excellence for the age of electronic media, including radio and (soon) television. Graham also maximized the opportunities afforded by passenger airplanes. Whitefield had tested the limits of how much one preacher could realistically travel by horse, wagon, and sailing ship. Graham's relentless schedule showed what a similarly motivated itinerant could do when he could arrive in cities around the world with just a day's worth of airplane rides. He would eventually speak live before more than 210 million people worldwide.

Like Whitefield, Charles Finney, and Dwight Moody before him, Graham particularly made his mark in America and England. In 1954, Graham held a monthslong crusade in London, with an estimated total attendance of over two million people. In 1955, Graham began a longtime friendship with Queen Elizabeth II. As monarch and the "supreme governor" of the Church of England, Elizabeth's warm reception to Graham was an essential vote of confidence at a time when many English church leaders dismissed Graham as a rube and a huckster. Graham's success in London also marked his long-standing trend of cooperation with virtually any Christian denomination, including Anglicans, Catholics, and Orthodox Christians. This led to significant criticism of Graham from more conservative evangelicals and fundamentalists, who thought that Graham should be more discerning about his ministry partners. Some conservative critics saw him as a publicity-seeker and a theological compromiser.

In 1954 Graham spoke at the liberal Union Theological Seminary in New York, and in 1957, the mainline-dominated Protestant Council of the City of New York hosted his crusade at Madison Square Garden. Many mainliners figured that partnering with Graham would do no harm, while Graham believed that as an evangelist, he should take any opportunity that meant a bigger platform for preaching the gospel. Critics on both the right and left remained unimpressed, however. Union professor Reinhold Niebuhr was irritated by Graham's success in New York, saying that the evangelist preached an oversimplified, "obscurantist version of the Christian faith." By the mid-1950s Graham was somewhat impervious to criticism, however, as he rocketed past Niebuhr and others to become the most popular religious leader in America. The formation of the Billy Graham Evangelistic Association in 1950 created a new parachurch structure through which Graham could operate independently of denominational restrictions. By 1952, Graham had also become a sought-after adviser to prominent American politicians, particularly Republicans. He was especially important in the transformation of Dwight Eisenhower (1890–1969) from a fairly secular military commander into one of the great architects of Cold War-era civil religion.

In England, the Fundamentalist movement of the early twentieth century never had the drawing power that it did in America. A number of religious leaders who called themselves "evangelical" in mid-twentieth century Britain did not accept the doctrine of inerrancy. The mixed reaction of many British evangelicals to Billy Graham led to a sorting of the British evangelical movement. John Stott, the rector of the Anglican All Souls Church, Langham Place in London, argued that Anglican evangelicals could avoid the "excesses" of American fundamentalism while adhering to the historic beliefs of the church, the inerrancy of Scripture, and the need for personal salvation through Christ. In 1958, J. I. Packer, then at Tyndale Hall, an evangelical Anglican college in Bristol, published the landmark book *"Fundamentalism" and the Word of God.* Packer argued that "fundamentalists" were drawing on a deep, respected tradition of "historic Evangelicalism." ("Evangelical" was commonly capitalized in the British context.) "Fundamentalism," Packer contended, was "just a twentieth-century name for historic Evangelicalism, though not, in our judgment, a very good or useful name." For Packer, the fight for the authority of the Bible echoed the spirit of the Reformers and the best of the Princeton tradition, as represented in the work of Charles Hodge and B. B. Warfield.

Packer explained why, despite its many critics, the doctrine of "inerrancy" remained essential to the evangelical movement. "Only truth can be authoritative; only an inerrant Bible can be used, as we shall hope to show, in the way that God means Scripture to be used." For Packer, the authority of the Bible was preeminent, and the church's biblical interpretation should also be formed by the great tradition. *Sola scriptura* never meant that believers should ignore the riches of the Christian tradition, in sources such as the great Puritan writers and the Westminster Confession of Faith. In a classic articulation of the great tradition, Packer wrote that "theology goes forward only by looking back—back through the Church's heritage of teaching to Jesus Christ and His apostles. Evangelicals seek to be traditionalists of this kind." Tradition could never be the ultimate authority. But faithful biblicism informed by faithful Christian heritage was infinitely preferable to a radical individualism in which the isolated Bible reader determined his or her own truth. Packer made his best-known contribution to the evangelical community through his best-selling book *Knowing God* (1973), which advanced Packer's historic evangelical model of a warm and intellectually serious devotion to the living God. In 1979, Packer permanently relocated to Regent College, an interdenominational, evangelical graduate school in Vancouver, Canada. Founded in 1968, Regent College has become one of the key institutional centers of evangelical academic life in North America.

> Disregard the study of God, and you sentence yourself to stumble and blunder through life blindfolded, as it were, with no sense of direction and no understanding of what surrounds you. This way you can waste your life and lose your soul.
>
> ---
>
> J. I. Packer, *Knowing God*, 1973

Cooperation and Compromise

Packer, Stott, and Graham represented the transdenominational bent of much of post-World War II evangelicalism. But key evangelical leaders such as Britain's Martyn Lloyd-Jones reflected an ongoing concern that evangelicals should exercise good theological judgment when selecting ministry partners. The strict separationist view of earlier fundamentalists, shying away from partners who showed the least dalliance with modernism, was waning. Strict separationism survived in quarters such as Bob Jones University in South Carolina, which remained comfortable with the name "fundamentalist" and whose leaders were critical of Graham's ecumenism (Graham had briefly attended Bob Jones in 1936). In the Graham era, a new rift opened between "fundamentalists" and "evangelicals," often over their clashing views of Graham himself. But the evangelical continuum regarding the priority of separation from Christians who were in theological error was broader than these two poles. Figures such as Martyn Lloyd-Jones stood in the middle between Graham, who partnered with virtually anyone who wanted to support his crusades, and Graham's fundamentalist nemesis Bob Jones Jr. (1911–97), the longtime president and chancellor of Bob Jones University. Bob Jones warned even against partnering with Christians who partnered with modernists, liberals, or Catholics.

Martyn Lloyd-Jones was a physician by training who became pastor of London's Westminster Chapel in 1943. A native of Wales, Lloyd-Jones was part of the Calvinistic Methodist movement which dated to Wales's Great Awakening of the 1730s and '40s. Lloyd-Jones was a boy during the powerful Welsh revival of 1904–5. This memory formed his belief in the Holy Spirit's power to enliven correct doctrinal (Calvinist) belief for revival. Lloyd-Jones was committed to promoting British evangelical unity but without the taint of Graham's broad-based ecumenism. (Lloyd-Jones did not participate in Graham's 1954 London crusade.) Tensions within the British evangelical movement came to a head in 1966, at a meeting of the National Assembly of Evangelicals. Lloyd-Jones called on evangelicals to be united only among themselves and stop partnering with liberals. John Stott, whose Anglican communion was as theologically mixed as any denomination, took exception and used his concluding address at the assembly to criticize Lloyd-Jones's view as unbiblical.

This moment reflected an enduring tension between evangelicals who remained within the Anglican Church and those who believed that partnering with Anglican leadership entailed theological compromise. In some ways, this debate echoed dynamics within the English Reformation. Puritans in the 1600s had pondered whether they could realistically reform the Church of England from within or whether they should separate from the church. For his part, J. I. Packer's Anglican congregation in Vancouver finally broke from the Anglican Church of Canada in 2008 over the Anglicans' approval of same-sex unions. In 2009, Packer's congregation joined the Anglican Church in North America (ACNA), a conservative denomination that maintains fellowship with Anglican provinces in the Global South, ones that have not affirmed same-sex marriage or ordained practicing homosexuals as clergy. By 2020, the ACNA counted almost a thousand affiliated congregations in the US and Canada.

Church Growth in the Global South

Those Anglican provinces in the Global South remind us that however significant these theological debates over separation in Europe and North America have been, the real action in Christian growth over the past century has moved to Latin America, sub-Saharan Africa, and south and southeast Asia. As important as Pentecostal denominations, including many local independent churches, have been to that story of growth, large transnational denominations including the Anglican Church and Roman Catholic Church still play a determinative role in the Global South. African Independent Churches (AICs) get a great deal of scholarly attention (as they should), but there are far more Catholic or Anglican Africans than those affiliated with AICs. People still tend to think of the Anglican Church as primarily white and British, but by the 2010s, about 60 percent of the worldwide Anglican communion was African. That number may be considerably higher if you only counted practicing Anglicans. Likewise, the number of African Catholics grew from 1.9 million in 1900 to an astounding 130 million in 2000.

Even the historic Christian denominations in Africa tend to be more charismatic than corresponding denominational churches in the West, however, in the relative exuberance of worship practices and their focus on divine healing. While the role of the prosperity gospel is controversial and disputed, the historic denominations—Catholic, Anglican, Methodist, and others—have checked the advance of the prosperity gospel in ways that it has not been constrained in the AICs. The relative prevalence of charismatic practices in Africa is a long and complicated story, but it is rooted in waves of Pentecostal-style revivals there dating to the early twentieth century. One of the major movements affecting a wide range of African denominations was the East African Revival, which began in an Anglican mission in Rwanda in the mid-1930s and spread across eastern and central Africa. While the East African Revival may have seemed novel in some ways—especially in its dramatic effects in traditional Anglican, Lutheran, and Presbyterian churches—it also drew on important aspects of the great tradition of Christian theology. Most notably, many influenced by the East African Revival were encouraged to read John Bunyan's classic *The Pilgrim's Progress*

(1678), a book which appeared in numerous African translations before and during the East African Revival.

The revival started at an Anglican girls' school in Rwanda in 1936. The awakening was marked by such intense and emotional repentance that some Western missionaries thought that the penitent girls and others had gone insane or were under demonic influence. But the confessions of sins including stealing, witchcraft, and sexual indiscretions followed long-standing patterns in the history of revivals. The experiences also took direct inspiration from Bunyan's *Pilgrim*; Bunyan began writing *The Pilgrim's Progress* with a heavy burden of sin strapped to his back. He desperately wanted to be free of it, as did the converts in the East African Revival. It was not unusual for church altars during the revival to be filled with pilfered, sinful, or idolatrous items that converts wanted to physically remove from their homes as a display of sincere repentance.

Sermons and conversion testimonies focused on the threat of judgment, the reality of hell, and the imminent return of Christ. One woman who had converted as a girl in 1936 later told an interviewer that those who came to Christ in the revival "used to shake, and there would be jumping and falling on the ground, and from that time we started cutting off the ornaments we used to wear, and we poured out the beer we were keeping at homes, and at night we went into churches, and we made a lot of noise, both men and women." Exuberant worship and radical, tangible expressions of repentance were hallmarks of new life in Christ and separation from the world.

Denominational officials routinely sought to check what they saw as the Pentecostal excesses of the East African Revival. For example, in 1940 George Chambers, the Anglican bishop of Tanganyika (now part of Tanzania), came to investigate an ecstatic outbreak in the town of Bugufi which was marked by tongues, trances, and other exuberant experiences. The skeptical Chambers wrote that "as darkness drew near, the waving hands and arms increased to the rhythm of profane hymn tunes and choruses. The clapping of hands took place, people began to sing different hymns at the same time and persisted in doing so, some finished their hymn with a rocking laugh, and then followed cryings, screamings, shoutings, making noises like those of animals such as catcalls, the yelping of dogs and the snorting of wild beasts. Two women groveled and wailed on the grass floor of the church, another woman crawled on the floor like a [snake]." Defenders of the revival insisted that many of these were biblical manifestations of the signs, wonders, and gifts of the Spirit that characterized true revival. Authorities sometimes became so concerned about the uncontrolled behavior in revival meetings that they called on police and intelligence services to investigate. Tensions over the appropriate limits of Pentecostal revival became an enduring theme in African Protestant churches. Many church leaders and missionaries balked at revivals' excesses, yet virtually every historic missionary denomination in East Africa was affected by the fervor. By the late twentieth century, the vast majority of the Anglican, Presbyterian, and Methodist clergy in East Africa had direct ties to the revivals.

As always in such awakenings, some converts in the East African Revival fell away after the initial excitement. Some were permanently estranged from the church, while others came back after a period of wandering. Future Anglican bishop Festo Kivengere (1919–88) was an instructive example. He experienced conversion in 1936. Even though he went to high school at a Church Missionary Society station, he soon fell away, became an agnostic, and began drinking heavily. Friends and family members pled with Kivengere to return to the Lord, and he despondently asked God to reveal himself in power. "Suddenly, as if in a vision," Kivengere recalled, "in front of me was Jesus hanging on the cross, as clear as anything I had ever seen with my physical eyes . . . I did not see just a helpless human being hanging on the cross like a criminal; I saw my God slaughtered for my sin." Like many of the converts, Kivengere immediately resolved to repent in public and to seek reconciliation with all those he had wronged. He went on to become a major Anglican leader in Uganda and one of the most influential African evangelists of the twentieth century. In 1973, Kivengere was forced to flee Uganda due to conflict with the dictator Idi Amin (d. 2003), who had begun a crackdown on Anglican authorities. Like the Anglican archbishop Desmond Tutu (1931–2021) during the era of apartheid and white minority rule in South Africa, African Anglican leaders such as Kivengere often found themselves taking on political leadership in addition to their ministerial work. In 1975, Festo Kivengere was one of the featured evangelists at the Billy Graham-sponsored "Eurofest '75" assembly in Brussels, Belgium, along with the Argentinian-American evangelist Luis Palau (1934–2021). Kivengere would also assist the Billy Graham Evangelistic Association in Australia in the late 1970s. African Christianity was growing at unprecedented speed, and the influence of the East African Revival was spreading globally via emissaries such as Kivengere.

Other key leaders of the East African Revival, including Joe Church (1899–1989), an English medical missionary to Rwanda, and his Ugandan co-worker William Nagenda (1912–73), toured throughout Africa, Europe and beyond to teach others about the revival movement. One such visit by Church and Nagenda to London in 1948 established contacts with Martyn Lloyd-Jones's Westminster Chapel and John Stott's future parish of All Souls, Langham Place. In a 1953 tour of North America, Church, Nagenda, and others spoke at key evangelical congregations including Harold Ockenga's Park Street Church in Boston, Oswald Smith's (1889–1986) Peoples Church in Toronto, and A. W. Tozer's (1897–1963) Christian and Missionary Alliance church in Chicago. Word of African revival was spreading across North America and Britain.

Revival in Brazil

One of Church and his colleagues' stops in 1959 was Brazil, a country that has become one of the epicenters of Protestant growth and Pentecostal revival. Brazil was part of a broader story of people in Latin America since World War II switching from Catholicism to Protestantism (or, in some cases, attending both Catholic and Protestant services). In Africa, many countries had little Christian history prior to the missionary overtures of the 1800s. Central and South America had deep Catholic roots that dated to the Spanish and Portuguese conquest of the region in the 1500s. By the time it gained independence from Portugal in 1822, Brazil was widely Catholic, although the nature of that Catholicism was perhaps different from what Catholic missionary officials hoped. Strong influences of Brazilian indigenous and African religions remained, especially among the slaves who worked on Brazil's sugar plantations.

Traditional Protestant missionaries made relatively little impact in Brazil. Brazilian Baptists and Seventh-day Adventists saw notable growth in the twentieth century, with both groups claiming around 1.8 million adherents by 2020 in a country of 210 million people. (Southern Baptists founded the first Baptist church in Brazil in 1882.) But no Protestant group enjoyed the type of success seen by Pentecostal missionaries, who began arriving in the early 1910s. Between 1940 and 2020, the number of Protestants (evangélicos) in Brazil surged from under 3 percent to about 31 percent of the population. Most of that growth occurred among Pentecostals. Conversely, the number of Brazilian people identifying as Catholics dropped from 95 percent to 51 percent over the same period. Assuming that these numbers are reasonably accurate, and that the trend persists, it seems likely that Pentecostalism will soon overtake Catholicism as the largest faith in Brazil. (Brazil is not alone: the number of Protestants and Catholics in Guatemala is already almost equal.) Pentecostalism has become so pervasive in Brazil that it has helped transform Brazilian Catholicism into a faith deeply influenced by charismatic worship practices, too.

The Assemblies of God (AG) is the most prominent Pentecostal denomination in Brazil. It was also one of the first Pentecostal groups to begin in Brazil, founded by Swedish

Image 25.2. *Assembly of God church, Brazil*

Pentecostals who came to Brazil by way of Chicago. (The Brazilian AG is loosely affiliated with the US branch of the Assemblies of God.) Reflecting similar international origins, the Christian Congregation (CC) denomination began in Brazil in 1910 through the work of an Italian immigrant, again via Chicago. Luigi Francescon (1866–1964) originally preached (in Italian) to working-class Italians in São Paulo. For its first two decades, the CC catered largely to Italian immigrants. In the mid-1930s the denomination transitioned to services in Portuguese. It remained centered in São Paulo, the nation's largest city.

According to historian Paul Freston, Brazilian Pentecostalism entered a second major phase of growth in the 1950s, led by denominations such as The Church of the Four-Square Gospel (FSG). This denomination was originally founded in the 1920s in Los Angeles by the popular and controversial preacher Aimee Semple McPherson (1890–1944). (Four-Square referred to the church's belief in the four biblical roles of Jesus as "Savior, Baptizer with the Holy Spirit, Healer, and Soon-Coming King.") FSG missionaries arrived in Brazil in 1953. They emphasized physical and spiritual healing, somewhat to the exclusion of sin, hell, and judgment, doctrines which had been central for other Pentecostal churches. Befitting the church's founding by McPherson, the denomination was unusually open to having women serve as pastors. The FSG was joined in 1955 by Brazil for Christ, the first of the nation's prominent Pentecostal churches founded by a Brazilian, Manoel de Mello (1929–90), a former deacon in the AG.

A third major phase of Pentecostal growth and denomination-founding in Brazil came in the 1980s, led by groups such as Edir Macedo's (b. 1945) Universal Church of the Kingdom of God (founded 1977). Macedo, taking cues from American evangelical and Pentecostal leaders, had the Universal Church acquire its own television station in 1989. The denomination also became heavily involved in electoral politics. The politicization of Brazilian Pentecostals became a pronounced theme of this third phase, a theme that has endured through present day. Whereas many early Pentecostals were relatively apolitical, seeing civic engagement as a distraction from piety and evangelism, many Brazilian Pentecostals in recent decades have believed that Christians should use their electoral sway to influence culture and politics. The Universal Church has retained traditional Pentecostal emphases such as speaking in tongues. It has put an even stronger emphasis on exorcism and combatting demonic powers that Pentecostals associate with Umbanda, an indigenous and Afro-Brazilian spiritist religion. The Universal Church is also deeply influenced by prosperity theology, or the idea that God will reward obedience—especially faithful giving to the church—with physical health and material abundance. Critics have noted that Macedo and others in his family have become enormously wealthy, with Macedo's personal wealth in the mid-2010s exceeding $1 billion. The Universal Church also opened a $300 million replica of Solomon's Temple in São Paulo in 2014.

World Evangelization and the 1974 Lausanne Conference

Christian growth in Latin America, Africa, and East Asia was a source of encouragement for many in the relatively stagnant churches of Europe and the US. In the late twentieth century, Pentecostal churches became the fastest-growing ones in Europe and North America, too, especially among congregations catering to immigrant populations from Latin America and Africa. By the early 2000s, it was typical for some of the largest and fastest-growing megachurches in European cities, from Kiev to London, to be pastored by ministers from Africa. But the rapid growth of the churches in the Global South also caused some institutional discomfort in organizations historically used to white, Western leadership.

Such tensions marked the Billy Graham-sponsored International Congress on World Evangelization in Lausanne, Switzerland, in 1974. Lausanne drew on the long-standing evangelical concern that effective missions required coordination between the many agencies and denominations which had missionaries in the field. Evangelicals had taken an ever-larger role in Western missions since the early twentieth century, when modernists had increasingly begun to construe "missions" as Christian service, not as proselytizing non-Christians. By 1974, evangelicals represented some 85 percent of the missionary personnel sent out from the US. Indeed, many mainline church leaders (and some delegates at Lausanne) were calling for a moratorium on Western missions sending to the "Third World," in order to "decolonize" missions. Lausanne's organizers sought to move beyond the model of Edinburgh 1910, a meeting which had been almost exclusively composed of representatives from Europe and North America. Half of the 2700 delegates at Lausanne were from Africa, Asia, or Latin America. Lausanne delegates held a range of views about the priority of social action in missions. Virtually all delegates were conversionist, but some—particularly the Ecuadorian René Padilla (1932–2021) and the Peruvian Samuel Escobar (b. 1934)—believed that social ministry was an essential aspect of missions, too. American and British delegates such as Carl Henry and John Stott tended to play mediating roles between social justice advocates and those who believed that evangelism alone should be the focus of missions.

Padilla came from an evangelical family in Ecuador, and as a teenager he briefly served alongside the American missionaries Jim Elliot, Nate Saint, and Pete Fleming, a group later killed when they sought to make evangelistic overtures to the Huaorani people of Ecuador. Padilla also became a translator for Billy Graham crusades across Latin America in the 1960s. At Lausanne, Padilla brought a critical word for missionaries and sending agencies, many of whom operated with an overly Western mindset, he argued. Citing Dietrich Bonhoeffer, Padilla contended that American missionaries in particular were selling "cheap grace" and merely trying to secure professions of faith. The watered-down American model of missions "can only be the basis for unfaithful churches, for strongholds of racial and class discrimination, for religious clubs with a message that has no relevance to practical life in the social, the economic, and the political spheres," Padilla concluded. Padilla and others created an ad hoc group at the congress to focus on "Theology and Implications of Radical Discipleship." The group issued its own statement alongside the general meeting's Lausanne Covenant. The statement declared that the "attempt to drive a wedge between evangelism and social action" was "demonic." Some leaders, such as John Stott, signed both documents.

For traditional evangelicals, there were many possible reasons to criticize the historic missions movement, including its tendency to confuse Western cultural norms with biblical mandates. There were also reasons to criticize evangelistic methods such as those employed by Billy Graham: mass meetings that generated many responses but which (despite the efforts of Graham's organization) often led to little follow-up or discipleship. Still, many at Lausanne agreed that proclamation of the gospel to non-Christians had to remain the center of missionary work because personal faith in Christ was God's exclusive path to salvation. This meant the difference between an eternity in heaven or hell. Conversionists may have sympathized with the call to make missions less Western and more focused on biblical discipleship, yet the call to gospel proclamation remained preeminent.

The most influential conversionist idea highlighted at Lausanne was that of "unreached people groups." Christ had commanded his followers to "make disciples of all nations," which missions advocates widely interpreted as common linguistic and cultural groups. Organizations such as Fuller Seminary's School of World Mission and Wycliffe Bible Translators (founded in 1942), helped to popularize the idea that there were many people groups in the world that lacked an indigenous gospel witness and/or a vernacular translation of the Bible. Though such advocates would not overtly support a moratorium on missions to "reached" groups, they did question why so much funding and personnel went to countries where there were already healthy churches, translated Bibles, and functioning Christian leadership. Why not focus on reaching peoples among whom Christ was not yet proclaimed?

The Lausanne Covenant ultimately reflected the ongoing primacy of evangelism, as well as evangelical tenets such as the authority of Scripture and Christ's unique character as Lord and Savior. (Framers of the Covenant decided to speak of the "infallible" nature of Scripture, an older and less controversial term than "inerrant.") The statement readily conceded the need for justice, reconciliation, and "liberation of men and women from every kind of oppression." "Liberation theology" was becoming a commonly used phrase in Latin American Catholicism. The use of the term "liberation" in the Covenant reflected the conviction that evangelicals should take what lessons they could from the liberation movement. "Although reconciliation with other people is not reconciliation with God," the Covenant stated, "nor is social action evangelism, nor is political liberation salvation, nevertheless we affirm that evangelism and socio-political involvement are both part of our Christian duty." However, the signatories concluded, "in the Church's mission of sacrificial service, evangelism is primary." Critics such as Padilla regarded the Lausanne Movement as something of a disappointment, with many leaders from the US in particular having "sidestepped the whole issue of social concern."

Evangelicals and Politics in the US

Evangelicals across time and place have always been involved in politics and social concerns, from the campaign against slavery, to temperance, to the anti-evolution crusade. The debate at Lausanne was more a question of what kinds of political and social concerns should be addressed and whether those concerns were as central to missions as was evangelism per se. Indeed, the years around 1974 represented a critical turning point for US evangelicals, who remained the most culturally and financially powerful evangelical community in the world. Since the 1950s, Billy Graham had been a power broker in politics, especially in the Republican Party. He had developed an especially close relationship with Richard Nixon (1913–94). Graham remained one of Nixon's staunchest supporters, even as the Watergate scandal engulfed Nixon's presidency, leading to Nixon's resignation in 1974, a couple weeks after the Lausanne meeting concluded. Evangelicals and Catholics in the US were still reeling from the Supreme Court's decision in *Roe v. Wade* in 1973, which affirmed a constitutional right to abortion. It is an often-repeated myth that evangelicals were initially silent about *Roe v. Wade*. The National Association of Evangelicals and *Christianity Today* both criticized the decision.

Although Jimmy Carter still successfully wooed many white southern evangelical voters in the 1976 election, Ronald Reagan and other Republican leaders had begun to recruit evangelical voters into the deepest core of the party's base. As seen in the case of Brazil's Pentecostals, there was nothing unique or unprecedented about a Christian movement becoming overtly engaged in partisan politics. But the white American evangelical mobilization around issues such as the pro-life cause and its 1980 fusion with Reagan's Republican Party would have cascading implications for US denominations and the global evangelical movement for decades to come.

Selected Bibliography

Anderson, Allan. *To the Ends of the Earth: Pentecostalism and the Transformation of World Christianity*. Oxford: Oxford University Press, 2013.

Atherstone, Andrew, and David Ceri Jones, eds. *Engaging with Martyn Lloyd-Jones. The Life and Legacy of 'The Doctor.'* Nottingham, UK: Apollos, 2011.

Chapman, Alister. *Godly Ambition: John Stott and the Evangelical Movement*. New York: Oxford University Press, 2011.

Freston, Paul. "Pentecostalism in Brazil: A Brief History." *Religion* 25 (1995): 119–33.

Jenkins, Philip. *God's Continent: Christianity, Islam, and Europe's Religious Crisis*. New York: Oxford University Press, 2007.

McAlister, Melani. *The Kingdom of God Has No Borders: A Global History of American Evangelicals*. New York: Oxford University Press, 2018.

Peterson, Derek R. "The East African Revival." In *The Oxford History of Anglicanism, Volume V: Global Anglicanism, c. 1910–2000*, edited by William L. Sachs, 211–31. Oxford: Oxford University Press, 2017.

Schmidt, Bettina, and Steven Engler, eds. *Handbook of Contemporary Religions in Brazil*. Leiden, The Netherlands: Brill, 2016.

Stanley, Brian. *The Global Diffusion of Evangelicalism: The Age of Billy Graham and John Stott*. Downers Grove: IVP Academic, 2013.

Wacker, Grant. *America's Pastor: Billy Graham and the Shaping of a Nation*. Cambridge: Harvard University Press, 2014.

Chapter 26

Civil Rights, Liberation Theology, and Culture War

Church history is commonly a story of churches changing in tandem with culture. Sometimes the church (as in the Reformation or the Great Awakening) molds culture, but often culture molds the church. A culture molding the church can be damaging, as seen in cases of churches' forced capitulation to dictatorial fascists and communists in the twentieth century. Sometimes culture influences the church in morally neutral ways, such as Christians' adaptation of the printing press or electricity. But one can hardly think of an era when Christian churches and the dominant culture, at least in the West, went through such profound social changes as the time from the 1950s to the 1970s. This was an era of convulsions including civil rights, sexual revolution, liberation theology, and (in the Catholic context) the titanic changes inaugurated by Vatican II. By the 1970s, the transformations wrought in Western culture and churches were profound, precipitating major conservative reactions in both Catholic and Protestant circles.

The Catholic Church and Vatican II

Perhaps the most significant structural reforms in Christendom during the 1960s came at the Vatican II assembly. Few would have predicted beforehand the upheavals that resulted from it. (The First Vatican Council was held in 1869–70.) Pope John XXIII (1881–1963), the former Cardinal Angelo Roncalli, had been elected in 1958. For a hundred and fifty years, the papacy had largely been a conservative institution, fighting against threats such as modernism and communism. At the time of his appointment, Catholic cardinals did not envision the seventy-six-year-old John XXIII as an epoch-making pope, but they were wrong. The pope summoned more than two thousand bishops to Rome for the new council in 1962. The assembly invited observers including some Protestants and Catholic women, who would not have been allowed at previous Catholic assemblies of this type. (Baptists were the only major Protestant tradition that declined to send observers.) John XXIII died in 1963, well before the council concluded, but he had set in motion a reformist impulse that traditionalists could not stop. The consequences of Vatican II were massive, complex, and subject to enduring debate. But some implications were clear: the delegates endorsed the concept of religious freedom, backing away from the historic view that Catholic nations ought to employ government force to suppress heresy and dissent. They also made major steps toward encouraging dialogue and tolerance of Protestants, Orthodox Christians, and non-Christians. Although the council left no doubt that the Catholic Church remained the unique guardian of truth, they only asserted that the true Church "subsists in" the Roman Catholic communion, headed by the pope. They even suggested that some "who do not know the Gospel of Christ or His Church" could be saved, if they genuinely sought God on the basis of what they did know about him.

Perhaps the change that made the biggest difference in the weekly lives of everyday Catholics was the encouragement for priests to celebrate mass in vernacular languages instead of using the traditional Latin. To many observers, this seemed like a dramatic turn toward the Protestant style of communicating the faith in the languages of the people. In Latin American-majority parishes in Houston, Texas, for example, priests began saying mass in Spanish by the late 1960s, but the overall tenor of the mass changed, too. In Houston's St. Joseph-St. Stephen Parish, Father Patricio Flores (1929–2017) introduced Spanish-language services and musical styles popular in Mexico and Hispanic Texas, including the use of a mariachi folk band to lead worship. Such changes did not necessarily foster enduring growth in mass attendance, but they undoubtedly helped to make Catholic services more recognizable in local contexts across the globe. For decades, however, some Catholic traditionalists regretted the loss of the Latin mass. They argued that the Latin mass should at least remain an option when parishioners preferred it.

Civil Rights and the American Church

The cultural transformations of the 1960s on civil rights inexorably affected all Catholic and Protestant churches. Sometimes churches helped to drive the changes. For example, the civil rights movement in the United States was inseparably connected with African American churches. In many ways, civil rights represented a continuation of moral reform movements dating to the antislavery crusades of the eighteenth and nineteenth centuries. In the early twentieth century, black churches had denounced the epidemic of lynchings and extralegal murders of black men that swept the nation, especially the South, through the 1920s. Black-led denominations such as the National Baptist Convention (1895) often found that though they shared similar theology with their counterparts in denominations such as the Southern Baptist Convention, leaders of majority-white denominations were commonly silent, equivocal, or complicit regarding the lynchings. Few white Christian leaders spoke against the segregation of public facilities across the nation under America's "Jim Crow" system, either. Not even the black churches could agree about the best approach to civil rights reform, however. One such disagreement led Baptist pastor Martin Luther King Jr. and his allies to break away from the National Baptist Convention USA (formed in 1916) and form the Progressive National Baptist Convention in 1961. Unlike the leaders of the National Baptist Convention, King and his supporters favored direct confrontation, marches, and sit-ins to challenge Jim Crow, instead of relying mainly on legislation and court cases to dismantle the legal system behind segregation.

King and similar advocates hoped that by provoking clashes with bigoted officials and white supremacists, civil rights activists could mobilize white moderate Christians on issues such as segregation. These Christians might sympathize with black complaints against the injustices of the segregationist and biased law enforcement systems, but they still advised caution and moderate reform. King specifically addressed his "dear fellow clergymen"—particularly white moderates—in his classic "Letter from Birmingham Jail" (1963). He spoke to those who expressed tentative support for civil rights leaders but simultaneously called their protests "unwise and untimely." King explained why blacks could no longer "wait" for reform, since in American history waiting usually turned into excuses for sustaining immoral systems. Citing sources including Augustine, Thomas Aquinas, and Reinhold Niebuhr, King argued that African Americans had waited "more than 340 years for our constitutional and God given rights." The time for waiting was over.

As influential as King was, he was also just one of thousands of civil rights activists in African American churches during the post–World War II era. Many of these activists were women, such as the Mississippi Baptist Fannie Lou Hamer (1917–77). Hamer's father was a Baptist preacher on a cotton plantation, and most of her literacy and learning came from attending Baptist churches. In 1961, Hamer was subjected to a hysterectomy without her consent, an all-too-common procedure performed on poor black women during that period. Hamer, grieved over this humiliating violation, began attending civil rights meetings in Ruleville, Mississippi, and organizing efforts for blacks to register to vote. She rose to national prominence when she appeared on television and challenged Mississippi's all-white delegation at the 1964 Democratic National Convention. Hamer framed her activism in biblical language, once even warning white policemen who beat her in a Mississippi jailhouse that they were going to be "miserable" when they had to "face God" at their deaths. She explained to her fellow civil rights workers that she believed they were exemplifying Christ's teaching that the church would be as a city on a hill, and a beacon that could not be hidden. "I don't hide that I'm fighting for freedom because Christ died to set us free," she declared.

> Hate won't only destroy us. It will destroy these people that's hating as well . . . You know the Scripture says "be not deceived for God is not mocked; whatsoever a man sow that shall he also reap."
>
> ---
>
> Fannie Lou Hamer, "Interview with Fannie Lou Hamer," *Freedomways*, Spring, 1965.

Unlike King, most civil rights activists such as Fannie Lou Hamer did not go to seminary, but they commonly had a biblicist theology formed by upbringing in the black church. There was also an emerging strain of formal black theology animating the work of leaders such as King, however. Perhaps the most influential African American theologian of the early civil rights era was King's mentor Howard Thurman (1899–1981), the dean of chapel at Boston University while King was doing his doctoral work there. Thurman had grown up in the black Baptist tradition in Florida. After attending Morehouse College in Atlanta, he received ordination as a Baptist minister and graduated from Colgate Rochester Theological Seminary, an American Baptist institution. Thurman gravitated toward an interfaith, modernist theology, however, especially after studying in 1929 with the Quaker theologian Rufus Jones (1863–1948) at Haverford College in Pennsylvania. Thurman became the dean of chapel at Howard University in Washington, DC, one of the most influential historically black universities in the country. In 1936, Thurman traveled to India where he met the anticolonial independence leader Mohandas Gandhi (1869–1948), who urged Thurman to bring Gandhi's teachings on nonviolent resistance to bear on the civil rights campaign in America. Thurman's most influential book was *Jesus and the Disinherited* (1949), which cast Jesus as a prophetic figure who advocated on behalf of the persecuted and oppressed people of the world.

Image 26.1. *Fannie Lou Hamer*

Following on the work of Thurman, the theologian James Cone (1938–2018) was arguably the most influential advocate of black liberationist thought in the civil rights era. "Liberation theology" first emerged from Latin American Catholicism in the 1960s, popularized especially by the priest Gustavo Gutiérrez's (b. 1928) book *A Theology of Liberation* (originally published in Peru in 1971). Gutiérrez and other liberation theologians and activists argued that ministry to the poor was not just one obligation of the church; the plight of the poor and oppressed should be the primary focus of the church. Liberation theologians cited Jesus's messianic proclamation of "good news to the poor" in Luke 4:18 as evidence of the centrality of liberation to the faith. They called their approach the "preferential option for the poor." Not that the church should despise or exclude wealthy people, but it should prioritize the needs and struggles of those whom the world oppresses and exploits. Gutiérrez himself had come out of an impoverished background as a person of mixed Spanish-indigenous ethnicity in Lima, Peru. He and his allies in the Catholic Church mixed Marxist philosophy about the structures of oppression with the Christian mandate to love your neighbor as yourself. Liberation theology's connection with Marxism led many Catholic leaders (most notably Joseph Ratzinger (1927–2022), the future Pope Benedict XVI) to register concern about this type of theology. While Gutiérrez and others had valid concerns about the poor, Marxist philosophy was fundamentally incompatible with Christian belief, the traditionalists warned.

Black liberation theologians picked up on the theme of the struggle of the oppressed against wealthy elites. They applied such ideas to the crusade for civil rights in America, in apartheid-era South Africa, and elsewhere. Especially after the assassination of Martin Luther King Jr., in Memphis in 1968, the civil rights movement turned more militant, questioning the value of Thurman and King's nonviolent resistance. Advocates like James Cone, who taught at Union Theological Seminary in New York, argued that care for the poor was not some quaint Christian mandate, but that liberation of the oppressed "is the gospel of Jesus Christ." In books such as *A Black Theology of Liberation* (1970), Cone declared that "any theology that is indifferent to the theme of liberation is not Christian theology." Moreover, liberation theology in America was fundamentally black theology, he taught, because oppression in American history ran along lines of race as much as those of class. Cone candidly wrote that his work was for the benefit of black readers, not whites, who were the audience traditionally presumed for most theology books. Cone said that "there will be no peace in America until white people begin to hate their whiteness, asking from the depths of their being: 'How can we become black?'" Black liberation theology, proponents such as Cone believed, was effectively a response to the moral failings of white-hued theology. The appearance of black liberationism was "due exclusively to the failure of white religionists to relate the gospel of Jesus to the pain of being black in a white racist society." Like Gutiérrez, Cone's views were shaped by his early years living in an impoverished, small, segregated Arkansas town in the 1940s and '50s.

Forms of liberation theology had parallels in the feminist and gay rights movements. Women had gained the right to vote in much of Europe and North America in the 1910s, culminating in the passage of the Nineteenth Amendment to the US Constitution in 1920. But by the 1960s there was a sense that women still lacked legal and economic equality with men. Many people wanted to give women legal access to abortion, despite traditional Protestant and Catholic resistance to abortion on demand as a means to terminate unwanted pregnancies. Within many denominations, there was also a push to ordain women as pastors and priests. Feminist theologians ranged from those who wanted women to have access to all churchly offices, to more radical voices who criticized Christianity and the Bible as inherently patriarchal and misogynist. Some rejected Christianity outright, due to men's traditional power in the churches and biblical passages such as the New Testament's ordinances for women's roles in the church and family. One of the most radical feminist theologians was the Catholic writer and activist Mary Daly (1928–2010), who taught at Boston College, a Jesuit institution. A self-described "radical lesbian feminist," Daly often restricted her courses to women students only. She indicted the Catholic Church for its millennia of complicity in the systematic oppression of women. Daly eventually drifted away from the Catholic faith, rejecting all forms of organized Christianity as inherently patriarchal and describing herself as a "post-Christian" thinker.

Most Protestants and Catholics influenced by feminist theology were not as radical as Daly. Some believed that a correct reading of Scripture would confirm "egalitarian" views of both marriage and roles in the church. The Evangelical Women's Caucus (1974), for example, affirmed both the authority of the Bible and the idea that all church offices should be open to women. Such groups often found it difficult to limit their activism to feminist concerns alone, however. In 1986, the Evangelical Women's Caucus split when the group endorsed the addition of "civil-rights protection for homosexual persons" to its roster of priorities. More conservative members were concerned that this would eventually entail affirmation of same-sex amorous relationships. More moderate feminists formed the Christians for Biblical Equality (CBE) organization in 1988. This organization served as a sort of doctrinal foil to the Council on Biblical Manhood and Womanhood (CBMW), founded a year earlier by leaders such as the Minneapolis-based Baptist pastor John Piper (b. 1946), and theologian Wayne Grudem (b. 1948), then of Trinity Evangelical Divinity School. The CBMW articulated the "complementarian" view that women and men were equal before God but that the Bible explicitly called them to complementary (non-identical) roles in the church and family.

Christianity and Postliberalism

The proliferating liberal ideas of the 1960s found their fullest expression in the "death of God" theology, pioneered by Thomas Altizer (1927–2018) of Emory University and William Hamilton (1924–2012) of Colgate Rochester Divinity School. They were echoing themes once developed by the radical German philosopher Friedrich Nietzsche. Altizer posited the possibility of "Christian atheism," writing that "it is the Christian who must murder God, or, rather, it is the Christian who must bury the decomposing God who continues to haunt our memory." Hamilton argued that Christians "do not know, do not adore, do not possess, do not believe in God . . . God is dead." This assertion was connected to a radical reinterpretation of the death of Jesus on the cross. On the cross, God actually died. In the resurrection he only came back in spirit as an inspiring example for others to fight for liberation of the oppressed. The "Death of God" theology earned a cover story in *TIME* magazine in 1966, but it proved to be somewhat ephemeral and easily dismissed by anyone with a stake in the great tradition of Christian theology. (Pastors undoubtedly realized that telling their congregations that God was dead was a surefire way to kill a church, too.) Evangelicals such as Denver Seminary's Vernon Grounds (1914–2010) mocked death of God doctrine as "graveyard theology" and "brash infidelity." If anything, death of God theology exacerbated the rift between traditionalists and many mainline religion departments and divinity schools. Some Methodists called for Altizer to be fired, but Emory officials explained that Altizer was free to express his views, especially since he was in the school's religion department and not in Emory's Candler School of Theology, which was traditionally focused on training Methodist pastors.

Some "postliberal" theologians continued Karl Barth's legacy of rejecting the excesses of modernist theology without embracing an inerrantist view of Scripture. The postliberal movement in the late twentieth century was centered at Yale Divinity School, especially in the work of Hans Frei (1922–88) and George Lindbeck (1923–2018). Frei came from a secular Jewish background in Berlin, but his family moved to America in the late 1930s to escape the rising Nazi menace. While studying at a Quaker school in England as a teenager, Frei became a Christian. In America, Frei went to Yale to study with H. Richard Niebuhr, eventually completing a doctorate on Karl Barth. Frei worked initially as a Baptist minister in New Hampshire but soon gravitated to the Episcopal Church. He received a faculty appointment at Yale in 1957.

Frei became best known for his 1974 book *The Eclipse of Biblical Narrative*, a study of the changing nature of hermeneutics (the study of biblical interpretation) during the eighteenth and nineteenth centuries. Frei posited that prior to the rise of higher criticism, there was a precritical consensus which assumed that the realistic (or "history-like") narratives in the Gospels and other books were sources of reliable information about God's dealings with humankind. "The words and sentences [in biblical narratives] meant what they said, and because they did so they accurately described real events and real truths that were rightly put only in those terms and no others," Frei argued. There was, within this consensus, no sharp division between the literary, historical, and providential understandings of Scripture. But higher criticism and the naturalistic tendencies within the skeptical Enlightenment fractured this consensus by primarily analyzing Scriptural narratives for their correspondence with (or lack of correspondence with) the "real" history behind the account. Frei proposed suspending the critical obsession with facts and historicity behind Gospel narratives and reading them the way the church had read them for centuries: as realistic, history-like accounts of the life of Jesus.

Frei's Yale colleague George Lindbeck grew up in China and Korea as the son of American Lutheran missionaries. A Lutheran observer at the Vatican II assembly, Lindbeck saw his work in the context of ecumenical relations, especially between Protestants and Catholics. His best-known book was *The Nature of Doctrine: Religion and Theology in a Postliberal Age* (1984), a work that helped to popularize the concept of postliberal theology. Borrowing from the work of the anthropologist Clifford Geertz (1926–2006) and the linguistic philosopher Ludwig Wittgenstein (1889–1951), Lindbeck argued that religion (including Christianity) was neither a set of doctrinal beliefs nor feelings related to the divine. In other words, both the conservative and modernist traditions had it wrong. Instead, religion was what Lindbeck called a "cultural-linguistic" system, or framework. There was no way to understand a religion without comprehending it in its historical and cultural context. Religions were not universal, instead they were profoundly grounded in the culture in which they were practiced. A religion was "not primarily an array of beliefs about the true and the good (though it may involve these), or a symbolism expressive of basic attitudes, feelings, or sentiments (though these will be generated)," Lindbeck explained. "Rather, it is similar to an idiom that makes possible the description of realities, the formulation of beliefs, and the experiencing of inner attitudes, feelings, and sentiments. Like a culture or language, it is a communal phenomenon that shapes the subjectivities of individuals." For Lindbeck, this cultural-linguistic quality of religion made it possible for postliberal believers to fully inhabit their religious tradition while setting aside the sort of universal truth claims that had caused so much conflict in the Christian past. At least in the US, Lindbeck's work set the terms of debate for much of the scholarly discussion of the nature of religion and doctrine for the next half century.

For many conservative Protestants, of course, the idea that Christianity was primarily a "cultural-linguistic system" was no more satisfying than Schleiermacher's emphasis on individual religious experience. Figures such as Carl Henry continued to argue that Scripture indeed revealed propositional truths, ones that applied universally to all humankind. One of the most influential of the mid-twentieth century's advocates for apologetics in this traditional vein was Cornelius Van Til, a former faculty member at Princeton Seminary and co-founder of Westminster Seminary with J. Gresham Machen. Many regard Van Til as the father of "presuppositional" apologetics, a perspective that has exercised enormous influence on popular evangelical thought since World War II. Van Til contended that truth was universal but that a person could only apprehend that truth by employing correct underlying presuppositions about God, man, and the Bible. In *The Defense of the Faith* (1955), Van Til argued that the essential issue in philosophy and theology was what presuppositions a person holds. "When man became a sinner he made of himself instead of God the ultimate or final reference point. And it is precisely this presupposition, as it controls without exception all forms of non-Christian philosophy, that must be brought into question." Every other thought system—even naturalistic reasoning about God—was man-centered and internally incoherent; only belief in God's sovereign will and his revelation in Scripture was the perfectly consistent philosophical system.

The Battle over Inerrancy

The world of evangelical scholarship was varied in its views of biblical authority, apologetics, the work of Karl Barth (whom Cornelius Van Til had denounced), and other key issues. But among many rank-and-file American evangelicals, including key theologians and pastors, there was a growing sense by the 1960s that lines needed to be drawn once again on the fundamentals of the faith, particularly regarding the inerrancy of Scripture. As we have seen, the battle over inerrancy had been fought (and generally lost) by fundamentalists in the major northern-based denominations in the early twentieth century. But the issue continued to fester in denominations such as the traditionalist Lutheran Church, Missouri Synod, and at evangelical institutions such as Gordon-Conwell Seminary and Fuller Seminary. (Gordon-Conwell, located in Hamilton, Massachusetts, was founded in 1969 in a merger of older Christian institutions.) Fuller dropped its requirement of belief in inerrancy during the 1960s in favor of the more flexible ideas of "divine inspiration" and infallibility.

Questions of inerrancy and higher criticism became especially pressing in the Southern Baptist Convention and its seminaries, starting in the 1950s. Growing concerns about modernist faculty were highlighted by the dismissal of thirteen professors at the Southern Baptist Theological Seminary in Louisville in 1958. But this was only the first of a series of episodes in which traditionalists in the SBC confronted reports that its seminaries were promoting higher critical views of the Bible, views that many SBC pastors and laypeople would have regarded as extreme or incomprehensible. In 1961, Ralph Elliott (1925–2022), formerly of Southern Seminary but now on faculty at the newly-opened Midwestern Baptist Theological Seminary in Kansas City, Missouri, published his book *The Message of Genesis* with a denominational press. The book dismissed the historicity of basic events and persons in Genesis, including Adam and Eve, Noah's flood, and God's command to Abraham to sacrifice Isaac. All these had spiritual meaning but could not be taken as literal history. Midwestern trustees fired Elliott in 1962. The denomination's "Baptist Faith and Message," originally adopted in 1925, already spoke of the Bible as having no "mixture of error." A 1963 revision did not do much more to exclude Baptist modernists. Soon, however, an interdenominational coalition of evangelical scholars, pastors, and writers determined that they needed to codify the meaning of inerrancy.

The product of the inerrantists' work was the Chicago Statement on Biblical Inerrancy (1978). The SBC's troubles over the Bible were loosely connected to broader American evangelical anxiety in the mid-1970s over what appeared to be a growing acceptance of non-inerrantist views in seminaries and among denominational leaders. Harold Lindsell (1913–98), Carl Henry's successor as editor of *Christianity Today*, bridged the gap between the SBC and the broader evangelical world, a community which tended to be dominated by northern figures such as Henry. Lindsell was born in New York City. He both studied and taught at Wheaton College in Illinois. But Lindsell was ordained as a Southern Baptist minister in South Carolina and had been a member at various SBC churches across the country. In his provocative book *The Battle for the Bible* (1976), Lindsell expressed special concern about the status of the SBC. The denomination "has numbers of people in it who deny biblical infallibility. They are challenging the historic position of the denomination and constitute a threat to its future," Lindsell warned. "Not only so, but it will be shown that some who have abandoned biblical inerrancy have also abandoned other cardinal doctrines of the Christian faith so that in any historic sense they have ceased to be Baptists as understood traditionally." In Lindsell's work among Southern Baptists and at *Christianity Today*, one began to see a synthesis of concerns that would help to produce the SBC's "Conservative Resurgence." By the mid-1980s, leaders of the Conservative Resurgence had started to transform the denomination into a far more uniformly evangelical organization than it was in the 1960s.

Prompted by Lindsell's arguments about the weakening of biblical authority in the evangelical world, the influential pastor James Montgomery Boice (1938–2000) of Tenth Presbyterian Church in Philadelphia (a graduate of Princeton Seminary and the University of Basel), organized the meeting in Chicago in 1978 to define the doctrine of inerrancy. In a series of affirmations and denials, the Chicago statement contended that inerrancy has always been an essential doctrine of the Church and was a characteristic belief of the apostles and authors of the biblical books. "We affirm that the doctrine of inerrancy has been integral to the Church's Faith throughout its history, from the Apostles and Church Fathers through the Reformers to the present day," they declared. "We deny that inerrancy is a doctrine invented by Scholastic Protestantism, or is a reactionary position postulated in response to negative higher criticism." Organizers and signers included well-known evangelical educators and preachers including Harold Ockenga, J. I. Packer, and Luis Palau; as well as D. A. Carson (b. 1946), professor at Trinity Evangelical Divinity School; Jack Hayford (1934–2023), a prominent Pentecostal minister in California; Hal Lindsey (b. 1929), the most popular eschatology writer of the 1970s; John MacArthur (b. 1939), an influential Bible teacher and pastor of Grace Community Church in California; the popular Christian apologist Francis Schaeffer (1912–84); R. C. Sproul (1939–2017), the head of Ligonier Ministries and a pastor in the newly-formed (1973) Presbyterian Church in America; and a number of Baptist leaders in the incipient Conservative Resurgence, including W. A. Criswell (1909–2002) of First Baptist Church Dallas and Paige Patterson (b. 1942), then the president of Criswell College in Dallas.

A number of moderate evangelicals (including many in Britain and Europe) either rejected inerrancy or did not wish to make it a test of faith. Even if these critics did not believe that the original Bible manuscripts contained errors per se, they thought that inerrancy depended too much on a concept developed primarily by nineteenth-century Princeton theologians, especially B. B. Warfield. They argued that the term inerrancy itself had virtually no role in the great tradition prior to the 1800s. Of course, none of the ancient and medieval documents of that tradition were written in modern English vernacular, thus the exact term "inerrancy" was not an option in those sources. But many figures from the Apostle Paul to Augustine to Luther spoke in their various languages of Scripture being "God-breathed," "perfect," "without error," etc. Inerrancy, especially in the American context, has become a hallmark of conservative evangelical belief. It is the official position of a range of denominations including the SBC (post-Conservative Resurgence), the Presbyterian Church in America, the Assemblies of God, and the Lutheran Church, Missouri Synod (the second-largest Lutheran denomination in America), as well as the Evangelical Theological Society.

The Legacy of John Paul II

Protestants and Catholics, then, both saw in the 1960s and '70s a great waxing of liberalizing tendencies, typically matched by important traditionalist reactions. (Of course, major doctrinal differences remained between Protestant and Catholic conservatives, too). We will speak more about the Conservative Resurgence in the next chapter, but among Catholics perhaps the most significant conservative development of the post-Vatican II period was

Image 26.2. *John Paul II visit to US, 1979*

the selection of Karol Wojtyla as Pope John Paul II in 1978. The Polish Wojtyla was the first non-Italian selected as pope in more than 450 years. Wojtyla trained for the priesthood at a secret Catholic seminary that Polish resisters kept open during the Nazi occupation of the early 1940s, receiving his ordination in 1946. During the 1950s he served as priest and bishop in Krakow, Poland, while also teaching at the Catholic University of Lublin, the only Catholic college to remain open in Soviet-dominated Eastern Europe. As a scholar and priest, Wojtyla was convinced that the Catholic heritage of Thomist thought and Christian humanism—a deeply Christian view of the value of human life—was the intellectual and spiritual answer to the challenges of Marxism, fascism, and the horrid outbreaks of war and persecution in the first half of the twentieth century. In 1963, Pope Paul VI appointed Wojtyla as the Archbishop of Krakow.

Paul VI died in 1978. Then his first replacement, Pope John Paul I, died almost immediately after taking office. The papal conclave chose Wojtyla as the new pope, and he took the name John Paul II. Perhaps the central theme of John Paul II's papacy was the God-given dignity of every human life, from conception to death. This foundational belief undergirded all the pope's views of war, peace, and human rights, and particularly the Cold War threats of Soviet oppression and nuclear annihilation. John Paul II's version of Christian humanism also made him a strong foe of abortion, which was becoming a legalized norm in the secular West after changes like the US Supreme Court decision in *Roe v. Wade*. (The Soviet Union had been a pioneer on the matter, legalizing abortion in 1955.) In his pro-life convictions, John Paul II was echoing and rejuvenating the official stance of the Catholic Church. He also complemented the pro-life ethos of leading Catholic missionaries such as Mother Teresa (1910–97), who ministered to lepers and other people in extreme poverty in India for much of the twentieth century. Mother Teresa said that abortion was the world's "worst evil and the greatest enemy of peace" when accepting the Nobel Peace Prize in 1976.

John Paul II also played an essential role in resistance against communist rule in his native Poland, making a triumphant tour of the country in 1979 that helped to spawn the "Solidarity" anti-communist movement there. In 1981, a gunman with connections to Soviet intelligence shot but did not kill the pope in an assassination attempt at St. Peter's Square. Across eastern Europe, the pope became a symbol of anti-communist resistance, especially for Catholics. When Soviet premier Mikhail Gorbachev (1931–2022) visited John Paul II at the Vatican in 1989, it was a tacit admission of the moral victory of the pope's Christian humanism over atheistic communism. The Berlin Wall had just come down in East Germany, and two years later the Soviet Union itself would collapse.

John Paul II also gave more direct attention to Latin America than any previous pope. Central and South America had become major centers of world Catholicism over the centuries of Spanish and Portuguese imperialism, a cultural legacy that continued after national independence movements swept the region in the early 1800s. But the papacy's physical distance from Latin America had largely prevented papal visits there until long-distance air travel became feasible. John Paul II repeatedly visited Latin America, including five trips to Mexico, where in 2002 the pope canonized Juan Diego as a saint. (Juan Diego, as we have seen, was reported to have received apparitions of the Virgin Mary in 1531, experiences which became the basis of the widespread devotion to Our Lady of Guadalupe.) Juan Diego was the first indigenous person from the Americas to be recognized as a saint by the Catholic Church.

John Paul II was attentive to the global Catholic Church in an unprecedented way, but he also registered grave doubts about developments associated with liberation theology. In a 1984 statement issued by the Congregation for the Doctrine of the Faith, headed by future pope Joseph Ratzinger and approved by John Paul II, the papacy warned about aberrant theology which was inspired by genuine care for the poor and oppressed but which embraced anti-Christian Marxist philosophy "in an insufficiently critical manner." They warned that "atheism and the denial of the human person, his liberty and rights, are at the core of the Marxist theory." Any "authentic theology of liberation will be one which is rooted in the Word of God, correctly interpreted." In a Catholic context, this "correct interpretation" meant as interpreted by authorized church authority, in light of church tradition. The impact of John Paul II's papacy was undeniable, but even some traditionalist critics noted that the pope did not do much to address the church's systemic global problems with clerical sexual abuse. To cite one example, John Paul II was made aware of allegations of serial sexual misconduct with seminarians and sexual abuse of boys by Cardinal Theodore McCarrick (b. 1930), Archbishop of Washington, DC, but the pope did not believe the charges and did not act. Catholic officials ultimately removed McCarrick from the priesthood in 2019.

Conclusion

In the post–World War II era, then, churches across a wide range of denominations and confessions grappled with challenges including secularizing elite culture, communism, and issues related to poverty, ethnic inequality, and political oppression. Some churchly responses to these challenges advocated radical theological adjustments, such as liberation theology, ones that traditionalists regarded as extreme, worldly, and violations of biblical-historic orthodoxy. Perhaps the greatest dilemma for traditional Christians in recent decades has been responding forcefully to the social and intellectual problems of a secularizing West without uncritically adopting answers offered by secular elites. Marxism, in particular, possessed an all-embracing theory that explained the root of oppression and inequality of all kinds (class struggle and the power of capitalist elites, who used religion as a tool of oppression). But could Christians import Marxism, or Marxist-informed theory, into the church, and remain distinctively Christian at the same time? Traditionalists were skeptical that they could.

Selected Bibliography

Bradley, Anthony B. *Liberating Black Theology: The Bible and the Black Experience in America.* Wheaton, IL: Crossway, 2010.

Brooks, Maegen Parker, and Davis W. Houck, eds. *The Speeches of Fannie Lou Hamer: To Tell It Like It Is.* Jackson: University Press of Mississippi, 2011.

Cannon, Katie G., and Anthony B. Pinn, eds. *The Oxford Handbook of African American Theology*. New York: Oxford University Press, 2014.

Harvey, Paul. *Howard Thurman and the Disinherited: A Religious Biography*. Grand Rapids: Eerdmans, 2020.

Holmes, Stephen R. "Evangelical Doctrines in Scripture in Transatlantic Perspective." *Evangelical Quarterly* 81, no. 1 (2009): 38–63.

Lamb, Matthew L., and Matthew Levering, eds. *Vatican II: Renewal Within Tradition*. New York: Oxford University Press, 2008.

Merrick, James R. A., and Stephen M. Garrett, eds. *Five Views on Biblical Inerrancy*. Grand Rapids: Zondervan, 2013.

Muether, John R. *Cornelius Van Til: Reformed Apologist and Churchman*. Phillipsburg, NJ: P&R, 2008.

Treviño, Roberto R. *The Church in the Barrio: Mexican American Ethno-Catholicism in Houston*. Chapel Hill: University of North Carolina Press, 2006.

Weigel, George. *Witness to Hope: The Biography of Pope John Paul II*. New York: Cliff Street Books, 1999.

—— Chapter 27 ——

Theological Conflict and a New Global Church

When it comes to the most significant denominational divides in early modern and modern church history, one immediately thinks of episodes including the Protestant Reformation of the 1500s or the fundamentalist-modernist controversy of the early twentieth century. In the American context, one might recall the denominational divides of the 1840s that tragically set the stage for the Civil War. But modern church history—at least in the Protestant context—has always seen persistent tensions within organized Christianity. Often these tensions have concerned the fate of the great tradition of Christian theology. Since the mid-1800s, modernist thought—sometimes denying the inspiration of Scripture, sometimes questioning doctrines such as the physical resurrection of Jesus—played a dominant role in elite academic theology in Europe and America. To what extent would that liberal thought filter into more traditional seminaries? To what extent would it inform the teaching diet of average churches?

Such debates were almost never just about abstract doctrines. They also had social, political, and organizational implications. To what extent would denominations, seminaries, and churches openly take positions on the great social issues of the day? In the past, such issues had included questions like the sale and consumption of alcohol or the morality of slavery. In the 1950s and '60s, the topics shifted to questions including civil rights, sexual ethics, and the role of women in church and family. Denominations might have a range of responses to such issues, but few could avoid confronting them. If some traditionalists had once viewed partisan politics as a distraction to the church's focus on the kingdom of God, by the 1980s overt partisanship (whether on the left or right) had become more common than ever in churches. American Christians took the lead in this politicization, led most controversially by Jerry Falwell, Sr.'s (1933–2007) Moral Majority organization, founded in 1979. Partisan engagement was tempting in nations such as the US, Brazil, or Nigeria where Christians could realistically aspire to influence electoral politics by voting as a bloc.

The SBC and the Conservative Resurgence

In America, the greatest denominational rift of the late twentieth century was in the Southern Baptist Convention (SBC), which by the mid-twentieth century had become the nation's largest Protestant denomination. The winners in the controversy called it the Conservative Resurgence; critics preferred labels such as the "fundamentalist takeover" of the SBC. As we have seen, the SBC had been dealing with instances of liberal theology, especially in its seminaries, going back to the modernist teaching of Crawford Toy at Southern Seminary in the 1870s. The SBC itself had been born in the mid-1840s out of the political controversy over slavery. But the fracases in the seminaries became more frequent in the 1950s and '60s. Those controversies became more overt and intractable as the convention faced new political and social questions including civil rights, abortion, and women's ordination as pastors.

Harold Lindsell's *The Battle for the Bible* (1976) was not focused on the SBC alone, but the book helped to crystallize the conviction among SBC inerrantists that decisive action was required to address the recurring problem of modernist theology. Some moderates in the SBC, though not modernists themselves, believed there was room in the seminaries for liberals. Moderates generally balked at the term inerrancy. Some believed that it was unwise to make inerrancy a test of faith, while others in the SBC simply did not believe that the Bible was inerrant, at least in matters of fact and science. Such liberals were comfortable with the conclusion that some apparent contradictions in Scripture revealed errors in narrative detail, if not more fundamental deficiencies such as ethical ones. SBC leaders such as E. Y. Mullins touted the ideal of "soul competency," or the idea that a Baptist's beliefs were ultimately between the individual and God. Baptist church historian Walter Shurden (b. 1937) argued that "soul competency asserts the inalienable right and responsibility of every person to interpret God for himself. There must not be a middle person save for Jesus

Christ." But many traditionalists increasingly heard "soul competency" not as a defense of the priesthood of the believer but as a cover for relativism, modernist theology, and radical individualism.

Paige Patterson of Dallas's Criswell Bible Institute (renamed Criswell College in 1985), and Judge Paul Pressler (b. 1930) of Houston, devised a plan for the Conservative Resurgence. It began with the election of traditionalist pastor Adrian Rogers (1931–2005) of Memphis as SBC president in 1979. A series of contested denominational elections followed, as well as efforts to replace moderate trustees, seminary presidents, and entity heads in the SBC with reliable inerrantists. The key showdown of the conservative campaign came at the 1985 annual meeting in Dallas, when the conservative Charles Stanley (1932–2023) of First Baptist Church of Atlanta defeated the moderates' nominee Winfred Moore (d. 2015) for the SBC presidency, despite ardent attempts by moderates to take the position back from conservatives. Stanley's election was widely perceived as the beginning of the end for the moderate movement and for tolerance of liberal theology in the SBC. In 1990, the Cooperative Baptist Fellowship (CBF) formed as a moderate Baptist organization. In 2002 the CBF cut ties with the SBC altogether. Some historic Baptist state conventions, such as those in Texas and Virginia, also resisted cooperation with the Conservative Resurgence. This led to the formation of alternative Southern Baptist state conventions in those states.

The composition of seminary faculties remained perhaps the most divisive issue in the SBC after 1985. The Southern Baptist Theological Seminary (Southern Seminary) became ground zero for resolving the question. Remaining moderates such as Southern president Roy Honeycutt (1926–2004) promised to bring more traditionalists and inerrantists onto Southern's faculty. But the seminary faculty still leaned moderate to liberal, especially on questions such as inerrancy and the ordination of women as pastors. Some Baptist groups had occasionally ordained women as pastors, or as eldresses, going back to the American colonial period. But Addie Davis (1917–2005) of Wake Forest, North Carolina, seems to have been the first woman ordained in an SBC church, in 1964. By the mid-1990s, there were perhaps three hundred women who had been ordained in SBC churches, although many of those women found it difficult to secure positions as senior pastors in established congregations. Still, at SBC seminaries like Southern before the Conservative Resurgence, support for women's ordination was widespread.

When Albert Mohler (b. 1959) became president of Southern in 1993, he mandated that the seminary hire only inerrantists and those who opposed women's ordination. Mohler had worked for Honeycutt during his doctoral studies at Southern, but Mohler was more profoundly influenced by evangelical leader Carl Henry, who in the 1980s became aligned with the Conservative Resurgence. Mohler initiated a massive turnover of Southern's faculty and administration. Soon the seminary had been almost entirely remade in line with the principles espoused by the Conservative Resurgence. Versions of that transformation happened at other SBC agencies and seminaries, including the controversial firing of moderate president Russell Dilday (1930–2023) at Southwestern Seminary in Fort Worth, Texas, in 1994. By the late 1990s, all the SBC entities were headed by conservatives.

Paige Patterson became president at Southeastern Seminary in 1992 and then at Southwestern in 2003. Patterson was fired as president at Southwestern in 2018, however, due to controversy over Patterson's alleged mishandling of sexual abuse allegations. Patterson's dismissal was part of a larger crisis in the SBC, precipitated by charges made by journalists at the *Houston Chronicle* and other outlets that there was a systemic problem in the SBC with sexual abuse and coverups. The *Chronicle* likewise reported charges of sexual abuse made against Paul Pressler. It was a controversy that echoed the sexual abuse crisis in the Roman Catholic Church.

The Conservative Resurgence played an unusual role in the context of modern church history. In American religious history, it was of enormous significance, due to the SBC's massive presence on the American Protestant landscape. But in global perspective, one could argue that it was just another instance of a national denomination suffering a controversy—albeit a particularly intense one—over liberal theology. In 2004, the SBC withdrew from the Baptist World Alliance (BWA), its primary conduit to the larger Baptist global community, over concerns about modernist theology and liberal social views in the BWA. The International Mission Board (IMB) of the SBC retains a massive global presence, with more than 3500 missionaries serving around the world as of 2018. The SBC controversy played out mainly between American factions, however. Other more fully global Protestant denominations besides the SBC have endured conflicts in which churches of the Global South have challenged the modernism and social liberalism of Europe and North America.

The Strength of Global Anglicanism

One of the most notable such controversies has transpired in the global Anglican Communion. Since the days of Puritan efforts to reform the Church of England, the Anglican Communion has been divided between liberals and conservatives, between advocates of low church and high church ecclesiology, and over other fault lines. Like the

Catholic Church, the Anglican Communion has remained a global denomination, but Anglicanism often followed geographic patterns molded by the history of the British Empire. In the twentieth century, the strength of the Anglican Church shifted dramatically to the Global South. As we have seen, the Anglican Church of Nigeria is probably the largest Anglican province in the world in terms of practicing members, with more than 18 million adherents. The center of ecclesiastical power in the Anglican Church remained in England, however, with the Archbishop of Canterbury recognized as the "first among equals" in his relationship to Anglican prelates around the world. In 2005, the growing power of Africa within the church was reflected in the selection of the Ugandan-born John Sentamu (b. 1949) as Archbishop of York, the second most prominent position in the denomination.

Image 27.1. *John Sentamu, Archbishop of York*, 2019

Anglicans in the Global South, and particularly in Africa, have drastically changed the dynamic of debates within the church on cultural and moral issues including homosexuality. There is a range of opinions even among African Anglicans on such issues. South African archbishop Desmond Tutu, for example, expressed support for same-sex relationships, including that of his daughter Mpho, herself a former Anglican priest, who married a woman in 2015. But outside of South Africa, the leaders of the sub-Saharan African churches tend to be more culturally and doctrinally conservative than their counterparts in England, Canada, and the US. Why this is so has been debated, but in general the religious cultures of Africa—whether Christian, Muslim, or polytheist—tend to be more socially conservative than those of the West. Most African countries have significant legal restrictions on abortion, for example, and did not follow Western countries' liberalization of abortion laws that started in the 1970s.

African nations also tend to hold traditional views on sexuality. African government leaders in recent decades have taken strong stances against homosexual sex acts. In 2014,

Uganda sought to criminalize same-sex relations, although the law was struck down in the courts. (By contrast, the US Supreme Court in 2003's *Lawrence v. Texas* invalidated state laws forbidding sodomy or other same-sex acts.) African political and religious leaders often characterize the West, including Western mainline denominations, as decadent and corrupt. They see liberal church leaders in the West as pompous elites who lecture Africans about the proper progressive view of cultural issues.

Such tensions came to a head in 2003, when the Episcopal Church (the branch of the Anglican Church in the US) consecrated Gene Robinson (b. 1947), a practicing homosexual, as bishop of New Hampshire. (Robinson and his former wife had divorced in 1986. He and his male partner joined in a civil union in 2008, then they divorced in 2014.) Also in 2003, the Church of England nominated Jeffrey John (b. 1953), who lived with a male partner, as bishop of Reading. The subsequent controversy caused John to withdraw from consideration for the post. Perhaps the most vocal critic of the Western churches on homosexuality was Archbishop Peter Akinola (b. 1944) of Nigeria. Akinola argued that acceptance and promotion of homosexuality, especially among church leaders, represented anti-Christian apostasy. When the Church of England sought to appoint Jeffrey John as bishop, Akinola declared that it was "an attack on the Church of God." He and other African leaders regarded the push to recognize same-sex relationships as transparently unbiblical. Liberal English and North American leaders, in turn, expressed open contempt for conservative Africans. Yet African and other conservative Global South Anglicans could not be dismissed or ignored, because unlike the plummeting Anglican and Episcopal membership numbers in England and North America their large churches were growing.

Following the controversies of 2003, Archbishop of Canterbury Rowan Williams (b. 1950) sought to contain the divisions between the warring Anglican provinces, trying to prevent a global Anglican schism. In 2008, Williams wanted the decennial Lambeth Conference to bring resolution to the tensions, but Akinola along with senior leaders from other Anglican churches in Africa, South America, Asia, and Australia, called conservatives to attend an alternative assembly, the Global Anglican Future Conference (GAFCON). Some bishops said they would go to both Lambeth and GAFCON, but Akinola said that "those of us who will abide with the Word of God, come rain come fire, are those who are in GAFCON. Those who say it does not matter are the ones who are attending Lambeth." Justin Welby (b. 1956) became Archbishop of Canterbury in 2013, but he had no more success than Williams at containing the global fracture over sexuality and marriage. At a 2023 meeting in Rwanda, GAFCON delegates announced that they could "no longer recognise the Archbishop of Canterbury as . . . the 'first among equals' of the [Anglican] Primates." This signaled the long-anticipated breakup of the global Anglican Church. GAFCON members are united in their support for traditional biblical views of marriage and sexuality, but they are less unified regarding the issue of women's ordination as priests or bishops.

In the US and Canada, the controversy over sexuality also produced a schism between conservative Anglicans, the US Episcopal Church, and the Anglican Church of Canada. The conservative Anglican Church in North America (ACNA) was founded in 2009, with the encouragement of attendees at the GAFCON assembly the year before. When Gene Robinson was chosen as a bishop, Bishop Robert Duncan (b. 1948) of Pittsburgh declared that the American church was in a state of "pastoral emergency," and called on Archbishop Rowan Williams to take decisive action. The US Episcopal Church, Duncan said, had "departed from the historic faith and order of the Church of Jesus Christ." Appealing to the principles of the great tradition, Duncan contended that the Episcopal Church had "denied the plain teaching of Scripture and the moral consensus of the Church throughout the ages." Duncan became the first archbishop of the ACNA, which aligned itself with Global South Anglican provinces instead of those in Canada and the US. The ACNA speaks of the Bible as the "inspired" Word of God, affirms the Apostles', Nicene, and Athanasian creeds, and (more specific to the Anglican tradition) receives the Thirty-nine Articles of 1571 as "expressing the fundamental principles of authentic Anglican belief."

Despite its controversies over cultural and theological liberalism, the Anglican Church has remained a bastion for broadly orthodox belief, even in its ecclesiastical and academic positions in Britain. As we have seen, the United Kingdom has tended to be more conservative in academic theology and biblical studies than elite institutions in Germany and the US. This is due in part to the established status of the Anglican Church, which has led to a relative openness to moderate or traditional Christian belief in British institutions. One can see this tendency in figures such as the literary scholar and Christian apologist C. S. Lewis (1898–1963), who taught at both Oxford and Cambridge during the mid-twentieth century. C. H. Dodd taught at Cambridge during the same period and defended the basic historic reliability of the Gospels. Such academic figures were generally not evangelicals, conservatives, or inerrantists. Compared to the elite theologians and biblical scholars in other nations, however, they embraced a kind of biblical traditionalism. Rowan Williams, for example, has been a vastly prolific author on a wide range of topics in church history and spirituality. Despite Williams' permissive views on sexuality and women's ordination, Anglican liberals have at times been exasperated with his seeming orthodoxy on matters such as the resurrection of Christ. Due to Williams's apparent traditionalism on historic doctrine, the radical liberal American Episcopal bishop John Shelby Spong (1931–2021) once reviled Williams as a "neo-medievalist." Spong suggested that Williams affirmed biblical doctrines that he simply knew were not true. Williams countered that he did in fact believe in the "empty tomb" of the resurrection, however exasperating that may be to figures such as Spong.

The recent Anglican writer and church official who has perhaps gained the widest popular audience is N. T. Wright (b. 1948). Wright served as Bishop of Durham as well as in positions at Oxford and at the University of St. Andrews in Scotland. Wright came out of an evangelical and Reformed background, but he gravitated away from that heritage during his biblical studies at Oxford and his preparation for the Anglican ministry. He continued to express respect for English evangelical leaders such as John Stott and J. I. Packer, however. Wright has been massively prolific and is perhaps best known for his magisterial series on "Christian Origins and the Question of God." These volumes have sought to reevaluate the early Christian church in its Jewish context. Wright also meticulously defended the idea (so long challenged in higher critical scholarship) that at its birth, the early Christian church believed in the bodily resurrection of Christ.

> The bodily resurrection of Jesus isn't a take-it-or-leave-it thing, as though some Christians are welcome to believe it and others are welcome not to believe it. Take it away, and the whole picture is totally different.
>
> N. T. Wright, *For All God's Worth: True Worship and the Calling of the Church*, 1997

Wright initiated a long-standing debate with evangelical and Reformed leaders such as Baptist pastor and theologian John Piper, however, over Wright's controversial writings on justification by faith. Wright went so far as to say that much of the church since the time of Augustine had misunderstood Paul's teaching on justification. "'Justification' in the first century was not about how someone might establish a relationship with God," Wright wrote. "It was about God's eschatological definition, both future and present, of who was, in fact, a member of his people." Wright's departure from the Augustinian tradition on justification prompted Piper to write a book-length response to Wright, *The Future of Justification* (2007). Yet both Wright and Piper commended the other as a faithful Christian, despite their sharp disagreement.

A final broadly traditionalist Anglican theologian is John Webster (1955–2016), who was a faculty colleague of Wright at the University of St. Andrews until Webster's death in 2016. Webster held previous positions at Aberdeen, Oxford, and Wycliffe College, Toronto. Webster's early work was on the Lutheran theologian Eberhard Jüngel (1934–2021), a student of Karl Barth. These studies allowed Webster to transition into work on Barth directly. Finally, by the early 2000s Webster began to develop his own work in dogmatic and systematic theology in books such as *Holy Scripture: A Dogmatic Sketch* (2003). While Webster's thought was heavily informed by Barth, he also interacted with scholastic and Reformed figures such as Thomas Aquinas, John Owen, and Herman Bavinck that were rarely cited (in a complimentary way) in elite theological circles. One of Webster's signature concepts was the recovery of "theological theology" (the title of a 1997 inaugural lecture he gave at Oxford). Theology was to center on God and the Scriptures; it was not a vehicle to make other political and cultural points, Webster insisted. "Christian theology is an exercise in concentration," Webster wrote, "required to fix its eyes not on everything but on the ways of God (Ps. 119:15); only in assent to this restriction will theology find itself having something to say about everything." Webster, Wright, and others have shown that broad Christian orthodoxy could still have a place at the table in Western academic institutions with high prestige, at least in the UK.

Struggles within the United Methodist Church

Across the Christian spectrum, denominations have struggled to handle differences within orthodox boundaries, as well as the kind of theological diversity that violates orthodox boundaries. This dilemma has presented special challenges for denominations such as the Anglican Church, historically rooted in England but which is now a profoundly global communion. Although not quite as world-spanning as the Anglican Church, the US-based United Methodist Church has faced similar problems over recent decades. Though the Methodist Church in America split into northern and southern branches in 1844, they reunited in 1939. In 1968 another denominational merger led to the formation of the modern United Methodist Church denomination (UMC). Shortly thereafter, United Methodists (like most denominations in Europe and North America) began dealing with questions about homosexuality, especially among clergy. The UMC decided that same-sex sexual activity was "incompatible" with historic Christian teaching. The denomination encountered periodic challenges to that policy, however, as well as to prohibitions on active homosexuals as clergy and bans on clergy performing same-sex weddings. Most of the other "mainline" denominations in America (such as the Episcopal Church) endorsed gay clergy and same-sex weddings. The Methodist situation was complicated, however, by the UMC's strong presence in Africa, the Philippines, and Eastern Europe. Like the Anglican Communion, United Methodists have a burgeoning church in Africa, which by the late 2010s represented about 5.5 million of the UMC's 12.5 million members worldwide. The Democratic Republic of Congo is especially strong for the UMC, with some three million members.

The non-Western delegates to the Methodist's quadrennial general conferences have generally kept North American delegates from liberalizing UMC policies on marriage and sexuality. Failed attempts and delays on those issues caused frustration among liberal Methodists. They knew that with every passing year, the conservative cohort of Africans, plus traditionalists in the US, was growing as a percentage of the UMC. By the mid-2010s, pro-homosexual UMC activists and clergy turned to ecclesiastical disobedience to try to shock the church into changing its policies. Before the 2016 general conference, more than one hundred UMC clergy and clergy candidates came "out of the closet" and announced themselves to be homosexual, effectively daring the church to discipline them. Also in 2016, the UMC's Western Jurisdiction selected a woman in a same-sex marriage as a bishop. The UMC's highest court in 2017 ruled that ordaining a practicing lesbian as bishop violated church law, but they also suggested they had no authority to act against the selection. In 2019, the UMC held a conference to seek final resolution to what had become a chaotic situation. Traditionalists at that meeting adopted a plan reinforcing the denomination's historic teaching on marriage and sexuality. This led to a breakup of the denomination and the formation of the traditionalist Global Methodist Church.

The Rising Influence of Global Catholics

The Roman Catholic Church has not suffered quite the same turmoil in recent decades over questions about sexuality. The Catholic Church's troubles during that period have focused more on widespread problems with clerical sexual abuse and inaction regarding it by the church hierarchy. Observers have also noted the apparent frequency of homosexual liaisons and relationships among certain Catholic priests and seminarians, despite the church's traditional understanding that homosexual acts are of "grave depravity," and that such sexual behavior is "intrinsically disordered." The Catholic Church sees similar dynamics in its global communion as those in the Anglican Church; African Catholic churches tend to be more conservative and more energized than their European and North American counterparts. Pope Francis, the former Jorge Mario Bergoglio (b. 1936), was selected as pope in 2013 and has made statements about not judging gays and lesbians and offering blessings to same-sex unions. African Catholic leaders have bristled at Francis's apparent moderation on issues of sexuality. As in the Anglican and Methodist cases, the Vatican can hardly afford to ignore Africa, which as of the mid-2010s was home to about 14 percent of the world's 1.2 billion Catholics. Estimates suggest that the fast-growing African Catholic churches may represent twice that percentage by the mid-twenty-first century. African leaders such as the Guinean prelate Robert Sarah (b. 1945) identify Western secular liberalism and Islamic radicalism as two great threats against the global Catholic Church. "What Nazi-fascism and communism were in the 20th century, Western homosexual and abortion ideologies and Islamic fanaticism are today," Sarah said in 2015.

Francis himself represented a remarkable recognition by the Catholic hierarchy of the church's global nature. Born to an Italian immigrant family in Argentina in 1936, Francis was the first pope ever to hail from the southern hemisphere, as well as the first who was a member of the Jesuits, or Society of Jesus. He served as the Archbishop of Buenos Aires prior to his selection as pope. The Catholic hierarchy had broken its long tradition of choosing popes only from Italy with the selection of John Paul II, a departure which it extended with the choice of the German Benedict XVI (Joseph Ratzinger) in 2005. Francis seemed to signal acceptance that the "Roman" church needed fully to turn its attention outside of Europe for leadership in the twenty-first century.

For decades prior to Francis's selection, there was concern among Catholic leaders that Latin America was "turning Protestant." They might have hoped that Francis would help stop South and Central America's torrent of defections from the Catholic Church, but his appointment did not seem to make a tangible difference. By the late 2010s, seven countries in Latin America and the Spanish Caribbean, including Honduras, Uruguay, the Dominican Republic, and El Salvador, had become majority non-Catholic. (This calculation represents a combination of Protestants and "nones," or people who identify with no religion in particular.) Brazil, by far the largest Latin American country by population and total area, was also poised to become majority non-Catholic by the early 2020s. Scholars and Catholic officials have debated the reasons why so many people in Latin America, especially among the poor, have left the Catholic Church, despite the church's noted turn toward liberation theology and the "preferential option for the poor." Most Latin Americans who remained connected to a Christian denomination have become Pentecostals. An (unattributed) witticism has become common among religious scholars of Latin America: "The Catholic Church opted for the poor, and the poor opted for the Pentecostals."

Unlike the tenure of John Paul II, the Vatican has shown relatively little concern under Francis about the massive defections in Latin America, perhaps reflecting Francis's relatively ecumenical and irenic bent. In 2019, the Vatican held a synod to discuss Catholicism in the Amazon region of South America, but virtually all the focus was on topics other than people turning to Pentecostalism. These topics included fighting environmental degradation (a top priority of Francis's papacy) and a move to allow married men to become Catholic priests in the region, due to an acute shortage of priests there. This much-discussed policy would not have allowed unmarried priests to get married, but it would have allowed already-married Catholic men to be considered for the priesthood. This would have represented a major departure from long-standing practice, but it would have only applied in the Amazon region. Francis ultimately decided not to approve the change, however. Prominent conservatives, including the former pope Benedict XVI and Guinea's Robert Sarah, opposed the suggested Amazon policy on married priests due to concern that it might lead to the widespread acceptance of non-celibate clergy.

The Overlooked Works of God

From the SBC to the Roman Catholic Church, major Christian denominations continue to struggle with challenges related to traditional doctrine and practice, as well as intensifying cultural pressures from a rapidly secularizing society. All the focus on large, historic denominations can miss much of the action in the changing Christian landscape of recent decades, however. As we have seen, the center of Christian gravity over the past century has shifted to the Global South, even though Christian resources and leadership tend to be centered in places like Rome, London, or Nashville, Tennessee (headquarters of the UMC and SBC). The most dynamic Christian churches and movements today tend to go under the media and scholarly radar. These groups are often of recent origin, are immigrant-led, and are disproportionately evangelical, charismatic, or Pentecostal. They are exactly the sort of churches likely to be missed in standard surveys of religion. They may have a loose (or no) affiliation with an established denomination, they may meet in a storefront or another church's building, and they may not offer services in the majority language of the host country (for example, a Spanish-speaking congregation in the US).

Yet in recent decades, the West has seen something of a Christian missionary reversal. People from Latin America, Africa, and southeast Asia have begun re-evangelizing and planting churches in areas that used to be the great engines of Christian missions. These include the urban northeast in the US and the cities of western Europe. In America, the number of new immigrants from places such as South Asia has surged due to a revision of immigration law in 1965. Immigration from countries such as Pakistan have significantly increased the number of Muslims living in the US. But the new immigrants of the past half century, especially those from southeast Asia, Africa, and Latin America, have been disproportionately likely to identify as Christians. Latin America is still the primary sending region for immigrants to the US, and a strong majority of them are Catholic or Protestant/Pentecostal. Even Arab immigrants are more likely to be Christians in comparison to the composition of their home countries. Especially during the civil wars in Iraq and Syria in the 2010s, many Greek and Syriac Orthodox, as well as members of other Christian groups, fled the Middle East and the anti-Christian violence of the Islamic State in hopes of finding sanctuary in Europe or the US.

> Over the last century, however, the center of gravity in the Christian world has shifted inexorably away from Europe, southward, to Africa and Latin America, and eastward toward Asia. Today, the largest Christian communities are found in those areas.
>
> ---
>
> Philip Jenkins, *The Next Christendom: The Coming of Global Christianity*, 2002

Some of these new immigrant Christians come as formal missionaries from their home countries. Others end up immigrating or fleeing for other reasons and practicing their faith in their new setting. In either case, they have changed the religious demographics of North America and much of Europe. To cite just one example, the Pentecostal, Nigerian-based Redeemed Christian Church of God (RCCG) has parishes in virtually every American and European town of at least middling size, from Gainesville, Florida to Anchorage, Alaska, and from Dundee, Scotland, to Belgrade, Serbia. In 2013, the RCCG dedicated a camp and a ten-thousand seat worship center (projected to expand to 100,000) outside of Dallas for its burgeoning number of adherents in the US.

Although Boston, Massachusetts, was once one of the great global centers of evangelical fervor and missions-sending, observers now regard it as one of the most secular cities in the US. But some scholars have noticed that the city has actually experienced a "quiet revival" over the past half century, which saw the number of churches in Boston double between the 1960s and early 2000s. Some of the growth has been driven by the conscious efforts of evangelical denominations, including the SBC, to plant churches in relatively unchurched areas such as New England. One of the region's largest megachurches is the African American-led Jubilee Christian Church, founded in 1982 and affiliated with the Church of God, Anderson, Indiana (a Holiness denomination). But much of Boston's recent change has been driven by immigrant-majority congregations. The RCCG lists sixteen congregations in the greater Boston area. And Haitian Protestants have an especially strong presence in the city. Boston's First Haitian Baptist Church opened in 1969, but by 2000 there were some fifty Haitian Protestant churches in the area.

Although the number of foreign missionaries and church planters in the US and Europe can be difficult to track, one estimate suggested that as of 2007 some 1500 missionary and church workers representing 50 different nations were laboring in Great Britain. One of the most notable and controversial was Matthew Ashimolowo (b. 1952), founding pastor of the Kingsway International Christian Centre, a RCCG-affiliated church with a reported attendance of 12,000 on Sundays at its main London facility. Its Miracle Centre had double

Image 27.2. *Iglesia de Dios Pentecostal, East Hollywood, Los Angeles*

the seating of the London landmarks Westminster Abbey and St. Paul's Cathedral, but the 2012 London Olympics forced the church to relocate to a new 24-acre site they called Prayer City. It was dedicated in 2014 by Enoch Adeboye (b. 1942), the Lagos, Nigeria–based General Overseer of the RCCG. Like some other megachurch pastors associated with the prosperity gospel, Ashimolowo has amassed personal wealth in the millions of dollars and has drawn charges of impropriety in the handling of the church's finances.

Many of the new immigrant churches primarily cater to people of a particular nationality or ethnic/language group, but that homogeneity is typical of long-established congregations in Europe and North America, too. These new churches are a signature characteristic of "global' Christianity today and are a primary growth area in the traditional heartlands of Protestant and Catholic Christianity. Adherents of the great tradition of Christian theology might question the doctrinal soundness of churches which teach versions of the prosperity gospel, or a transactional view of obedience and giving resulting in the worldly blessings of health and material wealth. Just how prevalent such prosperity views are among the new immigrant churches is unclear. Worldwide, prosperity teaching comes in both "hard" and "soft" forms. Soft prosperity emphasizes healing and abundance, without making the more overt promises that these blessings will always follow faith and obedience. Soft prosperity teaching has become quite common in evangelical and charismatic churches, including in the US. Whatever the tensions of such theology with the great tradition, there is no doubt that across much of the Christian world, a Pentecostal-themed, immigrant-driven movement of churches, rooted especially in African and Latin American diasporas, has become a major factor in the future of Christendom.

Selected Bibliography

Anthony, Andrew. "A Quiet Man Who Said Too Much." *The Guardian*, February 9, 2008. https://www.theguardian.com/world/2008/feb/10/anglicanism.religion.

Brittain, Christopher Craig, and Andrew McKinnon. *The Anglican Communion at a Crossroads: The Crises of a Global Church*. University Park: Pennsylvania State University Press, 2018.

Davidson, Ivor J. "In Memoriam: John Webster (1955–2016)." *International Journal of Systematic Theology* 18, no. 4 (October 2016): 360–75.

Gettleman, Jeffrey, and Laurie Goodstein. "A More Conservative Catholic Church Awaits Pope Francis in Africa." *New York Times*, November 25, 2015. https://www.nytimes

.com/2015/11/25/world/africa/a-more-conservative-catholic-church-awaits-pope-francis-in-africa.html.

Hankins, Barry. *Uneasy in Babylon: Southern Baptist Conservatives and American Culture*. Tuscaloosa: University of Alabama Press, 2003.

Hartch, Todd. *The Rebirth of Latin American Christianity*. New York: Oxford University Press, 2014.

Jenkins, Philip. *God's Continent: Christianity, Islam, and Europe's Religious Crisis*. New York: Oxford University Press, 2007.

Johnson, Marilynn. "'The Quiet Revival': New Immigrants and the Transformation of Christianity in Greater Boston." *Religion and American Culture: A Journal of Interpretation* 24, no. 2 (July 2014): 231–58.

Roberts, Alastair. "N.T. Wright: A Biography." Blog. September 11, 2006. https://alastairadversaria.com/2006/09/11/nt-wright-a-biography/

Rocca, Francis X., Luciana Magalhaes, and Samantha Pearson. "Why the Catholic Church Is Losing Latin America." *Wall Street Journal*, January 11, 2022.

Shepley, Randy, and Walter B. Shurden. *Going for the Jugular: A Documentary History of the SBC Holy War*. Macon, GA: Mercer University Press, 1996.

Tooley, Mark D. "The African Future of 'America's Church.'" *Wall Street Journal*, March 8, 2019.

Chapter 28

Global Churches Facing the Future

What are the most important future trends and challenges, especially for Christians who identify with the great tradition of Christian belief and practice? Historians are better at explaining the past than predicting the future. Yet some trends and challenges are ever-present in the life of the church and seem certain to recur in coming decades. One is the struggle to adapt churches to current culture without sacrificing the orthodoxy and orthopraxy of the great tradition. As we have seen throughout church history, changing cultures, mores, and technologies always influence the church. Even reacting against cultural trends involves change. But how do Christians and believers inhabit a changing culture without sacrificing beliefs and practices that characterize faithful Christians? This is perhaps the defining challenge of church history.

Issues Concerning the Family

To specifically address the contemporary era, global challenges facing churches today include issues of sexuality, declining fertility, growing secularization, tensions between Islam and Christianity, and the threat of persecution against Christians. (Sometimes these issues overlap, such as when Muslim jihadists persecute Christians, or when religious traditionalists across faiths face pressures to conform to secular elite views of sexuality or the exercise of religion.) There seems to be no question that Christians and churches will continue in coming years to wrestle with questions of sexuality, marriage, and the respective roles of men and women. Homosexuality is arguably the most acute concern in this constellation of beliefs about sex and gender. Homosexual practice is not new, of course, and is repeatedly and explicitly addressed in the Bible. What is new today is the growing acceptance of homosexual practice and marriage in the West, and the growing cultural, academic, and corporate pressure for Christians and other religious traditionalists to positively affirm the LGBTQIA+ agenda. That agenda has recently included the concept that gender is not fixed and can be changed depending on one's personal desires and inclinations. Mainline Protestant denominations have largely cooperated with this cultural mandate. Traditionalist evangelicals, Pentecostals, Catholics, and Orthodox Christians generally have not cooperated with it. Christian colleges and social-service ministries face special challenges due to their frequent acceptance of government financial assistance, which can be used to pressure such organizations to adopt the dominant culture's views. Particularly in North America and Europe, the range of ideas surrounding LGBTQIA+ ideology is perhaps the most salient challenge to the historic Christian tradition today.

Some of the most spectacular controversies over acceptance of the LGBTQIA+ agenda have transpired in the US. One illustrative example was the Supreme Court case of *Masterpiece Cakeshop v. Colorado Civil Rights Commission* (2018). This case involved an increasingly common scenario where a business owner—Jack Phillips, owner of the Denver-area Masterpiece Cakeshop and an evangelical Christian—declined to make a specialty cake for a gay wedding. The Colorado Civil Rights Commission determined that Phillips had discriminated against the gay couple, an act which is prohibited by state law. In a ruling that seemed limited only to the facts of the case (members of the Colorado commission had directly expressed contempt for Phillip's beliefs), the court majority found in favor of Phillips based on his First Amendment rights to free speech and free exercise of religion. Such cases against Christian-run businesses, Christians in government positions, or Christian colleges and ministries, seem likely to keep happening for the foreseeable future. This is hardly restricted to the US. In Australia, for example, the government debated strengthening its religious freedom protections in light of controversies such as the 2019 firing of popular rugby player Israel Folau. Folau, a Pentecostal Christian and ethnic Tongan, had averred on social media that unrepentant homosexuals were going to hell.

In Africa, the religious and cultural landscape on sexuality is quite different from places such as the US or Australia. At a minimum, church leaders and Christian politicians in Africa generally feel no hesitation about expressing opposition to the LGBTQIA+ agenda, portraying it as a tool of a culturally imperialist West. As we have seen, African traditionalists in the Catholic and various Protestant communions have tended to pressure Europeans and North Americans to curtail their liberal views on sexuality. Christian and non-Christian politicians alike in Africa have supported controversial bills in recent years to criminalize homosexual sexual activity and/or LGBTQIA+ activism. In Ghana, for example, an increasingly public role for pro-gay activists in 2021 led to a bipartisan effort in the nation's parliament to impose punishment for homosexual activity or pro-LGBTQIA+ advocacy. The bill was supported by prominent Muslim, Catholic, and Protestant leaders.

The leader of the Christian Council of Ghana (CCG), the Evangelical Presbyterian pastor Cyril Fayose, said in a statement that "As a Christian majority nation, the CCG has a mandate to espouse the position of the Christian faith on homosexuality to all citizens." Speaking on behalf of "we the people of Ghana," Fayose stated that "God considers homosexuality as an act of perversion and abomination that attracts His wrath." Sub-Saharan Africa is politically and religiously diverse, of course, and nations in the continent's south and southwest, such as South Africa and Angola, have taken more liberal approaches to LGBTQIA+ activity. South Africa was the continent's first country to legalize same-sex marriage in 2006, almost a decade before it was legalized in the US. Nevertheless, the cultural landscape of much of sub-Saharan Africa is far friendlier to traditional religious views than is the increasingly secular West.

Explaining why much of Africa has remained relatively traditional, while the native-born populations of Western Europe have become deeply secular and disengaged from institutional religion, is exceedingly complicated. Christians, of course, will at some level attribute such patterns of Christian growth and decline to the movements of the Holy Spirit and the providential plans of God. But on a this-worldly level, scholars such as Philip Jenkins have observed a strong correlation between national levels of fertility and relative levels of religiosity and cultural conservatism. (This applies to religions like Islam as well as Christianity.) Jenkins is careful not to attribute a causal role between fertility and faith, and the connection between religiosity and fertility is not entirely predictable. Nevertheless, there is a strong global pattern that suggests that when nations drop below replacement fertility level (about 2.1 children per woman), a drop in religiosity typically follows.

The reasons why are (again) quite complex. But one can readily imagine that a society that tends not to emphasize women's traditional roles as mothers will have more women in the non-familial workforce for more of their lives. Fewer people will marry and have children, or they will just have one child. This trend may help dissolve families' felt need for support structures at churches, many of which are built around family life stages (youth ministry, Sunday schools, etc.) and often feature regular teaching on family and child-rearing. With fewer families manifesting traditional models of parenting and sex roles, their resonance with conservative churches' assumptions about family and the value of fertility ("be fruitful and multiply") may also erode. Women are the majority of congregants in most Christian denominations. The weakening of women's ties to organizational religion represents an especially acute threat, then, to churches and other religious institutions.

Given these correlations between religiosity and fertility rates, it is no surprise that the highly religious sub-Saharan African nations dominate the rankings of the highest fertility rates in the world. Countries in Europe—particularly southern Europe—have some of the lowest. Much of Latin America, one of the new centers of Christianity in the Global South, has also gone through the demographic transition from high to low birth rates in recent decades. Signs would suggest that in some Latin American nations, that drop is correlated with declines in religiosity and growing levels of secularism and liberal cultural views. Brazil, for example, went from a fertility rate of about six children per woman in the 1960s to a rate below two today, significantly below the level needed to sustain a steady population. We have already noted the much-discussed number of Latin Americans turning from Catholicism to Pentecostalism. A parallel trend has emerged in recent years, however: a growing number of people in Latin America identify with "no religion in particular." The "nones" phenomenon is much-debated, and that self-description can mean many different things. But it seems indisputable that, especially among younger Latin Americans, increasing numbers have little connection to any church or organizational religion at all. Polls suggest that in countries like Chile, Honduras, and the Dominican Republic, the number of people who say they have "no religion" now runs from between 10 to 25 percent of the population. In Uruguay, one of the most secular and European-like of the Latin American countries, the number of "nones" is a whopping 40 percent. This is about 10 percent higher than in the US (roughly 30 percent), but still about thirty-five points lower than the intensely secular Czech Republic (72 percent).

Dropping fertility in Latin America has also come with more permissive social views. While most African nations still balk at abortion and same-sex marriage, these have become more accepted in Latin America. Countries such as Uruguay, Argentina, and Brazil have legalized homosexual marriage. Despite strenuous opposition from Catholic and Protestant leaders, abortion has been legalized in countries such as Uruguay, Guyana, and Mexico. In Pope Francis's home country of Argentina, the national legislature legalized elective abortions after a heated debate in 2020. Francis spoke out against the bill, saying that it was never right "to eliminate a human life to resolve a problem." Argentina's move reflected the declining cultural power of Catholicism in traditionally Catholic countries around the world. Ireland, once seen as one of the world's most staunchly Catholic societies, voted overwhelmingly to legalize abortion in a 2018 national referendum. Ireland's birth rate has also plummeted to around 1.75 children per woman over a lifetime.

Image 28.1. *Pro-life march in Argentina, 2018*

Until recently, the US has been something of an outlier in terms of traditional faith, fertility rates, and social liberalism. Unlike western Europe, rates of American religiosity remained comparatively high, even as it went through similar trajectories of economic development and patterns of cultural liberalization. The Supreme Court of the United States took an aggressive role in legalizing practices such as contraception, abortion, and gay marriage, usually over the protests of Christian traditionalists. In 1972, the court legalized birth control for all Americans. And in 1973, *Roe v. Wade* legalized elective abortion based on a woman's constitutional "right to privacy." (The 2022 *Dobbs* decision overturned *Roe*'s principle of a constitutional right to an abortion.) In *Lawrence v. Texas* (2003), the court prohibited laws against homosexual sex acts. Finally, in decisions culminating in *Obergefell v. Hodges* (2015), the court recognized a constitutional right to gay marriage.

One might assume that these changes would have been accompanied by plummeting religious adherence, just as western Europe has seen over the past half century. In the US, that decline was true for the mainline Christian denominations but not as much for Catholics and evangelicals. US birth rates dropped sharply in the 1970s, but they recovered to a comparatively robust 2.0 children per woman in the 1990s. The US has also remained a prized destination for immigrants from around the world, many of whom are devout Christians, especially in the first generation that relocates to America. This has increasingly seeded American congregations with new religiously observant families.

By the early 2010s, however, US birth rates began to drop sharply, to the (estimated) low rate of 1.64 children per woman in a lifetime by 2020. This placed US fertility below countries like Iceland, Sweden, and the United Kingdom, but still well above countries in East Asia like Japan, South Korea, and Taiwan, which tend to dominate the bottom end of such rankings. The COVID-19 pandemic which surged globally in 2020 seems to have exacerbated the trend of dropping fertility. Is the fertility decline, assuming it reflects a long-term development, leading to a correlated decline in religious commitment in America? Early signs would suggest yes.

Most gauges of religious commitment in polling, from service attendance to regular prayer to self-identification with a religion, have declined in America over the past couple decades. Again, there is good reason to take polling numbers on religion with a grain of salt. Even reputable polling agencies have struggled to replicate the representative samples of people they could take for granted in previous decades when the average American had a landline phone and did not have caller ID. Also, whenever people identify themselves qualitatively ("what religion do you identify with?"), the answers will include a fair number of obscure or idiosyncratic meanings. For example, we know that a significant minority of respondents who say they have "no religion" also attend church regularly. (Why these people say they have no religion is open to debate.) Nevertheless, the composite picture of overall decline, at least among nominal American Christians, seems undeniable.

The decline of the mainline American churches over recent decades has continued unabated, but even evangelical denominations—once seemingly impervious to such trends—have shown signs of weakening. The Southern Baptist Convention, for example (the largest Protestant denomination in the US), began losing overall membership numbers in 2006. From its high point of 16.3 million reported members, the SBC stood at 13.2 million members by 2022. (Denominational membership numbers are often clouded by inconsistent or misleading tracking of members, of course.) The traditionalist Presbyterian Church in America, a juggernaut of growth since its founding in 1974, has leveled off in the past few years and has shown signs of decline, too. Even the Assemblies of God USA, the major Pentecostal denomination that had been growing year-over-year through 2018, saw a decline in attendance in 2019.

Again, there are reasons not to take the membership/attendance numbers of large denominations as the final word on such matters. Some evidence would suggest that the number of American congregations is significantly underreported, perhaps by as much as 40 percent. The unreported congregations tend to be majority non-white, immigrant, evangelical, and Pentecostal, as well as traditionalist in their views of the Bible, sexuality, and other contentious issues. Nevertheless, it appears that at least in the short term, even denominational stalwarts like the SBC and Assemblies of God have begun slowly to decline. Many congregations were forced to stop meeting during the COVID pandemic of the early 2020s, and many struggled to return to the prepandemic levels of attendance.

In the longer term, predictions must be more tentative. Prophets of inexorable global secularization have almost always been wrong. Most historians today agree that religion and modernity have gotten along fine in many contexts. Some scholars have suggested that in places like Britain and America there is reason to believe that religion may have a robust long-term future, even if current trends look discouraging from a religious perspective. One possible reason for this strong religious future in the West is, again, immigration. A declining fertility rate means a greater need for immigrant labor, which will continue to draw people from the disproportionately religious Global South. Politics professor Eric Kaufmann, for example, notes that in recent decades, London has seen significant religious growth, even as smaller British towns and rural areas have experienced massive weakening of Christian adherence. By far the most important reason for the growth in London is immigration. Less than half the population of London is made up of white British people. Immigration from places like sub-Saharan Africa, Eastern Europe, or Muslim-majority Pakistan, has surged in the city. This pattern has reversed religious decline in much of the metropolis.

Kaufmann also puts great weight on data that show that religious traditionalists of all kinds—whether Jews, Muslims, Protestants, Catholics, Mormons, or other groups—have more children than do nonreligious or liberal religious people. In America, the fertility rate of regular church attenders outpaces that of nonattenders by about half a child, though this difference is currently obscured by the greater growth of nonattenders as a religious demographic group. But Kaufmann argues that in the long term, the major difference in fertility for devout believers of all faiths means that the future will belong to the practicing traditionalists and their more numerous children. Again, Christian observers will note that the rising and falling of churches and denominations is ultimately in God's hand. But one can also see that demographics, immigration, and fertility all play a role in sustaining religiosity.

Tensions between Islam and Christianity

It is also important to remember that the correlation between fertility and the religious future is not just a Christian one. It affects all major religions, including Islam, even as Christianity and Islam often clash in global hotspots like sub-Saharan Africa. Tension between Muslims and Christians is another major theme in the emerging global religious future. Fighting between Christians and Muslims is a much older story, dating to, for example, the Crusades of the twelfth and thirteenth centuries or the defeat of the Ottomans at Vienna in 1683. But events such as the fundamentalist Iranian Revolution of 1979 and the 2001 terrorist attacks in the US focused the attention of many in the West on the growing challenge of militant, jihadist Islam. Most of the world's Muslims are not involved with terrorism or religious violence, but modern Islam does have a special problem with terroristic radicalism, one that has become more conspicuous since 9/11. Jihadists' attacks are not always committed against "Christian" targets such as churches, of course. The 9/11 attackers destroyed the Twin Towers of New York City's World Trade Center and flew a plane into the Pentagon, symbols of American corporate and military power. But jihadists often view Western imperial power as Christian in nature, inspired by the same "Crusader" ideology that once led medieval Western Christians to try to conquer the holy sites of the Middle East.

As much as global Christianity has grown numerically over the past century, Islam has grown even more. Some of that growth has been through conversions to Islam, but much more of it has been due to fertility. Much of the Muslim world stood well above replacement fertility level for much of the twentieth century. But in recent decades, large swaths of the Muslim world also went through the kind of demographic transition of declining fertility that has affected the Christian world. Still, Christianity and Islam are by far the two largest religious communities on the planet. While the total number of Christian adherents will remain larger for the coming decades, Islam is rapidly increasing as a percentage of the world's population. This has put Christian and Muslim populations (of whatever level of personal devotion) in uncomfortable proximity in places such as Africa and the major cities of Europe.

Sometimes the clash between Islam and Christianity is revealed in radical Muslim violence against Christian missionaries, aid workers, and churches. For example, in 2002 a jihadist gunman in Jibla, Yemen, killed three staff members at a Southern Baptist-run hospital: William Koehn, the hospital administrator, Kathleen Gariety, a supplies purchaser, and Martha Myers, a doctor who had served in Yemen for 25 years.

Likewise, Islamic State suicide bombers in Egypt attacked two churches on Palm Sunday 2017, killing some forty-four people. The churches were Coptic Orthodox, the historic Christian church of Egypt. The Christian populations of North Africa and the Middle East have suffered many such incidents in recent decades, especially after the US invasion of Iraq in 2003. The Islamic State of Iraq and Syria (ISIS) proclaimed a caliphate in the region in 2014, leading to a horrific escalation of violence against Catholic and Orthodox Christian groups as well as adherents of other minority religions such as the Yazidis of northern Iraq. Christians in the region were often faced with a choice of fleeing, conversion to Islam, paying religious taxes to the caliphate, or death. Over the course of a decade and a half, the number of Christian adherents in the region dropped from about 1.5 million to 250,000, with many Middle Eastern Christians desperately seeking sanctuary from ISIS in Europe or North America. Such attacks and persecutions occurred in contexts where Muslims are in a strong majority, and jihadist violence is directed toward Christian minorities or toward missionary outsiders.

Image 28.2. *Dr. Martha Myers photo, International Mission Board*

Tensions over the place of Islam take on a different cast in nations such as France, which is historically Catholic but deeply secular. A strong Muslim immigrant population has developed in French cities in recent decades, representing some five million Muslims out of a total French national population of sixty-seven million by 2020. French authorities impose a relatively extreme version of secularism on society, including a prohibition on "conspicuous religious symbols" in schools, such as crosses for Christians or the headscarf (hijab) for Muslim girls. This secular mandate, combined with the widespread poverty among Muslim immigrants, has helped radicalize significant numbers of Muslims in France who feel like the nation's leadership is formally hostile toward them. This simmering rage has led to outbreaks of terrorist violence, including the 2015 attacks on the office of the satirical magazine *Charlie Hebdo* which had published denigrating cartoon images of the Prophet Muhammad. (Visual depictions of the Prophet Muhammad are generally prohibited in Islam.) Twelve people were killed in the *Charlie Hebdo* attack. The *Charlie Hebdo* incident has had ongoing repercussions, such as the 2020 murder and beheading of a French schoolteacher by a jihadist. The teacher had allegedly shown his class the *Charlie Hebdo* cartoons. Such actions show that secular countries like France have struggled badly to deal with the growing Muslim populations in their midst.

Along with the Middle East, one of the world's epicenters for conflict between Muslim and Christian communities is in Nigeria. Nigeria has by far the largest population of any African nation, and its Christian and Muslim populations (atypically) are roughly equal. Unlike in situations where Muslims are a majority (such as the Middle East or North Africa), or a minority (such as France), Christians and Muslims in Nigeria are evenly divided in population. Both communities are growing. In some Nigerian states, Muslims have created sharia courts as a sort of parallel legal system, normally used when both parties in a case are Muslims. Political conflict and endemic local violence have become common between Christians and Muslims, especially in areas of northern Nigeria that are especially mixed and proximate between the religions' adherents. As always, such conflicts are exacerbated by worldly issues including land use or ethnic animosity, but religion plays a powerful role. Boko Haram, one of the leading jihadist organizations in Nigeria, has perpetrated a series of murders, kidnappings, and church bombings, including the attacks on several churches in the north and northeast on Christmas Day 2011. One of these attacks, carried out on a Catholic church in Madalla, killed thirty-seven people. In 2014, Boko Haram militants kidnapped almost 300 girls, most of them Christians, from a public school in Chibok. Many of the girls were forced to convert to Islam and to marry members of Boko Haram.

Although the invasion attracted massive international attention and outrage, Nigerian officials struggled to rescue the girls. Many remained missing for years afterward.

Persecution in the Present

The Muslim-Christian violence in places such as northern Nigeria brings us to the final major challenge facing churches and Christians around the world today: persecution. "Persecution" is a much-debated and sometimes vague term, especially in the US where religiously-themed political and legal conflict sometimes gets labeled as persecution. Whether we should call the treatment of figures such as the Colorado baker Jack Phillips "persecution" or not is an open question. There seems no doubt, however, that America has not seen the scale or severity of religious persecution experienced in places such as Syria or Nigeria. After the 2020 murder of a Catholic seminarian in Kaduna State, the Catholic bishop of Sokoto, Matthew Kukah, lamented the complicity of "the northern Muslim elite" in Nigeria's vicious anti-Christian violence. Some observers argued that the troubles in Nigeria were not mostly about religion, but Kukah was incredulous about this claim. "It is what happens when politicians use religion to extend the frontiers of their ambition and power," he lamented.

We should also remember that as severe as the persecution of Christians has been in places such as northern Nigeria, in other places, persecution has fallen hard on non-Christian groups, too, including some Muslims in parts of southern Nigeria. One of the largest-scale waves of ethno-religious persecution in recent decades has come against the Uyghur Muslim community in northwestern China. The formally atheist Chinese government has launched a massive crackdown on the Uyghurs, leading to the detention of more than a million Uyghurs in concentration camps, along with campaigns of torture, sexual assault, and forced sterilization. China has perpetrated these wholesale human rights abuses against the Uyghurs in the name of containing the perceived threat of Muslim separatism and jihadism in the region.

Under the presidency of President Xi Jinping (b. 1953), China's communist regime has escalated its repression of groups it regards as insufficiently "Chinese" in orientation. This reflects an older Chinese fear of "foreign" influence through religious groups and missionaries, accompanied by a desire to decimate any religious group that could represent a source of resistance against government power. Chinese authorities take a suspicious view of any churches that will not join the state-controlled Three-Self Association. In the 2010s this suspicion led to a new crackdown on unregistered, underground, or house churches. At times, this campaign has resulted in the demolition or seizure of meeting facilities, bans on crosses adorning church buildings, requirements for congregations to display the Chinese flag and sing patriotic songs, the forced installation of surveillance cameras, or divulging the names of attendees. Church leaders and members who resist such edicts face fines and/or jail time.

In 2018, Beijing's Zion Church, reportedly the largest Protestant congregation in the city, was "dismantled" by authorities and subjected to crippling fines. Authorities pressured the church's landlord to cancel its lease. Members apparently scattered across the city and region, creating a series of small house meetings. Still, official pressure on the church continued, and in 2021 authorities arrested two of Zion Church's pastors. Citing the work and example of Dietrich Bonhoeffer, Zion Church's senior pastor asked for prayer for the detained ministers, saying, "Even though circumstances are difficult, we are not ashamed of the Gospel." Zion Church's struggles were not unique, as the Chinese Communist Party similarly devastated the Shouwang Church, once the largest house church in Beijing. When the Shouwang Church lost its lease in 2009, the church began meeting outdoors, but police disrupted the meetings and repeatedly forced the congregation to relocate. Although the persecution led to major media coverage outside of China, the constant harassment wore the congregation down, and by 2019 the church had apparently ceased to exist. Such persecution often garners short-term attention and support, especially if word gets out on social media. But it can be difficult for local churches and pastors to sustain their activities through years of struggle, intimidation, fines, and the arrest of key leaders.

One of the most poignant stories of anti-Christian persecution in China came out of Chengdu, a megacity in central China and the capital of Sichuan province. Early Rain Covenant Church, a Reformed congregation in Chengdu, was pastored by the former legal scholar Wang Yi (b. 1973). Wang became internationally famous due to his meeting with US President George W. Bush in 2006, and the extensive coverage by journalists, including by *New York Times* writer Ian Johnson, who profiled Pastor Wang in his 2017 book *The Souls of China: The Return of Religion after Mao*. Wang converted to Christianity in 2005 and helped to found Early Rain Church in 2008. Wang's theology is Calvinistic, and in his sermons he criticized the Three-Self churches as corrupted by state power. Wang also condemned the Chinese government's use of abortion and sterilization to support its long-standing policy of allowing no more than one child per family. (The government began revising this policy in 2015, when it became clear that it had produced massive demographic problems, including the survival of far more young men than women due to traditional Chinese preferences for male children.) Wang did not attempt to hide his criticisms of the Chinese government and Xi Jinping, calling the president a usurper who had destroyed the Chinese constitution by effectively granting himself life tenure in office. He also lamented Chinese violations of basic human rights against other groups, such as the Muslim Uyghurs. Wang Yi was repeatedly detained by Chengdu officials before finally being arrested along with more than a hundred Early Rain members at the end of 2018. In late 2019, a Chengdu court sentenced Pastor Wang to a nine-year prison sentence for crimes including "subversion of state power."

Pastor Wang Yi had, of course, anticipated his final arrest and imprisonment, and he prepared a "Declaration of Faithful Disobedience" to be released following his detention. The statement reflected the former lawyer's deep sense of the proper roles of state and church, as well as his steadfast commitment to the kingdom of Christ over the atheistic, persecuting Chinese state. "I am filled with anger and disgust at the persecution of the church by this Communist regime, at the wickedness of their depriving people of the freedoms of religion and of conscience. But changing social and political institutions is not the mission I have been called to, and it is not the goal for which God has given his people the gospel. For all hideous realities, unrighteous politics, and arbitrary laws manifest the cross of Jesus Christ, the only means by which every Chinese person must be saved," Wang wrote. Citing John Calvin, he stated that "wicked rulers are the judgment of God on a wicked people, the goal being to urge God's people to repent and turn again toward Him. For this reason, I am joyfully willing to submit myself to their enforcement of the law as though submitting to the discipline and training of the Lord. At the same time, I believe that this Communist regime's persecution against the church is a greatly wicked, unlawful action. As a pastor of a Christian church, I must denounce this wickedness openly and severely." Most importantly, he said, he would not stop proclaiming the gospel of salvation through Jesus Christ. This endurance was, Wang concluded, "the very reason why the Communist regime is filled with fear at a church that is no longer afraid of it."

> Genocides and persecutions can only cause this kingdom to gain more ground in China because the cross is the mystery of the church and the gospel. Since the church is the body of Christ, every time the true church is persecuted, it will bring forth the power of resurrection.
>
> ---
>
> Wang Yi, *Faithful Disobedience: Writings on Church and State from a Chinese House Church Movement*, 2022

Pastor Wang Yi's example is just one of the best-known among countless stories of Christian courage in the face of persecution around the world today. Wang Yi remains in prison as of this writing, and other Early Rain pastors and members have continued to be arrested. But Pastor Wang would undoubtedly remind us that it is far better to obey Christ and suffer than to compromise one's faith in order to achieve this-worldly freedom.

Selected Bibliography

Asiedu, Kwasi Gyamfi, Chinedu Asadu, Rodney Muhumuza, and Mogomotsi Magome. "Across Africa, major churches strongly oppose LGBTQ rights." *Associated Press*, October 20, 2021. https://apnews.com/article/lifestyle-africa-religion-relationships-united-states-3b1115a1a9ed40a1211dd508ae996141.

Jenkins, Philip. *Fertility and Faith: The Demographic Revolution and the Transformation of World Religions*. Waco, TX: Baylor University Press, 2020.

Johnson, Ian. "Pastor Accused of 'Inciting Subversion' as China Cracks Down on Churches." *New York Times*, December 14, 2018, https://www.nytimes.com/2018/12/13/world/asia/china-religion-crackdown.html.

———. *The Souls of China: The Return of Religion After Mao*. New York: Pantheon, 2017.

Kaufmann, Eric. *Shall the Religious Inherit the Earth?: Demography and Politics in the Twenty-first Century*. London: Profile, 2011.

Philpott, Daniel, and Timothy Samuel Shah, eds. *Under Caesar's Sword: How Christians Respond to Persecution*. New York: Cambridge University Press, 2018.

Qi Junzao. "Leading House Churches Targeted in China." *Bitter Winter*, May 10, 2021. https://bitterwinter.org/leading-house-churches-targeted-in-china/.

State Department, Office of International Religious Freedom. "2020 Report on International Religious Freedom: Nigeria." May 12, 2021. https://www.state.gov/reports/2020-report-on-international-religious-freedom/nigeria/.

Wang Yi. "My Declaration of Faithful Disobedience." *China Partnership* (blog), December 12, 2018. https://www.chinapartnership.org/blog/2018/12/my-declaration-of-faithful-disobedience.

ILLUSTRATION CREDITS

Image 1.1. Monument to Jan Hus, Old Town Square, Prague. Sculpture by Ladislav Šaloun, 1915. Photograph by Yelkrokoyade, 2019. Wikimedia Commons.

Image 1.2. Saint Catherine of Siena Receiving the Stigmata. Painting by Domenico Beccafumi, c. 1513-15. J. Paul Getty Museum. Wikimedia Commons.

Image 2.1. Title page of John Calvin's *Christianae Religionis Institutio [Institutes of the Christian Religion]*, 1536. Basel University Library. Public Domain.

Image 2.2. Statue of St. Ignatius of Loyola, San Xavier del Bac Mission, Arizona. Photograph by Donald Dickensheets, 1940. Library of Congress Prints and Photographs Division Washington, DC 20540.

Image 3.1. "Spaniards punish native Americans." Engraving in Dutch edition of Las Casas's *Destruction of the Indies*, 1620. Courtesy of the John Carter Brown Library, Archive of Early American Images.

Image 3.2. Frontispiece of Athanasius Kircher's *China Illustrata*, 1667. Folger Shakespeare Library, LUNA: Folger Digital Image Collection.

Image 3.3. *Kongo crucifix*. Solid cast brass crucifix by Kongo artist, 16th–17th century. The Metropolitan Museum of Art, Medieval Europe Gallery. Public Domain.

Image 3.4. "The Calling of St. Matthew." Painting by Caravaggio, 1599–1600. Contarelli Chapel, San Luigi dei Francesi, Rome. Public Domain.

Image 4.1. "A North West View of Westminster Abbey and St. Margaret's Church." Engraving printed and sold by Bowles & Carver, 1780. New York Public Library Digital Collections. Public Domain.

Image 5.1. Medal of Martin Luther, 1661. Yale University Art Gallery. Public Domain.

Image 5.2. "Siege of Magdeburg." Engraving by Matthäus Merian, 1642. Peace Palace Library, The Hague, Netherlands. Wikimedia Commons.

Image 6.1. "Assertion of Liberty of Conscience by the Independents of the Westminster Assembly of Divines." Painting by John Rogers Herbert, 1847. Parliamentary Art Collection, Palace of Westminster. Wikimedia Commons.

Image 6.2. Watercolor by William Blake, of a scene from John Bunyan's *The Pilgrim's Progress*, c. 1824–27. The Frick Collection, New York. Wikimedia Commons.

Image 7.1. Sculpture of San Felipe de Jesus, National Expiatory Temple of San Felipe de Jesús, Mexico. Photograph by ProtoplasmaKid, 2014. Wikimedia Commons.

Image 7.2. "Saint Rose of Lima." Painting by unknown artist, 18th century, Peru. Fogg Art Museum, Harvard University. Photograph by Daderot, 2019. Wikimedia Commons.

Image 7.3. Society of Friends Meetinghouse, Flushing, New York. Photograph by E. P. McFarland, 1936. Library of Congress Prints and Photographs Division Washington, DC 20540.

Image 8.1. "David Hume, Esqr." Lithograph by Antoine Maurin, c. 1820. New York Public Library Digital Collections. Public Domain.

Image 8.2. Ruins of San Ignacio Miní, Argentina. Photograph by Miguel Vieira, 2011. Wikimedia Commons.

Image 9.1. "Exorcismus der Täuflinge unter den Negern." Engraving in David Cranz's *Short, reliable news from the church UNITAS FRATRUM*, 1757. John Carter Brown Library, Archive of Early American Images.

Image 9.2. West Parish Congregational Church, Barnstable, Massachusetts. Photograph by Cervin Robinson, 1959. Library of Congress Prints and Photographs Division Washington, DC 20540.

Image 10.1. Frontispiece of George Whitefield's *The Christian's Companion*, 1738. Houghton Library, Harvard University Digital Collections. Creative Commons Attribution 4.0 International License.

Image 10.2. "John Wesley M. H." Mezzotint by John Faber, c. 1730–1756. Library of Congress Prints and Photographs Division Washington, DC 20540.

Image 11.1. Communion Token, 1843. Yale University Art Gallery. Public Domain.

Image 11.2. Cover page of "An Elegiac Poem" by Phyllis Wheatley, 1770. Beinecke Rare Book and Manuscript Library, Yale University Library.

Image 12.1. "Hell Broke Loose, or, The Murder Of Louis." Etching published by William Dent, 1793. Library of Congress Prints and Photographs Division Washington, DC 20540.

Image 12.2. "Thomas Paine." Engraving by William Sharp, 1793. Library of Congress Prints and Photographs Division Washington, DC 20540.

Image 13.1. Serampore College, India. Photograph by Biswarup Ganguly, 2017. Wikimedia Commons.

Image 13.2. Frontispiece and title page of Equiano's *Interesting Narrative*, 1794. Library of Congress Prints and Photographs Division Washington, DC 20540 USA.

Image 13.3. "Rt. Rev. Richard Allen." Engraving by John Sartain included in Daniel Alexander Payne's *History of the African Methodist Episcopal Church*, 1891. New York Public Library Digital Collections. Public Domain.

Image 14.1. Convento de Santa Rosa de Ocopa, Peru. Photograph by PoolPs, 2017. Wikimedia Commons.

Image 14.2. "Lorenzo Dow." Engraving, n.d. New York Public Library Digital Collections. Public Domain.

Image 14.3. Photo-postcard, c. 1908, of the Old Hay Bay Church, Ontario. From the collection of Kenneth Brown, loaned for scanning by the Deseronto Archives (Ontario), March 2011. Wikimedia Commons.

Image 15.1. "Inmaculada Concepción, la Niña." Painting by Bartolomé Esteban Murillo, 1668–69. Museo de Bellas Artes de Sevilla. Photograph by José Luis Filpo Cabana, 2018. Wikimedia Commons.

Image 16.1. "Stanley Meets Livingstone." Engraving arranged for by Henry Morton Stanley and published in the *Illustrated London News*, 1872. Library of Congress Washington, DC 20540 USA.

Image 17.1. "Samuel Adjai Crowther, D.D." Illustration in Frederic Perry Noble's *The Redemption of Africa*, 1899. New York Public Library Digital Collections. Public Domain.

Image 17.2. "Cottage of the Dairyman's daughter" at Shanklin, Isle of Wight. Photograph by J. Symonds, April 23, 1866. Getty Museum Collection. Public Domain.

Image 17.3. The Monastery Hodegetria Gonias, Crete. Photograph by Jerzy Strzelecki, 2009. Wikimedia Commons.

Image 18.1. "Shakers near Lebanon state of N York, their mode of Worship." Engraving, c. 1830. Library of Congress Prints and Photographs Division Washington, DC 20540.

Image 18.2. "The Mormon Temple at Kirtland, Ohio." Stereograph photo (right half) published by Underwood & Underwood, c. 1904. Library of Congress Prints and Photographs Division Washington, DC 20540.

Image 19.1. "The Discovery of Nat Turner." Illustration in Elisha Andrews's *History of the United States*, vol. 3, 1896. New York Public Library Digital Collections. Public Domain.

Image 19.2. "View of Roehampton Estate, Jamaica." Lithograph published by Ridgways, 1833. New York Public Library Digital Collections. Public Domain.

Image 19.3. "A Abolição 1888." Photomechanical print by or for Revista Do Ensino (a Brazilian teaching magazine), c. 1888. Library of Congress Prints and Photographs Division Washington, DC 20540.

Image 20.1. "Samuel Taylor Coleridge, Aged 42." Engraving by Samuel Cousins of painting by Washington Allston (1814), published by E. Moxon, 1854. Library of Congress Prints and Photographs Division Washington, DC 20540.

Image 20.2. "Mr. Spurgeon." Photograph published by Richard Smith, c. 1859–70. Digital Commonwealth, Massachusetts Collections Online. Public Domain.

Image 21.1. "Christelijk Batakkerkje aan Sumatra's Oostkust" [Christian Batak Church on Sumatra's East Coast]. Photograph by unknown author, c. 1935. Leiden University Libraries Digital Collections. Public Domain.

Image 21.2. "Miss Slessor and Children, Old Calabar." Lantern slide, c. late 19th century. Part of the International Mission Photography Archive, c. 1860–1960, at the Centre for the Study of World Christianity, Edinburgh. Wikimedia Commons.

Image 22.1. Crowd looking at "The Miracle of the Sun" during the Our Lady of Fatima apparitions, Portugal. Photograph by Judah Ruah, October 13, 1917. Published by *Illustracao Portugueza* on October 29, 1917. Wikimedia Commons.

Image 23.1. Field Marshall Allenby enters Jerusalem at Jaffa Gate. Photograph by American Colony (Jerusalem) Photo Department, December 11, 1917. Library of Congress Prints and Photographs Division Washington, DC 20540.

Image 23.2. "F. J. Grimké." Photograph by The Associated Publishers, Inc., 1927. New York Public Library Digital Collections. Public Domain.

Image 24.1. Aleksandr Solzhenitsyn. Photograph by Bert Verhoeff, February 14, 1974. Dutch National Archives, The Hague, Netherlands. Wikimedia Commons.

Image 24.2. Payton Hall, on the campus of Fuller Theological Seminary. Photograph by Bobak Ha'Eri. 2008. Wikimedia Commons.

Image 25.1. Billy Graham preaching in Norway. Photograph by unknown author, July 3, 1955. National Archives of Norway. Wikimedia Commons.

Image 25.2. Igreja Evangélica Assembleia de Deus de Telêmaco Borba, Brazil. Photograph by Simplus Menegati, uploaded 2020. Wikimedia Commons.

Image 26.1. Fannie Lou Hamer, Mississippi Freedom Democratic Party delegate, at the Democratic National Convention, Atlantic City, New Jersey, August 1964. Photograph by Warren K. Leffler, August 22, 1964. Library of Congress Prints and Photographs Division Washington, DC 20540.

Image 26.2. Pope John Paul II visit to US. Photograph by Thomas J. O'Halloran, October 4, 1979. Library of Congress Prints and Photographs Division Washington, DC 20540.

Image 27.1. Official portrait of The Lord Archbishop of York (John Sentamu). Photograph by Roger Harris, 2019. Wikimedia Commons. Source: UK Parliament website, license: 3.0 Unported (CC BY 3.0).

Image 27.2. Iglesia de Dios Pentecostal Movimiento International, Los Angeles. Photograph by Downtowngal, 2020. Wikimedia Commons.

Image 28.1. Marcha por la Vida, Argentina. Photograph by Eduardo Martín Schweitzer Benegas, 2018. Wikimedia Commons.

Image 28.2. Dr. Martha Myers. Photograph by unknown author, c. 2002. International Mission Board Photos. Used with permission.

INDEX

H

I

J

K

L

M

N

Q

R

S

T